Politics and Friendship

An early photograph of Carrie Chapman Catt and Rosa Manus.

Politics and Friendship

Letters from
the International Woman Suffrage Alliance,
1902–1942

Edited by
Mineke Bosch,
with Annemarie Kloosterman

Ohio State University Press
Columbus

Politics and Friendship is a revised version of *Lieve Dr. Jacobs: Brieven uit de Wereldbond voor Vrouwenkiesrecht, 1902–1942*, © 1985 Mineke Bosch and Annemarie Kloosterman.

Copyright © 1990 by the Ohio State University Press.
All rights reserved.

Parts of this book were translated by Nicky Williams and Mineke Bosch.

Library of Congress Cataloging-in-Publication Data

Lieve Dr. Jacobs. English.
 Politics and friendship : letters from the International Woman
Suffrage Alliance, 1902–1942 / edited by Mineke Bosch with Annemarie
Kloosterman.
 p.   cm.
 Translation of: Lieve Dr. Jacobs.
 Includes bibliographical references (p.
 ISBN 0–8142–0509–7 (alk. paper)
 1. International Woman Suffrage Alliance–Archives.   2. World
Center for Women's Archives.   3. Women–Suffrage–Netherlands–
History–Sources.   4. Suffragettes–Correspondence.   I. Jacobs,
Aletta H. (Aletta Henriette), 1854–1929.   II. Bosch, Mineke.
III. Kloosterman, Annemarie.   IV. Title.
JN5947.L5413   1990
342.6'23–dc20

                                                      89–72192
                                                      CIP

The paper in this book meets the guidelines for permanence and
durability of the Committee on Production Guidelines for Book
Longevity of the Council on Library Resources.

Printed in the U.S.A.

9 8 7 6 5 4 3 2 1

Contents

List of Illustrations *vii*

Preface *ix*

1. "Unity above Nation, Race, or Creed": An Introduction to the IWSA *1*

2. Politics and Friendship in the IWSA *21*

3. The Dutch Woman Suffrage Campaign and the IWSA *43*
   November 1902–September 1909; Letters 1–24 *51*

4. Strong-Minded Suffragists, Long-Time Presidents *91*
   December 1909–March 1914; Letters 25–42 *101*

5. Women United or Divided? World War I, the IWSA, and the International Women's Congress at The Hague, 1915 *135*
   October 1914–November 1918; Letters 43–56 *145*

6. Reconstruction in the Twenties *175*
   June 1920–October 1932; Letters 57–72 *185*

7. Crisis within the IWSA *219*
   April 1933–July 1942; Letters 73–85 *225*

   Appendixes *267*
      A. Abbreviations *269*
      B. Archives and Collections *270*
      C. Letters and Locations *272*

D. Countries Affiliated with the IWSA, 1904–42 *275*
E. Boards and Officers of the IWSA, 1904–42 *278*

Notes *285*

Bibliography *299*

Index *309*

Illustrations

Carrie Chapman Catt and Rosa Manus *Frontispiece*
Aletta Jacobs *11*
Rosika Schwimmer. The Hague, 1915 *13*
Clog dance during the 1908 IWSA congress in Amsterdam *19*
Aletta Jacobs and Anna Howard Shaw. Budapest, 1913 *24*
Rosika and Franciska Schwimmer. Budapest, 1919 *30*
Aletta Jacobs and Carrie Chapman Catt at the station in
Manila, 1912 *35*
In the garden of the American Club in Hangchow, China *36*
Rosa Manus and Carrie Chapman Catt at the arch of Constantine
in Rome, 1923 *39*
IWSA board in 1908 *45*
Cartoon in the weekly *De Groene Amsterdammer* during the 1908
IWSA congress *46*
Automobile used for canvassing during elections in the Netherlands,
1909 *47*
National Union of Women's Suffrage Societies caravan, England,
c. 1909 *48*
Anna Howard Shaw *76*
Lucy E. Anthony *76*
Alnwick Lodge, Anna Howard Shaw's house, 1915 *76*
Alnwick Lodge, porch, 1915 *76*
Carrie Chapman Catt and Aletta Jacobs at the station
in Shanghai, 1912 *96*
Carrie Chapman Catt and Aletta Jacobs en route to the
Manchu tombs at Mukden, 1912 *96*
At the tombs in Mukden, 1912 *96*
Sing Pey Zung, the "Christabel Pankhurst of China" *97*
Sing Pey Zung *97*

Carrie Chapman Catt and Aletta Jacobs with Chinese feminists, 1912   97
Mia Boissevain, Rosa Manus, and Carrie Chapman Catt during the
exhibition *De Vrouw 1813–1913* (Woman, 1813–1913)   118
Jane Addams   137
Women's Congress at The Hague   138
Delegation to the neutral countries in front of the royal
palace in Oslo, 1915   139
Rosika Schwimmer, Cornelia Ramondt-Hirschmann, Emily Balch,
Julia Grace Wales   140
Lida Gustava Heymann and Anita Augspurg with Charlotte Despard
of the English Women's Freedom League. Zürich, 1919   143
At the headquarters of the VVVK, Amsterdam   163
Board of the VVVK, 1918   163
Arrival in New York after final ratification of suffrage
amendment, 1920   172
Carrie Chapman Catt with "Victory Bouquet"   172
Carrie Chapman Catt and Mary Garrett Hay casting their first
vote for president   172
Catt addressing a meeting of women in Brazil, 1923   180
Bertha Lutz propagandizing for woman suffrage in Brazil, 1923   180
First leaf of birthday album given to Catt on her seventieth
birthday, January 9, 1920   182
Rosa Manus with Catt in a horse-drawn tram in Santiago, Chile,
1923   192
Aboard the *Little Venezuela*   192
Aboard the *Little Venezuela*   192
From Rosa Manus' picture album, 1923: Margery Corbett Ashby   193
Margery Corbett Ashby, her son Michael, Carrie Chapman Catt,
and two unidentified men   193
Carrie Chapman Catt and Rosa Manus at the Forum, 1923   193
At home in Baarn, 1923   193
IWSA board members relax. Berlin, 1929   206
The old guard. Berlin, 1929   206
Mia Boissevain and Rosa Manus, Wiesbaden   220
Rosa Manus and Carrie Chapman Catt. Paris, 1923   230
Rosika Schwimmer (with *Jus Suffragii* brooch) at her desk   236
The board of the IWSA in the newly opened IAV. Amsterdam,
1936   241
Rosa Manus, by Marthe Antoine Gérardin. The Hague, 1930   265

Preface

On December 3, 1935, three prominent Dutch feminists, Johanna W. A. Naber, Rosa Manus, and Willemijn H. Posthumus-van der Goot, placed their signatures on the charter of the Internationaal Archief voor de Vrouwenbeweging (International Archives for the Women's Movement; hereafter IAV). The aim of the foundation was "the stimulation of knowledge and the scientific study of the women's movement in the widest possible sense." The women had devised two ways of achieving their goals. The first was to build up an archive and a library in which women's heritage could be saved, expanded, monitored, and put at the disposal of the future feminist scholar. The second was to stimulate and encourage scholarly research and to publish its findings. Until the German occupation in May 1940, the IAV prospered and its collection grew steadily. Rosa Manus contributed the valuable personal papers and library of Aletta Jacobs, the Netherlands' first woman physician and indefatigable advocate of women's rights in many fields. It may be more accurate to say that the IAV was founded for the purpose of putting Aletta Jacobs' legacy to a worthy cause. In February 1940 Rosa Manus contributed her own archives, an embodiment of thirty years' work in the national and international women's suffrage and peace movement.

The other goal of IAV policy, research and publication, also promised well. In 1937 and 1938 two multilingual *Yearbooks* were published whose form and size attested that women had adopted a serious approach to the scientific study of the women's movement. Examples are Willemijn H. Posthumus-van der Goot's research into economic reasons for women to work (which also served as an argument in the political struggle against state restriction of female labor in the 1930s) and, in the same *Yearbook 2*, as the result of international cooperation, three articles on the problem of woman suffrage in France, Switzerland, and Belgium, two in French and one in German, with an introduction in English.

When we started to think of finding a suitable way to commemorate the fiftieth anniversary of the IAV in 1985, we decided to publish some of the source materials that nurtured this early period. The most obvious place to start was Aletta Jacobs' archive, which consists mostly of letters from women from many countries and covers the period from the 1880s to the late 1920s. We felt that a selection of these would lend substance to each element of the archive's name: *international*, *archive*, and *women's movement*.

After we had thoroughly examined the Jacobs material, we formulated a more detailed plan, one that slowly imposed order on our research and selection.

First, as a simple act of justice, we decided to portray Rosa Manus next to Aletta Jacobs, with the intention of drawing her out of the shadow that engulfed her contribution when the Nazis destroyed not only her life but also her archives. In June 1940 the IAV was sealed by the Nazis, and the archives were shipped to an unknown destination. Only Aletta Jacobs' papers, placed in a safe-deposit box probably long before the outbreak of war, and a few privately owned archives in the homes of individual women escaped the attention of the occupation authorities. Events have placed enormous restrictions on the research possibilities and therefore on our vision of the history of Dutch feminism. Though we did not have at our disposal the piles of documents Rosa Manus brought to the IAV in 1940 (we have never given up hopes of these being retraced), we did have two small collections pertaining to her which obviously had been sent to the IAV after 1945 by Carrie Chapman Catt and Anna Manus Jacobi, Rosa's sister. The Catt collection contained part of their correspondence from the 1930s as well as Catt's seventieth birthday album, which consists of sixty pages sent in by women from all over the world. Other letters made it clear that Rosa Manus had taken the initiative in compiling this album. The second collection consists primarily of letters of condolence to Anna Manus Jacobi from a surprising range of women. Both collections convinced us that Rosa Manus' activities were numerous, important, and until now greatly underrated.

Second, we decided to concentrate on the correspondence of Anna Howard Shaw and Carrie Chapman Catt in the Aletta Jacobs collection. The sheer quantity of their letters suggested "historical significance," either as a reflection of history "as it was" or as Jacobs wanted us and herself to see it.

Third, we felt that the selected letters, which we wanted to be printed in their entirety, should be firmly embedded in a narrative. As is most often the case, the major part of the correspondence is not sufficiently comprehensible to stand on its own, and without background information too much of its meaning would be lost to the general reader. With the four women— Carrie Chapman Catt, Aletta Jacobs, Rosa Manus, and Anna Howard Shaw— already selected, a contextual narrative seemed natural: the history of the International Woman Suffrage Alliance (IWSA), an organization which still exists as the International Alliance of Women (IAW). All four were actively involved in the Alliance: Shaw and Jacobs both as long-time presidents of their national suffrage associations, Rosa Manus as "special organizer" and officer of the IWSA, and Catt, of course, as the IWSA's president for almost twenty years. Having come this far we realized that it would be desirable to include more letters written by Aletta Jacobs and Rosa Manus than just those deposited with the IAV. This made us decide to sift through the papers of Anna Howard Shaw, Carrie Chapman Catt, and other people who had been involved, for example the Hungarian-American feminist Rosika Schwimmer. Thanks to a contribution from the Dr. Catharine van Tussenbroek Fund, I was able to visit the Smith College Library, the Schlesinger Library, the Library of Congress, and the New York Public Library for this purpose.

At first we were disappointed in our finds. Anna Howard Shaw seemed to have left far less extensive records than we expected. Although it was exciting to read in her diary vivid reports of trips she had made with Aletta Jacobs, she obviously did not save the letters Jacobs must have written to her over the years. Catt's collection was also discouraging in this respect. Mary Gray Peck, Catt's first biographer, mentions diaries devoted to the world tour she made with Aletta Jacobs in 1911–12, but these proved to be little more than scrapbooks with captions. Much of Catt's personal correspondence prior to 1923—including letters from Jacobs and Manus—had not been saved. However, the richness of the collection after this date, especially with regard to Rosa Manus, compensated for this partial loss. Our final surprise was the discovery that the Schwimmer-Lloyd Collection, described rather misleadingly in *Women's History Sources* as consisting of six trays, turned out to be three hundred meters in length, or 1,777 boxes! Rosika Schwimmer's papers not only contained a series of delightful letters from Aletta Jacobs dating back as far as 1902 but also a considerable chunk of the general history of the Dutch woman suffrage and peace movements (not to speak of material from the German and Austrian movements!): letters written by such Dutch feminists as Martina Kramers and the suffrage sisters Miel Coops-Broese van Groenou and Mien van Wulfften Palthe-Broese van Groenou, Dutch suffrage calendars, pictures of the nineteenth-century liberal statesman Rudolf Thorbecke, who in his function as prime minister granted Aletta Jacobs permission to enter the university as the first female student in the Netherlands, and newspaper cuttings and correspondence of the local Winschoten branch of the Vereeniging voor Vrouwenkiesrecht (Woman Suffrage Association) on speeches held there by Rosika Schwimmer.
Following our trip to the United States we determined to tell the story of five women—Carrie Chapman Catt, Aletta Jacobs, Rosa Manus, Rosika Schwimmer, and Anna Howard Shaw—in the context of the IWSA, through their private letters, or to tell the story of the IWSA through the private letters of these five women. The *or* is an inclusive one, for we have tried to do both things at the same time. That was our way of showing what the letters told us: that the suffrage movement was more than a collection of issues, political programs, constitutions, and congress resolutions, more

than just a political movement that aspired to one aim: woman suffrage. The voices of the women suffragists, speaking through their letters, told us that the suffrage movement could as well be conceptualized as a collective of *women*, active feminists, striking personalities, who debated together, intrigued, loved, and hated each other; women, moreover, who were human, sometimes maybe all too much so; who were corseted, or deliberately not when advocating reform dress; who used morphine occasionally; who admired queens while despising marchionesses in feminism (letter 62). We hoped to gain insight into the formalities as well as the realities of international suffragism (to use Mary Beard's terminology) and so to assess the importance of the notion of sisterhood in a history of suffragism—while at the same time exploring its limitations.

The main body of material from which we made a selection for this book consists of letters exchanged by Rosa Manus and Carrie Chapman Catt (70 and 94 letters, respectively, written between 1924 and 1940); letters from Anna Howard Shaw and Carrie Chapman Catt to Aletta Jacobs (71 and 81, respectively, written between 1905 and 1918/1929); and the letters from Aletta Jacobs to Rosika Schwimmer (55, from 1902 to 1915). Added to these are letters from other women, for example Lucy E. Anthony and Mien van Wulfften Palthe-Broese van Groenou. These letters have a special bearing on the subject, most often because of the writers' close relationship with one or more of the "main characters" in the book. Letters to and from Lucy E. Anthony were selected because Aletta Jacobs kept her correspondence among the letters from Shaw. To leave her letters out would be to apply an artificial selectivity and also to miss a certain continuity: it was Lucy Anthony who started the Jacobs-Shaw correspondence. Letters from Mien van Wulfften Palthe-Broese van Groenou are included because of her intimate connections with both Aletta Jacobs and Rosika Schwimmer (even long after the Jacobs and Schwimmer friendship broke up). Her and her sister's archives led us to suspect that Rosika Schwimmer was more important to Aletta Jacobs than Jacobs' autobiography and personal papers suggested: indeed, Jacobs destroyed all the letters and any other scrap that reminded her of Schwimmer.

In the last phase of the selection process, we were guided by less strictly defined selection criteria based on such questions as: Is it a nice, informative, passionate, or intriguing letter with respect to the central theme of the book? Does it fill in a gap in the material? The result is a selection of eighty-five letters.

In this English-language edition, the selection, which forms the core of the book, has remained unaltered. Otherwise there have been modifications, most of them in the sphere of adaptation of the texts for the non-Dutch reader, who, for instance, cannot be expected to be as well informed about the life of Aletta Jacobs as a similar Dutch reader. This is why the

Dutch title, *Lieve Dr. Jacobs* (Dear Dr. Jacobs), has been changed to *Politics and Friendship*. Other alterations involve corrections and updating. Not to have included an evaluation of the two recently published biographies of Carrie Chapman Catt (Fowler 1986 and Van Voris 1987) would prematurely date the book. And the general order has been slightly changed.

Some of the questions about how to edit the letters applied equally to the Dutch and the American editions. On the one hand, we asked ourselves, how we could prevent the letters from losing too much of their impact as a result of translation and the uniformity imposed by a printed text? Many of the letters were written in a style somewhere between spoken and written language. Most of Catt's letters, for example, were dictated, and Shaw's letters clearly illustrate that her powers of oratory far outshone her penmanship. Should we iron out all such irregularities, which might reflect the "truest innermost self," according to psychoanalytic text interpretation? What were we to do with Aletta Jacobs' clumsy German: "Ich war aber mit meiner Mann in der Schweiz, und dachte in dieser Zeit an keine Arbeit, keine Bücher, keine Briefe. Wir machten solche schöne Bergtouren in der Engadine, die Natur war ja schön; uns mit etwas anders zu occupiren dachte mir eine Profanation." Although it may strike the reader who knows German as being slightly comical, the passage demonstrates how Jacobs had no qualms about freely exchanging her ideas in a language over which she had little command. Indeed, where so much of the success of international, multicultural organizations depended on the ability to find a "common language," we did not like to blot out the fact that women like Rosa Manus and Aletta Jacobs took such pains to express themselves in a foreign language. To think they did so without making mistakes would not do justice to the situation. On the other hand, from the beginning of this project historical narrative rather than scientific source publication had been our aim, and this remained our policy. As a consequence, legibility, not literality or historical accuracy, has been the most important consideration in the editorial decisions we made about the letters. An additional list of letters and their locations refers the interested reader to the original texts.

To begin with the Dutch and German letters then, misspellings, grammatical errors, and phrases which were not idiomatic have been standardized in the translations. All different forms of address: Frau, Fru, Mademoiselle, and so on have been translated as Mrs. or Miss. In both translated and English letters names have been edited according to their proper spelling–difficult though it was to trace such correct spellings among the many different forms they have in different sources. Headings have been standardized to record place and date of sending.

As for the letters originally written in English–whether by native or non-native speakers–the original texts, errors and all, are given. All editorial emendations and explanations have been placed in square brackets. In the English texts the original forms of address have been retained since it shows how far the suffragists were willing to recognize national and language differences.

The writing of history deals with change over time. In the time that has elapsed since the publication of the Dutch edition in 1985 many changes have occurred. The saddest change was the bankruptcy of the feminist publisher Sara, who edited the Dutch version. The most spectacular change was the merger of the IAV with the Informatie en Documentatie Centrum (Information and Documentation Center) and the feminist journal LOVER (Survey of literature from the women's movement) into a rejuvenated and dynamic Internationaal Informatiecentrum en Archief voor de Vrouwen-beweging (International Information Center and Archive for the Women's Movement; hereafter IIAV). The new institute has three main sections: an archive, a library, and a documentation section. One clause in the new constitution ensures the unity of the collection of the old IAV (consisting of about 40,000 books and journals and more than 180 meters of archives and manuscripts) and all future acquisitions. Its name preserves the memory of the past: IAV collection. The Aletta Jacobs papers are still located in the IAV collection within the IIAV (=AJ-IAV-IIAV). We appreciate the interest the new board has taken in the translation of *Lieve Dr. Jacobs* and their willingness to return to Annemarie Kloosterman and myself the rights of authorship, which facilitated the editing process.

Annemarie Kloosterman and I worked in close collaboration on the selection and annotation of the letters, but the research and the writing, especially the revisions needed for the English-language edition, for the most part fell to me. Thus thrown upon my own resources, I have come to realize in full the importance of the innumerable conversations we had. Our shared commitment to the undertaking resulted sometimes in fertile discussions of questions that lie far beyond the usual boundaries of historical scholarship.

I would like to mention by name a few of the women who were very helpful to us in the early phases of this project. First is Edith Wynner, former secretary to Rosika Schwimmer and now consultant to the Schwimmer-Lloyd Collection at the New York Public Library. She was instrumental in speeding up the transportation of boxes of letters from the annex to the library. And when we deluged her with yet more questions from the Netherlands, she never failed to provide speedy answers. Her discerning interest in our project provided an enormous stimulus. Similarly, W. E. S. Coops and D. Kloppenborg-Coops were kind enough to talk with us about the past and give us permission to print a letter from Aletta Jacobs from their own collection. We were also greatly inspired by conversations with women from our research support group: Thera de Graaf, Maaike Meijer, and Marijke Mossink, all of them dedicated scholars.

As for the second "American" phase of the project, Annemarie's interest

and confidence never wavered, for which I am more than grateful. I do realize that it is not easy to see your coworker take up again the work that was
once started together. Vital in both the first and second phases was Nicoline
Meiners. I am always inspired by her never-ending search for and knowledge of women's books and archives; her editorial assistance and daily support were indispensable. Annette Mevis and Francisca de Haan stood by
me with their archivist's and historical skills. Maaike Meijer was an inspiration as ever. I want to thank Myriam Everard for her painstaking and constructive criticism and, of course, for braving the ocean with me to participate in the seventh Berkshire Conference on the History of Women. This
edition is the result of that gathering and of the enthusiasm of Leila Rupp
and Charlotte Dihoff, both connected with the Ohio State University Press.
However, enthusiasm alone is not enough. I am all admiration for Nancy
R. Woodington, who so carefully copyedited this manuscript. Without
Charlotte Dihoff – her skill and inspiring confidence – this English-language
edition would not have been possible. Neither "hartelijk bedankt" nor
"thank you very much" can adequately express my gratitude.

Mineke Bosch
Amsterdam

I

"Unity above Nation, Race, or Creed": An Introduction to the IWSA

Beginnings of International Sisterhood: The Foundation of the International Council of Women (Washington, 1888)

"In welcoming representatives from other lands here today, we do not feel that you are strangers and foreigners, for the women of all nationalities, in the artificial distinctions of sex, have a universal sense of injustice, that forms a common bond of union between them" (DuBois 1981, 210).

With these words Elizabeth Cady Stanton greeted an international assembly of women, gathered at her initiative and that of her friend Susan B. Anthony, in Washington in 1888. There was a special reason: "We are assembled here to-day to celebrate the fortieth anniversary of the first organized demand made by women for the right of suffrage" (DuBois, 1981, 209). She was alluding to the famous convention in Seneca Falls in 1848, where the drawing up of the "Declaration of Sentiments" gave the starting signal to an active women's movement which insisted on the equal rights of women. But the assembly did not just look back. The meeting of women of all nations in 1888 culminated in the foundation of the International Council of Women (ICW), which was, ideally, to become the umbrella organization for *all* women's organizations from *all* countries.

Stanton, President of the National Woman Suffrage Association (NWSA),[1] had originally planned to invite only suffrage organizations from abroad. But in 1888 the general meeting of the NWSA had voted for another setup: it had decided to bring together women from as many different organizations and as many countries as possible. This decision was the result of a growing desire in the North American woman suffrage movement to achieve the greatest possible unity among women, a desire shared by Susan B. Anthony. Nine foreign, primarily European, delegations were present, as well as representatives from more than fifty American women's organizations.

I

In her opening speech, Stanton spoke eloquently of universal sisterhood, the international solidarity of women, which was based on the subordination of women–present in varying degrees perhaps, but nevertheless universal: "There is a language of universal significance, more subtle than that used in the busy marts of trade, that should be called the mother-tongue, by which with a sigh or a tear, a gesture, a glance of the eye, we know the experiences of each other in the varied forms of slavery. With the spirit forever in bondage, it is the same whether housed in golden cages, with every want supplied, or wandering the dreary deserts of life friendless and forsaken" (DuBois 1981, 210). Nevertheless, the concept of international solidarity among women which underlay the foundation of the ICW bore all the marks of developments in the American woman suffrage movement. However well Stanton spoke, the hypothetical but heartfelt sisterhood she envisaged was not the same as the pragmatic, resolutely pursued sisterhood Susan B. Anthony had in mind, which would be embodied by the ICW.

Elizabeth Cady Stanton, Susan B. Anthony, and North American Suffragism

From the moment Susan B. Anthony had joined Elizabeth Cady Stanton in the still young women's movement in 1850, the two women had been virtually inseparable.[2] Both had, however, made their own contributions: Anthony as strategist and activist, Stanton as writer and philosopher of the movement, who, restricted in her actions by her duties at home–she had seven children–sent Anthony out with her ideas and speeches. Aletta Jacobs once described them on the basis of a cartoon she had seen: Anthony had been depicted as the "Napoleon of the Women's War," and "beautiful Elizabeth [as] her leading general" (Jacobs 1905, 11–12). In 1869 they had founded the National Woman Suffrage Association together, after having learned that even in the antislavery movement the rights of female Americans were put aside in favor of rights for Black Americans with the argument that it was now "the negro's hour."[3]

Partly because of the establishment of the more moderate American Woman Suffrage Association by Lucy Stone and Henry Blackwell, the "National" had been able to continue to steer a radical feminist course throughout the seventies under the guidance of Stanton and Anthony. In the "National," subjects like free love and divorce could at least be discussed. They also dealt with the organization of working-class women.

Gradually, however, Stanton and Anthony grew apart. Anthony felt an increasing need for organization and expansion. In the eighties she adopted more and more of the suffrage movement's new policy, which sacrificed diversity and radicalism to adaptation and unity in an attempt to seek alliances with various other fast-growing but less explicitly feminist women's organizations such as the Women's Christian Temperance Union (WCTU). In this process, discussions on a wide range of women's issues were increasingly avoided. The central theme became instead: "How can we reach as many women as possible?"

The expansion of the suffrage movement, which was the result of a reconciliation between suffrage feminism and the domestic feminism of more traditional women's organizations, is inextricably tied to the development which has been characterized as female institution-building, the building of a "woman's world" in the public sphere (Freedman 1979). The merger of the "National" and the "American" into the National American Suffrage Association (NAWSA) in 1890 constituted a milestone in this development. The movement increasingly consisted of and focused on white Protestant women. Single professional women began to take charge in order to become "professionally" active in politics. These women, very unlike their predecessors in the antislavery movement, did not avoid taking advantage of racist feelings and immigrant hatred. In her autobiography Anna Howard Shaw describes an incident at a Republican state nomination convention in South Dakota in 1890, where a referendum on the suffrage amendment was soon to be held. The woman suffrage delegation, led by Susan B. Anthony, was allotted a very obscure place by the organizing committee. The better seats had been taken mainly by "Russian laborers," says Shaw, "wearing badges with the inscription: 'Against Woman Suffrage and Susan B. Anthony.'" Suddenly there was some commotion. A delegation of Native Americans presented itself and was received with great decorum. Shaw, however, could see nothing but some colorful feathers: "I dared not look at Miss Anthony during this remarkable scene, and she, craning her venerable neck to get a glimpse of the incident from her obscure corner, made no comment to me; but I knew what she was thinking. The following year these Indians would have votes. Courtesy therefore, must be shown them. But the women did not matter, the politicians reasoned" (Shaw 1915, 250). Shaw concludes this passage with an analysis of the referendum. In the electoral districts consisting primarily of "American" residents, the suffrage amendment was carried; in districts where predominantly "foreigners" had voted, the amendment was rejected. She concludes:

> The fact that our Cause could be defeated by ignorant laborers newly come to our country was a humiliating one to accept; and we realized more forcibly than ever before the difficulty of the task we had assumed—a task far beyond any ever undertaken by a body of men in the history of democratic government throughout the world. We not only had to bring American men back to a belief in the fundamental principles of republican government, but we had also to educate ignorant immigrants, as well as our own Indians, whose degree of civilization was indicated by their war-paint and the flaunting feathers of their head-dresses.[4]

A shift of emphasis becomes apparent in the arguments used to advocate woman suffrage. In the period before 1890, women based their arguments primarily on natural law, appealing to justice. After 1890, their arguments were aimed specifically at convincing the public of the benefits of woman suffrage. If only women had the right to vote, it would be easier for them to carry out their reforms.[5] It was a strategic shift signifying that women now emphasized the common good instead of confidently demanding rights for themselves in their own interests, as they had before.

Shaw formulated the two approaches very clearly in a letter to Aletta Jacobs:

> If women could be made to see that through their political freedom, they would be able to bring to pass many of the things for which the good women of the Council are so eagerly working and yet which they fail to accomplish simply because they have no political power, I am quite sure that many women who now oppose it would give up all opposition and I suppose it will be the duty of our Committee to bring before these women the real purpose of women's enfranchisement rather than the theoretical one which so frightened so many very excellent women away from the movement in the past. [Letter 5]

Elizabeth Cady Stanton, the theoretician of the movement, who openly continued to stress that the "Woman Question" was a more complex one than could be solved by suffrage alone, became increasingly isolated in this process. At the NAWSA Congress in 1893 she was no longer present. She did send an "Address" entitled "The Solitude of Self " (DuBois 1981, 246–55). It is a strong plea in favor of woman suffrage and based on the argument that women and men are equally alone in moments of truth. Women should be given all opportunities freely to educate themselves, for which the right to vote is the prerequisite. Women might have the experience of subordination in common, but otherwise the subjects for their debate are manifold. Her emphasis on individualism implied a notion of sisterhood in which the differences and disputes among women were not covered up, but discussed and defined in a multifaceted political program – in addition to woman suffrage. She thus tried to reconcile the idea of sisterhood as a unifying force with the notion of intrinsic differences among women.

These notions did not tally with Susan B. Anthony's political program in the long run. Anthony had come to see sisterhood as the unification of the greatest possible number of women into one great women's movement, under the common denominator of a vague definition of womanhood, but with a fixed, unequivocal object: woman suffrage. In 1897 she wrote to Stanton: "The time is past when the mass of the suffrage women will be compromised by any one woman's peculiarities! We number over ten thousand women and each one has opinions . . . and we can only hold them together by letting alone their whims and prejudices" (DuBois 1981, 180). From the nineties onward, nonpartisanship and unity constituted the pillars of the North American woman suffrage movement, which in 1919 won the vote.

Anna Howard Shaw (1847–1919)

After the merger in 1890, Elizabeth Cady Stanton was president of the National American Woman Suffrage Association for only two more years. In 1892 she stepped down, partly because of her age—she was seventy-three years old—and was succeeded by Susan B. Anthony. Stanton was gone, but Anthony was not alone. During the international congress in 1888 she had managed to persuade Anna Howard Shaw to devote her energies to the suffrage movement. In her autobiography, *The Story of a Pioneer*, Shaw reports that she was still working happily in the Women's Christian Temperance Union at that time. "But," Shaw continues, "Miss Anthony's arguments were irrefutable, and she was herself, as always, irresistible" (Shaw 1915, 182). One night in particular was impressed indelibly on Shaw's memory. Long after one of the evening meetings, Anthony slipped into her room. Shaw describes herself as almost asleep, while the seventy-year-old Anthony was still as fresh as ever. Nestling down in a comfortable chair, she announced that she had much to say. Shaw propped herself up with a pillow behind her back and listened. "Hours passed and the dawn peered wanly through the windows, but still Miss Anthony talked of the Cause—always of the Cause—and of what we two must do for it."[6] From that moment, "we two" became inseparable in the suffrage movement.

Anna Howard Shaw was born in England in 1847. At an early age she and her family emigrated to the United States. She grew up in the woods of Michigan, where her parents built a new, hard life for themselves as pioneers. Under very difficult circumstances and parental disapproval she managed to become a minister. She then preached in her own parish for seven stormy years, successfully combining this profession with the study of medicine and work for the WCTU. Having found her place in suffrage work, Shaw remained very much a preacher with high ideals which she never ceased to defend passionately. But this is not the only way in which she can serve as a model of the development of the women's movement, for she also came out of the WCTU, had a university education, and made her own living. She remained unmarried and lived in a women's world which could be described as self-supporting. From 1890 she had an intimate friend and companion in Lucy E. Anthony, one of Susan B. Anthony's nieces, with whom she shared a house and who was also her secretary and housekeeper.[7] Her physician was a woman, and women architects were called in to build her a house. Eloquence was Shaw's greatest talent. Many different sources unanimously attest to her ability to inspire an audience, and although her later terms of office in the suffrage movement have been criticized by contemporaries and historians alike, such criticism is always compensated by praise for her oratorical talents and the zeal with which she applied them for the sake of the movement.

Carrie Chapman Catt (1859–1947)

Although Shaw was in every respect the most likely candidate to succeed Anthony, it was, dramatically enough, not Shaw but Carrie Chapman Catt whom Anthony recommended as her successor in 1900 (Shaw 1915, 184–85; Peck 1944, 108–9; see also chapter 4, below). During the relatively short period Catt had worked for the NAWSA on a national level, she had proved to be a brilliant manager, and this skill was badly needed in the movement. Catt grew up as Carrie Lane in a frontier setting on a farm in northern Iowa. She finished high school in three years and entered Iowa State College in 1877 after one year's teaching experience. Her father opposed her ambitions to higher education, which forced her to earn her own way through college. After receiving her B.S. degree, she started to work in a lawyer's office, having her mind set on a law career. But this was not to be. Within a year she had become principal of a high school in a nearby city, and after two more years, superintendent of schools, which was a position few women held. In 1885 she married Leo Chapman, owner and editor of a local newspaper, and became assistant editor. Their partnership was promising but short-lived. In 1886 her husband died, and in 1887 she took to the lecture platform, the same year she became involved in the suffrage movement. In 1890 she decided on a second marriage with an old schoolfellow, the engineer and businessman George Catt. It was a marriage of convenience: by a legally witnessed contract, she insisted on having several months each year in spring and fall for herself and the movement. Before long she drew the attention of leading suffragists in the national association, and she won Anthony's decided admiration for her work on the Organization Committee, which from 1895 set out to change the NAWSA into a well-defined, centralized, uniformly organized group.

Time proved Anthony's assessment of Catt correct. Catt demonstrated time and again her ability to inspire the movement and lead it to its final victory. She was a modern manager, diplomatic but decisive, and equipped with infallible political insight. Undemonstrative and reasonable, she was yet driven by "inner necessity," says Mary Peck, her friend and biographer (Peck 1944, 45). The presidency of the NAWSA, however, weighed heavily upon her, and she resigned in 1904. Anna Howard Shaw reluctantly took charge of the NAWSA at Anthony's insistence, and in the same year Catt began her career as the undisputed life and soul of the international woman suffrage movement.

Woman Suffrage and the International Council of Women

Many felt that the universal sisterhood envisioned by Susan B. Anthony had been achieved with the establishment of the ICW–but at the expense of the ideal underlying its foundation: woman suffrage. In order to keep together so great a number of heterogeneous women's organizations, the principle of unanimity was adopted at the first meeting. Decisions were to be made by consensus, rather than a majority vote. Unanimity was reached on three women's issues, but woman suffrage was not one of them.[8]

As early as 1899, during the Third Congress of the ICW in London, where 5,000 participants represented 6,000,000 women from eleven countries, the council's fragile unity was visibly shattered. The suffrage meeting failed when its organizers, who were in favor of woman suffrage, refused entry to opponents of the vote. This was in conflict with the view held by the coordinating committee of the congress, which stated that such anti-suffragists should have access to the meeting because they met the criteria for ICW membership. As a result, says Aletta Jacobs, Anita Augspurg and Lida Gustava Heymann,[9] two women from the radical wing of the German women's movement, took the initiative of convening an alternative meeting at which the foundation of an international alliance of woman suffrage was advocated (Jacobs 1924, 103; also Hurwitz 1977, 331–32, and Sherrick 1983, 656).

Most historical narrations of the International Woman Suffrage Alliance, however, do not begin with this subversive act, but with the international meeting in Washington in 1902, which was organized by Carrie Chapman Catt in conjunction with the annual NAWSA meeting.[10] In preparation for the conference, Catt had sent out questionnaires to collect information on the subject of woman suffrage in different countries. Eight countries seem to have had national suffrage societies, and all received invitations.

In all, women from ten different countries, though not all of them delegates from suffrage societies, gathered to discuss woman suffrage. Susan B. Anthony held the chair; Vida Goldstein[11] from Australia acted as recording secretary. It was decided that a permanent organization would be set up in Berlin in 1904, during a conference prior to the Third Quinquennial Meeting of the ICW. To prepare that conference and produce a draft constitution an International Woman Suffrage Committee was formed, comprising Susan B. Anthony, Carrie Chapman Catt, and Anita Augspurg, president of the newly founded German woman suffrage association. A "Declaration of Principles" closely resembling the "Declaration of Sentiments" from 1848 was also drawn up and approved. Its first and last principles ran:

1. That men and women are born equally free and independent members of the human race; equally endowed with intelligence and ability, and equally entitled to the free exercise of their individual rights and liberty. . . .

6. That the ballot is the only legal and permanent means of defending the rights to the "life, liberty, and the pursuit of happiness" pronounced inalienable by the American Declaration of Independence, and accepted by all civilised nations. In any representative form of government, there-

fore, women should be vested with all political rights and privileges of electors. [Schreiber and Mathieson 1955, 2–3]

These are remarkably radical principles insofar as they recapture the theoretical arguments of justice, which were considered much more extreme than the pragmatic arguments of expediency. By the time these principles were set forth, arguments of expediency were predominant in the American suffrage movement. One explanation for this anachronism might be that internationalism offered a possibility to compensate for expediency at home by a more principled attitude abroad. Another might be that by emphasizing woman suffrage as a fundamental issue of justice, the International Woman Suffrage Alliance clearly distinguished itself from the ICW in order to show that it was a new and vitally different international women's organization.

Berlin, 1904: Foundation of the International Woman Suffrage Alliance

Finally, in 1904, amid great public interest, the International Woman Suffrage Alliance (IWSA) was founded. Certainly the ICW looked with envy upon the younger sister organization that—even before its formal foundation—seemed to radiate vitality, if not revolutionary zeal. The news that Susan B. Anthony would preside at the suffrage conference decided many women to arrive in Berlin earlier. This caused the president of the ICW, May Wright Sewall, to implore Anthony not to participate in a public meeting of the newly founded IWSA because the ICW wanted to have the privilege of honoring her. Anthony gave in to this request, but Sewall could not prevent her from leading the talks of the international suffragists, which were widely reported. She won the sure sympathy of the press when, "in clear, but matter-of-fact tones," she welcomed the reporters who had been nearly forced to leave because of a motion of the Dutch representative, Aletta Jacobs.[12] And although Shaw described Anthony's obligingness toward the ICW as a heartrending act of self-sacrifice, Anthony got her share of the attention and more when, on the opening night of the ICW meeting, she was given a standing ovation of several minutes, while bonbons were presented wrapped in gold paper portraying her image (Hurwitz 1977, 336).

Eight countries (Australia, Denmark, Germany, Great Britain, the Netherlands, Norway, Sweden, and the United States) had national suffrage associations which joined the Alliance. Delegations from all eight countries except Australia attended the suffrage conference. In addition to this, there were women from countries where suffrage feminism had not yet been organized on a national basis: Austria, Hungary, New Zealand, and Switzerland. The main task of the conference was to consider and adopt a constitution. The goal of the IWSA was "to secure the enfranchisement of the women of all nations, and to unite the friends of woman suffrage throughout the world in organised cooperation and fraternal helpfulness."[13] Other articles of the constitution were concerned with membership, meetings, officers, and matters of organization. Article 3, which regulated membership, seems not to have been the sensitive item it became later, when schisms in national suffrage organizations provoked hot political debates about membership criteria. In 1904 it simply stated:

> Any National Woman Suffrage Society may become an auxiliary to the IWSA and be represented by six delegates at all international meetings by payment of the specified subscription. In those countries where no National Woman Suffrage Association exists, local associations of the same kind may unite in forming a National Committee of six, which may become an auxiliary to the IWSA on the same terms as a National Association. Any person can become an Honorary Associate on payment of the necessary subscription and have the same privileges as an auxiliary, except the right to vote. [Whittick 1979, 34]

At last an executive board of seven women was chosen, consisting of Susan B. Anthony (United States), honorary president; Carrie Chapman Catt (United States), president; Millicent Garrett Fawcett (Great Britain) and Anita Augspurg (Germany), vice presidents; Sophie Rodger Cunliffe (Great Britain), treasurer; Rachel Foster Avery (United States), secretary; and Johanna Naber (the Netherlands) and Käthe Schirmacher (Germany), assistant secretaries.[14]

Aletta Jacobs (1854–1929)

The Dutch women who were members of one of the seven official delegations present in Berlin were an impressive group. Feminist historian Johanna Naber was elected to the first board of the IWSA. Two years laters she was succeeded by Martina Kramers, who in 1906 became the sole editor of the journal *Jus Suffragii* (The right of suffrage).[15] But Aletta Jacobs stole the show.

Aletta Henriëtte Jacobs was the eighth child in a family of eleven in a liberal, assimilative Jewish milieu in the north of Holland. Her father was a country doctor. Though one of the central themes in Jacobs' *Herinneringen* (Reminiscences; 1924) is her often-repeated statement that the notion of struggle was absent in her life history, since she was driven by "inner necessity" in the face of injustice, still she did things that took a great deal of courage. Unknown to anyone, in 1871 she wrote prime minister Rudolf Thorbecke as a woman requesting permission to take up university studies, which at first he granted only for the period of a year. Definitive permission came in 1872 on black-edged paper: it had been one of the last decisions

Thorbecke ever made (De Wilde 1979). After receiving her doctorate in medicine in 1879 she went to England, where she met Elizabeth Garrett Anderson, another doctor (and sister of Millicent Garrett Fawcett, the long-time leader of the National Union of Women's Suffrage Societies), and other women physicians as well. It was also important for her that she became acquainted with the Malthusians Charles Bradlaugh, C. R. Drysdale, and Annie Besant, who openly campaigned for voluntary motherhood – an issue Jacobs took up immediately when she set up a practice in Amsterdam. Her experiences with the women in the Amsterdam slums convinced her more forcibly than anything else of the importance of contraception for women.[16] In the early 1880s she corresponded with a German doctor, Mensinga, about a pessary that some time later she began to prescribe. It was originally known as the "Mensinga-pessary," but later became famous as the "Dutch pessary" substantially because of Jacobs' efforts. It was characteristic of Jacobs that she not only acted in the face of injustice, but also openly defended her principles, translating her social campaigns into political issues. Typical small actions of hers were applying for membership in the all-male Amsterdam Reading Society and attending the Amsterdam Theater unaccompanied by a man. Greater steps were her attempt to register to vote in 1883, her public appeals for chairs for shopgirls, and the abolition of state regulation of prostitution. Since marriage was an outright injustice to women – until 1956 married women in the Netherlands were legally incompetent – this issue too was heavily debated, though usually in private with the party most nearly concerned, her intimate friend Carel Victor Gerritsen. In 1890 they decided to marry for the sake of the child they both wanted and the political career Gerritsen had embarked upon as a radical liberal. Jacobs, however, was to keep her own name, and they were to have their own quarters in the house they would share, with the dining room and the drawing room in common. Unfortunately, the child Jacobs bore lived only one day, a fact she bitterly ascribed to medical incompetence.

This sad event and her subsequent operation prevented Jacobs from attending the founding meeting of the Vereeniging voor Vrouwenkiesrecht (Woman Suffrage Association; VVVK) in 1894, though she sent a declaration of support and later took part in the deliberations of the committee charged with designing a constitution. In 1895 she became president of the Amsterdam section of the VVVK and in 1903 president of the whole association, a position she held until full suffrage was won in 1919. Jacobs' prominent role in the Dutch woman suffrage movement was the result not just of extraordinary talents but perhaps more of a balance of good qualities for the position. Of great importance was her reputation as the first university-educated woman in the Netherlands. Added to that were her administrative abilities. Her lack of skill in public speaking was offset by the ease with which she wrote articles, petitions, addresses, and requests. And although she was more a politician than a theoretician, she gave the movement in

Aletta Jacobs.

the Netherlands a broader philosophical basis by translating both Charlotte Perkins Gilman's *Women and Economics* (in 1900) and Olive Schreiner's *Woman and Labour* (in 1910).

Another factor which made Jacobs' position as leader of the suffrage movement in the Netherlands almost unchallenged was her international reputation. For example, she had already met many of the women who attended the 1904 meeting in Berlin. In her reminiscences she relates with satisfaction how, at the 1899 ICW Quinquennial in London, many foreign women remembered her name in connection with her medical studies or her attempt to register to vote in 1883. Susan B. Anthony had approached her in particular, and the topic of their converstation, apart from surprise about Jacobs' age, had been her experiences as the first woman doctor in the Netherlands, and their comparable efforts to vote, which had had such completely different results.[17]

To Aletta Jacobs, the 1904 conference in Berlin meant a reunion with many women. Among them were a number of Austrian women as well as one Hungarian, Rosika Schwimmer, whom she had first met in 1903. In that year Aletta had accompanied Gerritsen to a congress of the Interparliamentary Union in Vienna. She had made good use of the occasion by establishing relations with active Viennese women like Marie Lang and Marianne Hainisch.[18] She had inspired them to set up a *committee* for woman suffrage, since Austrian women, like their German sisters, were not allowed to form any association with a political goal. She later visited Budapest, where in 1904 a national council of women was established, partly due to Aletta's encouragement and Rosika's energetic approach.

Rosika Schwimmer (1877–1948)

Rosika Schwimmer impressed the congress participants in 1904 as a charismatic young woman who, fired by the events surrounding her, promised Catt, even before the congress had ended, to set up a suffrage association in Hungary. In her last letter to Rosika, more than forty years later, Catt wrote, "I well remember walking on the street by the side of you and your uncle."[19] Schwimmer's pacifist uncle, Leo Katscher, had undoubtedly played a part in forming her committed attitude to life. Born in Budapest in 1877, in an upper middle-class Jewish family of freethinkers, Schwimmer was raised in a small country town which had nothing to offer girls in the way of higher education. Her only unusual education, therefore, was six months at a commercial school for young men, which she was allowed to attend, properly chaperoned, after special permission had been granted. In 1895, when she was eighteen years old, she suddenly had to provide for herself because of her father's professional misfortunes. She did clerical work for several firms until 1904 while simultaneously pursuing a writing career. After 1904 she tried to make a living as a journalist and by giving lectures at home and abroad. In 1897 the family returned to Budapest, where Rosika began to develop her organizational ability. In that year she organized the Nötisztviselök Országos Egyesülete (National Association of Women Office Workers). In 1903 she established the first Hungarian Association of Working Women (Munkásnö Egyesülete), and in 1904 she contributed to the founding of the Nöegyesületek Szövetsége (Council of Women). In the very same year, after the Berlin congress, the Feministák Egyesülete (Feminist Association) was founded, as Schwimmer had promised Catt. Like most suffrage organizations in their initial phases, the Feminist Association worked for a broad range of women's issues, of which woman suffrage was only one. Vilma Glücklich, who had made a name for herself in the field of higher education for girls, assumed its leadership.[20] Franciska, Rosika's sister and companion until Rosika's death in the United States in 1948, also became actively involved.

Rosika Schwimmer. The Hague, 1915.

Rosa Manus (1881–1943)

Rosa Manus' association with the IWSA began during the congress in Amsterdam in 1908. At that time she and Carrie Chapman Catt sealed a lifelong friendship, which turned out to be a significant factor for the history of the IWSA and the Dutch Woman Suffrage Association. Rosa proved herself a major acquisition in the national and international suffrage and peace movements. In *Journey towards Freedom*, Schreiber and Mathieson (1955, 55) portray her not only as a "superb organiser whose insatiable energy and enthusiasm overrode all obstacles," but also state, "To her artistry was owed much of the pageantry of the congresses." Maybe her own initiation experience in the IWSA convinced her of the importance of suffrage culture. An often-repeated fact in her biography was that originally she had been asked to take part only in a clog dance, of which in a written account she seems to have reported laconically, "Despite the fact that I was no dancing type, I agreed. It was all in a good cause" (Posthumus-van der Goot and De Waal, eds., 1977, 140). It was just as well, because during the congress Rosa discovered that in fact she had always been a feminist.

Rosette Susanne Manus was born as the second child and eldest daughter in a wealthy upper-middle-class Jewish family in Amsterdam. Her father was a tobacco merchant and adhered to strict traditional values with respect to what was "done" and what was "not done" for a girl like Rosa. He had never allowed her to take up a profession or do paid work. She had not been allowed even to go to high school. Instead French and English governesses taught her at home, the only advantage of which being that she learned modern languages well. At the age of seventeen she was sent to a boarding school in Switzerland to give her education the usual finishing touch. Since marriage was not part of her plan, however, she kept trying to break her father's rule. She even went so far as to hire premises in what is still a good shopping area of Amsterdam for the purpose of opening a fashion boutique, but when found out by her father was forced to cancel the agreements. Her only alternative was philanthropy, and by making a virtue of necessity, she succeeded within a relatively short period in working her way up from serving soup to managing various kitchens.

Perhaps her organizational talents had already won some fame among Amsterdam women. Certainly she was also asked, together with Mia Boissevain, a former schoolfriend, to set up an information bureau for foreign guests at the 1908 conference. It is not clear exactly what sparked the friendship between Carrie Chapman Catt and Rosa Manus. According to one account, Catt was caught by Manus' impersonation of a jauntily dancing Dutch girl. Others say that she stole Catt's heart sitting behind her desk early each morning armed with maps, address books, folders, and guides over which she reigned with enthusiasm and efficiency. In any case, their friendship was to inspire Manus to an unequaled dedication to the cause on a national and an international level. After the Congress, she was appointed assistant to Johanna Naber, who was secretary to the VVVK. Somewhat later, together with Mia Boissevain, she set up the Dutch association's vibrant Propaganda Committee. During the 1909 international congress in London, Manus was already equipped to fulfill the important function of page to the president. In 1910 she became the IWSA's special organizer (Meijers 1946, 21).[21]

A Common Language

Transcending the differences among women of many nationalities depended on finding a common language. Latin was seen as the truly *international* language, though of course it could not function as a *common* language. Women in the United States especially kept raising objections to the name *Jus Suffragii* (see letter 25), and we know that Anna Howard Shaw protested against the adoption of the Alliance's motto in Latin (Whittick 1979, 51). The success of the Alliance in creating a common language was based on more day-to-day communication, and in the framework of the IWSA, suffragists all over the world managed to develop common ways of thinking and formulating their thoughts. This becomes clear, for instance, from the letters exchanged by Aletta Jacobs and Rosika Schwimmer. In spite of the totally different social and political situations in the Netherlands and Hungary, these two were able to describe all kinds of events in similar terms. The common language encouraged a feeling of solidarity, and indeed created that feeling.

A common language was also developed in the shared organizational vocabulary and the use of certain metaphors. Images of war and strife were widely used in suffrage discourse. "Like a true soldier, she would snatch a moment of sleep or a mouthful of food, where she found it, and if either was not forthcoming she did not miss it," Shaw (1915, 191) says of Mary Anthony. In her turn Mary Anthony, in response to Jacobs' letter of condolence following the death of her sister Susan, wrote, "If we fail, we shall only have to buckle our armor anew and work still harder for a victory somewhere."[22] In the same spirit Catt comforted Rosika Schwimmer after she suffered a distressing experience at the congress in Stockholm in 1911: "It is to be hoped that you are still living and that your meeting on Sunday has not placed you under the ground. You are having some of the experiences of pioneers and you will be glad that you have had them in after years. . . . We shall bind your wounds and give you soothing drinks and send you back recovered and ready for some other battle."[23] The report of the 1908 Amsterdam congress mentions such unusual posts as pages, chief sergeant at arms, and assistant sergeant at arms, in addition to ordinary posts like chairman (IWSA 1908, 149).

Another popular metaphor was the image of the IWSA as a distinct and separate empire of women, with Catt as the uncrowned queen surrounded by ladies-in-waiting, ambassadors, and subjects. In the much-quoted narrative of Catt's visit to Queen Louise of Denmark in 1906, shortly before the IWSA's third congress, the audience is described as a meeting of equals. The boundaries between image and reality, between the real and the artificial queen are vague, an impression reinforced by Catt's forgetting to kiss the queen's hand, a fact which is always mentioned only too eagerly (Peck 1944, 148). In 1911, in preparation for the congress in Stockholm, Catt went on tour and had the demanding schedule of a government official at least, if not of a head of state. According to Peck:

The four days in the little kingdom [of Norway] were filled with festivities and political interviews. Mrs. Catt spoke at the Norwegian suffrage convention in Christiania. She was honor guest at a luncheon at Voksenkollen. She had interviews with Premier Konow and the Minister of Foreign Affairs; was given a supper at the Grand Hotel at which the Premier made the address of welcome; was given a reception at the Women's Reading Club and a luncheon at the American Legation; made speeches at the University of Norway and the Radical Students Union; and finally had an interview with King Haakon. [Peck 1944, 176–77]

The passage concludes with a lavish description of the chambers Catt occupied in Stockholm during the congress, which "were worthy of an envoy of a great power on a diplomatic mission" (Peck 1944, 177).

IWSA Congresses and Suffrage Politics, 1904–14

The Alliance came to life neither through the "Declaration of Principles" nor through the constitution, but in swapping experiences, challenging viewpoints, thinking up strategies and plans of action, and helping to set up national suffrage associations. The energetic exchanges of ideas were reinforced at the biennial congresses and in the monthly journal *Jus Suffragii*. Direct contacts between women were fundamental to the existence of the IWSA. Women at the congresses were again and again enthralled by the vivid reports of delegates from various parts of the world. In Copenhagen in 1906, for example, the announcement that Marie Curie had taken the place of her deceased husband at the Sorbonne evoked a storm of applause. Astonished participants heard the Icelander Briet Asmundsson, in national costume, tell the story of how she set up a suffrage society by visiting remote villages on horseback and speaking with as many women as she could find. Finally, Annie Furuhjelm, the imposing Finnish delegate, who seemed to embody all the promises the franchise held for women, greatly heartened the audience with the assurance that after the general strike and her country's liberation from Russia women were given the vote by the revolutionary government because they had shown themselves worthy of it. In other words, it was extremely important that women prepare themselves for the franchise by educating themselves politically.

The Congresses in this period took place in Copenhagen (1906), Amsterdam (1908), London (1909), Stockholm (1911), and Budapest (1913). Their business meetings had three main recurring items: first, the president's address, which most often stressed larger and smaller victories for suffrage movements in different countries; second, reports like those described above from both affiliated and fraternal associations; and third, the adoption of resolutions. In the first ten years of the IWSA, resolutions were concerned with expressing satisfaction with the progress of woman suffrage in various countries. In 1908, for instance, congratulations were sent to the women of Finland upon their full enfranchisement in 1906 and for the election of nineteen women to parliament in 1907. Other resolutions concerned IWSA policy and the constitution.

Of course many issues that played an important role in the national associations, such as the striving for universal suffrage or the more limited aim of equality in matters of suffrage, could not be avoided in debates, which sometimes led to resolutions. The IWSA usually took a moderate stand on these issues, often referring to a bylaw introduced in 1908, which stated that "the Alliance by mutual consent of its auxiliaries, stands pledged to observe absolute neutrality on all questions that are strictly national; to respect the independence of each affiliated association, and to leave it entirely free to act on all matters within its own country" (Whittick 1979, 51). In other instances the IWSA carefully avoided speaking out plainly. On the sensitive issue of militant strategy (especially controversial in Great Britain) no resolution ever passed which explicitly condemned militancy. On the contrary, on many occasions militant tactics were praised for their having brought "votes for women" to the attention of millions. However, by deciding to admit the English Women's Social and Political Union not as an affiliate but as a fraternal association, the IWSA implicitly did take a more moderate stand.

During the first ten years of its existence the Alliance grew steadily. In Budapest the Seventh International Woman Suffrage Congress was attended by four hundred women (and some men) representing twenty-four affiliated associations from nations spread over four continents.

Besides the biennial congresses, other highly effective ways of establishing and maintaining new ties were the speaking tours and journeys undertaken with the aim of organizing women for membership in the IWSA. Best known of these is the world tour made by Carrie Chapman Catt and Aletta Jacobs in 1911–12 (see chapter 4). But many other less far-flung tours also helped, for example, the lecture tour Martina Kramers and Rachel Foster Avery made through Belgium in 1905 and 1906 with the aim of establishing a society. Although their efforts did not bring immediate success, they did sow the seeds of a Belgian society, which sprang up a few years later and added a new member to the IWSA.

IWSA Congresses and Suffrage Culture, 1904–14

In a short summary concluding their description of the Berlin congress in 1904 Schreiber and Mathieson (1955) wrote in *Journey towards Freedom*: "This foundation Congress of the International Woman Suffrage Alliance was a hard-working one, without entertainments or social functions. It wore the plain uniform of the midwife, with no frills" (p. 6). "The Congress at Copenhagen in 1906 presented, however, quite a different scene," according to Regine Deutsch (1929), another chronicler of the IWSA. "Here, for the first time, the International Alliance presented itself to the general public, whose interest had already been aroused by a clever propaganda, and for the first time business proceedings were blent with social activities, which lent future Congresses of the International Alliance their characteristic and special charm" (p. 14). No history of the IWSA is complete without an appreciation of the congresses as cultural manifestations of the political ideal of international sisterhood.[24] Not only the business meetings but the congress as a whole dramatized the two central ideas of the Alliance: the *unity* which the IWSA embodied in the visible presence of so many conspicuous differences in manner and dress, nationality, language and culture, social class and religion, as well as the *equality* of the women the IWSA represented. The IWSA lent reality to the idea of an essential unity and equality of women by the use of a recurring set of gripping images around notions of difference—in fact by exaggerating differences and romanticizing them. The emphasis on difference makes the centrality of the reports on the national representatives intelligible. These reports offered a means to elaborate upon national and even regional differences. In Copenhagen, for instance, the Russian delegate in her person represented hardship endured under barbarian absolutism, at least in the eyes of the women from predominantly Western democracies. In her report she quoted extensively from a letter to the Duma written by a thirteen-year-old peasant girl, the only person in her village who could write. The letter ended: "We are uneducated women and beg to be forgiven if we have not written well. We do not write our names for fear of our husbands and our rulers. There are old women among us and girls also from three villages" (Schreiber and Mathieson 1955, 6–7). Citing this passage in the context of a national report is just one instance of dramatizing differences among women (young and old, educated and illiterate, from agrarian areas and urban settings) while at the same time asserting solidarity, equality, and unity of principle. By reading the letter aloud to the congress, moreover, the almost inconceivable distance between the village women and the suffragists was breached.

Difference was present in the "text" even of the business meetings, but much more so in the visible "context." The use of folklore was important in visualizing national and regional differences. What made the report from Iceland so widely acclaimed at the Copenhagen congress was not so much its content as the fact that it was presented by one of those "picturesque visitors" who came from Iceland, "wearing their national costume, long black dresses and white head-veils held in place by a golden crown" (Schreiber and Mathieson 1955, 8, ill. 3). In the exaggeration for dramatic effect the boundaries between image and reality are often blurred. It is doubtful that Briet Asmundsson wore her traditional attire at home.

The social meetings offered an even more adequate setting for the play of suffrage images. In Amsterdam during one of the evening parties, a clog dance was staged. In it sons and daughters of the Amsterdam bourgeoisie displayed the different traditional costumes which were still worn in some

Clog dance during the 1908 IWSA congress in Amsterdam. Middle row, standing, far left: *Rosa Manus;* third and fourth from right: *Charles Jacobs and Anna Overduin.*

villages in the Netherlands (fig. 3). Another imaginative presentation of difference was the Pageant of Trades and Professions at one of the evening sessions of the London congress in 1909. At dusk a thousand women, representing ninety trades and professions, had gathered, all dressed "in medieval or national costume, academic robes, uniforms or factory overalls" (Schreiber and Mathieson 1955, 14). The women carried lanterns and boughs of evergreen and extended over five blocks when they set off for the Albert Hall. According to Lisa Tickner:

> There was great excitement as the five divisions of the procession paused in each of the hall's main entrances, and then filed into the brilliant interior from the stormy darkness outside. The detail of the emblems and bannerets now clearly visible, a small army of working women moved down the arena to the music of the organ and the cheers of the assembled delegates. As the applause faded away they were greeted by the president of the International Suffrage Alliance, Carrie Chapman Catt, with the memorable phrase: "You are an argument." [Tickner 1987, 101–02; see also letter 22]

Indeed, the London procession magnificently argued the transcending of class differences.[25]

The last example to be discussed, and, it may be said, the most dramatic one in the context of the IWSA, comes from the Budapest congress of 1913, which in general is described as the most impressive of the prewar congresses. Carrie Chapman Catt and Aletta Jacobs had just returned from their world tour, which had so moved Catt that, in her president's address, she soared to new heights in her statements about international sisterhood.[26] According to the chroniclers, however, what brought the congress participants practically to tears was the "moving ceremony" during the "roll-call in the flag-bedecked Congress Hall" (Schreiber and Mathieson 1955, 20–21), in which Aletta Jacobs presented the banner of the Chinese women to the IWSA, symbolizing the membership of women on the other side of the world who themselves could not be present. The silk banner had been shown to Catt and Jacobs before its completion during a reception given in their honor by the Chinese suffragists in Nanking. The motto, which was embroidered in large Chinese characters, had been explained to them: "Helping each other, all of one mind" (Van Voris 1987, 99).

2

Politics and Friendship in the IWSA

Prosaics and Poetics of Suffrage Sisterhood

"Leaders from Anthony and Stanton to Addams, Catt, Jacobs and Hey-mann spoke and wrote often on the themes of solidarity and sisterhood. It is not apparent, though, whether their rhetoric reflected, masked, shaped or distorted reality" (Sherrick 1983, 661). This was part of the conclusion of an article about the international women's movement. Sherrick's caution was our conviction: the decision to edit a selection of personal letters from women in the IWSA was at least partly based on the presupposition that personal letters, as the most primary kind of source, would be able to tear off masks and reveal the sisterhood in its true form.

Our confidence was based on inspiring examples of research into the history of feminism which assessed the importance of informal networks as part of a new, more radical feminist perspective on the history of women. Before this, most histories of women's movements—the suffrage movement in particular—aimed at writing the history of political movements in the public sphere. Suffrage feminism was related to and compared with other political "isms" such as liberalism, socialism, and the struggle for general suffrage. Gender, however, the fact that women organized themselves separately "as women" did not figure prominently in these histories. Also, this kind of historiography relied primarily on official sources: congress papers, committee reports, resolutions and public speeches—all the archival material which results from formal organization. But the "new approach" to the history of women in some instances explicitly favored the use of personal letters. Blanche Wiesen Cook, in her groundbreaking article about female support networks and political activism, marked the change from earlier methodologies. She shifted her attention from exclusive consideration of the *business letters* of women political activists to an orientation which included their *love letters*, writing:

In my own work, ten years of work on the historical peace movement—studies that included such significant women as Lillian Wald, Jane Addams,

Crystal Eastman, and Emma Goldman—I had focused entirely on wom-
en's political contributions. I wrote about their programs for social justice
and their opposition to international war. Nothing else. Whenever I came
across a love letter by Lillian Wald for example, I would note "love-letter,"
and move on. This paper is the long overdue recognition that the personal
is the political, that networks of love and support are crucial to our ability
as women to work in a hostile world where we are not in fact expected
to survive. [Cook 1979, 413]

Blanche Wiesen Cook articulates here what was happening in a wider
circle of feminist scholars. Many women's historians began turning away
from what now—with contempt for a superseded standpoint—was called
"compensatory contribution history," proudly presenting the new history
as one that was "women-centered" as well as "women-defined."[1] In the debate
on politics and culture in women's history organized by *Feminist Studies* in
1980 this shift was further elaborated, conceptualized, and generalized in
terms of the centrality of women's culture in women's history. A corollary
to that centrality was the idea that in a history of feminism "female solidarity," women's "primary identification as women," and the fact that women
self-consciously joined with other women as a result of their "awareness of
sisterhood" should take pride of place over women's political ideas or public
activities (Smith-Rosenberg 1975, 57, 59; Gerda Lerner 1969, 53; Dubois et
al. 1980).

All these developments fanned our expectations that a selection of
personal letters of several individual suffragists could give insight into the
extended-friendship network of the IWSA, where "sisterhood" was "experienced." Indeed the private, if not intimate, correspondence of Carrie Chapman Catt, Anna Howard Shaw, Aletta Jacobs, Rosa Manus, and Rosika
Schwimmer would inform us about the "female world of suffrage love and
ritual," to use Smith-Rosenberg's phrase, or, in other words, the informal
sisterhood of the IWSA. We also expected to gain new insights into the formal ideology and the political practice of the Alliance, that is, into the
sisterhood as a formal organization.

In the years that have elapsed since we articulated our first expectations, feminist theory has advanced new insights. Under the influence of
French feminism or poststructuralism, feminist theory has started to question the unexamined presuppositions of earlier women's studies, the most
important one being the assumption that women's experience "is," and not
only "is," but is so universal that we can build complete conceptual systems
on it: we women know what it is to be a woman, and science must of necessity be enriched by receiving analysis from our perspective (Lauretis 1986;
cf. *Feminist Studies* 14/1 [1988]). At the heart of the new feminist theory is a
different conception of the relation between language and reality. Reality
is no longer seen as distinct from language, since we know reality only
through language, as a construction within language. Far from being the

solid ground upon which "we" stand when practicing feminist studies, "women's experience," "the reality of women's lives," and "our subjectivity as women" now appear to be constructions without a fixed point of reference. From this perspective the concept of women's culture was again reviewed. Though it has always been more than the "romantic view" of women's history to which it has sometimes been reduced,[2] the concept of women's culture has not achieved the radical redefinition it aimed at. The desired shift in the meanings of such (traditional) notions as politics and culture, public and private, subjection and resistance has not been achieved. Instead the outcome has been an understanding of women's culture as the "real experience" of women.[3]

In due course, then, we came back to Sherrick's conclusion, though now with more appreciation for its cautious formulation: did the rhetoric of women's solidarity and sisterhood, which we began to understand as the "discourse of sisterhood," *reflect, mask, shape,* or *distort* the reality of sisterhood? The four possibilities Sherrick suggests reflect uncertainty about the relation between rhetoric, language, and reality. What would it mean to speak of the "reality of sisterhood"? *Is* there a sisterhood outside the rhetoric? What made us think that there is a distinction between personal letters (reflecting reality) and public utterances (masking, distorting, or shaping reality); between love letters (spontaneously reflecting sisterhood) and business letters (consciously constructing sisterhood)? Such questions also cast doubt on the traditional distinction between public and private. Our expectations that the personal letters of IWSA suffragists would be a transparent medium through which to see the true sisterhood of international feminism had to be abandoned. The letters do not reveal the international sisterhood of women as it was, but only how the international sisterhood of women was perceived—or how it was constructed.

The context of the IWSA discourse as we know it from official sources like congress reports was very much on the minds of the women when they wrote to each other. It is not difficult to see that "private" letters and "public" discourse both participated in the same project: constructing the IWSA discourse/sisterhood. As such the letters represent a sort of "prosaics" of suffrage friendship. But every correspondence has portions which go beyond the IWSA discourse, constructing a mutual understanding based on individual patterns of meaning. These portions of the letters represent the "poetics" of suffrage sisterhood.[4]

The "Prosaics" of IWSA Friendships

The first thing one learns from the letters is that no clear distinction can be made between personal letters and business letters, and consequently between the personal lives of these women and their lives in the movement.

Aletta Jacobs and Anna Howard Shaw. Budapest, 1913.

"We are like lovers," Anna Howard Shaw wrote to Aletta Jacobs on January 4, 1915. "[A]s soon as a letter comes from you we want to answer it at once sending love and good wishes." She ends the letter, "This is just a message out of the joy of getting your letter tonight" (letter 45). In spite of this, most of the letter is about a very sensitive political and strategic question. At that time Shaw was still president of the NAWSA, and she was trying to let Jacobs know, though indirectly, that she and her organization would not participate in the 1915 Women's Congress at The Hague, which was soon to be held at Jacobs' initiative. This information is all the more significant because Carrie Chapman Catt, president of the IWSA, did not support Jacobs' initiative, either. Shaw used all the possible arguments: it would mean the end of the Alliance; the women from the belligerent countries would be against it; she did not have enough money to go, now that the war had hit her financially; she was overworked. Finally she writes, "The best thing I can do for peace and a thousand other things is to get votes for our women." Shaw almost says it as an aside, but this last is unmistakably a political statement. It is also the NAWSA's official reason for declining the invitation to attend the congress at The Hague. Shaw's letter is not unique. Most of the letters in this book were written as personal letters, but they combine an exchange of confidences with political decisions and plans.[5]

The letters reflect how the personal lives of the women suffrage leaders were completely interwoven with the feminist politics they practiced. In this respect these women's lives were similar to those of women in more visible women's communities like women's colleges or settlement houses, which arose in the United States in great numbers during the second half of the nineteenth century (Freedman 1979). M. Carey Thomas, the well-known president of Bryn Mawr and a good friend of Anna Howard Shaw, lived and worked with her friend and colleague Mary E. Garrett within the walls of the college. Jane Addams and Lillian Wald, both from the settlement house movement, led comparable lives.[6] Suffrage work may not have taken place within such visible and clearly defined boundaries, but for the women who held prominent positions in the suffrage movement it was also true that they worked not only from nine to five, but day and night, for the cause. Everything that these women did and experienced happened in the context of the movement. Their overseas vacations, supposedly meant to provide an opportunity to recover from chronic fatigue, would turn into propaganda tours. Conferences were attended as vacations.

Shaw's living room functioned as an office, the household accounts could with difficulty be distinguished from the association budget, and friends were also colleagues. Jacobs once described Lucy E. Anthony as filling "the triple function of secretary, friend, and housekeeper for her [Shaw]" (Jacobs 1905, 37). Anthony lived with Shaw for almost thirty years and was paid $50 a month (Finn 1979, 23). Shaw in her turn received a monthly allowance for years from her friends M. Carey Thomas and Mary Garrett. In 1908 they collected $60,000 for that goal (Shaw 1915, 225). Shaw's suffrage work, they reasoned, would improve if she were not continually having to lecture in order to earn money. Much of the rest of Shaw's income also came in the form of personal gifts. Notes like the following often appear in Shaw's diary: "This morning received from Pauline Chapers Hodge of 31 East 28th St. NY $100.—check to be used as 'you see fit—you know best where and how it is needed most.'" Another time she decided to use a $2,000 gift for "my health in our cause hers and mine that I may do better work."[7] And Shaw, in her last letter to Jacobs (written shortly after Jacobs lost all her money in 1918), wrote, "I am enclosing the money I promised in my last letter and want you to use it in any way and for any thing you think is most helpful to you and your work" (letter 56). One wonders whether this sort of information can still be retrieved from somewhere in the association's records.

Carrie Chapmann Catt usually approached such matters more formally; at any rate, when she received a personal bequest from Mrs. Frank Leslie for about one million dollars "to the furtherance of the cause of Women's Suffrage" (Stern 1970, 182), Catt immediately established the Leslie Woman Suffrage Commission, which continued to make grants until 1941 (Van Voris 1987, 251–52 n. 8). Indeed, if Catt had not filed precise notes of all Mrs.

Leslie's earlier gifts, it is entirely possible that she would not have been able to win so many of the court cases about the validity and the interpretation of the will. Yet her financial operations can also be described at least in part as a mixture of personal and business finances. For example, when Catt, as the formal employer of Martina Kramers, decided that the Alliance had voted to fix Kramers' salary at too low a rate, she simply ignored the democratic procedures and, without telling the others, just added $100 per month. The source of those funds is not known.[8]

The knowledge that formal and informal relationships within the International Alliance cannot be easily distinguished is important for our understanding of the friendships between women. Within the movement friendships were indispensable. A life outside the cause was scarcely possible. Jacobs tried twice to visit her friend Shaw in the United States, but both times Shaw was not at home. "I am just heartsick to think we missed you at Alnwick Lodge. My only consolation is that you know we were both in the field for our cause. We give every thing of ourselves and miss the dear presence of friends in our home all for it," Shaw wrote to Jacobs in 1915 after one such attempt to visit (letter 52). Even Shaw seldom had the opportunity to enjoy the house, which she had built herself. "Is it not a shame that she has to be away from her new home this first Spring, and also the first Summer? I just know we will be anti suffragists the next time so that we will not feel the responsibility of the suffrage work, and can stay home and make our gardens," Lucy E. Anthony joked regretfully just before she and Shaw were to leave for the 1908 congress in Amsterdam (letter 18). In a letter written soon after that, Shaw was able to report the agreeable news that two more friends would be able to come with them to the congress, including her own doctor. If a personal life filled with friends and good cheer was not possible in addition to the cause, it was found *within* the cause.

The wave of "sympathetic analysis" (DuBois et al. 1980, 38), which focused on women and their mutual relationships, has expanded our knowledge of the love and friendships among them. As a result it has become possible to understand Lucy E. Anthony as more than just Shaw's secretary and housemate. An ordinary secretary, after all, would not write the following words on the last page of her employer's diary: "On the last night of the last day of the year which took away my Precious Love–Her Friendship–took away her who was the joy of my life . . ." (Finn 1979, 23). In spite of such plain emotion, however, one must remember that formal and informal relationships were intertwined to such an extent that Lucy Anthony was paid a salary by Shaw during all those years. If all friendship contains, in addition to spontaneous emotions, a healthy dose of cool calculation–unconscious or not–this is possibly even more true for the suffragists' friendships. In the women's movement the collective ideals of solidarity and sisterhood became a visible reality in many individual women's friendships.

"Here lie two friends, for thirty-eight years united in service to a great cause" (Peck 1944, 436) was the epitaph which Catt had placed on the double grave in which she and her friend Mary Garrett Hay were buried.[9] Their passion for the cause underlay women's friendships even as those friendships reinforced their sense of sisterhood. In order to strengthen the bonds between women and to help the organization function better, the women in the Alliance took great pains over their friendships, deliberately cultivating them.

In many respects it was worth lending fate a hand. Having friends in all countries made traveling for the Alliance easier. It was cheaper to stay in each other's houses–and also more fun. In 1906, when Rachel Foster Avery, who was living with Shaw and Anthony at the time, went to Europe to make a propaganda tour of Belgium, she stayed a few days with Jacobs in Amsterdam. Avery's housemates waited in suspense for news about the visit. After the news had arrived, a relieved Anthony wrote to Jacobs:

> We have also had letters from Mrs. Avery telling of her visit and meeting with you and of how much she admires and cares for you, and you say in your letter how much you admire and care for her, and that makes us all very happy too, for we wanted you two to like and love each other. Do you know that after we were in your home and you were over here I was just a little afraid that we might have praised you two to each other so much that in the contrariness of things in general you might not like each other as much as you would have otherwise–but now we are happy in the friendship which we are sure will ever be yours. [letter 11]

Mary Gray Peck,[10] in her biography of Carrie Chapman Catt, reveals how Catt inspired much of the emotional effort and dedication which the women devoted to the cause: "The enthusiasm felt by the young workers for the rising leader was often just this side [of] idolatry. Their rivalry in good works sometimes led to friction, but jealousy and resentment evaporated in Mrs. Catt's presence with uncanny celerity. She sublimated the affections of her lieutenants into work for the cause, and the persuasiveness of her appeal for a united front generally was irresistible" (Peck 1944, 96). Catt's talent for organization may have been based on this conscious or unconscious technique, a technique others were able to learn and use as well. Rosa Manus seems to have had the same talent "of enthusing young people" and making "ardent feminists" of them (Schreiber and Mathieson 1955, 55).

It is difficult to distinguish between these women's conscious policy and their spontaneous emotion, between the prosaics and the poetics of the friendships within the suffrage movement. At first glance, Shaw's frequent "love notes" and "gossipy letters" to Jacobs seem to suggest a great intimacy. From the beginning Jacobs was drawn into the intimate circle of friends around Shaw. On closer scrutiny, however, one begins to suspect that Shaw was consciously creating an atmosphere of love and friendship. When, before the congress in 1908, Jacobs asked for photographs of pioneering feminists, Shaw wrote that the photo of Susan B. Anthony would be the same as the one Shaw had hanging in her home. "Mrs. Avery and Lucy and I are going to have a copy of this picture made for you, your own dear self." Shaw repeats emphatically that the photo was a present from the three women to Jacobs: "So this is not a gift to the [Dutch] Association or by the Association at all, but just a little personal remembrance from us three who love you so very dearly and who are so interested in our good service and share in our admiration for our dear Aunt Susan."[11] Her feelings for Jacobs may have been honest, yet the distinction between their personal and business relationship is more rhetorical than anything else. One cannot escape the impression that Shaw's protestations of love are sometimes a little overdone, serving other ends as well. At least it seems so in the letter she wrote–confidentially–to Jacobs saying that she had had two ambitions in her life and that Catt had achieved both while Shaw had not. One had been to succeed Susan B. Anthony as president of the NAWSA; the other had been to go on a world tour like the one that Catt and Jacobs were making when she wrote:

> Had Mrs Catt known how with all my soul I had longed to do that very thing ever since the W.C.T.U. had sent its Temperance missionaries out, and how it made me ache all over to have to give up the ambition to be one of the first round the world woman suffrage missionaries she would not have misunderstood. I tried to tell her several times, but some[how] I never could open my heart to Mrs Catt. Not that she was ever unkind or unsympathetic, but because I felt she distrusted me because she had had distrust preached constantly to her. [letter 33][12]

It is highly likely that Shaw hoped that this information would find its way from Jacobs to Catt.

The intimacy Shaw invoked writing her many letters to "my dear dear Doctor" cannot be separated from her style of suffrage management. Shaw perhaps went further than most in identifying personal friendship with a more sentimental concept of sisterhood. In the North American woman suffrage movement the idea of a natural solidarity, a universal sisterhood of women, was much more powerful than in Europe. For instance, in 1910, at the NAWSA's yearly convention, where not a few internal difficulties arose (see letters 27–30), one woman, seemingly not embarrassed by the frictions, gave a talk under the rubric "The Sisterhood of Women." "We have plenty of work to do," she said, "but it is not that, it is not the organization, the growth of membership and the spread of theories that make me confident of success. It is the extraordinary spirit that animates the women who are working for suffrage, the sense of comradeship and community among them, rich and poor, educated and illiterate, old and young, mothers and daughters" (HWS, 5:283). Certainly the discourse of sisterhood allowed women to play with concepts of love and friendship in order to carry out a certain policy or to cover up less attractive dealings.

Although personal friendships were encouraged and cultivated in the context of the suffrage politics of sisterhood, such friendships were at the same time restrained by these very suffrage politics. Catt had a more pragmatic conception of sisterhood and in her role as president of the IWSA constantly stressed the need to work toward an impartial, objective, and therefore suprapersonal unity. In 1908, when she addressed the IWSA congress, she said: "Within our Alliance we must develop so lofty a spirit of internationalism, a spirit so clarified from all personalities and ambitions and even national antagonisms that its purity and its grandeur will furnish new inspiration to all workers in our cause" (Peck 1944, 161–62). In other words, work together, cherish a "sisterly sympathy" for each other, but do not involve yourselves too much in each other's private lives and personal convictions. This aspect of the suffrage discourse of sisterhood explains why the letters in this book are not so revealing about the personal lives and feelings of the women involved as one might suppose. Informal and formal bonds in the Alliance were intertwined to a great extent, but for the most part they were structured in accord with the organization's needs. Personal associations took place within the context of the Alliance and were limited by the organization's prescriptions and proscriptions. The letters in this book to a large extent reflect and even reinforce, rather than escape, the suffrage movement's economy of silence and speech. Their writers knew what could be said and done with propriety, and they respected the suffrage movement's taboos.

This tacit understanding may also explain why—notwithstanding the constant crossing of the personal and the political—women within the organization at least verbally adhered to a distinction between their public and private lives, between the public suffragist and the private woman. The letters frequently include such phrases as "but we had better not write about that." Jacobs wrote to Rosika Schwimmer before the 1906 tour with Catt:

> Can you tell me what exactly the women doctors want to know about Malthusianism? Surely they don't want a lecture? If they do, it will have to be in private without the press or any propaganda. It's not that I fear the publicity but it certainly would harm our cause. People are so stupid, they get the wrong end of the stick, and everything concerning sex may not be mentioned, it may only be done. I do not know Catt's views on the subject. Oddly enough, I have never discussed this with her. [letter 13]

Not so oddly, really. Jacobs apparently respected the ban for women suffrage activists on the public discussion of neo-Malthusianism even in her private encounters with Catt. She must have felt instinctively that she had better not talk about it with her friend the president. Jacobs' protest against the training and certification of laywomen by the Neo-Malthusiaanse Bond (NMB) to dispense birth-control information and devices, and her subse-

Rosika and Franciska Schwimmer. Budapest, 1919.

quent break of official ties with the NMB probably had political motives (Advokaat, Moll, and Niekus 1980, 116). At that time she became president of the Dutch Woman Suffrage Association, and if suffragism wanted to have any hope of success in the Netherlands, it was vital that someone like Jacobs not get involved in any other causes – and certainly not become a subject for gossip! Martina Kramers made a similarly conscious decision to pull out of the NMB in 1913, when the suffrage struggle intensified. Unofficially, however, Jacobs never detached herself from neo-Malthusianism. The meeting in Hungary with the women doctors was not the only time that she gave women information about "voluntary motherhood."

How much it became second nature for Jacobs as a suffragist to keep silent on this issue is revealed by an American newspaper account from 1925. At that time journalists interviewed foreign notables about their visits to the United States immediately after their boat had docked. The newspaper article in question reported the arrival of two European feminists: Helene Stöcker[13] from Germany and Aletta Jacobs from the Netherlands. Both women had the same destination. When asked what she was planning to do in America, Stöcker truthfully said that she was en route to a conference on birth control. Jacobs, however, told the journalists that she was planning to visit her old suffrage friend, Carrie Chapman Catt, which was not untrue, but certainly was not the whole story (*New York Times*, March 28, 1925). Yet even those in the midst of the movement were unsure about how much someone had a right to a private life and opinions. This lack of clarity left the women vulnerable and subject to manipulation. Martina Kramers was involved in one such ambiguous situation. Although the annals reported that Martina gave up her post as editor of *Jus Suffragii* of her own free will, this turns out not to be so. In spring 1913, a plan had originated to establish a new headquarters of the Alliance, with an international press office, in London and to publish *Jus Suffragii* from the new office. When Kramers did not immediately accede to Catt's request that she step down as editor and publisher, Catt—with the apparent cooperation of Jacobs—tried a different tack.[14] For years Kramers had had an extramarital relationship with a certain "Bobbie." Catt now used this fact as a lever to move Kramers, pressing her in a letter to leave quietly because, she said, in American circles rumors were rampant about Kramers' free love. Note that she did not reproach Kramers for her "illicit" relationship. Instead, she wrote: "In my judgment such matters are largely personal and must be governed by one's own conscience, but they cease to be personal or individual when one carries them into public work" (letter 38).

In her answer Kramers pointed out that Catt was using gossip and hearsay to get rid of her. When rumors had circulated about the homosexuality of two German women, Anita Augspurg and Käthe Schirmacher, or about Aletta Jacobs, suspected to be an abortionist, Catt had refused to lend an ear to the rumormongers.[15] She challenged Catt to have her case decided openly, and asked her not to influence organizational policy by personal manipulations. She ended her letter: "I hope soon to see that as President you refuse to discuss [the] personal life of candidates, and that as friend you will some time give me the opportunity to present to you the man I love."[16] Martina Kramers understood perfectly well that the politics of silence, which was based upon a vague distinction between public and private, made her a pawn, but she was not in a position to break out of the cycle. The threat of making her "secret" public was so great that she was powerless to combat it. During the Budapest Congress in 1913, she reported herself sick and left.

This unsavory incident might confirm the increasingly popular vision of the suffrage movement as a more or less conventional, unquestioning women's rights movement, in which "respectable women" aspired to merely superficial political changes, without touching the existing balance of power.[17]

And indeed, the suffrage movement can very well be described as a summary of opinions and political propositions which increasingly left out a disturbing number of feminist issues. But that does not mean that all the women who worked within the movement allowed themselves to be boxed in. For many, it is true, participation in the suffrage movement meant that they had to adapt friendships, activities, and opinions to the movement's policies, which in a number of cases promoted a political caution that resulted in stiff conventionality. Most of the correspondence in this book stays within the boundaries drawn by the movement. Yet, again and again the letters make it clear that what the women said or wrote was far from what they thought or did when they were off duty.

The "Poetics" of IWSA Friendships

Until now I have emphasized the rational and functional aspects, or the prosaics, of friendships within the IWSA. These can be built up from the letters, but by doing this one puts them in a rather unromantic light. For there were other aspects to it; it is not a single, uniform, lackluster suffrage friendship that the letters bear witness to. The various correspondences also give evidence of the so-called nonfunctional, accidental, loose, "natural," emotional, intellectual, and spiritual attraction between the women. If there is a prosaics of suffrage friendships, which sees the personal associations of women jealously guarded by IWSA politics and the discourse of sisterhood, there is also a poetics of suffrage friendships. These peek through whenever women cross the IWSA boundaries to construct individual patterns of meaning. In their individual ways women continually redefined IWSA sisterhood.

Aletta Jacobs and Rosika Schwimmer (1902–15)

The passage from Aletta Jacobs' letter to her younger friend Rosika Schwimmer cited earlier as an illustration of the circumspection women exercised even amongst themselves with respect to sensitive questions also reveals how openly those same questions could be discussed with carefully selected friends. This openness is characteristic of all the letters Schwimmer and Jacobs exchanged. Clearly these two trusted and knew each other so well that they felt free to discuss a wide range of issues. In one of her letters to Schwimmer, Jacobs wrote, "I should like to talk with you because I cannot write it in such a way that you will understand me," but in contrast with the earlier example, it is not caution that silences her here. What Jacobs meant to say is that the subject at hand, Schwimmer's predilection for morphia and its connection with her suppressed sexual desires, required a subtler treatment than Jacobs' written German would allow (letter 4).

Jacobs' letters to Schwimmer show that these women shared a broad feminist perspective, which allowed them to discuss subjects which in general were not publicly touched upon within suffrage circles: prostitution, white slavery, child protection, and birth control. A broad range of activities are also recounted in the letters. Moreover, Jacobs and Schwimmer discussed feminist theory. Jacobs, who translated Charlotte Perkins Gilman's book *Women and Economics*[18] into Dutch, inspired Schwimmer to do a translation into Hungarian. Schwimmer in her turn sent Jacobs many of her articles for criticism. This was a courageous act, for Jacobs could be severe: "I have read your short story with interest, but I don't understand it really. Did you ever meet a whore that already practiced such a long time and still cherished such ideals?"[19]

It is interesting to see that Jacobs in her letters to Schwimmer repeatedly identifies men or women as Jewish: "We have . . . recruited some good young workers. It is remarkable that they are always Jewish girls. With us and everywhere else. Courage and spirit are found most in these girls" (letter 10). This is quite a striking passage, since Jacobs always showed herself to be a child of the strongly assimilating, liberal Jewish community in which she grew up in Groningen. Suffrage emphasis on equality undoubtedly even reinforced this attitude. But in her confidential association with Schwimmer, she could discuss more things than with other, non-Jewish women in the movement. Very likely this had to do with the Jewish milieu to which Schwimmer belonged. She lived in Budapest in a political emancipationist atmosphere. There, in 1895, Theodor Herzl wrote his Zionist pamphlet *Der Judenstaat* (Romein 1967, 26). The Liberal Party in Hungary was made up almost entirely of Jews, and the suffrage movement was dominated by Jewish women and men (Evans 1979, 100). Schwimmer was more open than Jacobs in identifying women as Jewish. In an article called "Women Pioneers of a New International Order," she described Jacobs, Anita Augspurg, and Vilma Glücklich as "a few of the most brilliant Jewish women of our time" (Schwimmer 1924). The assessing of a "different," Jewish identity may have run contrary to the emphasis on equality and unity within suffrage discourse, but in the Jacobs-Schwimmer relationship it evidently had a role.

The correspondence between Jacobs and Schwimmer stands out from the other correspondences in the book in the range and depth of subjects discussed. This may have something to do with generational differences—Schwimmer and Jacobs both belonged to the pioneering generation of feminists in their countries, while Shaw, Catt, and Manus were members of the "second generation."[20] In part the spirited expression of ideas and convictions between Jacobs and Schwimmer can be traced to their common European background. European suffragism differed from American suffragism in its emancipationist claims. Even though the American model of a pragmatic and strategic concept of sisterhood had begun to be imitated in Europe by the turn of the century, European suffragism in general never reached the kind of unity the North American suffrage movement had.[21]

Aletta Jacobs and Anna Howard Shaw (1905–18)

Anna Howard Shaw made many protestations of intimacy in her letters to Aletta Jacobs, but her words must be read in context. The confidences she made were perhaps more the result of a consciously chosen style of management than anything else. This style seems to be intrinsically connected with Shaw's way of life and her self-perception. It is interesting to read her autobiography for her description of the female world of independent women she lived in. In this personal history she seems to mark every step by the women who stood by her at different times. Certainly she expressed her feminism in terms of a strong identification with women, for she had her own woman doctor, she hired a woman architect to design her cottage, she dictated her autobiography to a woman journalist, and, last but not least, she chose a woman as her life's companion. Set against this positive attitude toward women was a certain detachment, if not amused contempt, for men. This shows in numerous details in *The Story of a Pioneer*. She gives her opinion of her father unreservedly: "Like so many men, my father should never have married" (Shaw 1915, 27). Her first letter to Jacobs includes a variation on this theme: "My friends have often laughed at me because I have a list of six men of whom I say very often they have proved to me beyond doubt that it is possible to be as happy married as to be not married, but, since I was in Amsterdam and met your husband, there has been one more added to my list, so my friends are now laughing at me because my list is beginning to grow. But I am quite sure that such a list cannot be complete without the addition of your good husband."[22]

The most comical example of the way in which Shaw always decided the battle of the sexes in favor of women is the story of her horse Daisy— who would not allow men to get near her. It was an inconvenient trait in a horse, but Shaw decided to keep Daisy anyway. With obviously malicious pleasure, Shaw tells in one passage of her autobiography how a man whom she did not much care for insisted on proving that he could get along with Daisy. Shaw advised him most strongly not to try, but he persisted: "At his approach she rose on her hind-legs and when he grasped her bridle she lifted him off his feet. His expression as he hung in mid-air was an extraordinary mixture of surprise and regret. The moment I touched her, however, she quieted down, and when I got into the buggy and gathered up the reins she walked off like a lamb, leaving the man staring after her with his eyes starting from his head" (Shaw 1915, 137). The story is an outstanding model of feminist fiction. The female characters in this story are natural allies who unintentionally conspire to put the male protagonist in his place.

Shaw's *Story of a Pioneer* reflects many of the developments in the Ameri-

*Aletta Jacobs and Carrie Chapman Catt at the
station in Manila, 1912.*

can suffrage movement described in chapter 1, but it does not parallel these developments completely. Certainly her explicit emphasis on
the rich emotional texture of the female world she lived in and the centrality of women in her life/text were not equally appreciated by her
fellow suffragists. Her attitude may explain one aspect of the intimacy she
expressed in her correspondence with Jacobs. In her last letter to her Dutch
suffrage friend, written on Thanksgiving Day, 1918, she said: "Oh dear Doctor there are so few real friendships in the world that those which do exist
should be prized above all things, so today in recounting some of my blessings, they are so many that I cannot recount them all in the foreground
are my dear friends and out from the larger group a few for whom I am
especially grateful among them is my dear Doctor. So on this thanksgiving
day I am thankful for you" (letter 56). One can see Shaw's tendency toward
hyperbole here, but there is something more in these words, something
which escapes the context of suffrage discourse and gives us a glimpse of
the poetics of suffrage friendships.

Aletta Jacobs and Carrie Chapman Catt (1905–29)

The correspondence between Aletta Jacobs and Carrie Chapman Catt is in
many ways similar to that between Jacobs and Shaw, but the comparison
is incomplete because Catt would have been the last one to gush over a

In the garden of the American Club in Hangchow, China.

friendship. Her style was that of the true comrade, the congenial coworker. Her letters display the good, businesslike companionship and easy friendship that—especially during Catt and Jacobs' joint world tour—reached its apogee. Competition, however, also played a certain role. It is amusing to compare some of the passages from Jacobs' memoirs to Mary Peck's biography of Catt. Peck describes one incident during a tour through Europe in 1909 in the following terms: "In leaving Vienna to go to Budapest, the travelers met their only mishap during the trip, owing to Dr. Jacobs' misunderstanding directions, and in consequence piloting her companion on the wrong train" (Peck 1944, 156). Jacobs' interpretation is different: "We never could figure out whether the coachman was pulling our leg, and had therefore given the porter who carried our baggage the wrong information, or whether the porter simply misunderstood our intentions. It is certain, however, that someone put us on the wrong train, which pulled out of the station the moment we sat down" (Jacobs 1924, 108).

In a similar passage, describing their adventures in Budapest, Peck remarks: "The press gave unusual space to the meetings. Dr. Jacobs spoke German and needed no interpreter; Mrs. Catt's speeches had to be translated, but even with this handicap she received the lion's share of the publicity" (Peck 1944, 156). According to Peck, afterward Catt was given a beautiful scrapbook filled with the reviews (translated into English) of the speeches. According to Jacobs, the Hungarian women had been "so kind as to collect everything that had been published during those days and present the collection to us in a beautiful leather binding as a souvenir of the days we had spent in their city (Budapest)" (Jacobs 1924, 116). The best example of the competitive one-upmanship characteristic of the friendship is Jacobs' lengthy explanation of a difference of opinion which took place during the world tour about the names of two palm trees, the taliput palm and the royal palm. In her memoirs, Jacobs says simply, "after a while, Catt had confused the two names," which resulted in a disagreement whenever one of the two trees appeared. During a tour of the State Botanical Garden in the Dutch East Indies, an expert, at Jacobs' request, gave a positive identification of the two trees. Jacobs adds playfully but decidedly, "And it turned out that I had been right. We exchanged glances for barely a moment, but neither of us said a word" (Jacobs 1924, 288).

Catt refers to the episode one more time in a poem she presented to Jacobs when they had been traveling together for exactly a year. The theme of the poem is that, although everyone had predicted that they would be tearing each other's eyes out and would return home on separate ships, actually their friendship had only grown stronger.

> But then, my dear, I'd have you know
> It is the Taliput
> That palm they call the Royal one
> On that I'll stake my mut
> And if you will admit it is
> With you the summer seas
> I'll sail till death shall part us two
> If not, I'll say adieu. [Jacobs 1924, 289]

Afterward Catt noted in her diary:

> After the (traveling) party was reduced to us two, all was harmonious. We had the same wishes about traveling arrangements, both were businesslike in settling up accounts promptly. We had many arguments and did not agree on many things, but we came through fast friends. Her devotion to the cause of her sex, her information on many subjects, her good memory, her ceaseless energy, combine to make her a truly wonderful and great woman. It was with mutual respect that we parted, and we shall always have in common the memory of the most wonderful experience which ever fell to either of us. [Peck 1944, 206]

In 1924, Jacobs write in her memoirs:

> I have got to get it off my chest that, for the first time since the death
> of my husband, I had spent a happy year. It was a year during which I
> had spent my days in an atmosphere of affection and intelligence, due to
> an association with someone with whom I completely sympathized and
> whom I also esteemed highly. During that 16 month trip, I learned to value
> Mrs. Catt as one of those rare, superior women who, in an earlier age,
> would have been called saints. [Jacobs 1924, 295]

Their friendship had survived the test and would survive even more profound differences of opinion, for instance about the 1915 congress at The
Hague. The last line that Jacobs ever wrote to Catt was, "If I die conscious
it will be with a kind thought for you upon my lips (letter 66).

Catt's own judgment of Jacobs seems to have been milder than Peck's,
whose vision was probably somewhat clouded because the world trip with
Jacobs had taken Catt away from her for more than a year. Peck wrote that
Catt "sublimated the affections of her lieutenants into work for the Cause,"
but Catt's techniques for sublimating all that affection did not always work
equally effectively. This holds true for Peck's own feelings at least as much
as for those of many other women. Peck's descriptions of her friend sometimes reach lyrical heights. The correspondence between the two women
contains undisguised love letters, Catt often beginning with a tender "My
dearest Pecky Pan." At that time Catt was living with Mary Garrett Hay
and Peck with Dr. Frances Squire Potter.[23] In an undated (1910) letter to Potter in which Catt was trying to make an appointment with Potter, she
wrote reassuringly, "Miss Peck and I are making love to one another but
with you to watch her and Miss Hay to keep her eye on me, I expect it
will be some time before an elopement can be successfully planned!"[24]

Peck is not the only woman with whom Catt maintained a long, intimate
friendship. She had worked with Mary Garrett Hay (Mollie)[25] since 1895. Soon
after the death of Catt's second husband, Hay moved in with Catt, and they
stayed together until death parted them—literally. In 1928, Catt was talking to
her friend on Hay's birthday, when Hay suddenly had a stroke and fell back
unconscious on her bed. "What a wonderful death!" Jacobs wrote at the end
of a detailed report of the events in a letter to her Dutch friend Mien van
Wulfften Palthe-Broese van Groenou, ending the letter with: "Rosa is now going to America in November and is thinking of staying for a few months."[26]

Rosa Manus and Carrie Chapman Catt (1908–41)

Rosa Manus and Carrie Chapman Catt also conceived an ardent passion
for each other which had lasting consequences. All descriptions of their
first encounter during the IWSA congress in Amsterdam in 1908 indicate
love at first sight. Afterward, and in preparation for the next 1909 congress
in London, Catt wrote Manus "several charming letters" and asked her to

Rosa Manus and Carrie Chapman Catt at the arch of Constantine in Rome, 1923.

be her page during the congress. Not until their father had enjoined Catt to take care of his two daughters, Anna and Rosa, were "the girls" allowed to go at all. In an extensive report of the congress to another American friend, Mrs. McCulloch, Rosa Manus made no effort to hide her feelings. She was enraptured. Catt was "sweet and lovely" and "altogether a wonder," and Manus had worked herself to the bone trying to make sure that Catt wanted for nothing. No picture of Catt and Manus' relationship would be complete without a shade of eroticism. Catt had reserved rooms for the sisters right next to her own room. "Anna went off to stay at a friend's of hers at the country and so," writes Rosa Manus, "Mrs Catt and I had a glorious time together. . . . In between I was the only one who had a chance to be with her as I helped her dress, and took her home after the meetings and we always had our meals together too" (letter 22). One had one's friends—and one's special friends. In 1928, when Manus wanted to make it clear to Selma Lagerlöf who exactly she was again, Manus wrote: "I was at the time the special friend of Mrs. Chapman Catt, our much honoured President."[27] Catt and Manus often expressed their relationship in terms of a (step)mother-daughter relationship. "She always called me her little adopted daughter and she was really a perfect Mother to me. I grew passionately fond of her, I can tell you and she says she loves me very much" (letter 22). This adoptive mother-daughter terminology must be understood symbolically. It was quite common to describe an extraordinary, loving, and intense emotional bond between two women in these terms. When Susan B. Anthony, who was publicly known as "Aunt Susan," wrote a dedication to Shaw in the *History of Woman Suffrage, Part IV*, she began thus, "This huge volume IV I present to you with the love that a mother beareth. . . ," and she ended, "with unbounded love and faith" (Shaw 1915, 235).

What concepts were there to describe intense emotional feelings between women? Most common was the mother-daughter relationship, which in the last centrury seems to have involved much less overt tension than today (Smith-Rosenberg 1975). The emotional value of the terms *mother* and *daughter* in part runs parallel with the feminist ideology of motherhood. The turn-of-the-century feminist movement, with the help of various concepts of motherhood, tried to explode the deeply rooted ideas that womanhood and motherhood were biologically determined. Spiritual motherhood was a key concept which could be understood on various levels. Feminism, in this vision, was an abstract, large-scale form of motherhood. Women could express spiritual motherhood on a small scale by adopting children, taking in nephews and nieces, or coaching young women during their studies or at the beginning of their careers.[28]

As far as Manus was concerned, Catt was everything that life had to offer. Their relationship inspired her enormous devotion to the women's movement. "Yes, Lucy," she wrote to Lucy E. Anthony in 1926, "you are right in saying that for my love of Mrs. Catt I was inspired to give my very best to the Paris Congress; every minute and every thing I did for it I thought of her and it was dreadful not having her with us, however her watching eye and leadership was still with us" (letter 63).

Though her friendship with Catt inspired Manus to ever-greater initiatives, Catt was also inspired by Manus to undertake activities that she probably never would have ventured on otherwise. In 1933, for instance, Catt organized a protest against the Hitler regime's anti-Semitism. Rosa, who had just spent some time visiting Catt, wrote on the ship on her way back:

> It is a good thing you cannot see under which emotion I am writing this to you. But surely <u>real</u> friendship is the best thing on earth. My stay with you seems a wonderful dream, and when I let the days and hours go by since my arrival on July 14th so much seems to have been that is almost impossible that I have been only 5 weeks there. Seeing you at work for the protest of the Jews moved me more that I can tell you and the words written by one of those man [men] "you are a blessing to the world" is real true and the Jews of the world can never be grateful enough to you for having done this masterly piece of work. . . . All the work you have done in the past seems small in comparison with this wonderful, daring jest [gesture]. [letter 74]

Clara Meijers wrote in her biographical sketch of Rosa Manus, "As a modern Cassandra she predicted the disaster that was to come" (Meijers 1946, 59).[29]

Indeed, Manus' letters throughout the thirties reveal her premonition and growing awareness of what would happen later, and, so it seems, in all its magnitude. One wonders if it is a coincidence that Rosa Manus writes, on February 2, 1933, just three days after Hitler became chancellor of the German cabinet, that her "bowels seem to be quite in disorder," which in the next letter she attributes to a nervous breakdown.[30] Her health and spirits diminish more and more and sometimes prevent her even from writing to her beloved "stepmother." The events of Kristallnacht (November 9–10, 1938) seem to have been a real breaking point. She wrote to Catt that she could not stop thinking of the people who were suffering so in Germany, and she informed her of her decision to withdraw from the board of the Alliance. Early in 1940 Manus went through her things and brought all her archives to the IAV: "It will prove more useful in the future to have it all there" (letter 82). More than once Manus thanked Catt for the long friendship they had had, and on January 16, 1941, a few months before she was taken prisoner by the Nazis, she pondered: "You have always told me that a memory can never be taken away and you are right. In these days I just sit and think of all the nice things which have gone, the wonderful times I have had with you arise amongst them and it seems to be helping me to pull along, but it is difficult sometimes" (letter 83).

Catt's letters are comforting. She tried to encourage her friend to be a "fighting Rosa" (letter 80, note 9) instead of an "old maid sitting and knitting," but sometimes she missed the mark. For instance, when she heard about Manus' diet for her bowel trouble in February 1933, she joked: "You will be quite prepared to go to jail some day."[31] In answer to Rosa's announcement of her resignation from the Alliance board, she wrote: "I think, perhaps, you are feeling too sensitive about all the things that are happening to the Jews."[32] And in her last letter to Rosa Manus her optimism is poignant: "This is a birthday letter to congratulate you upon your sixtieth birthday. You will surely live as long as I have lived, twenty-two years longer" (letter 84).

Catt's love for Manus stirred her sense of justice and reactivated the old instincts. But for all her political experience, Catt's attitude was ambivalent. Her solidarity with the Jews in Germany was very much a solidarity with "the Others," to whom Manus does not—yet does—belong. It is *their* cause, Manus being one of "them" only implicitly. "Well, dear Rosa, . . . There is work for you to do," Catt concludes a letter from 1933 in which she informs Manus of Hitler's plans to "put [the Jews] down in Germany" (letter 73). Her role can best be described as that of an intermediary, between Manus and the National Council of Jewish Women, as well as between Jewish and non-Jewish women. She even asked Manus to write personal matters on different paper from information about Germany so that Catt could send the information straight on to the National Council of Jewish women.[33]

Though Manus confided all her fears and premonitions to Catt, she was seldom explicit about her Jewishness. Even when writing Catt to thank her for her "daring action," she speaks in terms of "the Jews," instead of "we Jews." In turn there is only one place in the correspondence where Catt positively identifies Manus as a Jew, urging her Dutch friend to take a trip to Jerusalem with a nice Jewish friend.[34] Suffrage politics and discourse helped in recognizing the dangers of totalitarianism, yet fell short of analyzing the sources and power of anti-Semitism. The Catt-Manus correspondence poignantly shows the importance of their intimate friendship to them as they tried to speak the things they never learned and did not dare to say. They did so to the very last moment. The idea that Manus left an unfinished letter to Catt on her desk when she was arrested by the Germans is deeply moving, and no account of their international suffrage friendship is complete without this image.

3

The Dutch Woman Suffrage Campaign and the IWSA

Aletta Jacobs and International Feminism

The true effectiveness of the IWSA can be seen in its influence on the national level. Did the IWSA have any influence on the Dutch suffrage movement? Certainly the fact that the woman suffrage claim was raised internationally gave the movement extra prestige. This was true in particular for Aletta Jacobs, who was held responsible for the international connection and who obviously benefited from international renown. Her extensive international contacts are repeatedly referred to by her contemporaries and are often put forward to explain why she sat so long and so firmly in the presidential saddle (*Gedenkboek* 1919, 10, 15). When in 1903 Aletta Jacobs was chosen as president of the VVVK, the Dutch association in a sense made a choice for the "American model," which can be described by the concepts of unity and nonpartisanship, internationalism being its natural ally. From then on, the VVVK definitely took the political line of linking as many different women as possible in pursuit of only one aim: woman suffrage. It is significant that one of the first decisions taken under Jacobs' presidency was that the VVVK become a member of the recently established International Committee for Woman Suffrage in Washington.

It is interesting to see how the letters in Jacobs' archives reflect the nature and the development of her international contacts, which in their turn reflect something of the development of feminist internationalism in general. From the 1880s there is a small but steady stream of letters from various individuals abroad about a range of women's issues. Most often the letters exchange information. Thus from 1882 there are two letters from Theodore Stanton in which he thanks Jacobs, first for the informative letter he plans to use for the chapter on Holland in his forthcoming book, and second for the admirable photograph for his collection of interesting European women.[1] From the early 1890s, there are two letters from Alexandra Gripenberg, a Finnish woman who played a prominent part in the ICW at that time. One of them contains questions about the position of Dutch women for a general survey on women in Europe; the other expresses Gripenberg's gratitude for the material sent to her.[2] Jacobs obviously made use of these contacts to add to the women's section of the Gerritsen collection.[3] Letters like these are testimonies to the growing international sisterhood, which existed, long before the ICW or the IWSA, in the shape of a regular but informal exchange of information. After 1899, however, there is a change. Not only is there a significant increase of letters from foreign women; almost all the writers have met Jacobs or make reference to the 1899 congress, and they present themselves as partaking in a common movement. The range of subjects remains broad, but suffrage begins to dominate.

After the congress in Berlin and Jacobs' subsequent trip to the United States with Gerritsen, this tendency grows stronger. At this time Jacobs began a regular correspondence with both Carrie Chapman Catt and Anna Howard Shaw.[4] Jacobs' cordial relations with Catt proved to be an asset when, at the beginning of 1907, internal dissension arose and a number of women left the VVVK to form the Nederlandsche Bond voor Vrouwenkiesrecht (Dutch Woman Suffrage League). The "separatists" took pains to present their secession as the result of an ideological decision and on this ground applied for membership in the IWSA. Catt, as president, formally asked all affiliated countries to pass judgment in writing concerning the admittance of the new Dutch league as a member. It is difficult to establish just what personal note Catt may have enclosed with her letter to the presidents, but the refusal appears to have been a foregone conclusion. From the moment the troubles began Jacobs received Catt's full support, as can be inferred from her having shown Jacobs the letters from W. Wijnaendts Francken-Dyserinck and E. C. Van Dorp, the instigators of the act of separation.[5]

Catt's gesture is understandable in view of her friendship with Aletta Jacobs, as well as within the context of IWSA policy. The women in the new league did not refrain from public – and often very personal – criticism of Jacobs, and the IWSA itself could benefit little, if at all, from such discord. Basic to suffrage politics was its pursuit of unity, which implied that only truly fundamental differences in strategy or principle could justify division. For this reason the IWSA's treatment of the Dutch Woman Suffrage League differs from its treatment of the Women's Social and Political Union (WSPU), the organization of militant suffragettes in England. In Copenhagen in 1906, the WSPU had submitted a similar request for membership to the IWSA. This had been opposed by the older National Union of Women's Suffrage Societies (NUWSS), a charter member of the IWSA. But the arguments and considerations behind this split were businesslike and had been brought forward in an open exchange of ideas. Militant strategy had been recognized as a fundamentally different course, one which might prove its viability in the future. And admiration and sympathy had been

IWSA board in 1908. Left to right: *Adela Stanton Coit, Martina Kramers, Carrie Chapman Catt, Rachel Foster Avery, Millicent Garrett Fawcett.*

expressed with the militants' suffering. Still, the congress had adhered to the policy of one national organization per country, admitting members of the WSPU only as fraternal delegates (Van Voris 1987, 68; Whittick 1979, 38–39; Schreiber and Mathieson 1955, 8–9).

The Fourth International Woman Suffrage Congress, Amsterdam, 1908

The IWSA influenced the movement in the Netherlands in yet another way. The Fourth International Woman Suffrage Congress, held in Amsterdam, June 15–21, 1908, was originally planned to take place in the Netherlands on the eve of a parliamentary debate about a proposed amendment to the Dutch constitution, which promised to clear away all impediments to "passive suffrage," i.e., the right for women to be elected to the parliament and to provincial and city councils (see chapter 6, n. 1). This would have paved the way for active woman suffrage. Some time before the congress, however, the political tide changed, the cabinet fell, and the amendment was shelved. With the actual propagandistic urge to organize the international meeting gone, the motivation behind the congress largely evaporated, but the perseverance of a small group of go-getters was amply rewarded (Naber 1923, 67ff.).

It has been generally assumed that the 1908 congress represented the

Cartoon in the weekly De Groene Amsterdammer *during the 1908 IWSA congress: "The New Oath of the Tennis Court." On the table is Carrie Chapman Catt; seated next to it is Aletta Jacobs.*

decisive breakthrough to the Dutch public which until then had stood somewhat aloof. The congress got a great deal of coverage, and, better still, was on the whole favorably received by the press. Woman suffrage began to be taken seriously in the Netherlands. Likewise the events had positive consequences for the VVVK, as membership increased from about 2,500 to 6,000, and, within a year, a Men's League for Woman Suffrage (Mannenbond voor Vrouwenkiesrecht) was established. The Men's League remained a faithful third, next to the Association and the League (*Gedenkboek* 1919, 33).

Johanna Naber wrote: "The Congress involved a great deal of work. It was stated during the setting up of the Regulation Committee that only women who in the final three months of preparation would be able to go without food, drink and sleep would be eligible. So I was appointed secretary to the Regulation Committee and was also assigned the task of Press Officer. We all survived" (Naber, ed., 1939, 207). At great financial risk the Concertgebouw was hired for the whole week. This setting inspired the Dutch composer and musical pedagogue Catharina van Rennes to compose and conduct a chorus of welcome for a choir of 400 women and children.[6] Other cultural manifestations were the staging of a play, *The Council of the Gods*, and the presentation of clog dances. Last but not least

Automobile used for canvassing during the elections in the Netherlands, 1909.

was the gala dinner. Naber's mother vividly described the event in a letter to her son: "The . . . main table was decorated in the colors of the Alliance, lilac and yellow, with an arrangement of golden chrysanthemums and purple irises. It was a splendid scene. The rule was that each person should dress in her best and wear her best jewelry. The English and American ladies were in full evening dress, low cut and with long sleeves. The Amsterdam ladies had brought out their jewels especially for the occasion— a very rare occurrence! A few English ladies wore tiaras" (Naber, ed., 1939, 232).

The business meetings went by in a glow of optimism. With few exceptions, the national delegations were able to report progress. Finland, where women had had the vote since 1906, now had nine women in Parliament. Norwegian women had the vote on virtually the same footing as men. In Sweden and Iceland, too, things were moving in the right direction. In Germany, the law now allowed women to become members of political societies as well as to attend universities. In France, a society had almost completely established itself,[7] and there were highly active suffrage committees in Austria and Bulgaria. Italian women reported on a feminist congress which had been subjected to the inevitable cartoons and lampooning in the press. This prompted Catt to comment in her presidential address: "Curiously the caricaturists of all lands show suffrage leaders as carrying umbrellas. In early days perhaps they imagined the umbrella to be the weapon with which women attacked governments. Mr. Asquith in England could teach them better" (Schreiber and Mathieson 1955, 9, 10). Indeed, militant

National Union of Women's Suffrage Societies caravan, England, c. 1909.

suffragettes (as distinct from "law-abiding" suffragists) in England were deploying far heavier weapons than umbrellas. Reports from that country overshadowed all others and were listened to with bated breath. Large-scale demonstrations took place in London both before and after the Amsterdam congress. The first of these was organized by the NUWSS–the English member of the IWSA–and the second by the suffragettes of the WSPU, a fraternal organization. Many American women had traveled to Amsterdam via London to show their support for their allies' demonstration. In a crowded Albert Hall in London, Shaw delivered an enthusiastic speech "which brought the English to their feet roaring with applause" (Schreiber and Mathieson 1955, 161–62). At the WSPU demonstration no fewer than 250,000 people gathered in Hyde Park, where they were addressed from eighty platforms (in this era before the microphone!).

Throughout the congress Catt managed to avoid clear-cut statements or resolutions on the sensitive issue of militancy–a considerable achievement in view of the intense and often contradictory feelings on the matter, which divided many of the national suffrage associations. When during the congress Schwimmer proposed that it adopt a resolution urging women to take part in the second demonstration, Catt thwarted the proposal. She even succeeded in diverting some of the attention from the success of the English suffragettes to the entire international suffrage movement. In her presidential address, she pointed out that with such events "the zenith of the world's half-century of woman suffrage campaigning was reached." It was not important where the first victory took place, she said, "since our Cause is not national, but international."

> Every victory adds momentum to the whole movement. We have heard much about the solidarity of the human race: we represent the solidarity of a sex. Therefore we must remain a united army, which in the words of Susan B. Anthony "knows only woman, and her disfranchised." . . . We must grow closer to each other. We must learn to help each other, to give courage to the fainthearted and cheer the disappointed of all lands. Within our Alliance we must develop so lofty a spirit of internationalism—a spirit so clarified from all personalities and ambitions and even national antagonisms, that its purity and grandeur will furnish new inspiration to all workers in our Cause. We must strike a note in this meeting so full of sisterly sympathy, so full of exultant hope, that it will be heard by the women of all lands and will call them forth to join our world's army. [Peck 1944, 160–61]

In 1908 Dutch suffragists, backed by their sisters from abroad, for the first time proudly presented their cause to the general public. The time for large demonstrations had not yet come, but from 1908 onward June 15 became the day of national propaganda by the VVVK. The Alliance's objective of "organized cooperation and fraternal helpfulness" certainly gave new impetus to the Dutch woman suffrage movement.

November 1902–September 1909
Letters 1–24

1. Aletta Jacobs to Rosika Schwimmer

[Amsterdam] 5 November 1902

Dear Mrs. Schwimmer,

You have not heard from me in a long time and I have not even thanked you for your books. I was in Switzerland with my husband, however, and during that time I had no thought for work, or books, or letters. We made such wonderful tours in the mountains of the Engadine, and nature was so beautiful, that it seemed a profanation to occupy myself with anything else.

But now I am back in everyday life, I have begun to work again, have given your books a good place and send you my warmest thanks for them now. I send you the 37 crowns by the same post.

I hope you will be able to unite the Hungarian women's associations this winter, and that this Federation of Hungarian Women's Associations will join the International Council of Women.

When you do not need my biographies at the moment, I should like to have them back, since I do not have many copies of them, and people often ask for them.

We are now governed by a Confessional Cabinet, which has so far taken only anti-feminist measures. We are losing ground, in spite of the efforts we make. But it has its good side. It stirs up the Christian women. Every day more and more of them join our ranks.

With best wishes for your health and kind regards.

Sincerely yours,

Aletta H. Jacobs

2. Aletta Jacobs to Rosika Schwimmer

[Amsterdam] 18 November 1903

Dear Rosika,

I left your letter unanswered for a long time, because I had no time. I wanted to buy picture postcards of Amsterdam and its environment for you and your friends Miss Willhelm and Grossman,[1] and had to find a spare hour in which to do so. After all, my husband had promised Miss Gr. to send postcards. Now you can all form a picture of what Amsterdam looks like. Amsterdam is often called "the Venice of the North," but in my opinion Amsterdam is more beautiful than Venice, if only it would not always rain so much here. For you I send a calendar of 1904. It is a calendar which

WITHDRAWN
SCCCC - LIBRARY
4601 Mid Rivers Mall Drive
St. Peters, MO 63376

is published by the "Association of Woman Suffrage" each year. One of our members makes the drawing, and others choose the mottos, so that it costs the Association only a little. All members buy one or more copies, so that our cash register makes a nice profit every year. The members make presents of the calendar and make propaganda for our ideas. Nothing much has come of the drawing this year, it was done by an 18-year-old member.

I enclosed the list of books that Miss Rosenberg[2] gave me. And now for the answers to your questions. I thank you for the three articles. One of them "The Struggle against the Trade in Girls" will be published in the women's periodical *Evolutie* this winter;[3] it will be translated by one of the editors, without any remuneration. Is that all right with you?

About the second article in *Die Zeit* certainly some more will be known.[4] So now Child Welfare on the part of the State exists in Hungary, and to what degree? Can you write something about that? You can describe the ideas in the article in *Die Zeit*, and even copy whole sections. Original articles are paid for, but only sparingly. In early April there is a conference here on Child Welfare, which is organized by the National Council of Women, which is why such an article is of great topical interest now. In Holland, child welfare on the part of the state does not exist, everything is done by private associations.

My husband and I have read your article with great interest and were astonished that the head of a young girl should produce such logical, radical ideas. You are destined for something better and higher, dear Rosika, than for the work you are now doing. This is no flattery, I mean it.

When the Hungarian Council of Women is founded, the Association of Women Office Workers does participate isn't it? Cannot your friends propose to choose you as a member of the Board? Surely Miss Rosenberg cannot mean that the entire Association of Women Office Workers will be ignored? Moreover, Mrs. May Wright Sewall[5] has been alerted to your person as a strong advocate of women's rights. So when you are not chosen on the Board, the decision will probably be criticized.[6] Influence will also be used in Berlin next summer. You must come and speak in Berlin. Tonight I am giving a lecture in Utrecht, tomorrow evening over here, and Monday in The Hague. And so on throughout the winter. My husband is also giving many lectures in political men's associations this winter, he has made us a promise to speak about woman suffrage in all of them, so the gentlemen will still hear of a subject they would rather not hear or speak about. You will understand, they will say afterward, "obviously the poor man is forced to it by his wife," since I am no favorite with the public either. I exaggerate, I stir up the women, I want to separate the child from its mother, and . . . I boss my husband around. I am the one that spoilt him, I turned him, for shame! into a feminist! The poor souls fail to understand that we would never have been a couple if poor Gerritsen had not been a feminist from the start.

The long, far journey has done us good; always in the open air in a wonderful environment, happy together, and not hearing a word from the outside world, has restored my strength.

Give our regards to your parents, all friends and acquaintances. And for you a sisterly kiss from your loving

Aletta H. Jacobs

Will you please have the other calendar delivered at Mrs. Malvi Fuchs?[7]

1. Sidonie Willhelm and Janka Grossman were coworkers of Rosika Schwimmer in the National Association of Women Office Workers.

2. Charlotte L. (Polak-)Rosenberg was a Dutch suffragist.

3. The Dutch feminist journal *Evolutie* (Evolution) was founded in 1893 by Wilhelmina Drucker and Theodore Haver. In 1889 Wilhelmina Drucker had taken the initiative to organize the Vrije Vrouwen Vereeniging (Free Women's Association), a forerunner of the Dutch Woman Suffrage Association that was founded in 1894. The Dutch Dolle Mina's (Rebellious Mina's), who practiced a playful feminist activism in the early 1970s and launched the second wave of feminism in the Netherlands, named themselves after this remarkable woman.

4. *Die Zeit* was an Austrian journal in which Schwimmer published several articles.

5. May Wright Sewall (1844–1920) was president of the ICW from 1899 to 1904. See NAW.

6. The Hungarian Council of Women, which in 1904 united fifty-two societies, was dominated by the nationalist (Magyar) gentry and aristocracy (Evans 1979, 99; Wynner 1974, 725).

7. Malvi Fuchs was a Hungarian journalist. She attended the ICW congress in Berlin as a delegate of the National Association of Women Office Workers.

3. Susan B. Anthony to Aletta Jacobs[1]

New York, Dec. 17, 1904

My dear friend—

I had a letter from Mrs. Harper[2] the other day, asking me to send you Volume 4, in leather, of the History of Woman Suffrage. I have put that up to go to you, and also, have put in my Life and Work, and some other documents, and hope you will be glad to get them all. I have written Mrs. Carrie Chapman Catt, 205 W. 57th St., N.Y., telling her that I have sent the books to the hotel to you, so I think you will get them without a doubt.[3]

I am greatly disappointed that I couldn't meet you while you are in this country, but my brother's sickness and death occurred about the time you passed through, I understand. I should like to know what you think of the people of this country. I wish you could stay here a whole year and watch us and see us work. Isn't it pretty good that the Territorial Committee at Washington declared that it was the woman suffrage letters from all parts of the country that moved them to strike out the whole clause from the bill which classed sex with idiots, criminals, etc. It really gives me hope when any body can be moved by the letters from women, and I should think that our women all over the country would take courage. You are not going to see Miss Shaw, either, for she is in Oklahoma and doing grand service there, but I am glad that you can see Mrs. Catt, and that we have one woman that can be reached. The International Suffrage Alliance grows apace, and Mrs. Catt is just the woman to be president of it.

Hoping to meet you at the International in London[4] two years from now,

I am

Very sincerely yours,

Susan B. Anthony

1. Jacobs received this letter while she was in New York.

2. Ida Husted Harper (1851–1931) at the request of Susan B. Anthony, who was impressed by her journalistic talents, became her official biographer. In 1898 she published the *Life and Work of Susan B. Anthony* in two volumes. After Anthony's death in 1906 a third volume was added. In cooperation with Anthony she also wrote the fourth volume of the *History of Woman Suffrage* (HWS), the monumental history of the suffrage movement in the United States. After suffrage was won, she completed this series with a fifth and a sixth volume in 1922. See NAW.

3. The two volumes of the *Life and Work*, with an inscription by Susan B. Anthony to Aletta Jacobs, are in the library collection of the IIAV.

4. The third conference of the Alliance took place in Copenhagen, not in London, in 1906.

4. Aletta Jacobs to Rosika Schwimmer

Amsterdam, 16 February 1905

My dear Rosika,

I was pleased with your letter, you have achieved a great deal in a short time. I have already written to Mrs. Catt about the invitation, you should get it. The aristocratic women, and those who are pleased to pass as such, are the same everywhere. In Denmark, Miss Norrie[1] has been expelled, the woman who got everything done there and who managed the entire Danish Council, and in my absence the same was done to my good Martina

Kramers.[2] I have used all of my influence to bring her back in, but whether I shall succeed, I doubt it. After all, I am not liked much myself, but so far they have not been able to manage without me.

Mrs. Perkins Gilman[3] is coming over on 5 March, and will stay with me until 9 March. Of course she was to give a lecture here, but that was a difficult matter. Not a single association wanted to invite her, not even my own Women Suffrage Association. Then I said, fine, there is not to be a quarrel, but Mrs. P.G. will speak here. I went to four aristocratic ladies, two of them are friends of mine. I knew that they had read her books, and together we formed a committee. I wrote an article in one of our daily newspapers and even before we have announced the exact date and place, we have sold so many tickets that in the end it turns out a good speculation.

I do not believe that she can come to Austria and Hungary now, since she has already booked her return passage, she wants to be back in New York before Easter. But you can try, in Holland her address is with me.

Of course I remember Vilma Glücklich,[4] she is not the kind of person one would ever forget. I liked her very much. She sent me the printed matter, but I cannot read it, it is all Hungarian, are there perhaps German articles about the new association? If you want to write to Mrs. Carrie Chapman Catt, her address is: 205 W. 57th Str. New York, but it can wait, I am sure she will write to you.

And now for your preference for morphia! Dear child, it is something completely normal. I am sure you do not want to believe me, women never want to, but it is very natural and always happens to unmarried women who are over 23 or 25 years of age. It is entirely physical. I should like to talk with you because I cannot write it in such a way that you will understand me without misinterpreting, but this is something you have in common with all women, only in coarse and less sensitive women it expresses itself differently. I have also experienced it for many years, it is because we live too respectably. It is the same with men when they lead a clean life. Which is why they don't. Very sensible; as long as they do not need prostitutes or make prostitutes.

I hope that your mama will soon be better and that you will not have financial worries. That is too bad! The other will pass, but very slowly.

My good husband has not been quite well since our return from America. He complains continually about nervous disturbances and has not yet been able to participate in public life. I hope it will pass, but now and then I am afraid it will be chronic. I for myself am completely involved again in all the feminist work, and feel very well. Receive the kindest regards from the both of us,

Yours, lovingly,

Aletta H. Jacobs

1. Charlotte Norrie was a delegate to the founding congress of the IWSA in Berlin (Peck 1944, 140).

2. Martina G. Kramers was a board member of the Dutch Council of Women from its foundation in 1898, resigning in 1904. She remained a board member of the ICW until 1909. See also chap. 1, n. 15.

3. Charlotte Perkins Gilman (1860–1936), feminist philosopher and publicist, met Aletta Jacobs at the 1899 congress of the ICW in London. Jacobs then promised that she would translate Gilman's *Women and Economics* (1899). See chap. 2, n. 18. On March 7, 1905, Gilman gave a lecture entitled "The Home and the World" in Amsterdam. See NAW.

4. In 1896 Vilma Glücklich became the first woman in Hungary to be admitted to the university. She studied physics and mathematics. In 1902 she became a member of the board of the National Association of Women Office Workers. In 1904, with Rosika Schwimmer, she founded the Hungarian Feminist Association, which campaigned for woman suffrage. In 1915 she headed the Hungarian delegation to the international women's congress at The Hague. In 1919 she was present at the Zürich conference, where the Women's International League for Peace and Freedom (WILPF) was founded. From 1922 to 1925 she worked for the WILPF in Geneva.

5. Anna Howard Shaw to Aletta Jacobs

Philadelphia, February 24th, 1905

My dear Dr. Jacobs,

It was with very great delight that I received a letter a few days ago from Mrs. Van Dorp-Verdam[1] that you had been appointed the member of the Committee on Suffrage and Rights of Citizenship for the National Council of Holland. I am so glad to have you a member of my Committee and was in hopes that they would appoint you.[2] But before I begin to talk of Committee work, I want to say how deeply I have regretted missing your visit and that of your good husband, while you were at my home. I have heard so much from Miss Anthony[3] about it and how much she enjoyed you and from our friends who met you, what a great delight they had in their visit. The same two Doctors are to spend Sunday with me and I am very sure that if they were here now that I am writing, they would wish to be remembered. My friends have often laughed at me because I have a list of six men of whom I say very often they have proved to me beyond a doubt, that it is possible to be as happy married as to be not married, but, since I was in Amsterdam and met your husband, there has been one more added to my list, so my friends are now laughing at me because my list is beginning to grow. But I am quite sure that such a list cannot be complete without the addition of your good husband. I will never forget his great kindness to us as well as of yourself. The more I think of it, the more I wonder at your taking so much pains with comparative strangers—more so because, when we left Amsterdam, we did not feel as if we were strangers, but more as if we were life-long friends. I hope that when you again come to America, I will be well established on my little farm outside of Philadelphia and that you will be able to stop a long time with us and let us have a genuine good visit.[4] How much we would enjoy it, I am sure, because we could bring together a number of excellent friends, whom I am quite sure you would be glad to meet, and Lucy has quite lost her heart to you both. Each day, as we tear a slip from our calendar, we are reminded of you so that no day passes without a thought of our good friends in Amsterdam and now I must, I suppose, say what I have to say about the Council work.

I suppose our principal work is not that of propaganda outside of the Council organization so much as it is to try to secure the cooperation of all the different members of the Council themselves. The difficulty is due largely to the fact that some organizations, who are members of the Council, are very progressive and others very conservative, and it will be impossible for us to push the work faster than the more backward members of the organization are willing to follow. Therefore, much judgment will have to be exercised on the part of the member of each Council as to just how far we can carry any aggressive lines of work.

I would like to ask you first of all, if you will kindly compile for me everything in regard to women's political privileges which may be enjoyed by the women of Holland? I want to learn exactly the status of woman's political freedom in all the countries represented in the Council body. I think one of the important things for the member of our Council to do in her own country will be to bring the subject of woman's political enfranchisement as often as possible before any of the meetings of the different organizations who compose the Council, especially those who are not at present favorably inclined to our movement, because I think one of the great difficulties is due not so much to the fact that women are particularly opposed to women's suffrage, but because they have thought very little about it and have read less and therefore, are not quite sure just what women desire by its use. If women could be made to see that through their political freedom, they would be able to bring to pass many of the things for which the good women of the Council are so eagerly working and yet which they fail to accomplish simply because they have no political power, I am quite sure that many women who now oppose it would give up all opposition and I suppose it will be the duty of our Committee to bring before these women the real purpose of women's enfranchisement rather than the theoretical one which so frightened so many very excellent women away from the movement in the past. As soon as I have more definitely thought of a plan of work, I will correspond with you and try to see if we cannot have some uniformity of action in all of the National Councils composing our international body. In the meantime, if there is any way in which I can serve you, I will be very happy to do so.

With sincere regards, I am,

Faithfully,

Anna Howard Shaw

1. Mrs. A. E. van Dorp-Verdam was president of the Dutch Council of Women from 1903 to 1908.

2. The ICW had several permanent committees. In 1904 the Committee on Suffrage and Rights of Citizenship was established under the presidency of Anna Howard Shaw. Aletta Jacobs was appointed as the Dutch member of the committee.

3. Lucy E. Anthony.

4. In 1908 Anna Howard Shaw moved into Alnwick Lodge in Moylan, Pennsylvania (Shaw 1915, 268).

6. Carrie Chapman Catt to Rosika Schwimmer

[New York] March 4, 1905

My dear Fräulein Schwimmer:

I have had a letter from Dr. Jacobs and she tells me that there has been organized in Hungary a new society, and that a part of its program is woman suffrage. I am very glad indeed to learn of this movement of progress. I felt sure it would come sooner or later, and now I hope its members will be quite willing to become auxiliary to the International Woman Suffrage Alliance. Very likely they will not see the necessity, nor recognise the benefit. To show to Parliamentary Bodies that there is an International Alliance composed of the women of many countries, who are fighting for their political freedom, is one of the strongest arguments we can use, and although the United States is supposed to be a very progressive land in reference to all things which concern women, we have found it of benefit even here, and I am perfectly positive you will find it of great benefit in Hungary.

Eight countries are now auxiliary and have paid their dues for the past year. These are: England, Australia, Norway, Sweden, Denmark, Holland, Germany and the United States. A new society has perhaps by this time been formed in Switzerland, and its dues have already been paid, but we do not yet count that as auxiliary for I am not sure that the work is quite complete. Before long Canada and France will also be members. I hope before the year is out that there will be an organization in Italy as well,—and so the movement grows! I cannot tell you how happy we should be to welcome Hungary into our Alliance, and I feel sure that in time the Alliance will help Hungary. I have just, today, received a letter from Berlin and one from Copenhagen, and both say that their suffrage work was given quite a boom through the fact of our International Organization.

I enclose a Constitution, which unfortunately is in English. You will see that new societies may become auxiliary by paying twenty marks per year when the membership is small, as I presume it is in Hungary. The money could be easily raised by asking each member to pay a trifle toward it. In 1906, we shall hold our next meeting in London, and we shall want a delegate from Hungary to come and tell us all about the new organization, and that delegate will learn what all the other countries are doing and will take home with her new inspiration and courage to continue the work there.[1] I beg you to urge the progressive women of Hungary to join the progressive women of all the world through our International Alliance. Our cause is the same whether it is in Hungary or Australia or in the United States, and we can help each other much through this fraternity.

Will you kindly tell me what the new organization is called, and also what it proposes to do?

I have very pleasant recollections of your bright face in Berlin, and I shall hope that I may meet you again in London.

With most cordial good wishes, I am,

Yours truly,

Carrie Chapman Catt.

1. This conference was held in Copenhagen in 1906, not in London.

7. Aletta Jacobs to Rosika Schwimmer

Amsterdam, May 7, 1905

My dear Rosika,

I am sitting now at the sickbed of my good husband. You know that we are having big elections this month, and Gerritsen has made such an effort that he is worn out now.[1] He has been ill in bed for a whole week. I hope he will soon recover, but you can never tell.

Do write about me and my husband in your book, you know us after all, and what you do not know you can ask me.[2]

Whether we are at home in August? I think so, but I cannot tell for sure. We want to stay at home, but when the elections are over in July, I don't know what condition my husband will be in. Four years ago I had to set off with him immediately, so terribly overworked was he then.

But I hope you will come and that everything will be well in the end. Tell your family and friends that we are at home, and then you must write to me on what day you arrive.

Do you know that Malvi Fuchs intends to come here at the end of the month?

Whatever is the matter with Miss Mohr from Vienna? I do not understand her letters at all. Is she out of her senses perhaps? Give my love to all your sweet friends, Glücklich, Grossman, and others.

I am the representative for Holland in the International Council of Women. There is nothing for you to do as yet, Reverend Shaw will write everything later. She was very ill at first and is now very busy in America, and there is no hurry.

We are all going to London next year, by the end of May, and you will come too, will you not? It is for the International Woman Suffrage Alliance.

And now I greet and kiss you. I must write more letters for my husband.

Yours, lovingly,

Aletta

1. Through these elections the Dutch House of Commons was chosen. Gerritsen stood for the Vrijzinnig Democratic Bond, a radical liberal party, and was elected.

2. Rosika Schwimmer was preparing a book on "marriage ideals and ideal marriages," which was published in German as: *Ehe-Idealen und Ideal-Ehen: Aeusserungen moderner Frauen auf Grund einer Rundfrage* (Berlin: Continent, n.d. [1905 or 1906]). In this final version nothing was published on the Jacobs-Gerritsen marriage. Was this because Aletta objected to it? See letter 8. The original answers to Rosika's inquiry into the marriage ideals of women like Anita Augspurg, Minna Cauer, Henriette Fürth, Charlotte Perkins Gilman, Lida Gustava Heymann, Ellen Key, Maria Lischnewska, Else Lüders, Anna Pappritz, Marie Raschke, Helene Stöcker, Bertha von Suttner, and others are in the Schwimmer-Lloyd Collection of the New York Public Library.

8. Aletta Jacobs to Rosika Schwimmer[1]

[Amsterdam, July 1905]

My dear Rosika,

The great sorrow has come, my good husband has passed away. All I could do was to nurse him, see to it that he felt no pain, that he was unaware of his suffering, but that was all. He developed a liver carcinoma in an unbelievably short time, and nothing could be done. Later, in a month, I shall write to you about our marriage. What you write is wrong. I am incapable of it now.

Tomorrow I am going to Hamburg with him. There is no crematorium here.

Your Aletta

1. This card was addressed to Rosika Bédy-Schwimmer. According to Edith Wynner, Rosika Schwimmer in 1911 married a certain Mr. Bédy, divorcing him in 1913. However, questions remain. When actually did Schwimmer marry, and why? It seems that in Hungary she is known as Rózsa Bédy-Schwimmer, and the form of address Jacobs used suggests that Schwimmer was already married in 1905. But why would Jacobs address Rosika by her husband's name, something she was known to detest if it happened to herself?

9. Carrie Chapman Catt to Aletta Jacobs

[New York] December, 1905

My dear Dr. Jacobs:

This budget will find you in Switzerland and I hope the fine air there is bringing you new life and health. I was at first quite prostrated, but I am improving and am growing stronger.[1] I am beginning to get interested again, altho' it is difficult to be so. I realize that there is much more in the world to be done, and that I must not shirk my duty because my heart aches. So I have adopted a motto and it must be yours too:

> To the wrong that needs resistance
> To the right that needs assistance
> To the future in the distance
> Give yourself![2]

I do not expect to be happy again but I shall try to keep others from knowing how I feel and to do the best work I can. At present, I am not able to do much, and I have been advised to travel while I am recuperating in body and mind. So I am thinking of going Westward to Australia and to make some study of the suffrage there. I think some young American ladies will go with me to Japan, but that I must go alone to Australia. Would it interest you to join me there? I must add that I have no definite plan as yet. First, I cannot go until my husband's estate is settled. I hope this may be done by May 1st, but some complication may arise, and our courts are exceedingly slow. Then my mother is a consideration for she relies upon me to come to her, should anything occur to need me. She is 72 years old, which is not very old in these days, but she thinks and feels that she is <u>very</u> old.

I think no death ever made a more profound impression upon me than that of your husband. It seemed so cruel and so unfair that so splendid and helpful a man should go out, when in the very midst of his usefulness. My sympathy with you was very close and tender, but now that I know the same sorrow and the same shock, I am sure that no one feels a truer and more understanding sympathy than I.

I am glad the women came to you with the work. It is best so. Work must be our comfort and our duty. I am so glad you have that splendid son.[3]

There is a dear American woman, who had a husband much like Mr. Gerritsen, a splendid reformer. He died in the prime of their lives, and she is now 88 years old! But she has been a blessing to all good things. She is an inspiration to me.

Lovingly, Carrie C. Catt.

1. Carrie Chapman Catt's husband, George W. Catt, died October 8, 1905. He was an engineer and owned a construction firm, which Catt inherited. This made her financially independent for the rest of her life.

2. These lines, which Catt often cited, are (according to Van Voris 1987, 83) a paraphrase of G. Linnaeus Banks, "What I Live For," from *Daisies in the Grass* (London: Hardivicke, 1865). In Van Voris' version the last sentence runs: "We give ourselves" (Ibid., 239, n. 14).

3. This "splendid son" was Charles Emile Jacobs (1887–1954), a nephew of Aletta Jacobs whom she more or less adopted after the death of his father, Julius Jacobs. From 1896 on he lived with her and Gerritsen in Amsterdam. They quarreled more than once, and it is suggested that Charles caused her bankruptcy in 1918. In Jacobs' *Herinneringen* Charles is not mentioned, and she tried to remove every trace of him from her personal archives.

10. Aletta Jacobs to Rosika Schwimmer

Hotel Belvedere, St. Moritz
1 Jan. 1906

My dear Rosika,

Now I must write to you. A little every day. Yesterday I received the newspaper, but could not read a word. Perhaps it is for the best. You discussed Helen Loring Grenfell,[1] I could see that. This is the best for you now, the people must know that women are also capable of holding public offices.

Mrs. Catt wrote to me last week if I want to travel with her to Japan and Australia next summer; I replied yesterday that she should come to Europe next summer and winter, and help the suffrage associations with their propoganda. Woman suffrage is à l'ordre du jour in all countries now, and we can all benefit greatly from a good propagandist. I should like to go with her in 1907, when Charles has to do his military service.

Yes, it is New Year's Day today. I try to forget it. What should one wish on people? I wish you all the best, always, also today. And your dear friends. The big meeting with Glücklich presiding and you as first speaker was wonderful.

How am I doing here? At first the change of air and surroundings did me a world of good, but then I experienced a setback. Suddenly I could not sleep any more and could have cried night and day. Now I am at rest. I sleep very well now, and feel so much better. We are staying here for another week, will travel on to Zürich first, then on to Frankfurt and will return to Amsterdam on 15 January. So, if you want to write me another letter, you must send it to Amsterdam.

It is terribly cold here. Today it froze −20° Celsius, or when you measure in Fahrenheit, the temperature was under 0. Still this cold, with its high, thin air is gratifying. You have to walk briskly; and the sun shines so beautifully and clearly. In Amsterdam we had not seen the sun for months.

Charles is obviously having a good time here. In the daytime he joins in all the sports, and he goes dancing in the evenings. Every night he has invitations to go dancing at various hotels. He asked me to send you his kindest regards.

I write and read a great deal here, always in the evenings. I have been able to finish some long articles so far.

What a pity that the English cannot accommodate us next summer. I have written immediately that the meeting of the Alliance should take place in Holland, in Sept. or October. I do not know what the Americans will say to this.

How is your mother? I should think she will have improved. Perhaps it is nothing but menopause. Many women in their fifties have similar nervous attacks.

Martina Kramers is active, but she could do better and more. She is held back by a wrong love. The man is not worthy of her, and spoils her life.[2] We have, however, recruited some good young workers. It is remarkable that they are always Jewish girls. With us and everywhere else. Courage and spirit are found most in these girls.

I hope, when I return to Amsterdam, I will be able to take an active part again in the public meetings and also resume my lectures. Until now I was always afraid I would get stuck; for if I do not keep my attention centered on the theme, my thoughts fly to undesirable places. And then I am done for.

When are you going to Vienna? Or have you already been there? How are Mrs. Hainisch and Marie Lang[3] and the others? I have not written to Vienna in a long time and therefore have not heard any news.

And now I greet and kiss you.

Yours, lovingly,

Aletta

1. Helen Loring Grenfell was State Superintendent of Public Education in Colorado. Aletta Jacobs wrote about her in the book *Uit het leeven van merkwaardige vrouwen* (Excerpts from the lives of remarkable women), 1906. Colorado had had woman suffrage since 1893. Within international suffrage circles Helen Loring Grenfell was often taken as an example of what happened to women in a society that had woman suffrage.

2. Probably this man (Bobbie) was not "worthy of her" because he was a socialist. Martina's own words also show tormented feelings. In a letter to Charlotte Perkins Gilman in 1904 she wrote: "That makes the misery of my life, for my best friend is a soc. democrat and my sympathies are all that way; only I will never join a party that is against the emancipation of women" (DC-Schl.). Cf. chap. 2; letters 38, 39.

3. See chap. 1, n. 18, for brief accounts of both Hainisch and Lang.

11. Lucy E. Anthony to Aletta Jacobs

Hotel Portland, April 30 [1906]
Portland, Oregon

My dear Dr. Jacobs,

I find myself quite unexpectedly away out here in Portland [to] help in the campaign. Miss Shaw found things in quite a bad way here and telegraphed for me to come and help.

Since arriving a lovely letter from you has been forwarded and Aunt Mary,[1] Miss Shaw and I thank you very much for it. I think that all of those who loved and were loved by dear Aunt Susan will always feel nearer together.[2]

We have also had letters from Mrs. Avery[3] telling of her visit and meeting with you and of how much she admires and cares for you, and you say in your letter how much you admire and care for her, and that makes us all very happy too, for we wanted you two to like and love each other. Do you know that after we were in your home and you were over here I was just a little afraid that we might have praised you two to each other so much that in the contrariness of things in general you might not like each other as much as you would have otherwise – but now we are happy in the friendship which we are sure will ever be yours. I came over to the office early this morning thinking that we were going to do a little extra moving about and fixing of things, but my helper did not arrive so I thought I would write to you inasmuch as there was a letter from Rachel saying what a lovely visit she had had with you – what an ideal hostess you are and how she does love that boy. I wonder dear Dr. Jacobs whether you are going to Copenhagen. I do not know that either you or Rachel have said anything about it. I do hope that you are going – but anyhow we will see you surely when we come over. We now plan to sail June 23 for Hamburg, and Rachel is going to meet us there.

I thought I was going to have more time to write – but will have to leave you now – with a great deal of love –

Lucy E. Anthony

1. Mary S. Anthony was Susan B. Anthony's sister, housemate, and companion.

2. Susan B. Anthony died on March 13, 1906. Immediately after all the necessary arrangements had been made, Shaw left for Oregon for one of the many suffrage campaigns that were being held in the United States.

3. At this time Rachel Foster Avery lived in Europe. See also chap. 1, n. 14.

12. Rachel Foster Avery to Aletta Jacobs

Midnight
Monday, April 9, 06

My dear Doctor Aletta,

I've decided to call you that – how does it sound to you? I hope you don't consider it too familiar on so short an acquaintance.

I had a very "comfy" journey – changes of cars at Emmerich, at Essen, at Hannover and at Lehrte – enjoyed very much the nice lunch you gave me which I supplemented by a cup of coffee at Essen and a cup of tea in the train about five o'clock. My bad (?) children <u>did</u> write me, but only to

Antwerp where I suppose the letter is lying at the hotel. They are both well and delighted at my return.

I found many letters which I have just finished reading. No, I've done more—I've written one to the Skandinavian-American Line at Copenhagen for berths on their boat sailing from there on Aug. 24. I found their circulars, price lists and a letter awaiting me. If I secure the accommodation I hope to, I will take the children to Copenhagen. I will probably take our bicycles along and make some trips after the I.W.S.A. meetings.

The ship also touches at Christiania[1] and, if it does not cost too much—we may go on up there. I think Anna Shaw will go with us and Aunt Mary Anthony—if she comes. Do bring Charlie and your wheels—we can have some nice times together. In the hope that you will consider the plan, I will send you word as soon as I receive the letter telling me whether I can get the room on that boat—Aug. 23 from Copenhagen and 24 from Christiania. Norway is so <u>lovely</u> and farther north, so grand in its scenery.

I owe you so many thanks for all your kind hospitality which I enjoyed to the full, I assure you.

Both the children want to meet you and Charlie. I've talked so much of you both to them already.

My home letters tell me how Anna Shaw was looking worn out and miserable when she left for Oregon—I hope she holds out to the end of that hard campaign.

Yours affectionately,

Rachel Foster Avery.

My cordial greetings to Miss Kramers and thanks for sending the Holland American Circulars.

1. Oslo was then called Christiania.

13. Aletta Jacobs to Rosika Schwimmer

Amsterdam, September 10, 1906

My dear Rosika,

It took a long time to reach a decision but I have finally decided I am coming.[1] Mrs. Hainisch wrote today saying that we should certainly go to Vienna. There will not be many people but there should be enough who are interested and the newspapers will no doubt do what is expected of them. She writes she is feeling unwell but she still insists on coming to bid me welcome. Dear old Mrs. Hainisch.

Today I'm sending you two copies of my photograph. Last week I was visited by a young man, a friend and member of the Feminist Association, I forget his name, but he was an extremely amiable young person. As it happened I was very busy and therefore could not offer him a particularly hospitable reception. Then I received letters from Ylda Sulyok in Italy asking numerous questions about coeducation and poverty laws. Johanna Naber replied to the first one and Mrs. Haver[2] saw to the second. And then Dr. Maday sent me a very useful book on *Le Droit de la femme au travail*.[3] So you see that I have been in touch with half of Budapest and should no doubt feel at home there. Mrs. Catt is now in Berlin, and we are to meet her in Dresden. She will take care of the arrangements; I don't have time for writing many letters. There is still so much to do before I leave.

Can you tell me what exactly the women doctors want to know about Malthusianism? Surely they don't want a lecture? If they do, it will have to be in private without the press or any propaganda. It's not that I fear the publicity but it certainly would harm our cause. People are so stupid, they get the wrong end of the stick, and everything concerning sex may not be mentioned, it may only be done. I do not know Catt's views on the subject. Oddly enough, I have never discussed this with her.

I am very sorry about what you told me of Mrs. Stritt,[4] but it's the same everywhere. As soon as an association begins to flourish everyone wants to take control, even if they are not acquainted with the skills of leadership. It is exactly the same here. No doubt you will arrange everything with Catt, so do write and let me know what you have decided. Charles sends his regards. He was out dancing at a ball last night, so he has retired early. I wish you all the best, dear. Send my regards to dear Vilma and all the other dear friends. I am looking forward to seeing them all again.

Night has fallen, so sweet dreams.

Your affectionate

Aletta

1. After Copenhagen Jacobs and Catt made a propaganda trip through Central Europe. See Peck 1944, 152ff; Jacobs 1924, 105ff.

2. Theodore P. B. Haver (1857–1912) was one of the founders of the Woman Suffrage Association and the editor of *Evolutie* (Evolution) and *Het Maandblad* (The monthly journal). She was chairman of the Amsterdam branch of the Dutch Association and for twenty-two years was secretary to the Free Women's Association. She was a good friend of Wilhelmina Drucker.

3. Dr. A. Maday was a Hungarian feminist and publicist. One of his books is *Les Droits de la femme hongroise dans le passé et à l'heure actuelle* (Budapest, 1913).

4. Marie Stritt (1855–1928) was a prominent German feminist. In 1894 she founded the Rechtsschutzverein für Frauen (Women's Legal Aid Society) as a local branch of the Allgemeiner Deutscher Frauenverein (General German Women's Association). She concentrated on divorce and the rights of unmarried mothers. She translated feminist literature, including Charlotte Perkins Gilman's *Women and Economics*, into German. In 1899 she became chairman of

the German council of women, in which capacity she chaired the ICW congress in Berlin in 1904. Hackett has described Stritt as philosophically a "radical," but a "moderate" in her associations. Her feminist orientation caused her downfall in the conservative German council of women. She resigned in 1910. See Weiland 1983, 261–62; Hackett 1976, 209, 236–46.

14. Carrie Chapman Catt to Aletta Jacobs

[New York] Mch 17, [1907]

My dear little doctor: –

I am grieved indeed to hear the news of the dissenting organization.[1] But let it trouble you as little as possible. Of course it cannot join the Alliance, and if they write asking affiliation I shall speak quite plainly to them. It is irritating to have it come just now, when suffragists should maintain a united front before the enemy, but it cannot be helped. I prophesy that it will soon die and leave you in peace. Do not waste any hours of worry over it, but be assured that when you are right yourselves, no harm can come to you. Martina Kramers has written me about it too.

I enclose the vote on the date and on Finland.[2] So you see you have it as you wish. I think that we should begin to correspond a little about the program, lest my Mother's condition shall prevent me from coming to Holland as long before the meeting as I had planned. Have you any new suggestions?

My Mother is no better, and I now think she will never be better, but will slowly grow worse. So I cannot tell what I may be able to do.

I have felt so lost without my home that I have rented an apartment and shall move into it this week. I may have to leave it at once and go to my Mother, but it will be a comfort to have it. I was too homesick to live in a hotel any longer. It was a mistake giving up my home, but I have a better one I think. It is farther uptown and is in a new building, with the vacuum cleaning attached to the building. I think I shall enjoy it but the moving is a process to be dreaded. I think you have given up the thought of giving up your home. I hope so. It is a mistake. I write hastily, just to assure you that I shall stand staunchly by <u>you</u>, my dear Aletta. I am very sorry about it because I admired Mrs Wijnaendts Francken[3] in Berlin, and Mrs. van Dorp[4] too. I am sure they are "seeing through a glass darkly."

Lovingly,

Carrie Chapman Catt.

1. In February 1907, the Dutch Woman Suffrage League was founded. The members of this League, in which men were permitted to sit on the board, called themselves "ethical feminists" in order to distinguish themselves from what they saw as the "ultra or rational feminists" of the Dutch Woman Suffrage Association. The division is comparable to that which occurred in German suffrage history between moderate and radical suffrage feminists. The distinction between ethical and rational is also comparable to the distinction made in the history of American suffrage feminism between arguments of expediency and arguments of justice. These categories, however, should be applied carefully when characterizing organizations or individual feminists. I wonder, for example, whether Kraditor's description of the development from arguments of justice to arguments of expediency is in fact, unequivocal and straightforward. See Kraditor 1981, 43–74.

2. Between congresses votes were taken using paper ballots. The date refers to the Amsterdam congress of 1908.

3. Esther Welmoet Wijnaendts Francken-Dyserinck (1876–1956) was a journalist and chairman of The Hague branch of the VVVK until 1907. She was one of the founders of the Dutch Woman Suffrage League in 1907 and was editor of *De Ploeger* (The plower). From 1925 to 1936 she sat on the publicity committee of the ICW. See further: Wijnaendts Francken-Dyserinck Collection, IAV-IIAV; van Raalte 1958; WWT.

4. Elisabeth C. van Dorp (1872–1945) was Holland's second female lawyer. She was one of the founders of the Dutch Woman Suffrage League. From 1922 to 1925 she was a member of the Dutch parliament for the Vrijheidsbond, a moderate liberal party.

15. Anna Howard Shaw to Aletta Jacobs

Swarthmore, Pa., March 26, 1907

My dear Dr. Jacobs: –

I received your letter in regard to the picture of the pioneer suffragists and I will attend to the matter at once. We will send you all of those that we can gather together for that purpose.

There is one picture, which we will send, however, which need not be returned and it is a picture of Miss Susan B. Anthony. We have one, the last one taken of her in November prior to her going away from us, which we consider the very best picture which she has had taken in these last few years. This picture has been enlarged. Lucy made me a present of one for my birthday and it hangs up now over our desks and seems like the living presence of Aunt Susan to us. Mrs. Avery and Lucy and I are going to have a copy of this picture made for you, your own dear self. This can be used at the Convention in Amsterdam, but when the Convention is over, it is to be given to you, or rather it will be given to you before by Rachel and Lucy and myself, and then when the Convention is over, you will take it home with you or do whatever you please with it.

It is a beautiful picture and we are so glad to be able to bring you this expression of our love for you and our sincere admiration for all you are doing for the cause to which Miss Anthony gave all that she was. So this is not a gift to the Association or by the Association at all but just a little personal remembrance from us three who love you so very dearly and who are so interested in your good service and share in your admiration for our dear Aunt Susan. Whenever you look at her picture, you will almost feel that she is ready to say something to you.

Lucy is leaving home today for Rochester and will be there for a few weeks while Mrs. Harper gathers up the material for the remaining book of the biography of Miss Anthony, in which will be included a sketch of Miss Mary Anthony's life.[1] We are very anxious to have this book completed and the history of that splendid life rounded out until the very last of her days among us.

Mrs. Avery is very busy with the large share of work, which she has taken up, and she is entering into everything with the earnestness and zeal which always characterized her service in the cause.[2]

The pages are deeply interested in their new society and at the present time are working very hard to arrange for a reception which their society is to give to me as the president of the National Association on next Wednesday evening.[3] It is to be a great event for these young people and is of the very first importance. I presume they feel its weight quite as much as you do in arranging for your Netherlands Convention in 1908.

We are all looking forward to that time and I am going to save up all the rest time which I ought to be taking between now and then, so as to make it longer when I come.

You may be quite sure we will furnish you with the pictures for which you ask, so you need not give them a second thought.

With sincere affection from us all, I am

Faithfully yours,

Anna H. Shaw.

1. Mary Anthony had just died. Susan and Mary had always lived in Rochester.

2. Rachel Foster Avery was vice president of the NAWSA from 1907 to 1909. Cf. letter II, n. 3.

3. Avery's daughters had apparently set up a suffrage club. One of Rachel's later letters indicates that the club flourished. See RFA to AJ, Nov. 18, 1908 (AJ-IAV-IIAV).

16. Aletta Jacobs to Rosika Schwimmer

Amsterdam, May 15, 1907

My dear Rozsa,

I have been meaning to write for several days and only now have found the time. I was very grateful for your prompt letters. I found your first and was able to make use of it just in time. Wijnaendts Francken has behaved so appallingly that various lawyers have advised me to sue for slander. I have decided against it. She already has done us so much damage that we would be better off keeping quiet. Our association has achieved so much popularity, so many members, and funds, as well as sister associations, which is what fires the anger of Wijnaendts Francken and van Dorp. Mrs. Catt often writes to me. She is continually concerned about the health of her seventy-three-year-old mother. Reverend Shaw and Foster Avery have had a picture taken for me of Susan Anthony which is apparently on its way.

You will have read in *Jus Suffragii* that we have hired the entire Concertgebouw for next year's Congress. You remember, we went one Sunday afternoon on your last visit to Amsterdam.

I was so sorry to hear about your ailments. Have you been working too hard? I don't think I shall be going abroad this summer. Charles has to stay at home, and if I am away he won't do any work. Little Bradlaugh Bonner[1] will be coming, and a few young girls will be staying for a few weeks. We shall be going to the country for three or four days at Whitsum. I forgot to send you the last edition of our *Monthly*, so now I'm sending you two. If you have time to read them I'm sure you'll find something useful for your speeches on woman suffrage.

How are things going with your magazine?[2] Are you satisfied? I'm sitting here surrounded by four large bunches of roses. Each day my dear friends send them together with lovely letters as a reminder of how many good friends and loyal colleagues I have. This is the pleasant side to these public attacks. I never used to be aware of how many good friends I had. Nor of how strong our association is, which is what has helped us through the winter, strengthened yet further by the battle.

Norway, Denmark, and Finland have written to us with the news that they have said no to Catt. And Anna Shaw in America also wrote to say that she believes only one association per country can join and she is strongly opposed to accepting a second.

Charles had his twentieth birthday yesterday. He is delighted to have reached such a mature age. I hope many of your colleagues will visit Holland next year; Catt would love to see you all again. Give my regards to everyone, including your mother. What are you doing this summer?

Affectionately yours,

Aletta

1. Bradlaugh Bonner was a grandchild of the English neo-Malthusian Charles Bradlaugh. See Jacobs 1924, 59.

2. At this time, Rosika was an editor for the Feminist Association's monthly magazine,
A Nö és a Társadalom (Woman and society), whose name was changed in 1914 to *A Nö* (Woman).

17. Aletta Jacobs to Rosika Schwimmer

Amsterdam, Dec. 16th. 07

My dear Rozsa,

The annual meeting of our W.S. Society lies behind me, now I find a
few moments' time to write you a few words. How are you? Did you receive
the copy of the book I send [sent] you "Studie-Materiaal voor Vrouwenkiesrecht"? This book is a great success. All papers write favourably about
it. A part of the press called it—"a good book that just came in time." We
received already from Germany from a publisher a demand to allow him
to let it be translated into German, and I think that in a few weeks the book
will be sold here till the last copy.

What are you doing this winter? Do you have again a lecture course
in Germany? What a satisfaction for you to have in Hungary now everywhere Central-Kitchens established. I read it with pleasure.

We go nearly everyday a step farther to our aim, the suffrage and the
right to be elected in all governmental bodies. Our society for Wom. Suffr.
contains now 3400 members. Mrs. Wijnaendts Francken and Miss van
Dorp are still working against us. They now tell the people that the Dutch
women are not yet ripe for the Suffrage and that it are only a few revolutionary women who make the noise. She and her Society has for aim to
educate the women for their rights, which they must not ask before they
are ripe for it. They published lately also a paper, what they called "De
ploeger," that will say, The plougher. One of our papers said of it: "How
is that, these ladies begin to plough again. The others have sowed already,
they wait only to begin to harvest. Should the ladies have slept all the time,
that they did not see how good the seed came out already, what others
sowed for them?"

Mrs. Montefiore is now working in the socialist party, who are against
Wom. Suffrage.[1] She wrote Martina and me lately, that she will only work
for Adult Suffrage and against ladies-suffrage. Martina and I found it a good
moment to write her that both of us preferred not to receive more letters.
Our correspondence could only be disagreeable for both parties, so we better found not to correspond any more with her.

Poor Mrs Catt has such painful days. She is waiting at the deathbed of her mother, who is incurable sick; every hour she lives longer, is an hour of more suffering, and she does not die. Two months ago she wrote me already that her mother could die every moment, but the old sick lady remains still on the same condition. How is the health of your dear mother now? And how are you?

Write me soon a few words, I am very much longing to hear something of you. With love for you and your dear friends,

Yours for ever,

Aletta.

1. Dora B. Montefiore (1850–1934) was an English feminist and socialist. She attended in 1904 in Berlin and was a delegate of the militant WSPU in 1906 in Copenhagen. She refused to pay income tax under the slogan "Taxation without representation is tyranny," and she barred her doors to the bailiff, an action which, in 1906, resulted in a six-week long siege of her house.

18. Lucy E. Anthony to Aletta Jacobs

Moylan, Penn. April 27, 1908

My dear Dr. Jacobs,

Just now the question has come up of Miss Shaw's going to Amsterdam by way of London, as they very much wish that she shall take part in the Suffragetts demonstration on June 13. In that case we would not reach Amsterdam until the morning of the 14th, and I wonder whether there would be any risk in that. Mrs. Fawcett[2] thinks not. I wonder whether it is morning afternoon or evening that Miss Shaw is to preach. Will you let us know about that please? She is very anxious to be at the London meeting for she has so much sympathy with the Suffragettes, and then they are going to have a banner for Aunt Susan and all of the people from the United States are expected to march under that. I am trying to change the date of our sailing—that is go on a faster boat and one which will take us right to London, but we may not be able to change the date—at least I am afraid that it will cost so much that we cannot afford it. I just thought that I would let you know of the possible change in plan although nothing is decided as yet. Mrs. Avery would still go on May 29 as we had expected for she has promised to help Mrs. Catt some a few days before the opening of the Alliance.

Miss Shaw is at present in the South and will not be home until the

Anna Howard Shaw.

Lucy E. Anthony.

Alnwick Lodge, porch, 1915.

Alnwick Lodge, Anna Howard Shaw's house, 1915.

8th of May. Is it not a shame that she has to be away from her new home this first Spring, and also the first Summer? I just know we will be anti suffragists the next time so that we will not feel the responsibility of the suffrage work, and can stay home and make our gardens. But then as we must go away, I am glad indeed that it is to dear Holland that we go, and to our precious Dr. Jacobs in Holland. I do think it is so lovely of you to include me in the invitation to your home, and want to tell you again how much I appreciate it. Thank you so much.

Will you please let me know what is the binding of your set of The Life and Work of Aunt Susan. We want to bring to you a copy of the third volume which is just finished. Mrs. Harper has done so wonderfully in writing it, and we are so grateful to her. Soon she and Mrs. Catt will be in Amsterdam.

Affectionately,

Lucy E. Anthony

1. Lucy was mistaken. The demonstration on June 13, 1908, was staged by the suffragists of the NUWSS. A week later, on June 21, the militants, or the suffragettes, demonstrated.

2. See chap. 1, n. 14.

19. **Anna Howard Shaw to Aletta Jacobs**

Moylan, Pa. May. 22nd, 08

Dr. Aletta H. Jacobs.

Dear Doctor Jacobs: –

Your letter was received yesterday and one from Mrs. Catt, which I will answer later. I am very glad to learn of the safe arrival of our good American friends and that they are so well situated and particularly that they are so near your home that it will be easy to see each other often after we arrive. There are two more of our friends going than we had expected, one is Mrs. Elizabeth Hauser, whose health is so poor that they felt it was wise for her to take a vacation and Lucy immediately put in word for her to go over to the Holland meeting and meet some new people and new life and so she sails with Rachel a week from today, and we are hoping that she can be accommodated in the same Pension with Mrs. Catt and the others. My good Doctor Medley is also going with Lucy and me and she will want to room in the same Pension[1] if it can be had. Mrs. Catt, in her letter this morning kindly offered to engage rooms for any of our American women so that we will make that Pension a sort of American headquarters, which will be delightful for all our friends to be together.

I understand about the church service, that I am to conduct the whole of it but if there was any other woman minister present I think it would be very nice to invite her to take part in the service and should be glad to do so if there is no objection on your part or on the part of the church. Of course I do not yet know of any woman minister who is to be present.

We are going to send an old fashioned picture by Rachel which belonged to Aunt Susan, it is a group of our most famous early women, except that it leaves Aunt Susan and Mrs. Stanton out. They were all Eastern women, their faces are so fine and they did such splendid service in the Anti-Slavery movement and the Anti-Suffragist[2] movement that I am sure the picture will be of interest. Rachel is going to get Aunt Susan's picture framed here so that it will be sure to be ready for the Amsterdam meeting.

We are beginning now to count the days before we start and I suppose very soon we will begin to count the days before we leave the ship and land on your side of the water.

We were glad to get word of the color of the binding of the set of Aunt Susan's life and will bring the third volume with us. We think Mrs. Harper has done wonderfully well with it.

Everything is looking beautiful here now and it is a pity to go away and leave it, but I am equally sure it will be as grand on your side of the water where I am told that Holland in June is Holland in its glory and I hope to see some of your famous tulips, if it is not too late.

I thank you so much for your kind thoughtfulness in saying that you would have a bed ready for me when I landed Sunday morning, but I am quite sure I shall be so glad to see you and there will be so much to talk about that it would be pretty hard work for me to go to bed.

With sincere affection,

Anna H. Shaw.

1. An entire floor of the luxurious Amstel Hotel was hired for the American delegation (Naber, ed., 1939, 207).

2. Suffrage movement. One of Shaw's not infrequent errors. She often admitted to being able to speak better than write. See, e.g., AHS to AJ, July 28, 1908 (AJ-IAV-IIAV). Shaw did not write her autobiography, but dictated it.

20. Anna Howard Shaw to Aletta Jacobs

Moylan, Pa., Dec. 14, 1908

My dear Dr. Jacobs:—

I did not know, until Mrs. Catt told me the other day, when I was at her home, that you were going to leave Amsterdam so soon this winter. You told me, when we were in Geneva,[1] you expected to go later on. If you are idling your time away in the mountains, I am sure you will be glad to get gossipy letters, and so you must expect to read mine whenever they come; but do not take any of your strength in answering them unless there is something particular you want to say to me.

There are some friendships which demand that you shall be frequently told of their existence; some people from whom, when you write, you expect a reply before you write again, and, if you do not hear from them, you are not quite sure of their attitude towards you. Now, the friendship I have for you, and which I believe you have for me, is of a vastly different kind. I could write you letter after letter for weeks and months and never hear a word from you and yet be quite sure that you were the same true and staunch friend you always have been. So whether I hear from you or not, I am going to write you all sorts of gossipy things, if there are any, and now to begin.

You will probably hear through Progress[2] of my trip to Denver and of my experiences on election day, so that I will not need to repeat them. However, I will say that my hopes for good results were more than realized, and that I was perfectly satisfied with the conduct of the women and men and with everything I saw there. There was, in the association of the men and women, a different attitude from that of any other body of men and women whom I have seen working together. That feeling of sex consciousness, which always makes both men and women conscious of each others existence, was entirely wanting, and they were simply a body of citizens interested in the public good and paid no more attention to the fact that some of them were men and some of them were women than if that fact did not exist. They were not at the polls as men and women, but as citizens of the commonwealth interested in the public weal.

Last week I spent several days with Mrs. Catt in New York, and she and Rachel and I went over the new Constitution, which is to be proposed at the London meeting, and we also planned many things in connection with the International Alliance meeting.[3] I do hope we will have a successful meeting and that we may accomplish some good results.

The aggressive attitude of the Suffragettes is interfering with our having any social recognition, because the people are so afraid that, if they admit them to their houses, they will create disturbances similar to those they have been creating in the private houses of London, so that I fear we will lack some of the social recognition which we have had heretofore in our Conventions.

The Interurban Suffrage Society,[4] under the direction of Mrs. Catt, had the largest and most representative meeting in New York City last week that has ever been held in this country. The leaders of the ultra-fashionable set were present and it was a magnificent success. I do not wonder Mrs. Catt was justly proud over the result. I am sorry to say Mrs. Catt is not feeling very well at present. She does not seem to get strong. She is in good spirits, however, and is working very hard.

Mrs. Harper seems to be very happy in her new home, and now has room enough to do her work well. More magazines and papers are coming out in behalf of our cause, and recently one of the papers of Philadelphia had a favorable editorial declaring itself staunchly in favor of suffrage.

Miss Hay[5] seems to be in the forefront of everything. She is living with Mrs. Catt and seems to take the responsibility of almost all the household in her own hands. I do not think there is any hope of breaking that affair off.

Rachel has started in with new vigor and seems like her old self again. She has taken the presidency of the Pennsylvania State Association and is doing splendid work.

Do take good care of yourself this winter and come over to London next spring full of vim and vigor, and let us have a jolly good time.

Lucy joins me in sincere affection.

Faithfully,

Anna H. Shaw.

1. The board and the committee members of the ICW met in Geneva from August 31 to September 4, 1908. Jacobs and Shaw had to attend as members of the Committee on Suffrage and Rights of Citizenship.

2. *Progress* was the official organ of the NAWSA from 1907 (cf. letter 25, n. 2). Women had had the franchise in Colorado since 1893. On election days there was always much interest at home and abroad.

3. The Alliance's fifth congress was held in London in 1909.

4. This refers to the Interurban Suffrage Council of Greater New York. In 1905, Catt had brought all suffrage clubs in New York under this umbrella organization, and in 1909, the Interurban Council was reorganized and renamed the Woman Suffrage Party.

5. Mary Garrett Hay had an informal influence as Catt's friend and, from 1905, as housemate. Her influence was vehemently disapproved by Anna Howard Shaw. See chap. 2, n. 13, and chap. 4, n. 3.

21. Carrie Chapman Catt to Aletta Jacobs

Budapest, Mch. 11 [1909]

My dear Aletta,

I have just received your dear letter. I will just say that I have been very well thus far. Next week is my time of trial and I cannot tell how it will be. I will not now reply to your letter, but I do want to tell you of a blunder I have made, and which is convulsing me with laughter. You see I do not feel sorry for it, as I should! I wished to go to Prag for a private meeting with the Czechish Committee and when I learned from Martina, I wrote them at once to say I would come on the same day—the 24. I thought it so very agreeable that we should travel there together and be in the meeting together. Now comes this morning a letter from Frau Hainisch, and she says it is impossible for us to go there together, or to be in the same hotel for Martina is to speak for the Germans!! I had taken it for granted that she was speaking for the Czechs! So look for <u>bloody</u> news from Bohemia after the 24th! Austria and Servia's proposed war will be as nothing compared with the German and Czech war over the two international suffrage visitors.[1] I think I will write the Czechs that I will come on the 25th! Then they will say we are having an international quarrel over Bohemia. Well, just now it seems tremendously funny.

Last night Rosika interpreted for me, and the people who know English very well say she did it extremely well. She is a wonderful girl. This pen and ink is <u>usual</u> in hotels.

I do not need Rosa Manus in London by April 1. Really, she would be more trouble than help just then, but do not say that to her. I have found an excellent stenographer and all will be well. When I return I will try to arrange that your room is near mine and Rosa's too.

Now I must make myself beautiful for a dinner at Frau Derment. I am sure I have spelled it wrong, but you know her.

Accept my love and believe it is as thick as this ink but more steady in its flow.

Do stay for a long rest in London.

Lovingly,

Carrie C. Catt.

---

1. Austria's annexation of Bosnia, for the purpose of thwarting Serbian nationalism, resulted in the first of a series of Balkan crises. See also Peck 1944, 152ff. on the relationship between German and Czech women in Bohemia.

22. Rosa Manus to Catharine Waugh McCulloch

Baarn, 2 June 1909

My dearest Mrs McCulloch—[1]

You will think me unkind not having written to you for such a long time however dont think I have forgotten you. As it is I wanted to write to you a long letter and therefore waited untill I had the time for it. I have often been thinking of you and missed you and Mrs Stewart[2] most frightfully at the London Congress. As I think you shall be interested I shall try and tell you a little about our doings. At first I never thought I could get the permission to go to London at all. Father was very much against it. Mrs Catt however wrote to me several charming letters and asked me specially to come to London with her, she said she would look after me as a daughter and so after long talks Father gave his consent. So Anna[3] and I marched off to London before Easter. Mrs Catt received us with open arms and had rooms quite close to hers for us.

Anna went off to stay at a friend's of hers at the country and so Mrs Catt and I had a glorious time together. Of course Mrs Catt was very busy. I tried to help her with little things as much as I could and I sort of looked after her a bit. You know she just needs somebody to wait upon her and spoil her a bit. She is so sweet and lovely and it seems so cruel for a woman like she is always to be alone. It is so very sad that she has no children she does feel it so very much poor thing and I feel so sorry for her. She always called me her little adopted daughter and she was really a perfect Mother to me. I grew passionately fond of her, I can tell you and she says she loves me very much, is that not sweet of her? Poor thing she was not at all well when I came over and at first I did not think she could get through the Congressweek. It seemed to me that in England all the work was on Mrs Catt's shoulders. Mrs Avery not being there it gave her all the more work.

We were in a very nice comfortable Hotel and every day more delegates arrived. It was so nice to see so many of the known faces from last year back and everybody was so very sweet to us. However I must say we did miss you very very much dear Mrs McCulloch. All the others were very nice but we did not seem to have made such true friends amongst them this year. The Congress was very interesting but it was a real hard working time. The revision of the Constitution took up a great part of the time and led to many discussions. Also the rules of order was a great work. I suppose you will have heard that the board of officers has been changed. Mrs Avery had no more time to be an officer, Dr. Augspurg[4] and Dr. Schirmacher[5] were not chosen.

I[n] their place came Signe Bergman[6] from Sweden—Annie Furuhjelm[7] from Finland—Frau Lindemann[8] from Germany. It seems to be a good choice and I hope they will be able to do some good work. My sister and I were made pages of the American delegation before we came to London and I was selected to be Mrs Catt's special one. My dear dont you call this a great honor? I felt so proud about it and enjoyed my post very much. Of course I was always on the platform and never missed anything. It was lovely to hear all the different discussions and to hear the opinions of all the clever women from all parts of the world. The way Mrs Catt managed the Congress was really more than beautiful everyone men and women were in high admiration for her, one afternoon it got really very hot and it looked as if they were going to have a real fight, but Mrs Catt always managed to say the right thing just on the moment it was needed. If it had not been for her nasty things would have happened.

The opening day was not a bit exciting. You remember last year the very nice afternoon when those dutch children sang. This all made such an impression upon all the foreigners and so in London it seemed so cold and unfinished. The St James Hall was very nicely decorated with different banners and flags, which had been designed and worked by the London "Artists League." This made a beautiful effect and all the different countries came to the conclusion that each of them ought to have an artist club amongst them.

On tuesday evening there was the great Albert Hall meeting. I suppose you read about it in the papers. Mrs Fawcett sat in the Chair that evening. I dont know if you know the Albert Hall well I can tell you I never saw any hall so big so gigantese as this one. It was crowded with people, all the boxes were filled and when we were seated, all the delegates on the Platform from 8 parts of the hall entered the processions. All the working women of all the different trades entered with a banner in their hand, to say of what they belonged. First came the docters and lawers and nurses, I think 56 different trades. Also the poor mineworkers came and there was a deputation of housemothers of cooks in fact of every imaginable thing in the world. It was just like a dream to see these hundreds of people pass and to think that all these women who all work hard to earn their living have nothing to say in the world. Miss Shaw and Mrs Catt enjoyed that evening very much and they would love to get up a procession like that in the U.S.

On Wedn[e]sday we had a dinner party in the Princes' Restaurant. I must say it was not half as nice as the Amsterdam dinner; after the dinner there was a reception and the actrices club played a comedy that is to say they performed waxworks; it was really awfully good. On thursday evening everyone was invited in the Albert Hall again where the suffragettes held a meeting. Mrs Pethick-Lawrence[9] was in the Chair and Mrs Pankhurst and Christabel Pankhurst[10] spoke. On the platform were seated all the women and girls who had been in prison. They were all dressed in white and wore the colors of the suffragettes, green – mauve and white. They held big banners and flags in their hands and every moment when one of these women said a word they approved off they all called out together–here here!! [hear hear!!]or if they disapproved–shame–shame. It is a ridiculous way. They wanted to persuade everybody that the militant tactics are the best and that only the vote can be obtained through the militant tactics. Everybody who at first thought they like the work of the suffragettes changed their opinion after that evening. However I think that they do a great deal of good as through them a lot is spoken about women but on the other hand I think they do no end of harm by the way they act and go about in their noisey ways. The men's League also gave us a reception which was very nice.

One very enjoyable evening we spent in going to an anti suffrage meeting [meeting], the nonsense they talked there was well worse [worth] hearing and as there were a good many delegates, and some of them got up to answer some questions it was a very animated evening.

Why was it that there were no Chicago women amongst the Americans? In fact there were not so many Americans as last year and not nearly as nice ones. One American Lady I liked very much she is Mrs Safford a reverant [reverend]. I did not get much opportunity to talk to her but what I saw of her I liked her very much.

Mrs Catt's address was beautiful and everyone says it was the best one she has ever given. I dont understand how she can possibly can [sic] speak like she does, her whole soul lies in her words and her quiet, earnest way of talking and her sweet smile and whitty [witty] words at times make her altogether a wonder! I suppose you will think me silly to talk in that way but really I am in one mass of admiration for such a great and noble woman. In between I was the only one who had a chance to be with her as I helped her dress, and took her home after the meetings and we always had our meals together too. You can guess how real sorry I was to leave after four weeks but my people at home wanted me back and I did not want to abuse of their kindness in sparing us both.

The next Congress will be held in Stockholm in two years' time and Mrs Catt has already invited me to be her special page there. You must try and come then too as otherwise you will quite forget your foreighn friends. Tell me how are your dear children getting on? have you had a nice winter with them? When is your son and those other friends of yours coming to Amsterdam. I hope it wont be in August as then we are away and I should so much like to see them and show them round a bit. So dont forget to tell them to come. Are you going to Seattle [Seattle]? I think that will be a very interesting meeting.[11] Miss Shaw wanted us to come along with her but there was no chance for us this time. However I do wish to come to the U.S. some day and visit all my dear friends. I should so love to see you again dear Mrs McCulloch, have you not forgotten us yet? Now I will finish. I see that I have talked rather too much to you and hope you wont find this letter too tiresome to read. Let me hear from you soon and tell

The Dutch Woman Suffrage Campaign

me what you are doing and how your dear family is. Lots of love dear Mrs
McCulloch and a fond kiss from your loving dutch friend

Rosa Manus

1. Catherine Gouger Waugh McCulloch (1862–1945), a lawyer from Chicago, was an American delegate at the Amsterdam Congress in 1908. In addition to having four children and her own legal practice, she was also an active member of the NAWSA and its vice president from 1910 to 1912. She published a great deal. See NAW.

2. Ella Seass Stewart was the American delegate to the Amsterdam Congress. See E. S. Stewart to AJ, May 18, 1908 (AJ-IAV-IIAV). Like Catherine McCulloch, she also came from Illinois. See NAW.

3. Anna was Rosa Manus' sister. She married a German physician, Dr. Felix Jacobi, and lived in Berlin. They had a daughter, Erica, who stayed behind when her parents fled to New York in the thirties. She died in 1941 trying to escape from the Netherlands.

4. Anita Augspurg (chap. 1, n. 9) sat on the Board of the Alliance from 1904 to 1909. She and Schirmacher were probably too radical for such functions. Anna Rueling was likely referring to them and Lida Gustava Heymann in 1905 in her "What Interest Does the Women's Movement Have in the Homosexual Question?" when she wrote, "I am convinced that the homosexual woman in particular is used for leading roles in the international movement for equal rights." In Faderman 1980, 88. Cf. letter 39.

5. See chap. 1, n. 14.

6. Signe Bergman, a Swede, was secretary to the Alliance from 1909 to 1913.

7. Annie Furuhjelm (1895–1937) was a Finnish feminist active in both the national and the international suffrage movement. Finland was the first Western country to adopt woman suffrage in its constitution (1906), which contributed to the general esteem for Furuhjelm in the Alliance. She was also a member of parliament in Finland from 1913 until 1929. See WWT.

8. Anna Lindemann, a German feminist, was active in the German council of women and the suffrage movement.

9. Emmeline Pethick-Lawrence (1867–1954) was an English suffragette and a key figure in the WSPU until the split in October 1912. From 1914 she was active in the peace movement.

10. Emmeline Pankhurst (1858–1928) and Christabel Pankhurst (1880–1958) were leading figures in the militant WSPU, which they founded in 1903. Their leadership gradually became more exclusive and the organization demanding of conformity. Even Sylvia Pankhurst (1882–1960), Emmeline's oldest daughter, who advocated a broader suffrage feminism, was dropped from the organization. With the onset of World War I things changed radically: the militant strategy was exchanged for a clamorous patriotism which did not appeal to many. See Spender 1983 for an appreciation of the vast and often unreliable literature about the WSPU. For a fresh approach see Stanley 1988.

11. The annual NAWSA convention was held in Seattle.

23. Aletta Jacobs to Rosika Schwimmer

Amsterdam, July 7th 09

My dearest Rosika,

I thank you very much for all the trouble you have taken for me. But here it is very rainy nearly every day and our newspapers tell us that this is the weather nearly over whole Europe. Especially from Austria and Hungary they speak of cold, dreary weather and under these circumstances I dare not decide to come over to you. If I will come at the first of August, I must write to an Hotel now and I cannot do that. Therefore I concluded to remain in Holland and when the wheather [weather] is fine in August go to Scheveningen.

I have had very much sorry [sorrow] during the last few months especially, but it was going on already from last winter. Under the bad influence of Anna Overduin[1] but more even under that of the family in the Hague, Charles was more than rude to me and did things he never can make good.

During the time I was in London, they upset him to me in such a grade, that I have had since that time only sleepless nights and sorry days. The result of this is, that Charles leaves the house and that he is entirely in the hands of his mother and brother and sisters and the family Overduin.

One of my sisters in law is staying with me now, but as her husband died last November and she has much trouble now with her only son, you can understand, that we cannot be a great consolation to each other, we only can cry together and help each other through these dark days.

Now you know, dear Rosa, why I did not write before and why I can not conclude to take a step in one of [or] another direction.

With many kisses,

Yours, Aletta

1. Anna Overduin (1887–1937) married Charles Jacobs in 1913. From 1914, she practiced medicine at the Institute for Physical Therapy in Amsterdam. The 1908 membership roster of the VVVK mentions her as a board member of the Amsterdam branch.

24. Carrie Chapman Catt to Aletta Jacobs

2 West 86th Street
New York City.
September 27, 1909

My dear Dr. Jacobs: –

I certainly owe you a big apology for allowing your letter to go so long without an answer. Indeed, I did write to Miss Shaw and Mrs. Harper about Charlie and asked them to write you a note of sympathy, and I presume they did, yet, I did not follow my own instruction. The plain truth of the matter is, that when I got home from London, I was about as sick as people ever get and keep out of bed. I concluded that I would go into the country where I might have absolute rest, and finally found a cottage in the mountains not a great distance from New York City, but it was several days before I was able to take the short journey there, and during the whole summer I was unable to do anything. Most of the time I spent on my back and was not able to even write a letter for many days at a time. I had access to no stenographer or typewriter and consequently what letters were written, I had to do myself by hand. Let this be my apology.

I have thought of you every day since getting that letter and had my poor old body been as willing as my mind, you would have heard from me long ago. While I am speaking about myself, I will say that I am now better and am hopeful that the change has come for good. Yesterday I actually went out and made a speech to a club of young Hebrews in Brooklyn. It took five hours to go and come and attend the meeting, and yet, I lived through it and feel pretty good to day. It was an appointment made long ago.

Some great changes have taken place in the suffrage work and some amusing things have followed. The National Headquarters have come to New York and Mrs. Harper is made the chief of the Press Department. As you have already read, this press department will be entirely supported by Mrs. Belmont.[1] The rest of the National work will pay rent for its office. The state organization of New York has also been given a headquarters in the same building free of rent by Mrs. Belmont. This fact has been heralded all over the United States until every crank has suddenly discovered that he or she is a suffragist and wants to get something out of Mrs. Belmont. There are bands that want to play for her, and playwrights who want her to put plays in the theatre. There are people who want to speak for her and all sorts of offers are made. On the other hand, she has given out one or two illadvised interviews which have given the press opportunities for critical editorials, and all this makes the situation rather amusing and exceedingly exciting. Our City organization also is planning to go a good deal of aggressive work and our whole city will be humming with suffrage doings about town.

Mrs. Pankhurst arrives on the 18th and will speak here on the 25th. She comes under the direction of Mrs. Blatch,[2] whom you know, I think. Mrs. Snowden[3] will arrive about November 2nd and will speak here November 6th. Mrs. Snowden will be my guest while she is here.

I do not wonder that your courage left you and that your health was broken after all your years' work and the shock of Charlie's sudden departure. It is impossible to think that he would have taken such action of his own free will. By this time you will have returned to your home in Amsterdam and I hope you will have found some comfort and rest in your trip to the Tatra. I am sure it will be lonely for you without Charlie and I hope for the time being you can find someone to come to you as companion and to help you forget that he has left you. I imagine however that he will be teasing you to come back before long. It must seem just now as though he thought more of others than of you, but I am sure this is not true for he certainly loves you very dearly. He probably does not appreciate all you have been to him through his early years for I believe no child ever does appreciate what it's home has been until he has had a little experience in life, but some day he will recognize it and be grateful to you. You at least have done your full duty by him and you have suffered enough so that you deserve his love and his gratitude, and I hope that neither will be long withheld from you. I think I know [w]hat this separation means to you much better than many do, and you have my earnest sympathy.

You ask when I may be coming to Europe again and say you may meet me in any country where I shall go. I have concluded that I will not leave home again until I have passed this trouble of mine. I have become so aenemic with the loss of blood from my hemmorrhages that my heart was much affected and I have no strength at all. Now I am trying internal electricity and they give me some encouragement that this may do the work. I do not know how much longer I will have to endure these losses, but if they continue a great while, I shall not be able to endure them. As it is, I am stuffing in order to make as much blood as possible. I drink a quart of buttermilk, and one glass of egg nog, besides some beef juice every day, in addition to my meals. That ought to kill or cure anybody. I am sure that I shall not go to Europe this year, and I do not think I shall attempt to go anywhere before it is time for the meeting in Stockholm.

I suppose that you know that the Council choose the same year and the same city for their meeting. I do not know what the Swedes think about it, but I think it is rather unfortunate.

I have had a letter from South Africa in which my correspondent said that the Dutch women there could get the suffrage for all women if they would. That re-affirms our opinion that you would do a good deal of good there, but apparently it is too late to get it in the present Constitution and doubtless a later time will do. I hope we may be able to go there together. I am hoping that after the Stockholm meeting I may be able to make many trips.

If you want to run away from all the troubles in Holland at any time come over here and I shall be glad indeed to take you into my household at any time when my one spare bed room is not occupied. I cannot promise to give you enough to eat nor Dutch tea, but you can carry a little lunch in your pocket.

With love and most cordial good wishes, I am,

Yours truly,

Carrie C. Catt.

1. Following the death of her husband in 1908, Alva Belmont (1853–1933) became a militant feminist. She was extremely wealthy and became the Maecenas of the suffrage movement. See NAW.

2. Harriot Stanton Blatch (1856–1940) was a daughter of Elizabeth Cady Stanton. She lived for many years in England, where she had contacts with the WSPU. Once back in the United States, she founded the Equality League of Self-Supporting Women (from 1910 called the Women's Political Union), which took English militant suffragism as a model. See NAW.

3. The Englishwoman Ethel Snowden (1881–1946) was a socialist suffrage feminist in the NUWSS. During World War I she was one of a group of women who, unlike the NUWSS president, Mrs. Fawcett, wanted to launch a pacifist antiwar campaign. She was one of the founders of the English branch of the WILPF. See Wiltsher 1985.

4

Strong-Minded Suffragists, Long-Time Presidents

Women at the Top:
Carrie Chapman Catt and Anna Howard Shaw

When Catt in 1928, on the occasion of her seventieth birthday, was presented with a memorial album containing tributes from women all over the world, Aletta Jacobs dedicated her album leaf to their joint world tour taken in 1911–12. As a caption for three photogaphs taken during their journey, she wrote: "What a time between then and now! How young and energetic we both were! I envy ourselves. I feel as old as Methusalem and as weak as a chicken now! The only thing what interest me now is how it will be in the world of the spirits, if there exists equality of the sexes. I hope not, if there was it would be too dull for me. You would there find enough to do, spirits always quarrel."[1] Jacobs seems to be referring here to the tact and strategic insight which Catt must have possessed to a large extent, for she systematically avoided trouble, differences of opinion, personal differences, or power struggles, and instead preferred to exert her energies elsewhere. The fact that she put so much energy into the international suffrage movement, including her world tour with Jacobs, can perhaps be accounted for by her peculiar relationship with Anna Howard Shaw. This may have induced Catt to step aside in the American suffrage movement.

In 1900, Catt and Shaw were the only two candidates from whom Susan B. Anthony could choose a successor.[2] "No easy task," wrote Shaw in her autobiography *The Story of a Pioneer*, "On the one hand, I had been vice-president at large and her almost constant companion for twelve years, and she had grown accustomed to think of me as her successor. On the other hand, Mrs. Catt had been chairman of the organization committee and, through her splendid executive ability had built up our organization in many states. From Miss Anthony down, we all recognized her steadily growing powers; she had, moreover, abundant means, which I had not"

(Shaw 1915, 284). Anthony's choice of Catt was a rational rather than an emotional one. Catt, through the Organization Committee, had structured, centralized, and professionalized suffrage work, and she had succeeded in reducing the distance between local branches and the national association. In her autobiography Anna Shaw took no pains to hide her feelings: "I will admit here for the first time that in urging Catt's fitness for the office I made the greatest sacrifice of my life. My highest ambition had been to succeed Miss Anthony, for no one who knew her as I did could underestimate the honor of being chosen by her to carry on her work" (Shaw 1915, 285).

Catt's position, however, did not go unchallenged. Just days after the 1900 convention she met with a resistance which could be accounted for by the fact that Shaw, still vice president of the NAWSA, had both grassroots support and Anthony's personal backing in the association—even though Anthony had chosen Catt as her direct successor. During the first meeting over which Catt presided, the Executive Committee of the NAWSA, which comprised branch presidents and the Board, demanded the dissolution of the Organization Committee (Peck 1944, 108–9). This meant nothing other than "away with Mary Garrett Hay," Catt's best friend and closest colleague and the most likely candidate to preside over the Organization Committee after Catt's move to the presidency of the association. It is no secret that Shaw vehemently disliked Hay.[3] After the meeting Catt shut herself away for hours, yet resisted her initial inclination to step down. This she did only four years later, in 1904, officially for reasons of health. But a term of four years is not very long during a period in which capable figures could and did lead suffrage associations for decades. Catt's resignation in 1904 is not the only example of sweeping changes being attributed to a person's ill health instead of to personal or power machinations.[4]

In 1904, Shaw, in spite of her admission that she had since lost all ambition to become president, was still the most likely successor, and indeed was finally "commanded" by Anthony to submit herself as a candidate (Shaw 1915, 286). Her leadership, however, did the movement no good. Although an excellent orator, she was not a satisfactory president. Her greatest assets were her powers of persuasion and her passion. Her administrative qualities were virtually nonexistent, and she was not gifted with tact (Flexner 1977, 256–57; Evans 1979, 55). Opposition grew, and matters came to a head during the annual convention of the NAWSA in 1910 because of Shaw's attitude toward Frances Squire Potter (letter 28, n. 2). Potter was a relative newcomer who less than two years earlier—at Shaw's personal insistence—was elected to the board. After that time Shaw became involved in a seemingly incomprehensible disagreement with her, so Potter stepped down along with two valuable veterans, Rachel Foster Avery and Harriet Taylor Upton (letters 28, 29, 30). Shaw remained, but her position grew increasingly untenable, most clearly at the annual national conventions, where dissension and controversy increasingly dominated the agenda. Strong sentiments were at stake. Susan B. Anthony on her deathbed had exacted a promise from Shaw that she would remain president as long as she was able to carry out her duties. Shaw had replied, "But how can I promise that? I can keep it only as long as others wish me to keep it." Anthony then had insisted: "Promise to make them wish you to keep it." After Shaw had given her pledge Anthony added:

> You will not have an easy path. In some ways it will be harder for you than it has ever been for me. I was so much older than the rest of you, and I had been president so long, that you girls have all been willing to listen to me. It will be different with you. Other women of your own age have been in the word almost as long as you have been; you do not stand out from them by age or length of service, as I did. There will be inevitable jealousies and misunderstandings; there will be all sorts of criticism and misrepresentation. My last word to you is this: no matter what is done or is not done, how you are criticized or misunderstood, or what efforts are made to block your path, remember that the only fear you need have is fear of not standing by the thing you believe to be right. [Shaw 1915, 231–32; cf. letter 25]

The Story of a Pioneer was published in 1915, and for all Shaw's purported naïveté, this moving account can also be read as a strategically timed public plea in which she justified her much-criticized actions. One can wonder how far Shaw felt herself bound by her promise to Anthony, and how much she used it to enforce the obedience of her fellow workers. Anyway, *The Story of a Pioneer* betrays her lack of confidence in its appeal to sentiments like the widespread veneration for "Aunt Susan." In December 1915, just before the annual convention, Shaw announced her resignation, and Carrie Chapman Catt automatically took up the reins. It must be said for Shaw that, once she finally realized her best contribution to the movement would be to step down, she put complete faith in Catt. In June 1916, she wrote to Lucy E. Anthony: "The new group is taking hold, and doing things splendidly. . . . I realise that my day except for speaking and 'inspiring' has gone by, and this is all right; I will speak and 'inspire' my best. I might do worse, I suppose" (Flexner 1977, 284).

Though it was undoubtedly due to Catt that a serious power struggle with Shaw or, worse, a schism within the NAWSA ranks over personal issues never occurred, this should not be interpreted as an act of pure unselfishness. True, by dedicating herself in 1904 to the international movement, Catt gave Shaw a clear field. Yet at the same time she won fame for herself as the great leader of a worldwide women's movement, which enabled her later to exact full obedience from her fellow suffragists in the NAWSA. She deserves respect for the way that she made full use of her organizational talents all the time. From the sidelines, and without Shaw's feeling threatened, she even succeeded in giving fresh momentum to the NAWSA.

When Catt returned to the United States after the 1909 congress in England, she had one purpose—to find an effective American alternative to militant behavior. She had been impressed by the enthusiasm and zeal of the English movement, which seemed only to emphasize the apathy within the American one. There had been no spectacular developments in the United States since 1896, when the franchise had been given in the Western state of Utah. Catt realized that if women wanted an amendment to the Constitution, a number of important Eastern states would have to be won over, New York being her first target. With this aim in mind, Catt proceeded to build a new style of organization structured on the lines of a political party. She skillfully made use of existing affiliates of the NAWSA, instead of breaking away. Following a short period of energetic scheming, the Woman Suffrage Party was founded on October 30, 1909, in Carnegie Hall, in the presence of women from all boroughs and voting districts of New York, all of whom proceeded to set up branches (Flexner 1977, 262). The Woman Suffrage Party not only appealed to the imagination of the general public but also fired the imagination of the women themselves. Shortly after the meeting, suffrage parties were established in other states along the same lines. To quote Peck, "The old trumpets were calling again to the suffragists of 1910. In that hour militancy lost its challenge for leadership of the suffrage movement. American women went political and constitutional instead of militant in 1909 (Peck 1944, 172).[5]

Toward the end of 1910, this new strategy yielded its first fruit, and the state of Washington became the fifth state in which women were given the franchise—finally breaking the fourteen-year-long impasse. Catt, however, had had a difficult year and was recovering from a serious operation. She had decided meanwhile to go on the world tour which she had been discussing with Jacobs since 1906. Somewhat sorrowfully, she wrote to her friend Mary Peck, "There has come a mighty opportunity to our movement and here I am, in the midst of the opportunity I've prayed and waited for, for the past twelve years, running away from it—throwing away my weapons and making a grand skiddoo" (Peck 1944, 175).

Carrie Chapman Catt and Aletta Jacobs on World Tour, 1911–12

The IWSA's sixth congress was held in Stockholm in June 1911. From there Catt traveled to London, where a banquet was given in her honor. Leaders of the militant movement as well as of the constitutional suffrage movement attended. Catt left London together with Amelia Cameron, a friend of hers from New York, en route to South Africa, the first leg of their world trip. They were joined in Madeira by Jacobs and a friend, Nettie Boersma. Their journey took them from South Africa, via the Red Sea, through the Middle East (Jersualem and Beirut), and then back to Egypt, where Cameron and Boersma left the party. Catt and Jacobs traveled on to Ceylon (Sri Lanka). They toured India, calling at Madras, Bombay, Jaipur, Delhi, Lucknow, Benares (Varanasi), and Calcutta. They went overland to Burma, then via Singapore by sea to the Dutch East Indies (Indonesia), where the tireless pair visited Sumatra and Java. Then they journeyed on via Hong Kong to the Philippines, back to Hong Kong, and thence to Canton. The last leg was by no means the least adventurous. From Shanghai they proceeded to Nanking before penetrating the Chinese interior as far as Hankou (Wuhan). Peking (Beijing) was the last stop before Japan, where they visited Kyoto and Tokyo. At this point they parted company, Catt sailing via Hawaii to San Francisco, and Jacobs taking a train from Vladivostok to Amsterdam. By fall 1912, both were back home.[6]

A simple geographical description cannot convey the full richness of this tour or the varied impressions Jacobs and Catt gathered. And yet personal accounts are not necessarily the most reliable: Jacobs' extensive and lively report of her meeting with Olive Schreiner in *Herinneringen* is at variance with Peck's (almost firsthand) description. Far from being pleased with Schreiner, as Jacobs wrote, Peck says she returned from her one-day visit thoroughly disapproving of Schreiner's life-style, which she described as an "utter mental stagnation while making a home for her husband" (Peck 1944, 183).[7] Such personal accounts, however, do give an impression of the travelers' versatility and responses to variety. In South Africa, for example, where women were busily campaigning for the introduction of state-controlled brothels, Jacobs, staunchly opposed to such measures, paid more attention to prostitution than to woman suffrage. In addition to the usual sightseeing trips, Jacobs and Catt visited numerous women's hospitals, girls' schools, and women's associations. Catt's fascination with matriarchal societies took them on a trip to the Menankabau of Sumatra, on which subject she later wrote a number of articles for publications like *National Geographic*. In China both Catt and Jacobs were overwhelmed by the determined militancy of their sex. Women refusing to marry and ex-members of the revolutionary "dare to die" clubs—who had started out as couriers in the Sun Yat-sen liberation movement and later fought in women's regiments against the Manchu dynasty—were prepared to resort to violence on their own behalf now that the revolutionary government was bluntly ignoring their demands for woman suffrage. Jacobs' and Catt's unstinting admiration for the Chinese women held no hint of the skepticism which continued to color their feelings about the militancy of the women in England.[8] But then China was not England, which perhaps goes some way toward explaining

Carrie Chapman Catt and Aletta Jacobs at the station in Shanghai, 1912.

Carrie Chapman Catt and Aletta Jacobs en route to the Manchu tombs at Mukden, 1912.

At the tombs in Mukden, 1912. Standing, left: *Carrie Chapman Catt;* seated on the steps, right: *Aletta Jacobs.*

Sing Pey Zung, the "Christabel Pankhurst of China."

Sing Pey Zung.

Carrie Chapman Catt and Aletta Jacobs with Chinese feminists, 1912.

the doublethink process to which even such seasoned international feminists as Catt and Jacobs could be subject.

It is worth asking what the direct contact with women from so many non-Western cultures did for their ideas of international sisterhood. In a fine example of subtle analysis, Harriet Feinberg focused on the *Reisbrieven* (letters from the journey) that Aletta Jacobs wrote for the Dutch newspaper *De Telegraaf* asking: "What happens when a woman committed to an egalitarian feminism and to a worldwide movement for women's social and political rights, yet with internalized, barely questioned notions of 'higher' and 'lower' races, 'advanced' and 'backward' societies, which are the result of lifelong conditioning, comes into direct contact with colonial societies? Or more simply: does her international feminism triumph over racism and Eurocentrism?" (Feinberg 1988, 5)[9] The answer she framed on the basis of aptly chosen citations is not a simple one. Feinberg detected a gradual movement in the letters toward a recognition of people of color as fully equal beings, as well as a condemnation of colonialism. This movement, however, is not linear, and Jacobs seems again and again to have lapsed into old prejudices as soon as she distanced herself from a direct experience. On more than one occasion she contradicted herself. Thus she fulminated against the general British attitude of contempt toward Indians, while in an earlier letter she did not express herself particularly sensitively when she wrote: "The natives of South India evoked my deep revulsion—and that of my travelling-companion, too" (Feinberg 1988, 9). Otherwise Feinberg discerned in the *Reisbrieven* a pattern she has found in various other accounts of Western and third-world women. She calls this pattern the "circle of inspiration" and describes it as follows:

> A woman of color feels moved to take action to help her people. She is somewhere in this process touched and influenced by Western concepts of liberty and equality—through a teacher, governess, or correspondent, through books, through travel, or study. With other women she takes action to start something—a school, a dispensary, lecture series, cooperative, protest action—that puts her in a nontraditional role but in her view moves her people forward. She and her comrades in turn become an inspiration to Western women who exclaim, "These are our sisters!" and are helped past their isolating racism to write, speak, agitate for—depending on their politics and the particular situation—better conditions in the colonies, better treatment for a minority population, independence, an end to racism. [Feinberg 1988, 12]

It is not easy to define what the world tour did even for Catt and Jacobs personally, and this becomes more difficult when one considers the effect on the IWSA as a whole. In South Africa, local societies for the first time came together in a national convention; in Egypt, an effort was made to establish a suffrage committee. In the Dutch East Indies, Jacobs devoted a great deal of time to setting up local branches of the existing suffrage society. In the Philippines, a society consisting of four American and four Filipino women was founded. And finally, in China, one of the existing suffrage societies was invited to join the Alliance. Perhaps the most immediate result of the whole trip was that it enriched the discourse of international sisterhood with the language of personal experience. When the IWSA met in 1913 in Budapest for its Seventh Congress it seemed to have a new perspective. On behalf of the Chinese women Jacobs presented a banner which ratified membership of the Chinese branch. In her presidential speech Catt, in a formulation derived from imperialist discourse, boasted that the sun would never again set upon her empire of international woman suffrage: "The North Star and the Southern Cross alike cast their benignant rays upon suffrage activities" (IWSA 1913, 84). It was the last time that such an optimistic utterance was heard.

December 1909–March 1914
Letters 25–42

25. Anna Howard Shaw/Lucy E. Anthony to Aletta Jacobs

December 11th, 1909

My dear Dr. Jacobs:

I am wondering if you have left Amsterdam, and are now at St. Moritz or some other place for the cold weather;—just what has become of you. I need not ask you what you are doing, for I know very well, whether in Amsterdam or St. Moritz you are up to your eyes in suffrage work.

We have had some nice letter[s] from the little Manus girls, and little Anna seems to be interested in the new line of work which she is taking up. I am very sorry I cannot keep up a steady correspondence with them and with you all but my work is such that I cannot even think of friends, let alone keep in touch with them.

We never had such a suffrage boom in our lives. It is either suffrage meetings or anti-suffrage meetings continually, until I should think the people would get sick and tired of them. I feel as if I should have to run away. Lucy went down to Moylan yesterday to open up the house and get things ready for me. I go today; so that I can have just a little breath of the country and roam through my little grove and sit on my great big boulders and watch my little stream, and gaze over the whole country, for you know we can see for miles in all directions from my house. Sometimes I think there is no such great big fool as I am in the whole world: to think that I should leave that home and all it means to me, and the quiet of the country,—after all the years of difficulties I had to get it together, and come to this great big cold city, where the people do not care whether I was in Moylan or not, and have to mix in with so many uncomfortable and unpleasant things. When I feel that way I feel I cannot do it any longer. Then again, I feel the presence of Aunt Susan; I feel her hand on my head just as I did when she died, and I remember my promise to her not to give up under any circumstances.—I do not think that she really expected I would leave home and live in a little suite of apartments looking out on a lot of old tin cans and wash boilers, instead of out on my own beautiful land and grove and stream.—I do not know whether I have got grit enough to keep it up very long, or not.—I do not mean the work; it is the petty jealousies and little contemptible feelings, and the feeling of superiority of so many people who are fresh in the work, who know nothing about it, and yet who think they understand everything. It is so easy to sit and dictate letters, and to attend meetings, and to go to banquets when you have an organization back of you to settle the bills and look after all the expenses; but when you have to get the money and be responsible for it it is not so easy;—but you know how that is, because you have had to do the same thing in Holland, with the same attitude confronting you.

Mrs. Catt's health seems to be improving. I saw her last night at a bazar

103

which she is holding for her city societies, and she looked better than I have seen her for a long time.

If I do not forget it, and the probabilities are that I will, I am going to send my views and Lucy's to the Holland Society. I wear the Holland button all the time, and the reporters take great interest in it,—much more interest than they do in our American button, and it has been copied a great many times in the press here. I received the one that you sent for my friend Dr. DeBey[1] and she was very much pleased.

There was some misunderstanding between Miss Conners and Mrs. Upton[2] in regard to Jus Suffragii, but I do not know just exactly on what ground the misunderstanding arose, but I hope at the Business Committee meeting which we will have in a few days, we will be able to straighten it out. I shall feel sorry if the paper was not kept up, and if we could not get any subscriptions in this country; but the name hurts it here. The people do not want it by that name.[3]

My dear Dr. Jacobs,

Miss Shaw left the above letter and went to Moylan for a rest of a day or so and when she returned she was not able to go on with her work, but had to cancel all of her dates and is now in a private hospital in a lovely room overlooking the park and where she has every attention and care. The Dr. says that the principal trouble is her stomach and nerves and he hopes that in a short time she will be all right but she simply must have rest for a time. I am just adding this note and with a great deal of love and wishing to let you know just how Miss Shaw is. So please do not worry, but know that everything is being done that can be and that she has every care.

Love again,

Lucy.

1. Dr. DeBey was a Dutch doctor in Chicago about whom Peck told an amusing anecdote. When the Russian peasant activist Catherine Breshkovskaja was visiting the United States, she was taken from one social engagement to another.

> She dressed very plainly in peasant-like clothes and while she was in Chicago she was entertained in a palatial home and given a reception to which the guests came arrayed in purple and fine linen. One of the last to arrive was Dr. Cornelia DeBey, a well-known Chicago physician who always wore tailored suits. As soon as the Russian caught sight of her she made a bee-line for the doctor, who she had never seen before, threw her arms around her and whispered urgently in her ear, "I want to go home with you!" Needless to say she went. [Peck 1944, 142]

2. Harriet Taylor Upton (1853–1945) was originally opposed to woman suffrage but from 1890 became the pivot, together with Shaw, of the NAWSA (1894–1910) and publisher of *Progress* (1902–1910). She was reelected to the council in 1910 but stepped down because of problems with Shaw. She did remain active in Ohio. See NAW.

3. We were unable to find out who Miss Conners was and which misunderstanding was referred to. There was probably a continual tug-of-war behind the scenes about the publishing of the Alliance's magazine, and many no doubt disliked Martina Kramers' having complete control of *Jus Suffragii* for such a long period (1906–13). Its title was also a vexed point.

26. Aletta Jacobs to Rosika Schwimmer

Amst. April 8.10

My dearest Rozsa,

Your post-card arrived at this moment and I must answer you at once. I am very glad you got that position on a daily paper, as well for the financial support it will bring you, as for the reason that your country-people at last found out your great power and ability as a yournalist [journalist]. Do you think that Fl. 100.00 a month, is not very much, you know in our country they would say it is very high paid and I believe that we have not one woman-yournalist who is paid as much as that. But once being placed in that position, you will climb till the highest spot, I am sure of that.

I was also glad to receive a few words from you, because I was afraid that you were ill, or so much overworked that you could not write. I am glad it is not as bad as that, but you ought to have a vacation this summer. My rest in Tatra-Lomnicz last summer has brought me a part of my health again. I am much and much better than a year ago, and I can do much more and better work than for years. This summer I will take again a complete rest. Perhaps I shall go to one or other place in Tyrol, but I must remain in Holland till the Intern. Congr. of the N. Malth. League is over.

Now about Charles. In the middle of February he passed his first examination as a lawyer and two days before, he had send [sent] Mr. van Straaten[1] to me, asking, if he passed his ex. well, I would receive him then? Of course I did. And so he came to me, asking forgiveness for what he had done to me and allowing him to come again in my house. Since than [then] he comes regularly and two or three times a week, he takes dinner with me. But Annie has not yet been here and as he never mentioned her, we never speak of her.

But as Charles is now coming here and everything is over, you can imagine that it is not the same boy to me as he was before. There is something broken, what never can be mend[ed] again.

Miss Gill proved a good surrogate for Miss Corbett.[2] She spoke very well, especially when she could tell about the Norwegian women. We gain daily new members and from time to time new branches, but this Government of ours does not give us any hope. We are going again to our Queen in May, but I do not expect any good of it.[3]

Mrs. Catt wrote me a long letter. I do understand from it that she is not at all well and that she prefers to travel abroad than to stay at home. She asks me to take a long tour together after the Congress in Stockholm. I will try to go with her for at least 3 or 4 months than [then].

And now I must go to Joh. Naber for our Maandblad, I have no time more. With many kisses,

Yours, <u>Aletta</u>.

1. E. W. van Straaten was a member of the Men's Society for Woman Suffrage.

2. Miss Corbett, an Englishwoman, later Margery Corbett Ashby (1882–1980), was a member of the Alliance board and in 1923 succeeded Catt as president, holding that position until 1946. She was also an active member of the British Liberal Party. Whittick's history of the Alliance pays extensive tribute to her role in the IWSA. See Whittick 1979.

3. In 1910, the queen was presented with a rundown of all "sexist legislation" in the Netherlands (*Gedenkboek* 1919, 30).

27. Lucy E. Anthony to Aletta Jacobs

New York, June 10, 1910

My dear Doctor:

Some weeks ago we had a very lovely letter from you, but we have both been so very busy that it has seemed as though all friendly correspondence had been left out of our calendars for some time. I am just writing a note now to let you know that tomorrow morning Miss Shaw sails for England on the "Cincinnati" of the Hamburg American line. She will go right to London and be there a few days before starting on a vacation motor trip with Ray Costelloe.[1] During her stay in London, in fact all the time she is in England which will be about six weeks, her address will be "care of American Express Company, No. 6 Haymarket."

Miss Shaw has been very very tired and finds herself in need of a complete change and rest. Her plan was to spend the summer in her own home at Moylan, a privilege she has never yet had since she has had her home, but she realized that should she stay there she could not get away from the cares of the suffrage work and from her correspondence. So all of her friends have joined in urging her to go away, and she starts tomorrow morning.

I do hope you are going to see each other for I know Miss Shaw wants to see you very much indeed, both for the love of you, and some things of mutual interest which she wishes to talk over with you, and things which you said in your letter you wanted to hear about.[2]

We are so glad that you are better, and I trust you are now started on the pathway of health which will keep you well all of the days to come.

You may have heard of the fact that Mrs. Catt has at last had the operation which I think you suggested so long ago and said she must have. It is now eight days since the operation, and she is progressing finely. They say that yesterday she asked to have some one read to her and seems to be getting on as well as possible.

This is all for this time, but with a great deal of love, yes, and to Charles too.

Lucy E. Anthony.

1. Ray Costelloe (1887–1940), better known as Ray Strachey, was an English suffragist. She spent a number of years in the United States, where she studied at Bryn Mawr College. She was a niece of Bryn Mawr's president, M. Carey Thomas. It was probably while she was a student that her friendship with Shaw began. Once back in England, she became Fawcett's right hand within the NUWSS. After World War I she was political advisor to England's first woman member of Parliament, Lady Astor. She wrote several biographies and a history of the English women's movement, *The Cause* (1928).

2. Jacobs wanted to hear about all the problems which had flared up during the 1910 NAWSA annual conference. See letter 28.

28. Rachel Foster Avery to Aletta Jacobs

Philadelphia, July 14th, 1910

My dear Aletta:—

I was so tried with the bank at Munich, when I received your nice letter telling me that you had written me twice to that address. I went there faithfully every day and I was in Munich during the entire week at the very time I had told you to write me there. Of course, I never received either of your communications. The Oberammergau Post Office did have the grace to return the letters which were lying there during the very time when I was begging them for mail twice daily! I suppose it is the same with post offices and postal clerks the world over, but it is surely especially provoking in this instance, for I should have so much liked to see you and Martina.

Your second letter, written after your London trip and seeing Miss Shaw, has been here now some days. I appreciate the justice of your withholding judgment since you have heard only one side of the difficulty between Miss Shaw and myself.[1] There seems to me no use going into the details further than to say that you will surely realize that nothing less than a profound conviction that injustice was being done to a third party could have made me take the stand which I did against Anna Shaw and her regime in the National work. It involved more for me personally than it possibly could involve for anyone else concerned in it. Did Anna tell you that in the matter between her and the new Secretary of last year, Frances Squire Potter,[2] the entire Board of Officers stood with Mrs. Potter? That is the fact, and surely the judgment of six women who have given much of their time and effort to the support of the woman suffrage cause, and especially of the National work, ought to count for something when it is pitted against the extreme personal feeling of even the President of the organization. I do not mean that we felt Miss Shaw was entirely to blame, for although she was chiefly responsible for the election of Mrs. Potter to the Secretaryship, at the Seattle Convention last year, the rest of the Board having finally (with one exception) yielded to her over-powering desire to have Mrs. Potter in that position, the members feel that they were, in a measure, responsible for having Mrs. Potter put upon the Board in a very important position, when she was entirely new to the work and inexperienced. The personal disagreement between Miss Shaw and Mrs. Potter is something which is quite mysterious to all of us and probably will never be understood fully, or judged of from the same point of view, by any two of us. It is unfortunate that it happened, but Anna has had a number of such strong and passionate attachments to other women, which have broken up in some tempestuous fashion as this. However, heretofore, they have not involved anyone but the two women concerned and their immediate friends. It has been most unfortunate that in this case it involved, to a certain extent, the whole National work.

It has also changed my own plans very materially, but when I took the stand against Miss Shaw, at the Convention, I knew that these other changes were also involved in it. Julia will not go to Bryn Mawr College[3] and I shall keep house at Swarthmore for another year, and then probably both the girls will go to Wisconsin University. That in itself, however, is quite a gain, from my point of view.

Of course, there is no room for me now in the National work, and I think I am justified in feeling that I have given a fair contribution of both time and money to International and National work, and that I may well be excused from any more of it. I can do a good deal of State work, and perhaps later, some local work, which may be of value.

My dear friend, I know how badly this breach between Miss Shaw and myself has made you feel, but I fear there is no healing of it to be expected. Do not let it worry you. The stand I took was made on principle and not for personal reasons. Elizabeth Hauser[4] expressed my position, when she said to me as long ago as last November, speaking of the differences then already existing between Mrs. Potter and Miss Peck[5] on the one hand and Miss Shaw and Miss Lucy Anthony on the other: "I tell you, Mrs. Avery, if it came to a showdown as between these two parties, my heart would be with Miss Shaw but my judgment would be entirely with Mrs. Potter." The break-up of the friendship between Miss Shaw and myself is no small thing in my life, but Miss Shaw herself has choosen her way, and is not to be moved from it by the fact that the rest of her Board disagreed with her, and that many of her old friends cannot approve of her course. She has many new friends. Perhaps they will make up to her for the loss of those old friends from whom she has separated herself by her injustice to Mrs. Potter and Miss Peck.

I spent two days last week with Mrs. Catt. The operation was five weeks before my visit to her and I think she has done wonderfully well during that time. She has a splendid appetite and the doctors allow her to eat about everything she wants. She took her first outing while I was there, a ride for an hour in a motor cab. The one danger for her is that she may be too ambitious and over-exert herself. Miss Hay is taking very good care of her. I used to doubt the depth of Miss Hay's affection for Mrs. Catt, but lately I have come to believe that she really loves her. In any case, she is certainly taking very good care of her, and I do not know what Mrs. Catt would have done without her at the time of the operation.

I was on the ocean at the time and Mrs. Upton, of whom Mrs. Catt is very fond, is tied at home by her father's condition. He is very old and gradually growing more and more feeble. I believe that Mrs. Catt has taken a new lease of life and that she is going to be able to give splendid service to the cause, both local and international. She has no desire to go into the National work.

If Martina has heard anything about the disagreements over here and you think it well for her to see this letter, please feel entirely free to send it to her.

I am going West very soon to see my grand-child. Rose[6] is in Chicago now visiting her sister. Julia is in camp up in Canada, where I have sent her for several summers and where she lives an out-door life, going bare-headed and bare-footed most of the time. Rose and I hope to get up to the camp before the end of the summer. Julia is very anxious to have us do so, as this is probably her last year there.

Yours very affectionately,

Rachel.

1. Rachel Foster Avery had just resigned as NAWSA's vice president, along with Harriet Taylor Upton and others, in protest against what she saw as Shaw's ineffective leadership. She also severed all personal contact with Shaw.

2. See chap. 2, n. 23.

3. Julia, Rachel Foster Avery's daughter, could not go to Bryn Mawr because M. Carey Thomas was a good friend of Anna Howard Shaw.

4. Elizabeth J. Hauser (1873), who came from Ohio, was present at the Amsterdam congress. For a long period she was secretary at the headquarters and chairman of the press committee of the NAWSA.

5. See chap. 2, nn. 10 and 23.

6. Rose was another daughter of Rachel Foster Avery.

29. Carrie Chapman Catt to Aletta Jacobs

New York, July 16, 1910

My dear Aletta,

It was good to receive your letter and all the good messages it contained. You were right as to the nature of my operation. I think I boasted of my improving health when I last wrote you. I took electricity all winter and certainly improved under it. Then my menses ceased altogether and I was quite hilarious. I thought I had come quite to the end of my troubles. But <u>pride</u> falls, and just when I was most sure that all was well, I began to flow. I had many severe hemorrhages, and grew weaker and weaker. After 72 days of flowing I had four days of hemorrhages. My maid washed 150 napkins as the result of two days flowing and as these were stuffed with cotton wadding, you will see how severe the trouble was. I could not turn over in bed without severe heart symptoms. So they took the news to me that I could not go through another such April, as I had little blood left. There was nothing left for me but the operation. Now, all is well, but I am in doubt as to how long it will take me to recuperate. The doctors tell me I should not expect to be fully well under a year. It is now six weeks and yesterday I walked two blocks on the street which is doing pretty well.

New York is giving us one of her hot summers. Last night we slept under a <u>blanket</u>, but it is the first time for a month. How do you think you would like it, with nothing but a sheet for a cover? Of course, the Doctor tells me I must go to a cool place in order to grow well faster, but there is no place to go except to big hotels and alas! I cannot wear <u>clothes</u>. That seems the hardest thing to do. So I am going to a Sanatorium where there are pretty walks, baths etc. and shall return in about six weeks. I hope I shall be well enough to work with comfort, for work I must at that time. I hope to retire from all offices connected with the local work here this autumn, and to allow myself a rest, before going to Sweden. It is a pity, though, for the American work is so in need of workers just now, but it has been my plan for some time to extricate myself from work here and to spend the remainder of the time while in International office in International work. I mean to stick to that program, for I know the American work will still be calling for workers when I am released from the International in 1913. I cannot yet make very definite plans, for I am not sure of my health yet. But if all is well with me I shall go to Sweden in advance of the convention (as usual). Then I shall go to London to print the Report. When that is done, if I am well enough, and if you are well enough, and if they want us, how about South Africa? That is for us to think about. So much about myself.

Now, about yourself. I am sorry to hear that you are not well. I expect if you were an American your malady would be called nervous prostration. You have overworked, I am sure. The trouble with us all is, that when we overdo, we do not take time enough to recover and it is easier to overwork again. I think you must work in a substitute for president while you go to So. Africa. I hope the Sanatorium will do you all the good so short a time can do. Try to be a dunce, or an anti-suffragist, which is the same thing and forget your sex. Empty yourself of all obligation and the process will do much for you. If you think at all, remember your good members. That is glorious. The joy of that memory ought to do you good. But you must be satisfied for the moment, and not wish that you had 10.000.

So you have been in London and marched with the Suffragettes.[1] I thought you were not in sympathy with them. I'll tell you what I think. When the suffrage is gained in England, the suffragists all over the world will fall to quarreling over the question: Did the Suffragists or the Suffragettes do it? I am reminded of the intense anger of Miss Naber when the thought of the possibility of a procession in Holland and a foreigner marching in it. She was indignant over Miss Shaw then. Do you remember it? I hope she will not get angry at you!!

You are right. Miss Shaw needs a longer rest. I fear she is in a sad plight. She might have been released from her office of President last winter, but she insisted upon standing for re-election, and no woman would be a candidate against her. I am sorry she told you about the difficulty at Washington, for such matters are quite unintelligible to the people of another country. I know she did tell you, for Rachel was here, and read me your letter to her. She was much disappointed not to have seen you. It is too bad that the mails went so badly. Had you seen her, I presume she would not have mentioned the difficulties here, but since Miss Shaw has told you her side, I hope you will insist upon Rachel telling her side. It is a hard story to tell and will be a harder one for you to understand as it involves so many personal relations. Stripping the story of all personalities, I will tell you my version.

Miss Shaw is a great orator, and as all orators are, is impulsive, quick tempered etc. All accede her greatness in this direction. She is not executive nor capable of constructive forward work. She is a great Leader from the platform, and no Leader at all from an office. I think this is no criticism, for I know of no man orator in all history who has been an executive Leader. To be a superb orator seems to have been all Nature would offer to any one man. Public sentiment here as everywhere is on the increase and the situation demands a master hand. Instead, Miss Shaw is on the platform quite constantly (where she ought to be) doing splendid propaganda work for the general cause. This would be well enough if she would allow other members of her Board to do the executive part, but she will not and this has been the cause of a constantly growing irritation ever since she was president. This is what her officers say, and I believe them for I have served on the Board with most of them and with her. The personal difficulties which have embittered Miss Shaw as well as many others have all sprung from this fact. Her entire board were a unit upon the matter which led to the climax, and two members had refused re-election because they would not serve with her under the conditions which they could not change, and two more resigned after election when further evidence was brought them. If Miss Shaw would willingly, cheerfully retire from office, her followers would love and honor her so long as she lived and she would always be in popular demand for speeches. She might have a chance to rest too and thus live longer. As it is, she is making enemies, and wearing herself out in a position which will never be any easier for her. The entire difficulty has come from Miss Shaw herself, and is due to the fact that she is out of place in an executive office. She is to be greatly pitied for she is bringing worry and ill-health upon herself, and the Association is not prospering as it should. I would not have mentioned this had I not learned that you had learned something about it.

But American women are superior to those of some other countries. They have difficulties which become almost unbearable, but they do not sulk, nor quit. They keep it out of the papers and work right on. If they cannot work on a Board, they work off from it—the main thing is that they work, and when necessary to work with other women in whom they have lost confidence, they do it.[2]

It seems as if every Land was destined to have divisions and difficulties as soon as the cause grows a bit strong. It is a pity.

I shall write to Martina and tell her I approve of her vacation for August.

May every minute bring you rest, peace and joy and may you live long and prosper.

Lovingly,

Carrie C. Catt.

1. This was the largest demonstration so far organized by the WSPU, and Shaw also took part. The motto was "From Prison to Citizenship." Members of the WSPU carried a hunger strike banner. Among Aletta Jacobs' papers is a letter from Emmeline Pankhurst in which she thanks Jacobs for her participation. See Tickner 1987, 111–15.

2. Catt is clearly comparing the American suffrage movement favorably with the European suffrage movements, which in most countries were strongly divided. See Bosch 1989.

30. Anna Howard Shaw to Aletta Jacobs

S.S. Minneapolis
At Sea
August 5 [1910]

My very dear Doctor Jacobs,

I was so glad to get your last letter and to know that you had arrived home safely and were getting ready for your summers rest. Mine has done me an immense lot of good and though I cannot think of returning without a sinking of the heart and a dread still I am going to do my best. I had a letter from Rachel a few days before I sailed just as full of unkind and untrue accusations as were her others. She has simply lost her grip of things and is giving head to all sorts of stories told her by other people. I have written her that she must see me and talk things over and see where she is wrong and that her statements are untrue. That I do not believe she wants to be wrong and to tell any thing she thinks is untrue, but if she continues to refuse to talk things over with me and does talk them over with those who are seeking my overthrow that I shall be forced to believe she does not want to know the truth and that she no longer desires my love. I also told her I would not take any ones word for it but her own, I am so sorry for her for I am sure she is unhappy.

I am going dear Doctor to try to follow your good advice and not think of the unhappy things any more than I can help. There is so much real work to be done and so many good and true friends and life is so short that one cannot spend it looking at the clouds or at false things in life. Rachel is at heart good and true I believe but she is far off the right track at present.

I am going to do my best to find and keep the right path myself and if I can help Rachel to do so I certainly will not let any thing she has said or done keep me from it.

Well I wonder if you know I went back to London to speak at the Trafalgar Sq. meeting and again on the 23d of July I went to Mrs Pankhursts demonstration.[1] I marched at the head of the American delegation all the way from the Embankment to Hyde Park, and then spoke from Mrs Lawrence platform. It was a wonderful sight as I stood on the platform and looked over the Park, it was one mass of humanity clustered about the 41 platforms. When the bugles sounded and the resolution was put it was a most marvellous sight. I would not have missed it for any thing, and I am glad I was a part of it.

I do hope dear Doctor matters have straightened themselves out in your country and that your work is going more smoothly. I suppose as the work is built up and as more and more people come into it there will be more jealousy and more difficulties to meet and especially more people to keep from running things to pieces.

Every new person thinks she knows just what should be done and that she is the only person to do it, and that those of us who have given our lives to it are keeping things back because we do not do things their way. We must expect this more and more and if we did as we would like we would give the whole thing up and take our ease and enjoy ourselves, but we must face the fact that two ways lie before us, one the way I think we would most like and the other to just keep our eyes on the thing desired and to go ahead, without fear or favour and do our best and trust the result with God and our conscience. I am going my dear Doctor to try the latter plan and go ahead and do my best as soon as I reach home.

I sailed on the 30th July and expect to reach New York on the 8th Aug. So far the winds have been head ones and delayed us, but the sea has not been rough and I have both slept and eaten well. So that I hope to reach New York on Monday looking so well my friends will not know me.

Ray was a dear friend and all her family did so much for me and made my vacation such a good one.

It does not seem like going to Europe any more when we can have such precious homes open to receive us as yours, Mrs Coit's[2] and Ray's people, one hardly realizes she has been away from home.

I shall be glad to see Lucy and Moylan and all the good friends. How good it is that Mrs Catt is doing so well.

Affectionally,

Anna H. Shaw.

1. See Tickner 1987, 115–19.

2. Adela Stanton Coit was English. From 1907 she was on the board of the Alliance.

31. Carrie Chapman Catt to Aletta Jacobs

[New York] May 15, 1911

My dear Aletta:

About now you were to be home again. You say you went to gay Paris to kiss friends good bye, but I suspect it was a Paris bonnet you went after! Well, well, I'm content to leave you the leadership of fashion, it is not in my line!

I have forty yards of things to say about South Africa, but I must boil it all down to a few inches. I found letters here from all the points where I had written. All will take us. They are politely hospitably [hospitable], but they impress me as not ready to wear crape if we should fail to get there. It will be necessary to ask one of them to arrange the itinerary, I have written to all saying that we <u>are</u> coming and that they will get the date later. I have told them the probable time of our arrival. I have also ordered some maps and books which I've known about through these letters and I think we can make up our own itinerary to some extent. I shall have these by the time you get here. I find in an advertisement such that the Union Castle Line has a Steamer which goes from Durban every 28 days to England via Pt Said with several stops in Eastern Africa. I have written to ask when our steamer will arrive and when that Steamer leaves. We could, if sailing dates permit, go from Cape Town to Durban, touching at all the chief towns and points of interest and then take that Steamer without having to retrace our travel. This would bring us to Egypt direct and would save time and expense too. Of course it would cut out Portugal and Spain. Both of these countries I wish very much to visit, but they are not ready for us and more, we could visit them at another time as they lie within our range. For that reason I should be glad to cut them out. I find that Palestine lies within a few hours of Pt Said also. Now, one place I never cared to visit is Palestine. The clergymen from the U.S.A. visit it in great numbers. But, if we could go overland across Palestine and through <u>Persia</u> to India. That is merely a suggestion to be considered later.

A letter from Miss Cameron says the trip now is so different from that first discussed, that she is unwilling to engage to go on it until she has more definite information as to what we are really going to do. You said you would have to pay the first instalment on our rooms before leaving. Now, give me your agent's name, and I will send the amount on to London. Your man will get his commission just the same. I shall have to pay on my own berth and ask them to reserve the other until some date which I shall give them. I think you said the amount to be paid was £2.105. What is the price through to Cape Town? I am getting prices on the itinerary in S. Africa.

I think I should like to go on July 15, and spend a week in Madeira also, if I can get through my work. I'm not sure as that is an agreeable time for those Islands.

I hear that many Dutch are coming up quite a time before the Congress. Let me know when you are coming if it is convenient.

Hastily,

Carrie Chapman Catt.

32. Rosa Manus to Anna Manus

[Stockholm, June 1911]

My dear sister,

I am afraid there is no time to write a long letter. It is gorgeous here, and such a shame that you can no longer take part.[1] This portrait is not very good, but I am sure you would like it. Miss Shaw is so kind to us. Just imagine – Ray has suddenly married. Margery Corbett is married, too. She was also here, but without her husband. Mrs Catt's address yesterday was splendid, as usual. Goodbye, and warm regards from everyone and your Rosa.

1. The IWSA's sixth congress was held in Stockholm in June 1911.

33. Anna Howard Shaw to Aletta Jacobs

[New York] 16 July 1912

My dear good Doctor,

It is a long time since I have written to you but not a long time since I have sent loving and proud thoughts to you and Mrs Catt. I have rejoiced in every step of your journey and in its success not merely for what you are both able to accomplish on the trip itself but for what it will mean afterward. May I tell you that I have had but two overwhelming ambitions in my life, and one of these was to take the trip you and Mrs Catt are taking in just the same kind of work and I longed to take it with Mrs Catt. I felt that we could do it successfully and without friction just as we did our campaigning here for years before an outside influence prompted by jealousy felt it would weaken our influence if our friendship were broken. Then I realized I would probably not be able to carry out my part of the plan, for two reasons. First because Aunt Susan forced me into the National Presidency, and secondly because I had not the financial means to carry me through without using up what I had saved for old age if it ever should come to me. I was eager to have Mrs Catt do it and I did all I could to persuade her to take it up after her husband passed away. She needed something to take her out of the horror of his death and the awful strain which followed by her splendid courage and loyalty in carrying out his wishes in regard to his body. I have never admired her for any thing more than for that, and yet it must have torn her very heart to do it. She needed a change for body and mind, and she needed it in different company from those who had been with her through that experience.

If Miss Hay had gone with her it would have been impossible for either of them to have forgotten it. However, my intrest [interest] was misunderstood and misinterpreted. Had Mrs Catt known how with all my soul I had longed to do that very thing ever since the W.C.T.U. had sent its Temperance missionaries out, and how it made me ache all over to have to give up the ambition to be one of the first round the world woman suffrage missionaries she would not have misunderstood. I tried to tell her several times, but some[how] I never could open my heart to Mrs Catt. Not that she was ever unkind or unsympathetic, but because I felt she distrusted me because she had had distrust preached constantly to her.

Nevertheless I glory in what you are both doing and am so glad you were able to do it, and that you are keeping well.

I knew you would find Mrs Catt a good travelling companion. We had some experience with her and she was always cheerful and not easily upset by discomforts. I think those of us who had had our training in woman suffrage campaigns learn to put up with discomforts and not be overcome by them.

I do not know what started me off on this line of thought in writing you but think it had been on my mind for a long time because of my joy and gratification that you are finding it interesting and that Mrs Catt seems to feel a deep interest in it and that it has been worth while. If she [had] not I should have almost felt responsible.

I am very sorry that there is no prospect of having you both at our National Convention in Phil. Nov. 21st to 26th. It would have been a great card for the Convention and we could have had a greater number from different parts of the nation to welcome you. Mrs. Laidlaw[1] told me a few days ago that there was no hope of Mrs. Catt being back for the National Convention. I suppose while she is there she feels she must do it well for it is too far to go and at too great an expense not to finish it, but we did want her very much, and those of us who knew you want you also. I had a long letter from Rosa a short time since telling of the plans for Amsterdam and asking me to go to the International meeting via Holland.[2] Then came your letter asking us to come to you. I am so sorry that there is no prospect of your being here, as there is not if you go to Russia, but I know that what you do will be done with the cause and its interests in the foreground. If I go to the International I promise to go via Holland, and Holland without you is not Holland to me, so that I shall gladly come to you if I go at all.

Now for the work here. There never was such a lot of different kinds of work nor so many people interested and working, some wisely others unwisely, but with earnest purpose. The interest which has been shown in the Ohio campaign and the number of women who have offered their ser-

*Mia Boissevain, Rosa Manus, and Carrie Chap-
man Catt during the exhibition* De Vrouw 1813–
1913 *(Woman, 1813–1913). Amsterdam, 1913.*

vices without price and the number of workers whose services have been
contributed by New York State, Mass., R.I. and Pennsylvania have sur-
passed any thing I have ever known in any previous campaign. It is rather
interesting to note that while the Western states cry out against the East
whenever it comes to personal sacrifice and money raising they always turn
to the East for it and it responds splendidly. I am so proud of them this
year in their splendid generosity. Even the woman Suffrage Party which
rightly feels that it has a tremendous work to perform in taking care of New
York city has done more for Ohio than have all the western states put together. The east has not the strong state rights feeling which either the
south or west have and has always been as eager that the west should win
as for themselves. It is splendid of them.

I am sorry not to have much hope for Ohio, nor Michigan, but feel
there is a chance for Wisconsin, Oregon and Kansas. I have little belief in
what so many people say that the men are ready to grant suffrage but the
women do not want it, and yet I feel that if the women would only get
down to good hard unselfish work in all the states where campaigns are pending there is not a state which could not be carried. The women could this

year inspire the men as they will not have a like chance when the progressive people themselves become machine ridden as they will in a few years.

As to my health. I cannot say it is as good as I wish for my head gives me much trouble but I am so much better than I was two years ago that I dislike to complain.

Yes, I am very busy and will be more so. About the middle of August I start out to the campaign starts. I begin in Ohio and stay until after the election Sept. 31. Then go to Michigan for two weeks. Then to Wisconsin. Then to Oregon and then, Kansas, giving each state two weeks before the election in Nov. and get back in time for the National Convention. You see I have a task laid out for myself. I have asked each state to have my route all arranged before I arrive so that I need not waste a day but can speak each day. If they do this I shall be able to make a lot of speeches and I hope help to win the victories the few who are really working deserve. I am sure even if Mrs Catt is not here to take a hand at this time. She will feel as I do that the hard service we did in past years is a great factor in the present success, and that we have a share in each victory.

Our greatest need is money. Our country is so large and our distances are so great that campaigning is very expensive. I do not know what they would have done if it had not been for a fund given me last year by a friend of suffrage who wished me to controle its expenditure. It has saved us in every state.

Politics among men have been so hysterical and disgraceful this year that the better class of men are feeling that their only hope is in woman suffrage. Certainly the women delegates to the National Republican and Democratic conventions were an example to men and won a lot of praise.[3]

I shall write Mrs Catt a gossipy political letter in a few days. Lucy joins me in love and dear Doctor I want [to] say I am so thankful for your friendship and confidence and I esteem it all more than I can tell. I hope you will feel I have an unfaltering affection for you which is as enduring as life.

Affectionately, Anna.

1. Harriet Burton Laidlaw (1873–1949) had been interested in the woman suffrage movement since 1893. She became active in the Woman Suffrage Party in New York. Her husband, James Lees Laidlaw, was active in the Men's League for Woman Suffrage. See NAW.

2. The seventh IWSA congress was held in Budapest in June 1913. Manus seems to have asked Shaw to visit the exhibition *De Vrouw 1813–1913* (Woman, 1813–1913), which she and Mia Boissevain had initiated.

3. The presidential election of November 1912 resulted in victory for the Democratic candidate, Woodrow Wilson.

34. Carrie Chapman Catt to Aletta Jacobs

[New York, December 7, 1912]

My dear Aletta:

This American monkey has been swung by her <u>tail</u>, so vigorously ever since she stepped on this Continent, that she is dizzyheaded; her body is tired, and her <u>tail</u> sore! I am sure the <u>Dutch</u> monkey is having the same experience. In San Francisco I was kept going with one public meeting and many dinners and luncheons so that I was glad indeed to get away after six days. I did however enjoy the election day for I spent it all on a motor going about the City and saw some of my old suffrage friends vote.[1] It was great. (Here is a point, <u>every</u> candidate in California, for any office which had any thing to do with making law or enforcing it had taken the utmost pains to assure the new women voters that he stood right on the question of the white slave traffic. That is good argument, isn't it?) I came straight on to Albany where I spoke and then home. Here I found notice of packages at the post office. I went after them at once with a taxi, and had them in the house two days before I discovered that one was from Kioto. I thought they had all come from James Eades & Co. I just love that Japanese lady and am so happy to have it. Thank you a thousand times for her ladyship. Everyone admires her, and when my cabinet comes, she shall have a nice place in it.

They had a Welcome Home in Carnegie Hall for me and it was great, but I didn't enjoy playing the heroine and hearing complimentary speeches which I do not deserve. Mrs Nathan[2] had got up a sort of pageant in which girls dressed in the costumes of the various countries we had visited marched before me and each gave me a flag. They said it looked very pretty but I felt silly! Then I went to Philadelphia to the National Convention where I spoke on the slave traffic, not white but yellow and brown in the Orient and showed how even the slaves are pitted against each other by their competing owners. The convention was the largest, and had the most representative women in it of any ever held, but it was <u>stormy</u>. Miss Shaw gained many friends among the uninitiated and lost as many among the old, on account of her position on many questions. The opposition had no candidate but it cast 155 votes against her. Poor Miss Shaw! If she could see herself as others see her—she would be saved much suffering and would always hold an honoured place for her immeasurable services to the great cause. The Journal business was the chief subject of the <u>storm</u>.

Well, later I had a Citizen's Welcome Home by the People's Institute at Cooper Union and then I went to <u>bed</u> with a cold and I am still voiceless. I got a stenographer and it takes nearly all her time to decline the invitations to speak which come pouring in from all over the nation. I have refused all outside of New York before February and have made few dates here. The reason is that my business affairs are in a tangle. There is no financial difficulty yet, and none expected but I am devoting about half my time to my own dollars and cents at present and that I shall continue to do until I find out just where I am. I shall not bother you with the details.

I did not find the pile of letters I expected and no word from Hungary, but I have gone to work just the same. You probably know that Denmark may get the parliamentary vote before Budapest.[3] I am going to suggest that one afternoon be given to speeches—How the vote was won—In California, in Arizona, in Kansas, in Oregon, and Michigan (if we get it—that is still in doubt) in Denmark if we get it, we must add the story of the campaign in Bohemia etc. Do you not think that would make a good program?

I want you to present the Chinese barman. I shall tell you later when and how. Just now there is such a pressure of many things all crying for attention at once that it is difficult to keep calm. The queer thing is that I do not feel that I am any part of things here. I think you are having the same experience there to adjust your mind to the situation. I too, long for the peace of globe trotting and wish we could take our astral bodies out of our skins and fly off together for a visit over all the things which have happened to us since we parted.

I shall send you Mr Shusters book about Persia which you must read to learn what nice countries England and Russia are![4]

You had a most unfortunate homecoming and my heart ached for you when I got the first letter, but as the joy came later I hope all is well now. I do not see how it can be quite right with one officer dead and another hopelessly ill,[5] but perhaps you have found others.

I shall write Martina as soon as I can see daylight and will let you know just when I do it. I am glad you are going to be so agreeably fixed at Mme Bataerds. Give her my love.

My dear Dutch monkey, what a lot of fool things I did buy!—My ivory God's head is split open already with our dry air! When I go again, I shall buy nothing and travel with a suit case. There are many yards I'd like to write but I cannot. You have been an angel to write me two letters.

Lovingly,

Carrie C. Catt.

1. California women had won the vote on October 10, 1911.

2. Probably Maud Nathan (1862–1946), a social welfare leader and suffragist. She was vice president of the Equal Suffrage League of New York and also active in the NAWSA. See NAW. According to Peck (1944, 171) it was Frederika Cooke who set up the pageant.

3. Danish women won the vote in 1915.

4. In May 1911, the American W. Morgan Shuster arrived in what was then Persia as financial advisor. The Russians thwarted the plan, and Shuster and other foreign advisors were finally forced to leave. The book is W. Morgan Shuster, *The Strangling of Persia: Story of the*

European Diplomacy and Oriental Intrigue That Resulted in the Denationalisation of Twelve Million Mohammedans (New York, 1912).

5. When Jacobs returned from the world tour Theodore Haver had just died, which meant that the festive welcome was postponed. Jeanne van Lanschot Hubrecht was probably the woman who was ill. See letter 46, n. 4.

35. Carrie Chapman Catt to Aletta Jacobs

[New York] Feb. 26, 1913

My dear Aletta:

Your first letter came yesterday and scared me stiff. I went around the house half dazed all day at the thought of what I might not hear from Amsterdam. I was on the point of cabling several times, but discretion told me I had better wait a bit. Today your second letter is here and worms seem such dear dainty little innocents compared with what might have been, that they seem like nothing at all. I congratulate you on your worms! and I feel happy and relieved indeed at the news. Poor Dutch Monkey! The doctors will chase the worms out in short order and as soon as the cause is gone, you will soon be in splendid health and looking youthful once more. Now, what nationality are the worms? I hope the doctors can tell. Do they speak English?—then they must be Filipinos! Well, well, I shall talk no more of health for by the time this reaches you you will be far on the road toward recovery. I do not think I got any of these eggs for I have had good digestion since I came home. I must have escaped them.

I am going off for a two weeks lecture trip soon. First I go to Washington where Miss Shaw and I and some others speak on Sunday in a theater and then there is a procession on Monday and we speak again at the close. The following week I go for my longer trip. I shall visit Michigan which will take another vote on woman suffrage in April. I am sailing for London on April 19th arriving on April 28th or 29th. I am recommended to stop at Dr Keyser's Royal Hotel. Isn't that the place where you were and thought it horrid? I'll let you know where I go, but you could write me in care of Mrs. Coit in any case.

I had intended to go to Budapest as fast as I could from London, but Rosa asks me to speak at the Exhibition and I think you may need looking after. Perhaps they will send you away to recruit somewhere and in that case you may not be in Amsterdam in early May. But if you are and if that is the time for the speech I shall try to come. I cannot stay longer than two days.

What do you think that woman suffrage Committee in the Philippines is doing? They gave Christmas presents to 1200 children and are now taking care of the <u>infants</u> of Manila to the mutual satisfaction of brown and white. The two races are working well together—but not for suffrage!

The work here is simply overwhelming. Michigan votes in April and we think Maine will vote in Sept.

Several States will vote in 1914 and New York and Penn. in 1915. When the next Congress meets in 1916 we may have a <u>big</u> story to tell and perhaps we shall have a backset—Meanwhile every body is working themselves to the limit. Miss Shaw, who never spares herself, is speaking every day and sometimes three times a day. She ought to rest in Europe instead of speaking, but she <u>will</u> <u>speak</u>. These are great times though. You can just <u>see</u> the movement grow, day by day.

My Japanese furniture is very pretty and my cabinet filled with my many treasures is very nice. It may all fall to pieces before you get over here to see it. I think you better pay a visit to America and set yourself to converting the Dutch of New York.

Well, it looks as if the militants didn't know what to do next and I really think Mrs. Pankhurst will starve herself to death and think while she is doing it, that it is the only way out of a very trying predicament.[1] Woman suffrage is certainly occupying the center of the stage of the whole world. I hope we shall all hold out to see the end if not to cast a vote.

I have had a tremendously busy winter, but I've done most of my work at home. I've had a stenographer all winter and my time has been mainly filled by correspondence but I've written several articles and made a good many speeches. I've had my own food to eat and my own bed to sleep in and in spite of steady work I've grown stronger and more rested and intend to go somewhere with Miss Hay after Budapest where I can just eat and sleep and walk and take a real relaxation, so that when I come back in the Autumn I can give my entire time to the work here.

Miss Hay, if she goes over at all, which is not yet certain, will go later than I and will meet me in Budapest. She is far from well, and I am not sure that rest is all that she needs. Her condition worries me, but like all the rest, she is worked nearly to death.

My dear, precious friend, I hope the last worm has departed ere this reaches you and that every day is making you strong and hopeful. The world would be a much poorer place were you not in it. I hope we, who have worked so long together may continue to the end of our campaign and then we must go of course.

With love, deart [dear] Heart, and all good thoughts for you. I am filled with gratitude that [it] is only worms.

Lovingly,

Carrie Chapman Catt.

1. Emmeline Pankhurst was arrested on February 24, 1913, and went on hunger strike. This resulted in the Cat and Mouse Act—imprisoned suffragettes who went on hunger strike and suffered from ill health were temporarily released. But once recovered, they were liable to rearrest.

36. Aletta Jacobs to Mien van Wulfften Palthe-Broese van Groenou

Amsterdam, May 16, 1913

Dear Mien,[1]

I have just received a letter from Miss Shaw in which she says she will arrive at your place on Monday morning. The Americans don't seem to distinguish between Amsterdam and The Hague; she is expecting to see me there, but I can't possibly be in The Hague before 4 or 5 o'clock, so I was hoping to stay until Wednesday morning. Then on Tuesday I shall be able to put in an appearance at the Women's Council, do what is expected of me, and go to the reception in the evening.

I appreciate your kind invitation, but would it not be expecting too much of your hospitality? I feel I must decline.

How wonderful that the husbands of the ladies Br. v. Gr. are all pleasantly cooperating in furthering our cause. How mettlesome those English suffragettes are! I respect their tremendous courage and vigour. They are certainly putting the government to work.

Kind regards to you all,

Yours,

Aletta H. Jacobs

1. Frederika Wilhelmina (Mien) van Wulfften Palthe-Broese van Groenou (also: Mrs. Palthe) (1875–1960) was a good friend of Aletta Jacobs. Jacobs spent her last years in her home. Mien's sisters were also active within the movement—Emilia (Miel) Coops-Broese van Groenou (1876–1966) and Susanna (San) van Rees-Broese van Groenou (1878–1967). See De Wilde 1984a.

37. Martina Kramers to Rosika Schwimmer

Rotterdam, June 2, 1913

Dear Rosika,

Well, would you believe it![1] I also had to rub my eyes and to read it a few times before I could believe that for the sole purpose of getting me out of the way, Catt thought up a plan of a news agency in London,[2] which she had earlier rejected. And now, because I refuse to step down, she is constantly critical of my work. For example, I didn't have the right to cancel the June edition of Jus [Suffragii], and I should have had my bookkeeping checked by an accountant etc., etc.

And Aletta Jacobs now posing as an advocate for morals! Suddenly, after thirteen years! You know what's behind it: if I make a quiet exit, Holland, where the movement has been so successful and has gained international acclaim, will still need a representative in the International Board. My friend Aletta says I should step down to avoid the scandal affecting my brother and sister.

When you have read my letter and Catt's, let me know whether you think I am right in not tolerating interference in my personal affairs and whether those responsible shouldn't be exposed. If Catt makes my leaving a condition for her staying on, and her party votes against me and the newspapers are full of my immorality, I shall never return to Holland. Bobbie says he'll go with me.

That's how it goes in the movement. One is worked to death and exhausted by overloading, and now, simply because I have worked according to my own principles and in the position to which I am most suited, they want to get rid of me. Let us call on the assistance of Marie Stritt and Anna Lindemann and Signe Bergman and Drysdale[3] and all other sensible people.

Your Martina.

1. Letters 38 and 39 were enclosed in this letter.

2. Kramers is referring to Catt's proposal of using a news agency in London for the publication of *Jus Suffragii*.

3. Charles Drysdale was a champion of neo-Malthusianism and cofounder of the British Malthusian League in 1887. Kramers and Schwimmer knew him through their participation in the Women's Branch of the International Neo-Malthusian League.

38. Carrie Chapman Catt to Martina Kramers

Budapest, May 21, 1913

My dear Martina,

For two years I have postponed writing you about a matter which seems to me and many others a very grave one. I have postponed it because it was a painful thing to do, and I feared you might misunderstand. You have confessed to three American women of my acquaintance, certain moral trangressions of yours. I do not think any one of them is a gossip, but they have repeated the tale you told them and it has continually spread into larger circles. Other Americans have learned the same story in Europe, perhaps in Holland, and have told it in the U.S.A. Many of these you probably never heard of and thus have never seen you, but they tell it of an officer of the Alliance. It has come to a point where it is seriously damaging the standing of the Alliance in the United States and in England. I do not know [how] much of it is known on the Continent. I am not a gossip myself and I do not question people about such matters.

In my judgment such matters are largely personal and must be governed by one's own conscience, but they cease to be personal or individual when one carries them into public work. To my mind had you been a sincere, true suffragist, you would never have accepted an office in the Alliance knowing as you must that in time the story of your violation of prescribed moral order would be known and especially as you seem inclined to confide of living your own life as you liked or of being an apostle of woman's political freedom. You cannot have both without so seriously injuring your official mission as to make it less serviceable to the cause than would be the work of some other woman in your place. In other words I feel very strongly that it is now your duty to the cause we represent to give up your post. It may not be easy to feel it, but a possible opportunity arises which may offer a way. The British Society want an international press bureau. They are not particularly anxious to have it in London but of course that is the press center of the world. It follows very naturally that if it is established it will save labor and money to combine this new press-scheme with "Jus Suffragii" and thus remove it to London. It would not be necessary in such an event that any other explanations of your withdrawal be made.

I judge that you must consider your action as justifiable and may not care who knows of it, but for the sake of our common cause, I hope the change may be effected without the stirring up of a scandal. Of course you will not think that your private life can effect [affect] a great cause, but that is because you do not understand the horror and repugnance with which such things are regarded by most enlightened people.

Believe me, personally I have always liked you and do still. I appreciate fully all you have done for the Alliance and were it a private business I could work with you to the end of time. But I consider it my duty to see that the Board of Officers of the Alliance is above reproach of public critics and so come to you plainly and frankly with the difficulty. I am sure you will be willing to make the sacrifice of withdrawal in the interest of the common cause.

Yours truly,

Carrie C. Catt

39. Martina Kramers to Carrie Chapman Catt

Rotterdam, June 2, 1913

My dear Mrs. Catt,

I thank you for writing frankly and I will answer in the same spirit, putting the interest of the international woman suffrage movement before personal considerations. Now if you do really like me (as I do you) and appreciate my work and do not really want to get rid of me, I will here provide you with an answer that will silence interfering people as effectively as in the cases of Anita Augspurg, Käthe Schirmacher and Mr. Stanton Coit[1] accused by many gossipers of homosexual intercourse and of Anna Wicksell,[2] accused of not being married in the right form and Aletta Jacobs of having anticipated marriage and of practising abortus, in all of which cases you have constantly refused to listen to detractors. I will here give you some facts.

I am not a propagandist of free love first, though I am a Neo-malthusian as Marie Stritt, Aletta Jacobs and Rosika Schwimmer are; indeed I never appear in public with my left-hand husband with whom I have been united these 13 years, and most of the Dutch suffragists and my nearest relations (to begin with my brother and sister and their children) would be most astonished at being informed of the truth.

A proof of this is that in December 1912 at the last election of our W.S.A. (Woman Suffrage Alliance) Executive, there were 1367 votes cast, Aletta Jacobs obtained 1339 and I 1313, the other two officers elected having 1155 and 704 votes. I am one of the principal workers in our Executive, and of late years nearly every official document issued by the Dutch W.S.A. has been written by me. Last year the Moral Education Congress invited me to come to the Officers' table and attend the whole congress and translate. They honored me and recognized my services by all sorts of compliments and a gift of f. 100. Now would these things be possible if I was considered an immoral person, as you say the Americans term me? You see, if you do not choose to heed slurring of my character you can answer it by these facts.

You must know that you are going to inflict great grief upon my sister and my brother in whose family I am now filling the place of his deceased wife and upon all those of my fellow-workers who do not know of my relation to my friend. Your disclosures will possibly also cost the cause of W.S. (woman suffrage) in Holland the asset of my work, in the very moment that I am gaining ground step by step to make the Socialists realize that the women's movement is not hostile to theirs. But you think that blasting my position is little compared to the "moral" gain you strive for in expelling me. If so, you must act as your conscience dictates just as I do. But you shall do it openly and have all the credit for it which the Americans who regard me with "horror and repugnance" will give those who vindicate their morals. You say that I have the choice of living my own life (something like a Parisian Grisette?) or of being an apostle of woman's political freedom. But you are mistaken there, since my own life is propaganda for the enfranchisement of women and the working classes. The companionship and constant collaboration with my friend makes it possible to me to do a great deal more than I could do alone. I wish I had an opportunity to present him to you, surely that would be a pleasure to both. He is a superior man with some literary talent and broad-minded enough to see farther than most socialists do and understand that the women's movement does not hinder but advance socialism. Working together we can accomplish much more than one alone could. To explain to you that we are cheating nobody and how it is that his legal wife is never satisfied with the sum we can offer her and continues to refuse a divorce, that is better for a talk than for a letter. Also why I entrusted my secret to three Americans whom I considered as friends concerned about my personal welfare or as students of the new sexual moral which is to result from the freedom of women. They may have betrayed my secret, but I have certainly never tried to bring others to follow my example or made a point of preaching the abolition of marriage, my special aim being the political enfranchisement of women.

As to the work of international communication through the press, I hold that the I.W.S. (International Woman Suffrage) Alliance is better off with my services as editor of its organ than with those of any other worker that I know of. Are the "better women" whom they wish to put into my place able to read nine languages and have they friends and correspondents in all nations? As for my reputation, nowhere in Europe, beginning with my own country, are people so convinced of my immorality as they seem to be in America; so I see no reason why you as President should not give the U.S. the satisfaction of voting against my re-election and let the other countries vote as they please. As for me, my love of my work and my sense of duty towards the International women's movement does not in the least prompt me to give up my position. In so doing I think of Susan B. Anthony and her firm stand for the Mormons whose sexual morality differed from that of the rest of American society.[3] The only attitude that a body like the Alliance, only existing to obtain the enfranchisement of women, can take is to judge of the merits of a person by what he does for this aim and for the organization, leaving personal likes and dislikes out of the question. In case there are suffragists (even voting delegates) unable to make this discrimination, that will appear from the result of the poll. I think that you as president—and all wise suffrage workers for that matter—should make a point of making people understand that they are not voting for or against the institution of marriage but pronouncing whether or not they will entrust the organ of the I.W.S. Alliance to the hands that have built it up (in two editions) since it was started. Indeed I believe that you are above using your influence to intimidate me or my friends into serving the aims of upholders of certain moral conceptions that are not at issue here.

Think of it, if the I.W.S.A. convention were to inquire into the private life of every candidate for office! What would not be said against everyone of us (perhaps only with one or two exceptions) and what precious time in which we should build up a basis of common suffrage action would go to that kind of investigation. Don't you be enticed into using your authority to take sides in such questions. Let the ballot pronouce; that is what it is secret for. Is not the essential part of the task of a President to make people understand exactly what they are voting for or against and so do away with all confusion of issues?

I hope soon to see that as President you refuse to discuss [the] personal life of candidates, and that as friend you will some time give me an opportunity to present to you the man I love.

Yours

Martina

1. Dr. B. Stanton Coit was the husband of Adela Stanton Coit. He was active within the socialist church movement in England and wrote a book, translated by Kramers, on neighborhood associations. (Crezee 1978, 117).

2. Anna Wicksell was a long-time Swedish suffragist who had been at the founding congress of the IWSA in Berlin in 1904. In 1920 she was elected to the board of the Alliance. Later she became active in the peace movement and was the Swedish delegate to the League of Nations.

3. Many feminists wrote on the subject of the Mormons' polygamy. For recent articles on Mormon women and suffrage feminism see *Feminist Studies* 10/3 (1984).

40. Carrie Chapman Catt to Rosika Schwimmer

[Budapest, June 1913]

To Rosika Schwimmer,

Paula Pogany,[1] and any others implicated in the awful crime of present-ing me with the beautiful badge[2] that I received last night. I am no "un-crowned queen" as your card announces. I am a CZAR and although I shall proudly wear the badge and bequeath it to my grandchildren (not so numer-ous as I could wish) as my most precious possession and shall always love and value it. I am very angry at my extravagant "subjects." As soon as the Congress is over I shall order you all boiled in hot oil, but when you are all dead, I shall attend the big funeral it will make as the most sorrowful of all the mourners. Remember the awful fate which awaits you and repent your sins while there is time, but if your repentance goes so far as to come to take the badge back, I shall hide it. Meanwhile,

Lovingly,

C. C. Catt.

1. Paula Pogany was a good friend of Rosika Schwimmer and active within the Hungar-ian Feminist Association. She was also editor of *A Nö*.

2. Compare letter 69.

41. Anna Howard Shaw to Aletta Jacobs

Florence, July 11th, 1913

Dear Doctor,

I suppose by this time you are away from Amsterdam and up in the mountains, like a sensible woman that you are, resting and getting some good out of the summer. I did not plan my summer well from the first and I have not gotten out of it as much as I should in one way while I have gotten some things I did not expect.

Out of all the rest there is one new friend who stands out above all the others and is ranked in my mind with the old friends and that is Mrs. Palthe. Of all the new women I have come to know this year she stands out as true and sincere and genuine. A woman to be trusted to stand true to what she believes to be true. It is worth a whole summer to find one true soul. Then dear Doctor it was good to see you. To be with you in your home and to have had a nice visit with you as I did when I was there. I am so glad to think of you in that precious little new home and to know that while it is large enough to be most pleasant and comfortable, it is not so large as to absorb all your time and strength, and leaves you free to go and come as you please. The trouble with my place is it is too big, not the house but the grounds and outside things and I cannot leave it easily. However, it is mighty pleasant to go back to and I am looking forward longingly to getting there.

I regretted so much not having a chance to talk with you after the meeting at Budapest. I wanted to know your real opinion of it and of its management, not the Budapest peoples part but the working part of the convention. To me it was the most unsatisfactory convention we have ever had from a working point. In fact I am wondering if an international body can ever be a working body. If its real mission is not more as a band of union between suffragists of different countries and a means for propaganda and inspiration for workers. In that light I think the whole round of meetings were helpful.

Mrs Catt never presided so poorly. She seemed absentminded and far away, as if she were in a sort of dream. In fact she has seemed that way ever since she returned from her trip. I think it is that being out of things for a couple of years among different people of differing conditions she has not just gotten back into touch with home things again. Then I think she really did not want to take the International Presidency again. I think she sees that there is nothing larger that the International can really do, and that the work in our country has grown so big, that there lies the largest field for her activities. Mrs Catt is, and always has been ambitious, and ambition well controlled is not a bad thing. If it were not for the influence of Miss H.[1] over her I should not fear for the future in our country but as it is I do in some ways. Yet one cannot be a special providence for all time and there must arise some one who can counteract what every one who knows her feels to be the wrong kind of influence of Miss H.

I am wondering about Miss Kramers and what the outcome of her trouble has been to her. Oh how I wish she had remained at Budapest, for whatever she might have suffered there. The press both there and at home would not have gotten hold of the trouble and she would have gone back without feeling that we were all personally antagonistic to her. She was angry with me, and for what I do not know for I did not speak of it to any of the members of my delegation and was surprised to know they were all familiar with even the details. I think Mrs C. told Mrs Harper and Mrs H. told whom ever she wished. I had not in all the time I was with her mentioned it to Rosa, and she did not know a thing of it until it was discussed in her delegation. The only thing I did was to urge Miss Kramers to stay by and if she had taken the advice to do so it would have been a great deal better for her in every way. There are so many likable things about her that I am sorry she has deliberately cut herself off from the friendship of many of us who would gladly be her friends. However, we must accept what comes and do our best. It may be that Mrs Catt could have managed it more wisely than she did, as some say but it is a great deal easier to tell what is wise after than before a thing is done.

I hope dear Dr. the outlook with the new government is better for suffrage than it was under the old.

May your summer get you far the best year of suffrage work you have ever had. With the tenderest affection for you dear Doctor, and a heart of love,

Anna H. Shaw.

1. Mary Garrett Hay.

42. Anna Howard Shaw to Aletta Jacobs

New York, March 19, 1914

Dear dear Doctor,

The mail has just brought your letter and I hasten to reply. The Womans Journal[1] seldom gets anything correct about me and when it stated that I had recovered from my accident and had gone to fill my engagements in the south it was about as far from being correct as it is in regard to the Holland news.[2] Yesterday was the first time I went out and I went to New Haven to speak before the Yale Students. It was the first time a woman had been permitted to speak in their great Hall. I promised them a long time ago that I would go, and they had made big preparations for it and there were 2500 people. Nearly all the professors, such a lot of students. It was an enthusiastic meeting. Four men carried me up stairs in a wheeled chair and wheeled me on the platform. I stood on one foot with my knee resting on a chair 1½ hours and talked and gave them a great day. It was well worth while though my well foot got so tired and swelled up and cramped all night so that I could not sleep but it paid. It was a great meeting.

The doctor is to take off my cast for good tomorrow. Then I will feel like a human being again.

Fortunately I was with Mrs Catt when the accident happened. We had been speaking the night before in Cornell University and it was a cold and icy morning. We had been on the train all night and got back on my birthday and then it happened. Not a good birthday for me. It was five hours before I could get to the X ray doctor to have it photographed. The storm was so severe that we could not get motors or carriages, and the snow so deep that they could not run. We had a fearful time.

I had arranged to take a tour of the south and had planned the best list of meetings I could make in Texas, Louisiana, Georgia, Alabama, Florida and South and North Carolina, and they all had to be canceled. It had taken me months to arrange them and I was fearfully disappointed and so were they.

You asked to have Lucy write you. The poor girl is worse off than I am as far as writing is concerned. She fell the night before Christmas and broke her right elbow joint and has been unable to write or to do any thing with the right arm since. It is however improving and the Doctor thinks now it will be almost right again in time, but she cannot comb her hair or feed her self with that hand very well. We have had rather a hard time of it and are rather a broken up couple.

We hope however that when we see you as we hope to in Rome. How glad I am that you are going, that we will both be all right again. Oh, Doctor, do be sure and come to Rome[3] and then let us have a jolly good time of it there. I wish Mrs Palthe could go too. I long for you all when I hear from any of you. I always think of the true and loyal friends that some of you foreign women are, and am so thankful for you.

We have been having a pretty hard time with a lot of young women here who got their training under Mrs Pankhurst and who are trying to introduce her methods in a mild form here, but they are hurting us fearfully.[4] I think by their unwisdom they have put us back ten years in Congress. It is pretty hard to work for years and years to bring the cause up to a point where it has some chance of going through and then have a lot of young things who never did any thing to build up the cause, attempt to run things their way without being responsible to any one. The only comfort I have is in the thought that nothing that any one can do can keep it back long. It is coming, I may not see it but it is coming, and I am glad I had the privilege of helping it along. That is a comfort no one can rob us of.

Mrs Catt is doing splendid work, and is working I am sure beyond her strength. If any one can carry this state through and make a success of the campaign she can. There will be a lot to talk about when we meet. Do be sure to go to Rome. I am in a hotel in New York but in ten days will go to Moylan. Lucy sends love, and I my dear Doctor send you warm hearts affection.

Anna.

1. *The Woman's Journal* was founded in 1869 by Lucy Stone and from 1887 was published by her daughter Alice Stone Blackwell.

2. Shaw broke her ankle and used the time she was laid up to dictate *The Story of a Pioneer* to a well-known American journalist, Elisabeth Jordan (1865–1947). See NAW.

3. The Quinquennial Congress of the ICW was held in Rome that spring. Activities

included a large-scale international suffrage demonstration. Afterwards Shaw, Lucy Anthony, and Jacobs left for a few days in Naples and Capri. See Shaw diaries, May 1914 (DC-SCHL).

4. Shaw is referring to Alice Paul and Lucy Burns, who had both been imprisoned in England for militant suffrage activities. When they returned to the United States in 1910 they were assigned the organization of the Congressional Committee, which lobbied Congress for a constitutional amendment. Their high-handed policies resulted in 1914 in the establishment of the Congressional Union, later renamed the Woman's Party. Like the WSPU, the Congressional Union held the ruling party responsible for the absence of woman suffrage. Each member of the majority party, even if he was in favor of woman suffrage, was harassed. The historiography of the suffrage movement has long been dominated by the NAWSA, and it is worth noting that neither Paul nor Burns is mentioned in NAW. But in the last five years of the fight for suffrage a militant movement was at work in the United States. Shaw's remark is a classic example of selective tolerance. She admired suffragettes in England, but not in the United States. See Stevens 1976, and, for Paul's international activities, Pfeffer 1985.)

5

Women United or Divided?
World War I, the IWSA, and the International Women's Congress at The Hague, 1915

In July 1914, even as telegrams foretelling the start of the First World War were crisscrossing Europe, Carrie Chapman Catt was at the headquarters of the IWSA in London. In the midst of this crisis situation the IWSA, "true to its principles of international sisterhood" (Schreiber and Mathieson 1955, 24) issued a manifesto which was presented to the British Foreign Secretary and to various ambassadors in London. It began: "We, the women of the world, view with apprehension and dismay the present situation in Europe, which threatens to involve one continent, if not the whole world, in the disasters and horrors of war. . . . Powerless though we are politically, we call upon the governments and powers of our several countries to avert the threatened unparalleled disaster" (Whittick 1979, app. 2; Oldfield 1984, 178). It ended with a call to use every possible means to arrive at reconciliation and arbitration. In a sense, an old theme of the international women's movement was now being played again; back in 1888 one of the policies of the founding congress of the ICW had been permanent arbitration. Its first standing committee, which was set up in 1899, was the committee on peace and international relations (Sherrick 1983, 656).[1]

Talks considering the IWSA's best course of action began immediately. It was decided that an attempt should be made, at whatever cost, to keep the Alliance alive by continuing the publication of *Jus Suffragii* and distributing it as widely as possible. The 1915 IWSA congress, scheduled to take place in Berlin, was canceled, and pleas poured in from all sides for an alternative IWSA congress in a neutral country, where women could mount a protest against the war. Aletta Jacobs became the spokesman for such requests when, in the December issue of *Jus Suffragii,* she officially launched a proposal to hold a "business congress with no festivities" (Internationaler

Frauenkongress 1915, xxxviii), which she offered to organize in Holland. No such clear-cut pacifist course was taken, however, for the motion to hold such an IWSA congress to discuss the war failed.[2] In the end the only official measure the IWSA made with respect to the war was its decision to cooperate in an International Women's Relief Committee led by Chrystal Macmillan and Mary Sheepshanks. From the IWSA headquarters in England, this committee would offer aid wherever possible.[3]

In addition to this official gesture, women of the Alliance and of other groups, as individuals as well as in national organizations, began seriously to pursue numerous antiwar activities. Thus Rosika Schwimmer, who had visited Lloyd George on July 9, 1914, to explain to him the gravity of the incident in Sarajevo, went that fall to the United States to submit a protest to President Woodrow Wilson on behalf of European women and to ask him if he would be prepared to act as mediator. Carrie Chapman Catt, who had access to the White House, helped Rosika arrange an audience and accompanied her. Somewhat later the former militant suffragette Emmeline Pethick-Lawrence[4] joined Schwimmer in the United States, and together they went on tour, making speeches to win public support for active mediation. In the meantime Julia Grace Wales, an instructor in the English department at the University of Wisconsin, drew up a comparable plan for "Continuous Mediation without an Armistice."[5] At Christmas the English pacifist Emily Hobhouse, who once had achieved fame through her reports on the concentration camps of the Boer War, addressed an open letter to the women of Germany and Austria, writing of the common fate of women and mothers in countries engaged in war. Lida Gustava Heymann, a German, distributed a pamphlet entitled *A Call to the Women of Europe* which urged that a meeting to protest the war be held (Internationaler Frauenkongress 1915, x; Posthumus-van der Goot 1961, 150). And finally, in January 1915, at a meeting in Washington chaired by Jane Addams and Carrie Chapman Catt and attended by 3,000 delegates of American women's organizations, the Woman's Peace Party was born (Lemons 1975, 5).[6]

The fact that Aletta Jacobs' proposal for an IWSA meeting had failed did not put her off for long. In February 1915, she took another course and in her private capacity offered a proposal to individual women to hold an international women's congress in the neutral location of The Hague to discuss matters of war and peace. As such the congress was not a strictly legal offspring of the IWSA, but it could be seen as a natural offshoot of the Alliance. All the broad experience built up within the Alliance was brought into force, and the available channels of information were put to use. Most of the important speakers had been schooled in the Alliance in international feminist politics. Jacobs' compromise proposal was enthusiastically hailed by a great many women, and Jane Addams, who seemed to embody the appropriate combination of pacifism and suffragism, agreed to chair the event. It was a cautious but combative sisterhood which gathered

Jane Addams. The Hague, 1915.

in the *Dierentuin* (zoo) at The Hague from April 28 to May 1, 1915. More than eleven hundred women from neutral and belligerent nations were there sitting together, and nothing remotely like it had been seen before. The participants had to brave criticism and condemnation even more intense than they had experienced before at international suffrage congresses. In particular, women from countries at war were suspected of betraying the cause of victory and undermining a whole range of patriotic and other principles. A group of 180 Englishwomen was prevented from crossing the Channel, and the German delegates were arrested upon their return home. Many a participant was shadowed after the congress by agents of any number of secret services. Aletta Jacobs' name appears in the archives of both British and German intelligence.[7] Jane Addams did not escape unpleasant attention, either. When she returned to the United States in July 1915, she was immediately

Women's Congress at The Hague, 1915. Left to right: *Florence Holbrook (U.S.), Mia Boissevain (Neth.), Thova Daugaard (Den.), Fannie Fern Andrews (U.S.), Jane Addams (U.S.), Rosa Manus (Neth.), Aletta Jacobs (Neth.), Chrystal Macmillan (G.B.), Kathleen Courtney (G.B.), Emma Hansson (Nor.), Anna Klemán (Sweden), Rosika Schwimmer (Hung.).*

caught up in the "bayonet charge." In her address at the reception for her in Carnegie Hall, she had explained how troops were given dope to enable them to engage in bayonet charges; the press had interpreted her remarks as an attack on military valor, and a flood of hatred and vituperation followed (Randall 1964, 198).

Circumstances, difficult and threatening though they were, at the same time contributed to the sense of solidarity and exultation among the participants. The women involved clearly felt that the congress was a great success. According to Kraft (1978, 21) the women passed "the best synthesis thus far formulated of an enlightened post war program, including Miss Wales' plan for a neutral conference for continuous mediation." With an eye to the future an International Women's Committee for Permanent Peace was formed. It was to organize a second women's congress during the official peace negotiations, wherever and whenever they might be held.[8] The determined vigor with which they pressed and adopted numerous resolutions drew the admiration of many outsiders. This was true in particular for Rosika Schwimmer's last-minute proposal to submit the resolutions personally to the leaders of warring and neutral nations. Despite opposition from prominent women at the congress, this resolution, after a passionate plea by Schwimmer, was carried by acclamation (Randall 1964; Wiltsher 1985).[9]

As a consequence of this resolution two delegations were appointed. The one to leaders of the belligerent countries and Switzerland comprised Jane Addams, the Italian suffragist Rosa Genoni, and Aletta Jacobs; the second, which would travel to the Scandinavian countries, was made up of Emily Balch, Chrystal Macmillan, the Dutchwoman Cornelia Ramondt-

Delegation to the neutral countries in front of the royal palace in Oslo, 1915. Left to right: *Emily Balch, Cornelia Ramondt-Hirschmann, Rosika Schwimmer, Chrystal Macmillan.*

Hirschmann, and Rosika Schwimmer.[10] In the two months following the congress, these women—and some personal friends who accompanied them unofficially—visited foreign secretaries and foreign ministers, chancellors, prime ministers, and even the pope. The Addams-Jacobs party, after an interview with the Dutch prime minister, from May 7 to June 6 traveled to London, Berlin, Vienna, Budapest, Berne, Rome, Paris, and Le Havre (where the Belgian government in exile was located). From there Addams left for the United States; the others went to Amsterdam. The northern delegation in the meantime toured the Scandinavian countries. Here the women were received by the king of Norway and, in Stockholm, were encouraged by the Swedish foreign minister Knut A. Wallenberg to collect the opinions of all belligerent powers on the idea of continuous mediation initiated and led by European neutrals. Part of the team went on to Russia, where it induced the foreign minister to sign a statement that he would not

Rosika Schwimmer, Cornelia Ramondt-Hirschmann, Emily Balch, Julia Grace Wales.

consider such mediation an unfriendly act. After this first round the women compared notes in Amsterdam, then started immediately on a second round, which brought Balch and Macmillan to London, Schwimmer and Ramondt-Hirschmann to Berlin, and both delegations to Sweden to discuss the consenting but otherwise noncommittal responses with Wallenberg.

The ease with which the women–Jacobs and Addams especially–gained access to government leaders may seem astonishing. It even looks as if the international women's movement, through its envoys, was capable of performing the entire mediatory function by itself. Although Addams was the first to put the events of 1915 into perspective (Randall 1964, 179), feminist historians in general have tended to idealize the enterprise as a true sign of the strength of universal sisterhood. From the vantage point of this book, such an interpretation is inaccurate, because the IWSA, until World War I a vital international feminist network, did not survive the Women's Congress of 1915 undamaged.

First there was an irreparable breakdown of the relations between two notable women of the IWSA, Aletta Jacobs and Rosika Schwimmer. After 1915, they never spoke to each other again. The conflict arose in part from their differing views on strategy.[11] Instead of mobilizing public support for the congress resolutions, Jacobs inclined to adhere to the more cautious tactic of persuading the United States, via diplomatic channels, to act as mediator. Behind this, as it turns out, was an informal message Jacobs had received from the Dutch prime minister P. W. A. Cort van der Linden and which she was requested to carry to President Wilson. This clashed head on with Schwimmer's idea of openly presenting the suffrage resolutions to government leaders. Schwimmer's approach had no place for the establishment of (secret) diplomatic relations; her aim was to gain as much attention as possible from the press. When in 1915 she and Chrystal Macmillan followed Jacobs unannounced to the United States, her intention was to rally public opinion there to "democratically" pressure the President to act as mediator.[12]

More important than this personal split, though, was the fact that IWSA president Carrie Chapman Catt did not side with the Hague initiative, and this may have permanently divided the international sisterhood. It is unclear why Catt remained aloof so completely. She had herself considered such a congress (letter 44). Perhaps it was beyond her capabilities under the circumstances. To quote Peck: "During the few days she was on the ocean [from England to the United States, July/August 1914] the burden of international work had been lifted from her shoulders and flung to the wind, and when she reached home, she was free to devote her whole energy to the New York Campaign" (Peck 1944, 215). This was even more true a year later, in December 1915, when Catt succeeded Shaw as president of the NAWSA. War in Europe offered Catt the opportunity to devote herself to American suffrage. And she did, unreservedly. In 1917, she produced the "Winning Plan," an ingenious strategy which aimed–with all available forces, from every corner of the suffrage movement–to exert the greatest possible pressure on all necessary elements at the federal level to get the suffrage amendment adopted (Kraditor 1981, 9; also Peck 1944, 267ff.; Van Voris 1987, 142ff.). It is also just as likely that political motives lay behind her aloofness. In September 1914 Catt walked in the silent women's peace demonstration in New York, and she was involved in the organization of the founding conference of the Woman's Peace Party in Washington in January 1915. Apparently at that moment peace propaganda still seemed to her the most effective way of ensuring the support of women. A month later, however, she and the NAWSA decided to support the government in the event that the United States intervened in the war (Van Voris 1987, 122ff., 137; see n. 5 above). A too blatant peace manifesto did not seem appropriate, and a visit to The Hague would not have been a good tactic.

Whatever the exact reasons, it is clear that the Women's Congress threw Catt into something very like confusion. She wrote to Jacobs of her doubts about the right course of action, even raising the possibility of disbanding the IWSA (letter 48). Catt's misgivings may have thrown doubt on the validity of their relationship. Was Jacobs a rebellious subject, or an overzealous minister taking over the reins unnoticed? Anything was possible in this explosive atmosphere. There were figurative mines between Europe and the United States as well as literal ones, and for the remainder of the war Catt ceased to correspond.

Anna Shaw, however, continued. Although feminist politics was not discussed as it had been before—Shaw had withdrawn from the suffrage movement and did not involve herself with the International Women's Congress—the letters are invariably tinted with matters of war. Shaw wrote mostly about her work as president of the Women's Bureau of the National Council of Defence. For the first time since her entering the ministry, she was working beside men. Finn (1979, 24) describes her activities as follows:

> Publicly she fulfilled the duties of her office—making speeches in support of the war, promoting government programs to conserve food and fuel, selling Liberty Bonds, and recruiting secretaries for government offices. But behind the scenes she waged a secret war with the government officials to gain employment opportunities for women, to remedy individual cases of sex discrimination, and to give women a voice in decisions which affected their lives. To accomplish her goals, she used every means, both fair and foul, learned in her long career. She badgered, harassed and threatened the men of power, hinted at resignation, an action which would have greatly embarrassed the administration. She could not win all her battles, but even William O'Neill, sharply critical of her suffrage leadership, judges that "as a guerrilla fighter in the halls of power she was magnificent."

Shaw's letters to Jacobs during this period reflect this struggle, which in her formulations takes the shape of a battle of the sexes. She complained, for instance: "The great obstacle is the interference by young men, well intentioned, who know as little about womens organizations as they do about the man in the moon and yet they cannot get it into their young conceited heads that women can do anything without being supervised and controlled by some young chap that has no more idea about how the work should be done than a baby" (letter 54). Her pen was very likely sharpened by the experiences of war.

This draws our attention to the paradoxical effect the war had on the IWSA. On the one hand, it considerably strengthened the (rhetorical) sex war, encouraging the concept of a close-knit international sisterhood clearly distinct and different from the brotherhood of men. On the other, it permanently disrupted the unambiguous nature of this same unified, close-knit, active sisterhood. Aside from suffrage, peace had come into its own as a concrete feminist issue. The Women's International League for Peace and Freedom developed alongside the Alliance, and many Alliance members became actively involved with the WILPF—even as the IWSA was broadening its field.

A no less paradoxical result of the war and the intensified battle of the sexes was that women were given the franchise in twenty countries. When,

Lida Gustava Heymann (left) *and Anita Augspurg* (right) *with Charlotte Despard of the English Women's Freedom League. Zürich, 1919.*

following a fourteen-year impasse in the American suffrage movement, women were given the vote in Washington state in 1910, Catt is reported to have said: "I can stand defeat, but victory is almost too much for me" (Peck 1944, 174). This comment is more than anecdotal. In all countries where suffrage was won during or in the aftermath of the war the principal raison d'être of the national suffrage movements suddenly ceased to exist. Of course it was clear to the suffragists that there was more to woman's emancipation than the single issue of the right to vote. But how and for what newly defined purpose were all the old forces to be reorganized?

October 1914–November 1918
Letters 43–56

43. Lucy E. Anthony to Aletta Jacobs

Moylan, Penn. October 7, 1914

My dear Dr. Jacobs,

When your letter came to Miss Shaw I read it before forwarding. I was sure that you would not mind and I was so anxious for news of you. Your letter was certainly most satisfying and I hope and pray that Holland is not going to have any special trouble, although every moment must be frought with terror as you cant know what is coming next.

Rachel and Julia had to come home steerage and had a pretty hard time. The first person we met after leaving the train at Moylan was Rachel and she came forward to shake hands and quite insisted on it—I shall have to confess that it went against the grain with me very much because I can never forget how much she has made Miss Shaw suffer.

We have thought of you so many times, and I shall always be so glad that we had that lovely trip together and I know that we will all always remember it. We will have to do our next sightseeing together in the United States I feel sure. Do you think that we will have an Alliance meeting next year? It would seem as though it would have to be here does it not?

Poor Miss Shaw is travelling and working hard—speaking many times each day and sometimes the train stops three times en route for her to speak to the people assembled. No soldier ever went to battle who took his life in his hands more than did Miss Shaw when she started off on this long trip. She was risking her health and strength in doing it, and it was certainly a very great sacrifice on her part to do it. Just think our peach trees were bearing for the first time—and she had to leave them. O how delicious they have been and I do not think I have eaten one without thinking how she would enjoy them.

I am sorry to have to say that my arm is not improving very much of [if] any, and when I saw my nice Swedish doctor in New York last week she fears that there is some bony obstruction and wished me to have two more X Ray photographs. So I am to have them taken tomorrow. I do hope it will soon be better for I am so handicapped now.

October 8.

I am just home from having the photographs and one shows a big bunch of cartilage on the inner lower arm which prevents motion. So far as could be seen there was no bone obstruction. The picture was wonderful showing muscles and even blood vessels. Surely that X-Ray is a wonderful invention and a blessing. This mornings paper confirms the rumor that Mrs. Catt has inherited $800,000 for suffrage work.[1] Is not that too splendid? One can hardly believe it. I know that she will be most wise in its expenditure and that suffrage will receive a wonderful impetus. O but I am glad and happy over it. How glad Miss Shaw will be and so relieved, that we will not have to struggle so hard to get money to pay postage stamps and necessary expenses.

This is just to send you some love messages and the hope that all is going well with you. My love to Charlie and his wife.

Affectionately,

Lucy E. A.

I was most touched by something you said in your letter—just at the last about what you would do under certain exigencies—think I would better not repeat—but it made me weep.

1. Mrs. Frank Leslie's inheritance. See Stern 1970. The amounts mentioned differ. Flexner (1977) speaks of $2,000,000, Van Voris (1987) and Stern both of $1,000,000.

44. Carrie Chapman Catt to Aletta Jacobs

[New York] November 13, 1914

Dear Dr. Jacobs:—

It has seemed to me that letters hardly express one's feelings in these days. I received your letter telling me that the suffragists in Holland were giving themselves up to relief work.[1] At that time mails were uncertain and I did not reply.

I have received a protest from Denmark and Sweden against the use of the name of their societies in the petition presented to the President. I believe they thought it was the printed appeal which Mrs. Schwimmer had sent to the various countries after she had secured their cabled consent to some form of petition.

I have thought best, therefore, to write the enclosed letter to the presidents, but I am only sending it to Sweden, Norway, Denmark, Finland, Switzerland, France, Mrs. Coit, Mrs. Fawcett, and Miss Macmillan. It seems to me strange that the pacifists who have held their congresses for years and who have been agitating for peace and trying to find the means of abolishing war, should at this moment be so inefficient. We hear nothing of the regular pacifists, but other people are trying to do something, each effort seeming to be a little more inane than the one which preceded it. Meanwhile the appeals for help for the victims of the war are coming thicker and faster and our people on this side are being organized to secure relief and food funds. It strikes me that it would be more sensible to stop creating victims than to find the means of taking care of them after they are made. But who, and what, can bring anything to bear against this madness which has taken hold of Europe? Surely by this time the masses of the people must know the devastation which has already been created and must long for peace. We read that even the Kaiser's hair has turned white.

We of the neutral nations ought to do something – but what? Can we hold an International meeting in a neutral country and there make plans for something practical?

I know you are in the thick of the relief work with a heart heavy with distress and sadness at this time. Please accept my sympathy. I do not think there is an intelligent person anywhere in the world who is happy these days. In the back side of his head he is conscious all the time of the terrible thing that is going on in Europe.

Lovingly yours,

CCC

P.S. Since dictating this letter Rosika has been in town and gone again. She told me she had spent $200 for cables since she came here and a big sum for typewriting. I wonder if she is a little mad over all this world's madness. Her plans for peace are impractical. Mrs Lawrence is here. She wants a worlds peace movement among women (militancy seems unpopular just now) Mrs Lawrence doesn't believe in Rosika's plans nor Mrs Lawrence in hers. Christabel is here too, but no one talks of her. Militancy has not the hold on the imagination that it had before the men went at it.

Rosika is going to try lecturing. She will begin with a bureau at a big price. But she will never have any money I think. The suffragists cannot afford to employ her. She says she has always had big prices in Europe, but has given free lectures when she wanted to do so.

Lovingly,

Carrie C. Catt

1. Catt is referring to the Women's Relief Committees set up immediately following the outbreak of the war.

45. Anna Howard Shaw to Aletta Jacobs

[New York] Jan. 4th, 1915

Dear My Doctor,

We are like lovers just as soon as a letter comes from you we want to answer it at once sending love and good wishes. It is always a joy to hear from you even when the letters are sad as all letters of thoughtful people must be these days. We are passing through a fearful time testing of hearts and character, not knowing whether each day will swamp our country in the whirlpool of destruction.

There is a great effort among some of our people to increase our army and navy and to fortify our ports. Could there be any thing more insane than such a move at this time. It is all a move of military men and manufacturers and ship builders.

There is to be a peace meeting of women at Washington on next Saturday and Sunday the 9th + 10th of this month. I was in to see Mrs Catt this morning and she and I are going to see if we cannot keep it out of the hands of the militant suffragists and Mrs Pethick-Lawrence, and the Congressional Union. If we cannot we will not have anything to do with it. There is nothing that would kill our movement at this time so much as any suggestion of militancy. As soon as the meeting is over I will write you again telling you all about it.

Now in regard to the meeting in Holland next spring I do not know what to say to you that will convey my thought in regard to it, for I have not the least hope that it would be possible to hold such a meeting even among the neutral nations, a spark would create a blaze in a moment that would make any future meeting of the Alliance impossible.

The women from the beligerant [belligerent] nations so far as heard from protest against it and I feel we would be treading on thin ice if we met at all. I do not want to seem to oppose it if you and others want it, because it will be impossible for me to come over this spring. Many things are against it. I have not the means to spare for one thing. The war is hitting us hard in many ways and financially every thing is dead and money is at a stand still. Then that nervous dyspecia [dyspepsia] from which I have been suffering more or less for years, has been, because of overwork and anxiety very much worse of late, and the Doctor has ordered me to stop work and go south for a good rest. I shall leave home for Floriday [Florida] the first day of Feb. if all is well and will not return until the middle of April. Then I will have to start with the campaigns and give to them every day I have until the election. I feel that my first duty is here. That the best thing I can do for peace and a thousand other things is to get votes for our women. You see, Doctor dear, I am not so young that I have much time to lose and now is our time to win in this country. We have not a day to spare, there is so much to do and so few of those who could do the work who are ready to give them selves to it, and so few who are fitted of those who want to do it. There is a kind of work on the platform that I can do Doctor, perhaps better than any other woman among us, and campaign time is when I need to do it.

I am sure if you were here in my place dear Doctor wild horses could not get you away from it. I do not have any expectation that we will win any of the states next year but we must put up a big fight for it, or it will not be possible to win another state for years to come.

Mrs Catt for the first time looked old to me this morning, she is wearing herself out. She has not the endurance that I have. In fact I don't know any one who has. If it were not for my dyspecia [dyspepsia] I would be all right. That makes me feel life is not any easy thing, though I am better than I was two weeks ago.

I am more than usually depressed tonight for I am very tired. I was on the train last night and the night before and all last week was back and forth to Boston. My eldest brother was taken suddenly ill and died on New Years day and was burried yesterday. He was a dear brother to me and his going seemed like the beginning of the end of our family.

There were eight children of us, four of whom died years ago. It has been a long time that the other four of us have been together, now he the eldest has gone. I have two brothers left, but none of them were as near to me as James was. He was a Doctor and dearly beloved by his patients. I am the youngest and you see the prospect is that all must soon pass on. As I saw him resting so quietly in this casket yesterday I wondered if he were not the best off of any of us, and if his New Years day was not in fact the gladdest New Year of his life.

Dear Doctor I will write you more about the peace meeting after the one in Washington acts.

This is just a message out of the joy of getting your letter tonight. I had not intended to do any thing but go to bed when I reached home, but I felt as if I wanted to talk with you. The brightest part of the old year was our trip together. I wish we might take it again. I wonder if we ever will.

Lucy sends dear love and I long to hold your dear face in my hands and kiss it. With love ever

Anna H. Shaw.

46. Aletta Jacobs to Mien van Wulfften Palthe-Broese van Groenou

[Amsterdam] February 5, 1915

Dear Mien,

I trust you have received an invitation from Rosa Manus to attend a meeting at the American Hotel at 10am on Friday the 12th and, if required, on Saturday, February 13. Invitations have been sent to Germany, etc., and here in the Netherlands to members of Board of W.S., members of the Nat.

Comm.,[1] and to members of the Council of Women, Mrs. Wibaut, Miss Ankersmit, and Mrs. Kapteyn.[2]

An organization-sponsored congress will not be taking place, but individual women from England, Germany, and France are now hoping to arrange an international gathering for individuals from all countries. The preparatory meeting, which again will be organized by individuals, will be held here next week, and we shall see what we can achieve. Attending the meeting is in no way binding.

I have appointed a small committee to assist with the preliminaries— J. van Lanschot Hubrecht, Dr. Docters van Leeuwen–van Maarseveen,[3] Mia Boissevain, and Rosa Manus. Mia has not responded yet, but the others have accepted and have been set to work.

I have not yet been able to find a few Belgian women. In any case, if you come and are able to bring your companion, she will be very welcome. She should know, however, that some German women will be present, and whether she can bear to meet them. I have been having trouble with the Belgian women, as none are able to rise above a hatred of all that is German, including German women who are totally innocent with regard to the war. If you are unable to come and Miel[4] is willing to take your place, she will be more than welcome. Do bring her anyway.

Let us know in good time if we may count on your presence and if your companion will be accompanying you.

Affectionately yours,

Aletta H. Jacobs

1. Probably the National Women's Relief Committee.

2. Mathilde Wibaut and Heleen Ankersmit were invited as representatives of the League of Social Democratic Women's Clubs. Action was also taken against the war in the social democratic women's circles. In spring 1915, twenty-eight women from warring and neutral countries gathered in Bern. The resolutions adopted were not published because some delegations, notably the French and the German, were not supported by their rank and file. See Outshoorn 1973, 70ff.

Geertruida A. Kapteyn-Muysken (1855–1920) may be regarded as an anarcho-communist. She was at first active in the suffrage movement but broke away when her unconventional ideas were rejected.

3. Jeanne van Lanschot Hubrecht (1864–1918) was originally on the Association's Amsterdam propaganda committee. She later became secretary of the board. She was also active in the nurses' trade union, Nosokomos. In 1915, she joined the International Women's Committee for Permanent Peace, at which time she was already seriously ill. See letters from Emily Hobhouse to AJ (AJ-IAV-IIAV). She died before the war ended. *Gedenkboek* 1919, 64.

G. W. P. Docters van Leeuwen-van Maarseveen belonged to the first generation of women students in the Netherlands, though she graduated in Zürich in 1897. She sat on the executive committee of the Woman Suffrage Association and was editor of *Het Maandblad*.

4. Miel is Miel Coops-Broese van Groenou.

47. Aletta Jacobs to Rosika Schwimmer

Amsterdam, April 7, 1915

My dear Rosika,

Today you are leaving the U.S. and every day will bring you nearer to us. Your kind, glad letter, which you have sent from Boston, was received today.

You ask me whether I could call together a small informal meeting of those who belong to the I.W.S.A.

Let me first tell you that from that board only Miss Macmillan will be present and then probably Miss Sheepshanks.[1] Both of those women are too broad-minded to have a bitter feeling against you. I am sure they have not. They love you as before and admire the splendid work you have done. And the Dutch women? We all are so glad that you are coming, we all love you just as ever, and we feel sure that what you and Mrs. Catt have done, you did with the best intentions.

I do not believe there is time to call such a meeting together. We cannot spare a minute. Besides I really do not know, whom I should invite to address such a meeting.

As soon as the Congress is over, we will give you the opportunity to tell us all you think we ought to know and then you can advise me who to invite.

You must not forget that we have to arrange everything for this Congress in 2 months' time, and that we have now also to do the International work, what otherwise has been done by an international board.

We know now already that at least 75 from England are coming and more than 40 from Germany. Three societies from Italy send delegates. Your Hungarian women, with Countess Teleki[2] as president do splendid and we expect a lot of them. From Vienna we got a letter from Kulka, Olga Misar and Rosa Mayreder[3] that they are coming, but we expect more. Denmark is splendid but Norway is not too awake. Spain sends a lady, Palestina [Palestine] and Brasil also.

We have you put on the list of the speakers. Mr. Giesswein[4] is here in Holland and he will come and see us at the end of the week. He has sent us a most encouraging letter.

And now I must finish, dear Rosika, I feel very glad that you have had such a success in the U.S. Both of us are going to stay with de Palthe's, so we will have plenty of time to talk.

Heartily yours,

Aletta.

1. Mary Sheepshanks (1872–1958) became secretary at the Alliance headquarters in London in 1913. She was responsible for *Jus Suffragii*. See Oldfield 1984.

2. Iska Teleki was active in the Hungarian suffrage movement and was president of the congress' preparation committee. Shaw stayed with her at her castle in the Tàtra mountains after the 1913 congress in Budapest. Shaw 1915, 334.

3. Leopoldine Kulka and Olga Misar both attended the Budapest congress, Misar as official delegate and Kulka on behalf of a sister organization, the Austrian women's council.

Rosa Mayreder (1858–1938) was one of the founders of the Allgemeine Österreichische Frauenverein (General Austrian Women's Association) and coedited *Dokumente der Frauen*. Two years after Otto Weininger's mysogynist but influential book *Geschlecht und Character* (Sex and character), she refuted his arguments in various essays in *Kritik der Weiblichkeit* (Critique of femininity) (1910). After 1915 she became active in the Austrian branch of the WILPF.

4. Alexander Giesswein was a pacifist clergyman from Hungary.

48. Carrie Chapman Catt to Aletta Jacobs

[New York] June 30, 1915

My dear Aletta,

Your letter from Bern was enroute about four weeks, before it came into my hands. Mails are decidedly uncertain in these days. I had a call a few days ago from one of the Chicago delegates who brought me a letter from Miss Macmillan and messages from Rosika. This lady told me that it was the plan for all those who had visited the various capitals to return to the Hague and to exchange their experiences there. I therefore suppose that you will have returned to your home by the time this reaches Amsterdam. This lady said that it was the possible intention to remain at the Hague and to see what further good offices concerning peace might be attempted.

So far as I know nothing has been heard here concerning Miss Addams' return, although the American papers interview her at every capital. We have just had an interview from Paris in which she announces that she will go next to the Hague and then probably return home, at which time she will go to see the President. I think you have been travelling with her to all the other capitals; why do you not finish your job and come over here and go with her to see the President? Were these ordinary times I should assure you of my own hearty welcome and to make promise that I would accentuate it in some demonstration worthy of you. As it is, I am in and out of New York continuously, with definite appointments long ahead which could not be easily set aside. I should hope, however, that your coming would be at such time that I would have the opportunity to do something to show you that I still love you.

The Peace Party here in New York is talking of getting up some kind of demonstration of welcome for Miss Adams, in which you would be an honored part, were you with her. They are anxious to make plans, but do not know when she will return.

It was interesting to observe in the resolutions and also from numerous letters that the International Peace Committee proposes a Congress in the city or country where negotiations for peace will take place. It is curious that this idea originated with Mrs. Fawcett, who did not approve of the Peace Congress at the Hague and with the Swedish Society, which also disapproved of that Congress. Since her suggestion appeared in JUS SUFFRAGII some months ago, the Swedish Association suggested that it might be well to have such a Congress, but as this was during the time when the proposals were pending as to holding a Congress under the direction of the Alliance, I did not regard it as a definite proposal. Later, it was made in official form and I sent it to the headquarters in London with the request that Mrs. Fawcett should write a letter of her own in connection with mine before it was sent out. They afterwards wrote me that the mailing was long delayed owing to the absence of Miss Macmillan to whom they desired to submit it, so it seems that we have two proposals before our members. I say "before our members" because the Congress in the Hague was most assuredly organized and called by that minority of the Alliance which voted to have a Peace Congress under the Alliance. It would seem, therefore, that the minority in the Alliance and the majority are likely to agree upon this proposed Congress to be held at the time of the peace negotiations. Two congresses at the same time and in the same place give rise to embarrassment, and I am therefore writing to Mrs. Fawcett, who originated the idea and to Miss Bergman who submitted the proposal, to ask their opinion concerning further action. The questions which arise are as follows:

1. Shall the Alliance hold a separate Congress without regard to that of the Peace Committee[1] with a view to secure, if possible, a suffrage resolution from the conference of the powers?

2. Shall the Alliance combine with the Peace Committee in holding one conference?

3. Would the Peace Committee desire the help of the Alliance even if it should be willing to render it?

4. Would it be advisable to have two congresses, ours merely to solicit a resolution concerning woman suffrage from the peace conference, the other to go into a discussion of future war and peace conditions?

Of course the Alliance could not assist in the propagation of the Peace Conference resolutions since it has not adopted them. I think it could not go much further than a suffrage resolution and possible action concerning women in time of war.

The Hague Conference, quite apart from the work it has undertaken, and has done, seems to have made a profound impression upon the Alliance itself. The minority desiring a Peace Congress organized the Hague Congress. As a result of agitation concerning that Congress (about which I do not feel that I am fully informed) several members of the Board resigned from the Board of the National Union.[2] Apparently, as a result of this agitation disagreements arose in the International Headquarters and Miss Sheepshanks has resigned as editor of JUS SUFFRAGII. I have been so completely occupied with the campaign work in New York that I have not given much serious consideration to the future of the Alliance. When thoughts have come to my mind, I have put them away in the back side of my head with private comment that no plans or theories could be evolved now which would be of any value, since no one could tell what the further developments of the war would bring.

It has, however, occurred to me that this minority which organized the Congress may prefer a different international organization, which shall be linked together with peace propaganda rather than a non-partisan and neutral suffrage organization. I have always felt that a strong minority going out of an organization do those who remain a great injustice in not telling them what they propose to do, as they often leave the responsibility of a dying and useless organization on the hands of those who are its unfortunate officers.

If the Alliance is going to be useless in the future, I think it would be much wiser to properly disband it so as to leave all its organizations free to go into a new organization, if they prefer. We are bound by our Constitution to hold a Congress in 1917. I cannot think that it will be possible that the war will not be at an end long before that time. We read that little Holland may be drawn into the war, and, indeed, so may the United States—God forbid! If your country gets into the war I don't know where there is a neutral land left which could take care of the Congress in 1917. That I think we must hold and at that time determine whether we shall go on or whether we shall stop. Of course at that meeting I go out of office no matter what happens.

I am myself hopeful that there will be a great democratic movement in Europe and especially in Germany after this cruel war is over. If that be true, then woman suffrage must be pushed as never before. These are hard days. Do come over to America and let us talk it over.

I want to say that I am glad that you held the Congress. I feel sure that it will bear some permanent results. I do not suppose we would exactly agree as to what its immediate results are, but that it was good to have held it we are sure to agree on.

Lovingly yours,

P.S. Since this was dictated I have seen Miss Addams who has safely returned. I hear that Miss Sheepshanks has concluded to continue as Editor of Jus Suffragii.

More, the man in Canton who entertained us at dinner, took tea with us yesterday! The nice young man who went home with us and one of the Assembly women members who dined with us that night have been shot! – for believing as we do!!

Carrie C. Catt.

1. Catt means the International Committee of Women for Permanent Peace.

2. Catt refers to the English National Union of Women's Suffrage Societies (NUWSS). For more specific information on the complex English situation see Wiltsher 1985, Vellacott 1987, and Oldfield 1984.

49. Aletta Jacobs to Jane Addams

New York, Sept. 8th 1915

Dear Miss Addams, Let me begin to tell you that I arrived here yesterday after a very comfortable journey as a result of your kindness of arranging such a good room in the railway for me.

As you will see from the letters of Rosika & Chrystal Macmillan they both arrived here to-day. They have not received our cablegrams. They have been interviewed, photo'd and everything else, all is in the papers to-night. I explained to them the situation here and begged them not to give interviews or not to do anything before they had time to study the situation here in the U.S.A. or before they have seen you. But it did not help; in the short time I was sitting there, we were 3 times interrupted by photographers who took photo's of both of them and reporters who interviewed them.

I received a letter from Miss van Lanschot Hubrecht and one from Emily Hobhouse.[1] Both tell me how Rosika made at the meeting, from which we read the minutes, the Peace Committee pay her expenses. Miss van Lanschot Hubrecht writes, that in the minutes was said that there was so much in cash, but Rosika did not copy, that after her bills were paid, only a small sum was left. Rosika has made all her expenses (also between her first and second visit to Germany and Stockholm) [paid] by the Committee, only by saying that she, as the acting president, had a double vote.

Miss Hobhouse, apart from Miss v. Lanschot Hubrecht, writes me in the same sense.

Rosika & Macmillan arrived here in the middle of the day, just in time to attend to the Luncheon Miss Anna Shaw gave in honor of Mrs Quincy Shaw[2] from Boston. After that lunch we had our talk. To-day I told them my experience, to-morrow-morning they are coming here to tell me what they have planned to do.

We shall send a letter or telegram to Chicago to tell them there that we are willing to come for a meeting some day after this week or next week.

Although Miss Hobhouse's letter is a private one to me, I believe she would not mind you reading it; therefore I include it and hope you will return it to me. You will better judge if you have read it, than when I tell you all what is in it.

Miss van Lanschot Hubrecht writes a Dutch letter. She writes that the report was not finished, Macmillan only had gone over the first correction and in a very nervous way, so that there is much work left undone and she and Miss Hobhouse have to do it all. She never believes it will come out well done.

I hope you are feeling every day better and are growing stronger and that you will and can come here to see these two firebrands.

With love to you and your two nice friends, Miss Smith and Miss Wald.[3]

Affectionately yours,

Aletta H. Jacobs.

1. This is letter 50.

2. Pauline Agassiz Quincy Shaw (1841–1917), one of the wealthiest women in New England, financed numerous progressive projects and from 1900 was an important sponsor of the suffrage movement. See NAW.

3. Mary Rozet Smith, intimate friend of Jane Addams, largely provided for Addams and also financed the house at Bar Harbor where they spent part of each summer. See NAW, s.v. "Addams," and Cook 1979, 417–19. For Lillian Wald, see chap. 2, n. 7.

50. **Emily Hobhouse to Aletta Jacobs**

Amsterdam, Aug 21, 1915

<u>Private</u>

Dear Dr. Jacobs

I can't help feeling that the cable, being sent to you today, which will greet you on yr arrival, will upset your plans and your mind and prove very disconcerting. It was extra bad that it should have been sent the very day yr card arrived from Falmouth expressing the underlined wish that we three should *all* remain at this post till your return. Miss Manus & Mme Hubrecht and I all did our best without avail. You know however what yr friend Rosika is, and what she will do when her mind is made up. Miss Macmillan who is & should be immersed in the Report was more than half dubious but was overpowered by Frau Schwimmer's insistance. I cannot see how the Report can possibly be finished and the proofs corrected in time for her to start on the 28th & I fear the delay may greatly impede you. I nourish however the hope that you & Miss Addams will go your own way & disregard the cable, for from what was said it would appear that the motive of the journey is more to make an effect on the American public than for any further contribution of great import, that can be brought to put before Wilson.

I felt, as you can imagine, aghast when it was proposed that I should stay & do the work of the office alone–and hoping it would act as a deterrent, I demurred to this & said I could not consent to idle my time in an office where there was no one to direct affairs & I myself was devoid of authority. They at once obviated this difficulty by proposing to elect one assistant secretary & clothing me with official authority, and of course this does give me power to sign letters & to carry on the work with greater confidence & I hope all will be found in good order by your return. However before I was elected to the executive the question of this joint journey to [the] U.S.A. was put to the vote. 2 voted for it & 2 against. Then, as this decided nothing, it was proposed that Rosika who was Chairman should have a second vote & in this was [way] I believe it was carried–Mrs Ramondt[1] was present but had no vote, and my opinion which was asked was given against but was of course valueless.

Not only does it necessitate doing the Report in a hurried way, but it is another heavy cost. Yet to my mind neither of those is so important a drawback as the fact that you & Miss Addams may be seriously upset in your plans and delayed. My hope is you won't change or delay or modify your plans.

I am writing late in bed & very tired so please pardon incoherence. Hoping you rested well en voyage,

Yours affect.ly,

Emily Hobhouse.

1. See chap. 5, n. 10.

51. Aletta Jacobs to Rosika Schwimmer and Chrystal Macmillan

New York City, Sept. 13, 1915

My dear friends,

After I thought it over this night I must write you that I am not going to Bar Harbor again. I have had long talks with Miss Addams and we settled every question which we thought that ought to be discussed. You want to talk with her about your own plans in the U.S., but that are personal questions and I have nothing to do with it nor our Intern. Committee. As every dollar more or less I spend here weighs heavy with me I do not feel free to take that expensive trip for a second time.

I am sorry to say that I feel very angry this morning after I read the papers. I told you that I took the greatest care not to be mentioned in the papers in connection with the work I hoped to do here, and I asked you not to give any publicity to your plans before you have seen Miss Addams. Have you than [then] the right to use our names for publicity without informing us? You know that you cannot see the President, now you will make it impossible for me too. Miss Macmillan knows that I never would have gone to the U.S. if I could have presumed that you were coming. What does this all mean? I have now spent my money, time etc. for nothing else than a dangerous trip.

I feel too angry to tell you all this and therefore write it.

Sincerely yours,

Aletta.

52. Anna Howard Shaw to Aletta Jacobs

[Moylan, October 6, 1915]

Dear Doctor,

I was just heartsick when I got home for a few hours only last night to learn that you had been here and that no one was at home. It is just too much ill luck for any thing, but Lucy and the car and I were out in Massachusetts and New Jersey and the last we heard was that you did not think you could get here.

I hope you saw the outside if you were not welcomed by us as I would have been so glad to welcome you to the inside.

It is such a pity your stay in this country is so short. How I would love to have had you at our big thing in November and at our National Convention as our Guest of honor as you would have been if you had remained here.

I am sending you my book with my love and the hope that it may interest you a little on your voyage.

It was good to look into you[r] dear face if only for a minute or two, and I hope to see it again in a World's Peace conference.

I am just heartsick to think we missed you at Alnwick Lodge. My only consolation is that you know we were both in the field for our cause.

We give every thing of ourselves and miss the dear presence of friends in our home all for it.

How I wish our war for freedom as well as the cruel war of Europe was over.

With dear love to you,

Ladee

53. Anna Howard Shaw to Aletta Jacobs

Moylan, April 18th 1916

My blessed Doctor,

It was a joy to see your letter in the mail yesterday, even though it had been opened and read by the censor. But we were disappointed that you do not think you will be able to come to us this spring. We had looked forward to it with such pleasure in the hope of repaying you for a little of the kindnesses and the hospitality you had shown us. It is a very late spring, at least two weeks later than usual at this time of the year. January was like April and April is like January. The whole world seems to be turning upside down weather included. We are very glad however that you are not going to risk your precious neck on the Ocean until Germany comes to feel that the murder of women and children neither adds to her glory or honor. Oh: it is brutal business and God alone knows how long it will take to make men and nations human.

We hear rumours of the Netherlands mobilizing her army and no one seems to know whether it is a threat against England or Germany? In fact the whole world seems going mad and no one knows what it is fighting for or what it wants. I have not half the respect for mans judgment or common sense that I used to have, that they are such fools as to go out and kill and be killed without knowing why.

I would like to have a long talk with you about so many things that I cannot understand in regard to that peace trouble. I am not in touch with any of the people and since the illness in December I have not seen any of the suffragists, so know nothing of what they think of the whole matter.

You speak of Miss Addams' contradictory letter. That is Jane Addams. You can never be quite sure what she is. We have had our great trouble the past few years because of her being on both sides of so many things in the suffrage that you could not depend upon her taking a stand and keeping it. However in spite of every thing the work goes on.

I reached home on Sunday night. Left Florida on the 31st March and came to Summerville So. Carolina, one of the most beautiful spots in the world. A friend met me there who is a great walker and who made me walk every day for a week until I could walk five and six miles. Then on the 9th of this month I came to Atlantic City[1] where I got the wonderful air and sunshine of sea and sky for a week and on Sunday night reached home, just four months from the time I was taken sick. Never in all my life have I had four months of such rest and care, and now I must go to work again. I began yesterday on the big pile of mail which awaited me and shall keep right on.

My first job in New York will be to marry a couple next Saturday and the next week is full of work meetings and a banquet to welcome me back again and a very busy time, and until the 5th of May I shall be very busy there. I shall rest for two weeks and then go into the campaign in Iowa; I am not going to do much work before September. Then I shall give myself to it, in the campaigns. I have made up my mind to take a portion of my time for myself and my friends, the time I have left of life for I have given forty and more years to steady work in fact fifty and more and now I begin to realize that the more one does the more she may.

Mrs Catt as National President is doing splendid work this year and my only regret is that I have not been able to help her more. So many of our dear women are working so hard expecting immediate results and that the end of the struggle is at hand when in fact we are only in the midst of it.

Mrs Catt is now in Iowa. I have not seen her since the 19th of December and she will not be in New York when I am there next week. I am sending you the new letterhead that you may see the names of the new Board. Mrs Catt selected them all and they are an uncommonly fine lot of women. Very much in favor of Mrs Catts methods of work and all of them devoted to her.

I am going to Bryn Mawr to stay the night with Miss President Thomas. She came to see me several times while I was ill but I have not seen her for two months. She kept my room a bed of roses, every other day fresh bouquets came and all my friends were very lovely to me.

I wish I could see and talk so many things over with you. One does not care to have censors reading ones thoughts and hope[s] and ideals even if there is no treason in them.

At the headquarters of the VVVK, Amsterdam. Left to right: *Aletta Jacobs, Rosa Manus, G. Docters van Leeuwen-van Maarseveen, C. Groot, S. Gomperts-van Emden, J. van Buuren-Huys.*

Board of the VVVK, 1918. Seated, left to right: *V. C. van der Meer van Kuffeler, F. van Balen-Klaar, Aletta Jacobs, Rosa Manus, J. van Buuren-Huys;* standing: *B. Bakker-Nort, S. van de Hoeve-Bakker, C. Mulder van der Graaf-de Bruijn, E. van der Hoeven, C. Groot, S. Gomperts-van Emden, Martina Kramers, G. Docters van Leeuwen-van Maarseveen.*

We are having more and more trouble with Mexico.[2] I rather think we are in for a long siege there.

Give my love to Rosa and Charlie and his wife and our congratulations on the advent of their son.[3]

I hope you got the letter Lucy wrote you about two weeks ago. She joins me in sincere and affectionate thoughts to you.

Affectionately,

Anna H. Shaw.

1. To the apartment of M. Carey Thomas. See letter 54.

2. Germany tried to turn Mexico against the United States. The famous Zimmermann telegram was one such attempt.

3. On February 23, 1916, Charles Erik, son of Charles Jacobs and Anna Overduin, was born.

54. Anna Howard Shaw to Aletta Jacobs

[Washington, August 30, 1917][1]

Dearest Aletta,

I am thinking of you and of the other dear friends in Holland so much these days, when one danger after another threatens the happiness and lives of our dear friends across the sea. Not only those who are at war, but those who [are] trying to keep from it are being crushed between the conflicting foes on every hand.

The question[s] of food and fire are the burning ones for you now. We have heard nothing but "food production and food conservation and the elimination of waste" for months, and everybody is trying her best to save her share of the seven hundred million dollars the male experts say women waste in their households every year. Not a word however is said over the millions of dollars men waste in smoke and drink. I got tired of having the women attacked day after day so some time ago I turned the tables and said in a speech which got into all the papers because I was attacked so much for it, that as long as thousands of acres of the most fertile land in Massachusetts, Pennsylvania and Connecticut, which would raise immense crops of wheat was put into the cultivation of tobacco I would not do without bread or eat corn meal to save flour. That started the women and since then the men have had to take it from us as much as we have from them. You would have thought to hear the learned young chaps talk here in Washington that most of the time of the average woman was spent throwing away good food especially bread. I know we are an extravagant people but the extravagance is not confined to women. Before the war is over men will learn a lot about themselves and women will do the same and things in this world will never again be as unequal between men and women as they have been.

I never realized how difficult it is to get things done in the government as since I have been at the head of this womans committee.[2] Every body is afraid of every body and each so jealous for fear the other will tread upon his department. It is so childish at times that it is laughable. Men I am convinced never grow up and of all the animal creation are the least capable of reason.

The one great excuse for not passing an amendment to the National Constitution granting suffrage to women is the fact that a little handful of willful women are picketing the White House and annoying President Wilson, in spite of the fact that there are more than two million women in our national suffrage association who are working with all their might to support the President and to help to carry the war to a successful issue.

Here am I working nights and days giving up my home and the beautiful country and living in one room in this hot city, without one cent of compensation not even my board, and cutting myself from earning anything, taking no vacation and no rest and what I am doing hundreds of other women are doing for the government and yet all that counts for nothing as compared to a hysterical young girl or a fanatical woman waving a banner at the gate of the White House, and yet they try to persuade me that men reason.[3] They have absolutely no sense of proportion or else their excuses are base hypocrisy. I am rather inclined to think it is the latter. However it is coming and I am sure another year will bring it through National legislation.

I have no hope that we will carry either Main[e] or New York this fall. Though some of the earnest women will be fearfully disappointed if we do not.

I have been able to stay in Washington during the hot weather because I have spent most of my week ends at Atlantic City or Moylan. I am going to Atlantic City tomorrow and will meet Lucy there and stay until tuesday. Miss Thomas the President of Bryn Mawr has a beautiful apartment right on the ocean and she loaned it to me for the summer while she is in China and it has been my life saving station.

The work of the womans committee grows more and more interesting as the possibilities unfolded in it present themselves. The great obstacle is the interference by young men, well intentioned, who know as little about womens organizations as they do about the man in the moon and yet they cannot get it into their young conceited heads that women can do anything without being supervised and controlled by some young chap that has no more idea about how the work should be done than a baby. I have a lot of quiet amusement when they come to us from the departments with such a wise expression and say "you must be very careful how you deal with such and such a matter. It takes expert knowledge to understand it. Have you your plans well worked out.["] Then, innocently to say [to] them, no, not yet we waited for suggestions from you. How do you think we would better deal with it? The poor fellows just ooze perspiration as they back out and say, Just make out your plan and then submit it to us and we will go over, and see if we approve it. When they are gone we have a merry time over the poor chaps.

Dear Doctor, I hope all is well with you as it is with me. My health is good, and I am living in hopes that the beastly war will soon end and that we may meet again.

With love, Anna.

1. The United States declared war on April 6, 1917.

2. Shaw was chairman of the Woman's Committee of the Council of National Defense.

3. Between June 1917 and spring 1919 more than five hundred women were arrested for peacefully demonstrating at the White House. Of these, 170 received prison sentences. See Stevens 1976.

55. Carrie Chapman Catt to Aletta Jacobs

New York, September 4th, 1918

My dear Aletta:—

I watched the papers with great anxiety for news of the Dutch elections. There is at this time so much news coming over the cables from Europe concerning the war that matters which formerly would have been considered very important frequently get squeezed out. So it happened that for many days we saw no mention of the results of your elections. At last in the Christian Science Monitor there appeared a report that they had been held and that one woman, a Socialist, had been returned.[1] I do not know at this time whether this is a correct report or not, but I take it for granted that you did not secure the election. I am very sorry indeed that you did not. You wrote at one time that you would be glad because of financial circumstances which were embarrassing you to receive the salary of a member of Parliament.[2] I am very sorry indeed that you are deprived of that. You did not have the votes of the women behind you and that was the trouble. I should think that the canvass of the women for votes would greatly increase the sentiment for woman suffrage and that the Parliament will soon be willing to grant it.

One cannot read the newspapers these days without realizing the very delicate and critical position in which Holland is placed by the efforts of the two conflicting powers to get at each other. Holland has maintained its neutrality in splendid fashion and has won the respect of the whole world by so doing.

Our country has been transformed from a land of peace wherein a soldier was rarely seen and where military affairs were rarely discussed, into a military nation. Soldiers are now seen on every hand. Long trains of them are continuously passing to and from the training camps and from the camps to Europe. Everybody is now a part of the big war machine. It is a strange experience. Many things in this connection would prove of great interest to you were it considered wise to talk of them freely at this time. Out of respect to the censorship regulations I will confine my comments to those subjects which are not taboo.

We often talked of the wonderful capacities of the bamboo and the palm. The war is developing similar capacities in our corn (maize). Long before the United States entered the war, olive oil chiefly imported from Spain and Italy, was difficult to secure, and the price was high. We are now using oil made from cotton seed and from corn. I cannot say that it is quite equal to olive oil but it is very good indeed and is used in making French dressing and mayo[n]naise most satisfactorily. Corn has also produced a very good syrup which having little flavor beyond sweetness is very successfully used in place of sugar. Corn was always used in this country in the form of meal and coarse flour. It is now ground finer and is made into a flour which mixed with wheat flour makes a very good bread. I think it a very wonderful thing that from one product, sugar, flour and oil can be secured. As this country has every possible variety of climate and is exceedingly productive, it is not difficult to substitute one article for another. We have such quantities of fruit and vegetables that they eke out our menus and allow us to save the flour and sugar and meat which go to the army and to the Allies. We here in this country have plenty to eat. Prices are going up. We have our profiteers as every other country seems to have had, but the Government is after them heavy and fast. Wages have gone up also, perhaps not quite so fast as the cost of food. You spoke about the need of coal in Holland last winter. The trouble is that there seems not to be coal enough in the world at this time to keep us all customarily warm. We had great coal troubles ourselves. The difficulty was mostly with the transportation facilities and the coaling of so many ships all at one time. The Government has tried to make people buy their coal in the summer so as to avoid the difficulties of last winter. We are now informed that we should be willing to live in houses of 64 degrees Fahrenheit next winter in order to save coal, and we are encouraged by the assurance that this temperature is very much healthier for us than that to which we are accustomed. I have no doubt there is plenty of truth in that statement. But you can imagine how many Americans will shiver, if that regulation is really carried out. The entire country is very obedient to all requests of the Government for conservation and seems to be very united in every respect.

Women in large numbers are engaged in doing the things which in the other belligerent countries they have been doing for some time. For instance they are running many of the elevators in New York City; they are serving as conductors on street cars, as ticket sellers in the railway stations, and we have quite a reserve of women police. I do not think the work of the women in this country in substitution of the work of men has been as picturesque as in the other countries. Those women blazed the trail and proved that women could do certain things which nobody in the world had believed they could do at all. Therefore our women simply slipped into these positions without much public comment.

The general opinion here seems to be that the war will not end for at least a couple of years. There is no doubt in anybody's mind as to how it will end.

Our Suffrage Amendment is held up in the Senate for the want of two votes.[3] Only 96 men are members of that body and within this one Congress there have been ten deaths. That fact is unprecedented. As a matter of fact these men who hold their positions for terms of six years grow old in the service and never seem to retire. It naturally follows that they will die some time and will still be senators when they do. Of the ten who died, seven were our friends. Had they lived we would have gone through the Senate long ago. It is a curious and spooky thing, this feeling that the hand of death has entered in this fashion to turn the direction of woman's progress. There are at this moment two vaca[n]cies in the Senate created by recent deaths. Our fate depends upon the kind of men who will be appointed to fill their places. We shall know soon. If they are favorable we shall go through directly. If they are unfavorable we are likely to have a long delay. It is very tedious, exacting and depressing.

I learned through the London Headquarters, and probably you have learned from the same source, that Miss Furuhjelm's two brothers were shot by the Reds. We do not know very much about the real truth of what has been taking place in Finland. That they have had a revolution everybody knows. I believe Miss Furuhjelm's brothers were standing, as I believe she would, for the continued independence of Finland and for the right to control their own affairs, and that that was the reason they were shot.

Miss Shaw is still serving as Chairman of the Woman's Committee of the National Council of Defense. She is speaking as well as ever and is in great demand. She keeps up wonderfully well although at times she looks tired and worn. I have made 31 round trips between New York and Washington within the last twelve months. My last trip was by motor and Miss Shaw drove back with us from Washington to Philadelphia.

One rarely sees the name of Jane Addams these days. I understand that she is keeping up fairly well because she takes good care of herself. I believe she is affected by some malady that will take her off in due time. I hope she will survive the war. She was greatly misunderstood and I think considered it the better policy to keep silent for a time. If she lives until the war is over you will probably hear from her then.

The women of New York are exercising for the first time their right to vote. There were three by-elections in which a few women had an opportunity to vote last winter, but this is the first statewide opportunity. It is the primary election for nomination of candidates. Large numbers of women registered and presumably there will be a large vote. It has been extremely amusing to observe the manner in which the men now treat the women. There is nothing that they would not offer them by way of favors with the expectation that their candidacy or their Party may reap the benefit. The most amusing of these attentions was given to several of our leaders in the New York campaign, among them Miss Hay who was the leader in Greater New York, and Mrs. Tiffany, the present leader of Manhattan Borough, the largest and most important of the five Boroughs that make up Greater New York. Each belongs to one of the dominant political parties and one party tried to outdo the other in conferring honors upon them. Miss Hay was made Chairman of the Resolutions or Platform Committee in the convention held by her Party. It is the most important committee in a convention in this country, and heretofore the big men of the Party have been its members and the chairman has been selected from among those most honored. Members of the Committee included some members of Congress, our two United States Senators, some members of the State Legislature, and a few of what we call old wheel horses. The bitterest antis in the State were members of that committee over which Miss Hay presided. Everybody has been chuckling about it ever since. Not to be outdone by Miss Hay's Party, Mrs. Tiffany's Party offered her the permanent chairmanship of the entire convention, a very distinguished honor which is coveted by and is given as a sort of reward to men who have attained distinction for valuable service to their party.[4] Probably you have learned that the State of Texas has given the women the vote for the primary elections, and that 350,000 of them voted recently. Their votes defeated a bad man who would probably have been nominated otherwise. The President of the Texas Association who was the real leader in defeating this man against most powerful influences and did a really remarkable work in accomplishing the object of the women of that State, has been chosen by the men to occupy the important position of chairman of the State Convention of her Party. In Arkansas the women also have the right to vote in the primary elections and 400,000 of them voted. Arkansas is a smaller state than Texas and both results were splendid.

I had three weeks' vacation this summer in the mountains and at the hotel where I was staying a young man gave weekly lectures on travel with moving and stationary pictures. I therefore travelled with him once more through Java, Japan and India. It brought back all our many experiences. It seems so long ago that we went on our journey it might have been in another incarnation. I long to see you once more, and hope that the prognostications as to the length of the war may be more gloomy than the realities, and that peace may soon return.

Lovingly yours,

Carrie Chapman Catt

1. Dutch women gained passive suffrage (the right to be elected) following a constitutional amendment in 1917. Suze Groeneweg of the Sociaal Democratische Arbeiderspartij (Social Democratic Labor Party) was the first woman to be elected to parliament.

2. Faulty investments by Charles Jacobs probably resulted in Aletta Jacobs' losing a great deal of money, after which she was supported by friends, Mrs. Jeannette Broese van Groenou-Wieseman, her three daughters Miel Coops, San van Rees, and Mien van Wulfften Palthe, and Mrs. Betsi van den Bergh-Willing. See VWP to RS, June 11, 1947 (SL-NYPL).

3. The constitutional amendment had been passed by a narrow majority in the House (Jan. 10, 1918). One member had even been taken in on a stretcher. Another voted on the day of his wife's funeral—she had been a fervent feminist.

4. Mary Garrett Hay and Katherine Tiffany were important in the New York Suffrage Party. They played a significant role in New York State's last major suffrage campaign, which is known as "the Decisive Battle." See Peck 1944, 221–23.

56. Anna Howard Shaw to Aletta Jacobs[1]

[Washington] Thanksgiving day, 1918

Dear, dear, Doctor,

Even Holland with the Kaiser on its hands has something to be thankful for today.[2] The cessation of hostilities on the battlefield is a great blessing and now if those of the beligerant [belligerent] nations who have become so accustomed to killing other people, do not turn on each other and will settle down to secure the wellbeing of the people and rebuild the moral and industrial life of the world there is much to be thankful for and to look forward to with hope.

Well I am thankful for you and for your dear friendship and that let come what may there are some things which do not change. Oh dear Doctor there are so few real friendships in the world that those which do exist should be prized above all things, so today in recounting some of my bless-

ings, they are so many that I cannot recount them all in the foreground
are my dear friends and out from the larger group a few for whom I am
especially grateful among them is my dear Doctor. So on this thanksgiving
day I am thankful for you.

Lucy left Washington for Florence Villa yesterday and I hope to follow
her by the end of Dec. I shall be so glad to get away from here, from all
the rush and uncertainty into a place of quiet and peace. No one knows
from one day to another when we will land or what we will do.

We have been advocating having a woman on the peace commission.[3]
We had no expectation that it would be done but we felt the women had
a right to a representative and that we ought to say so, and it has created
quite a sensation. The fact of it all is that unless at this time women insist
on recognition things are going to slip back, and be worse than they were
before. Now is our chance to assert ourselves and if we falter we will lose
it for years to come.

Jane Addams called on me this afternoon to tell me that she did not
think there would be any chance to get passes for our women to go to the
Womans Congress for some time.[4] That may be but I have no doubt that
by April the Suffrage Alliance will meet somewhere.

Miss Addams said it would not be allowed for German women to go
to a neutral country until peace is declared. She is going to see Sec'y Lansing[5] tomorrow and will perhaps be able to tell more. She is looking very
well and says she feels like herself again: the long rest and care she has had
has done her a lot of good.

Lucy started for Florida as I said, and is full of happy prospects of un-
packing and settling up the house there. She has had for her a very enjoyable time buying furniture and things for the little cottage and I am anxious
to follow her and see how it looks.

Mrs Catt is very anxious for fear we will not get our Federal amendment passed in time to get it ratified by the State legislature this winter,
and she is also much disturbed about the Alliance meeting. I hope it may
be held this spring, and if it cannot be held where the peace Conference
is then in some country.[6] I hope it will not be delayed for I want to go to
it and get away from here for a time, where I cannot be reached by telephone or telegraph.

We are all at sea to know what is to be done with our committees,
which ones are to be kept and which given up. It seems sure the womans
committee will not be given up for some time yet but just how long we
do not know. We are hoping that we will get some definite information
when the President makes his statement in Congress on Monday. Then we
can make some plans. What ever happens if there is an Alliance meeting
in the spring I shall if I am able and can get a pas[s]port go to it.

We were all ag[h]ast by reading in the papers this morning that Rosika
Schwimmer had been sent to Switzerland as an Embassador by Hungary.

Arrival in New York after final ratification of suffrage amendment, 1920. In the middle are Carrie Chapman Catt and Mary Garrett Hay.

Carrie Chapman Catt with "Victory Bouquet."

Carrie Chapman Catt and Mary Garrett Hay casting their first vote for president.

I hope that is not true. Not that I object to a woman embassador but I do not think she is the kind of a woman who should be selected. The worst of our movement as of all other reforms is the wrong people too often profit by it. If a woman is given such a position she should be an unusual one.

I am enclosing the money I promised in my last letter and want you to use it in any way and for any thing you think is most helpful to you and your work. You know I belong to Holland as I am a member of your Frauenkisrecht. I don't think that is spelled correctly but I often don't spell things correctly. Here is my Thanksgiving love for you dear Doctor. Give my love to Rosa.

Affectionately,

Anna.

Dear Dr., I had to sign a paper at the Bank saying what the money would be used for and I said for refugees or other needed services so that you are free to use it as you like. As soon as you receive it please send me a line addressed to my Florence Villa Florida.

1. This is probably Shaw's last letter to Jacobs.

2. On November 10, 1918, Kaiser Wilhelm II fled to Holland.

3. Shaw means the American delegation taking part in the peace talks which took place in Versailles beginning in January 1919.

4. The International Committee of Women for Permanent Peace planned to organize a woman's congress to discuss the resolutions of the peace conference at Versailles. This woman's congress, which was also the founding congress of the WILPF, eventually took place in Zürich in May 1919. See chap 5, n. 8.

5. Secretary of State Robert Lansing.

6. Catt had been concerned since 1915 (see letter 48). In fact, a woman's congress took place in Paris during the peace conference, at the initiative of Lady Aberdeen of the ICW and Mrs. de Witt-Schlumberger, president of the French branch of the IWSA. This Inter-Allied Suffrage Congress peitioned the Supreme Council of the Allies that women's organizations should be heard. See Whittick, 1979, 70ff; Reinalda and Verhaaren 1989, 49–51.

6

Reconstruction in the Twenties

Growing "Inter-Internationalism," 1920–29

The IWSA succeeded in reviving itself after the chaos of the First World War, but it was no rejuvenated phoenix. The first postwar IWSA congress in Geneva in 1920 was notable not so much for the topics considered as for the fact that it took place at all (Deutsch 1929, 22). The Alliance indeed carried on, but no longer with the natural idealism of the prewar period; nor was the sisterhood so "universal" as before. In particular, there was an inevitable gulf between the delegates from suffrage nations and those from nonsuffrage nations, the dividing line roughly running between west and east, rich and poor nations. The actual presence of countries like India, China, and Japan enlarged the scope of the IWSA. At the same time, however, it diluted the ideal of unity, which had been central, in the symbolic representation of difference. Deutsch, in her 1929 history of the IWSA, unwittingly proves this point when she says that there could hardly have been a greater contrast between the Chinese representative's report in 1920 and Aletta Jacobs' report on China in 1913. Women in China, according to Mrs. Chu Chia Hua, had always been held in high esteem, and were never so looked down upon as in Japan (Deutsch 1929, 24). Symbolic difference was replaced by real differences between women, a task the old IWSA feminists were not yet ready for. Again Deutsch's words are enlightening. About the 1920 congress she wrote: "Representatives from India, Turkey and Japan proved in their speeches how like and yet unlike their women's aims were to our own. It is difficult to arrive at a full understanding with these women, more bound by tradition and faith than are we. None the less we have seen with astonishment how rapidly the Turkish women, urged it is true by strong government pressure, have responded to new ideas and conditions (Deutsch 1929, 25). The perspective is clearly that of the Western feminist, who naturally speaks in the first person plural when she expresses IWSA policy and sentiment.

The majority of women at the 1920 congress came from the prosperous Western countries, and they set the tone of the conference. Since 1913 twenty-one of these countries, either in the midst of war or in the turmoil afterward had granted women the vote. In the United States, the suffrage amendment had passed both houses in June 1919, just before Anna Howard Shaw died. In the Netherlands a constitutional amendment made women eligible for election in 1917. In 1919 Dutch women gained the right of active suffrage through the so-called Jacobs law. They did not exercise their newly won right until the 1922 elections, however.[1] Women did not win suffrage on the same footing as men in all of these countries, but even so the change from the prewar situation was great.

In many countries women had been elected to legislative bodies and were now proving "women's influence" in political affairs. Jeannette Rankin was exemplary, being the first woman in the United States Congress and the only member of it who voted against American intervention in the war in 1917. Many of the new members of various parliaments were present, and the public meeting which they held was, according to Adele Schreiber, who herself had just been elected to the German Reichstag, of exceptional interest (Schreiber and Mathieson 1955, 28). There were even a few official government delegates.

The emphasis during this congress lay on the reorganization of the IWSA for the benefit of this group. To begin with, the objective was broadened. The IWSA now pledged: "to secure the enfranchisement of the women of all nations by the promotion of woman suffrage and such other reforms as are necessary to establish a real equality of liberties, status, and opportunities between men and women" (Schreiber and Mathieson 1955, 29). Necessary reforms were equal pay for equal work for men and women, the right of women to retain their nationality after marriage, equal family rights for wives and mothers, and an equal moral standard for the sexes. For each issue a study group was appointed (Deutsch 1929, 26). The IWSA also decided to keep close track of developments in the League of Nations, established as a result of the peace treaties, and where necessary to introduce and defend women's rights and interests. The importance given to these broader objectives was underlined in 1926, when the name International Woman Suffrage Alliance was changed into International Alliance of Women for Suffrage and Equal Citizenship. This name was always abbreviated as the even more all-embracing International Alliance of Women (IAW).

Interestingly, the Alliance took the same course as the ICW, for which the League of Nations was also a decisive influence, and which set up study groups on exactly the same subjects. The absence of a clearly defined format and objective of its own prompted the Alliance to grow close to the ICW again after so many years. After 1920 a merger with the ICW was considered more than once, and it is probably only for historical and personal reasons that the two organizations did not become one. To give a paraphrase of one of Rosa Manus' evocative descriptions: How could one merge with an organization whose chairman was a daunting marchioness who, even after she had dozed off, "conducted" a joint peace congress with the feathers on her hat (letter 62)? Far-reaching cooperation, however, did take place. The boards of the two organizations met regularly, combined meetings were held, and in 1926–at the instigation of the president of the ICW, Lady Aberdeen–the Joint Standing Committee of Women's International Organizations was established, which included the IAW, the ICW, and other international women's organizations.[2] The objective of the Joint Committee was to act as a pressure group, a women's lobby, to get more women into the male world of the League of Nations to represent women's interests. The committee was so successful that in 1931 the Liaison Committee of Women's International Organizations was established. It consisted of the organizations in the Joint Committee as well as some others but had a broader objective. The Liaison Committee in turn founded the Disarmament Committee (or Dingman Committee, after its chairman, Mary Dingman) in 1931 to coordinate the disarmament activities undertaken by women's organizations in anticipation of the first international Disarmament Conference, which was to be held in 1932.

Posthumus-van der Goot,[3] in her book *Vrouwen vochten voor de vrede* (Women fought for peace), summed up these and other instances of concerted action in Geneva, then wrote: "It is quite possible, worthy fellow traveler, that at this point you will heave a sigh of boredom and wonder why women can join forces only through all these committees!" She admitted that her summing up was not particularly startling:

> But the reality was. These women all had diverse viewpoints and were all very critical of one another. The formation of these cooperative committees proves that the women, "inter-internationally," were putting their twenty years' experience to good use. The courage and ingenuity with which they jointly besieged, and occasionally penetrated, the bastion of the League of Nations is also proof of a profound faith within these diverse associations in the influence of women as a force for peace. [Posthumus-van der Goot 1961, 209]

This sympathetic analysis, however, is somewhat too optimistic. There is another side to the story. If we look at it from the perspective of the IWSA, such inter-international cooperation marks the international officers' increasing isolation from their national supporters. The IWSA clearly needed the other women's organizations in Geneva to reformulate international policy, now that inspired direction and clear-cut objectives were lacking in the national organizations. One big divisive issue that arose after the vote had been won was the question of what to do with it, a question indissolubly connected with the reconstruction of the national suffrage associations. Did women have to join the male political parties of their preference and reconstruct the suffrage associations into general women's organizations, or should the former suffragists favor separatism in parliamentary politics and reorganize their suffrage associations into women's political parties? A letter from Carrie Chapman Catt to Aletta Jacobs in 1920 illustrates the dilemma:

> I have urged women to go into political parties when their consciences call them in that direction. Many of them are so partisan that they could not do otherwise. I have not myself, however, joined any political party and do not intend to do so at least for the present. I have never advised them not to join parties for if they feel as I do they need no advice.
>
> It was a very great misfortune that the vote came to women in the midst of a very hot campaign full of bitterness, and with no clear-cut issues. The result is that we will find after Election that many women will have left us for their respective parties, without really understanding why we should still remain together for a time. However, if we shall lose some, we will gain others as the women are realizing here, exactly as the Dutch women have already realized, that the women must stand together until they win emancipation as well as enfranchisement. [letter 58]

It is a typical Catt analysis in that it touches only the matters at hand, in the end not saying much at all. Her observation that the Dutch situation is so much beter than that in the United States was not very realistic. In the United States the National League of Women Voters was born in 1919, even before the suffrage amendment had passed. When in the Netherlands in 1917 discussions started on which course was to be taken after woman suffrage, the journal of the VVVK endorsed the idea of a separate women's candidates list at the coming elections in 1919. At about the same time a new women's association was founded to campaign for such a list, many of its members coming from the VVVK.

When the elections came, however, Jacobs decided on a different course, standing for the Radical Democrats in Amsterdam.[4] This unexpected maneuver may not only have weakened women's position in politics–neither Jacobs nor the women's candidates were elected–it may also have closed the issue of women's separatism in the Dutch political arena.[5] Thus in the Netherlands, as in the United States, women–even women like Aletta Jacobs–"left for their respective political parties." At the same time the suffrage associations were reorganized into general feminist organizations. The VVVK was transformed into the Vereeniging van Staatsburgeressen (Association of Women Citizens) and the Dutch Woman Suffrage League into the Nederlandse Unie van Vrouwenbelangen (Dutch Union of Women's Interests). As in the United States, both organizations had links with state and city politics, but during the twenties many women lost interest.[6]

Feminism was no longer "modern," and as Jacobs wrote in a 1926 letter, truly emancipated women were on an equal footing and therefore on comradely terms with men (letter 65). There was little attraction left in the notion of sisterhood. In this context the merger in 1930 of both organizations, into the Nederlandse Vereeniging voor Vrouwenbelangen en Gelijk Staatsburgerschap (Dutch Association for Women's Interests and Equal Citizenship [always abbreviated as Women's Interests]) may be seen as another example of the vital need of women to combine forces in a way similar to the inter-international cooperation in Geneva.

"We are too old, and the young lack energy and devotion"

Carrie Chapman Catt's letters around 1920 clearly show the confusion in the mind of this pragmatist without a cause. Catt was not really capable of accurate political analysis in the new situation, and she attributed the IWSA's loss of impetus to the attitudes of the new generation. In 1920, she complained that a younger person than herself should have been chosen president (letter 58). She was not alone in this opinion. In 1923, during the IWSA Congress in Rome, Jacobs wrote to her friend Miel Coops-Broese van Groenou: "The old guard is proving to be infinitely more vigorous and more progressive than our followers." But what could one do about it? "This morning Catt said, 'If only I could make the old guard twenty years younger, together we could restore order, peace and prosperity in the world. But we are too old, and the young lack energy and devotion.' And she is right!" (letter 61).

This was, however, only partly true for the women we talk about, and it seems as if Catt was unconsciously trying to disguise her own lack of inspiration. The vacuum which developed in the IWSA cannot be explained simply by a generation gap (letter 58). In fact her observations make sense only in the case of the aging Jacobs, who throughout the twenties was suffering from poor health and retired. She wrote her *Herinneringen* (Reminiscences) in 1924, was paid overwhelming tribute on her seventieth birthday as well as on her golden jubilee as the first woman doctor in the Netherlands, but only occasionally attended a congress. For the other women we are concerned with in this book, Catt's observations have no substance. True, Rosika Schwimmer, who in the past so often had been a vibrant element at the suffrage congresses, had left the ranks. In 1920 she started a new life in the United States, and the conflicts of 1915 and later prevented her from returning to the Alliance, but her age was in no sense a contributory factor. Nor was Catt herself too old to set out on new adventures, or at least so it seems. In 1922–23 she went on and enjoyed an "inspection tour" throughout Europe and Latin America, by which she hoped to ensure the orderly handing over of a still-growing international woman suffrage empire.

On this trip she was accompanied by Rosa Manus, "her little stepdaughter," as Manus—now forty-two years old—was still addressed. From Rome, where they witnessed the arrival of Mussolini's Blackshirts at their "March on Rome" in October 1922, their tour took them via Vienna and Budapest to the new democratic state of Czechoslovakia, where Catt shared lunch with President Masaryk. The two women then traveled to Berlin and

Catt addressing a meeting of women in Brazil, 1923. Seated to her right is Rosa Manus.

Bertha Lutz propagandizing for woman suffrage in Brazil, 1923.

were received by President Ebert of the Weimar Republic. Catt was the first foreign guest to address the Reichstag. She then fell ill and was nursed for several weeks in Berlin by Rosa Manus' sister, Anna Jacobi-Manus. Recovered, and seemingly inexhaustible, she stopped over on her way to Latin America to meet in London with the IWSA board to prepare for the 1923 congress in Rome, which Catt preferred to have relocated to another place. She did not think Mussolini's Rome the right setting for an international women's congress. Discussions also took place with the ICW about a possible merger. In Latin America she assisted in the setting up of several suffrage societies, as well as general women's organizations (Peck 1944, 363–90). At the last minute, Catt managed to muster the support of Bertha Lutz, her "Brazilian daughter," as Bertha described herself in her contribution to Catt's seventieth birthday album.[7] Nor, in 1925, was Catt too old to set up the Conference on the Cause and Cure of War and turn it into a broad-based American women's peace movement (Peck 1944, 409ff.)!

Finally, Catt's judgment that the IWSA was hampered by a generation gap was proved wrong by Margery Corbett Ashby and Rosa Manus. Catt's successor as president of the IWSA in 1923 was in all respects appropriate: Margery Corbett Ashby had every bit as much devotion and energy, and although she belonged to the younger generation, she was in a real sense one of the old guard—as a young girl she had been with her mother and sister in Berlin in 1904. She held the presidency even longer than Catt, until 1946. In 1923 Rosa Manus, who since 1908 had developed her organizing talents to an international level, had no alternative but to take on an executive post. Characteristically, she became vice president—a largely unseen driving force behind the organization, in which function she would be "a superb organiser whose insatiable energy, good temper and enthusiasm overrode all obstacles" (Schreiber and Mathieson 1955, 55).

Manus' strength lay in her power to combine a bird's-eye view of the organization with an eye for detail. She always created a positive atmosphere and carefully monitored and nurtured not only public but also private affairs. When Jacobs celebrated her seventieth birthday in 1924, Manus made it a day to remember for Jacobs personally as well as for the Dutch women's movement at large. When Catt reached the same age in 1929, she again took on the job of organizing the celebration. Far in advance she asked people all over the world to write a page for the presentation album, to send back a native recipe for an "international woman suffrage cookery book," and, last but not least, to send seeds for the "international suffrage garden" at Catt's new home.[8] In 1934, when Catt celebrated her seventy-fifth birthday, it was again at the prompting of Rosa Manus that a set of records with speeches by many different women was made. The records were played during a reception given in Catt's honor.[9]

In 1926, at the IWSA congress in Paris, Manus became secretary to the newly instituted Peace Committee, which was to organize several interna-

First leaf of birthday album given to Catt on her seventieth birthday, January 9, 1920, by her friends in the international woman suffrage movement.

tional study conferences. In this function she also played an important role in the organization of the women's petition in favor of disarmament.[10] Eight million signatures were collected for this petition, and its presentation to the secretary-general of the League of Nations was coordinated by Manus. In 1936, at the request of Lord Robert Cecil, she became General Organizing Secretary of the Rassemblement Universel de la Paix, a true effort to unite as many peace organizations from as many countries as possible.

Catt's analysis of the changes within the organization were clearly inadequate, though it is quite understandable that Catt should be confused. She was, in fact, struggling with the very same problem that many others after her have formulated: how, after gaining the vote, could feminism and the women's movement virtually have disappeared?

There are a number of theories. Many believe the cause to be the erosion of the symbolic function of suffrage, which, during the growth of the movement, changed from being a means to being an end. Kraditor writes:

When Mrs. Stanton was in her prime, women had not yet won many of the rights they took for granted by 1900. To her the vote seemed to be a means to acquisition of precisely those rights, to their entrance into professions and graduate schools, to equal guardianship of their children, and so on. Those later suffragists to whom these rights seemed the sum of the equality they desired in the most desirable society imaginable could not visualize the vote as a means because it was virtually the only right they aspired to that they had not yet won. Hence it stood alone and appeared to be the end. [Kraditor 1981, 262]

Freedman (1979) believes the reason behind the disappearance of the women's movement to be the gradual breakup of women's institutions, which she sees as a prerequisite for a powerful women's movement in the public sphere. Some seek a solution to the problem in a redefinition of the terms. Feminism as an ideology identical with suffragism may have died, but feminism as a "world view that ranked gender a primary category of analysis or explanatory factor for understanding the unequal and unjust distribution of power and resources in society" may have survived woman suffrage.[11]

In the letters of this chapter the correspondents often look back on days gone by, and when there are new initiatives, they are surrounded by reminiscences of a common suffrage past. These letters may reflect some of the historiographical problems posed by the period "after woman suffrage."

June 1920–October 1932
Letters 57–72

57. Rosa Manus to Lucy E. Anthony

Genève, June 1920

My dearest Miss Lucy,

I feel I cannot leave Switzerland before sending you a few lines. I am so sorry not to hear from you any more. After our dear Miss Shaw died I have written to you quite often and never had any answer, however I feel you must have been overwhelmed with letters so don't make any excuses please, I quite understand. Well Lucy the Congress was a great success although we all missed dear Lady Shaw very very much. Mrs Catt was as lovely and splendid as ever and everyone adored her. I have been helping her again like usual and I think she quite enjoyed her stepdaughter again. Mrs Catt has invited me to come to New York this winter to stay with her, so I truly hope I shall be able to see you then some time Lucy. We have women of 36 countries so really splendid and women of India Japan Turkey all were there. I am sending you also a picture of the Congress as you will like it I guess. My thoughts so often wonder [wander] to you and I am afraid you must feel very lonely at times. I just thought you should have come over to Geneva, but then it would have been almost too sad for you. Mrs Catt was elected once more as President although she had absolutely made up her mind to resign. However she felt she must lead these two years again and then in Paris where the next Congress will take place we certainly must find another President.

Our evening meetings were a great success and we all think that it made a lot of propaganda for the Swiss men, who after this will perhaps h[e]arten a bit and give their women a vote.

Quite a good many of our old friends were there—Annie Furuhjelm, Fru Quam (oh she was funnier than ever).[1] On the foto you can see the board and also me sitting at the back of the platform, well my usual place. Mrs Corbett Ashby is one of the officers now, and Mrs Rathbone, both Gr. Br. as Mrs Coit and Mrs Fawcett both resigned, then Adele Schreiber from Berlin was elected, Anna Wicksell, Sweden, and Ancona, Italy and Girardet, Lausanne.

It will be quite different for Mrs Catt as she was so accustomed to work with her old staff.

I am spending a few days in Lausanne and visited my old school where I have been for a year—it was so very nice to see all back again. Miss Lucy I do wish you would send me some of the last pictures from Miss Shaw, I saw them at Dr. Jacobs and would love to have them myself too. I am so awfully pleased and proud that Miss Shaw gave me her book herself. I did love her so very much and had so longed to see her again. Well dear Miss Lucy, goodbye, this note is only to show you I think of you very often.

Much love from an old admirer from your Lady Shaw and your friend

Rosa Manus.

1. Marie Quam (1843–1935) was a veteran of the Norwegian suffrage movement, which she helped found in 1898. She was also vice president of the Norwegian Council of Women from 1904 to 1913.

58. Carrie Chapman Catt to Aletta Jacobs

[New York] October 11th, 1920

My dear Dr. Jacobs:–

It was a great pleasure to receive your two letters and to learn about the Congress in Christiania.[1] I will comment on the first one.

I have urged women to go into political parties when their consciences call them in that direction. Many of them are so partisan that they could not do otherwise. I have not myself, however, joined any political party and do not intend to do so at least for the present. I have never advised them not to join parties for if they feel as I do they need no advice.

It was a very great misfortune that the vote came to women in the midst of a very hot campaign full of bitterness, and with no clear-cut issues. The result is that we will find after Election that many women will have left us for their respective parties, without really understanding why we should still remain together for a time. However, if we shall lose some, we will gain others as the women are realizing here, exactly as the Dutch women have already realized, that the women must stand together until they win emancipation as well as enfranchisement.

I believe in Geneva that all the women had a feeling of this sort, but some way the work to be done was so indefinite that we did not know how to get together and to formulate a program. Perhaps we did all we should expect–to come together and talk things over as friends. Perhaps next time we will do a better job, I hope so.

Many thanks for news of the Christiania Congress.

I agree with you that it is the task of women to save the world from the results of this terrible man-made war, but I am sure I do not know how to go at it. You are nearer to the problem than are we, and when you learn what is to be done you must let us know.

Mme. Chaponnière-Chaix[2] is too old and too timid to be the president of a very live society. I can see plenty of work for the Alliance to do, but somehow I do not feel the same interest to take hold of it that once I did. I am tired and want a chance to rest. I am vexed to find myself president again. It needed someone with more energy than I seemed to possess. We really ought to go hot and fast after those Spanish countries and wake the women up to demand their rights.

Yes, I think Rosa will come over but I do not know whether she will meet me in London where I go for an International Board meeting the middle of November, or whether she will come later. It will be a pleasure to have her here.

I will send your letter to Ida Husted Harper for she will be tremendously interested to learn all you have said about the Congress in Christiania. She has always been so interested in the Council.

Thanking you again for your two letters and promising you a better letter when our Election is over

I am, lovingly yours,

Carrie Chapman Catt,

President.

1. The first postwar ICW congress took place in Christiania (Oslo).

2. P. Chaponnière-Chaix (1850–1934) was cofounder of the Swiss Council of Women. From 1920 until 1922 she was president of the ICW. See WWT.

59. Clara Hyde to Rosa Manus

[New York] Sept. 29th, 1922

Dear Rosa,

I just have time for a hasty line by the s/s Rotterdam leaving to-morrow. It is already five o'clock, and Mrs. Catt has just come into the office from the farm, which has finally been closed, good-byes said, tears shed and the last chapter there closed. We have to go over a lot of things late as it is, so as explained I can only just barely say a word. The principal thing I want to tell you is that I have sent off by parcel post by the Rotterdam a package containing the Corona typewriter ribbon (blue) also paper and envelop[e]s to fit the machine. Then I have sent you three dozen pencils–the kind Mrs. Catt likes best. Also I have enclosed as many press photographs as I could lay my hands on. I have not been able to get any press material at all, either French, German or English. If there is a moment which I can devote to it next week, I shall do it and send by the same steamer that takes Mrs. Catt to Italy, or by a later steamer to some other point where I know you will be. I am not bothering Mrs. Catt to take anything at all to you. She has so many packages already that she is most frantic. She and Mollie are now at the Hotel McAlpin, where the Chief will remain until she sails Saturday.

Well, Rosa dear, I know you will enjoy being with your adored one

and will take the best of care of her. The Chief calls me—so a hasty goodbye.

Lovingly,

[Clara Hyde][1]

1. Clara Hyde was Catt's secretary.

60. Rosa Manus to Clara Hyde

Rome, Italy, April 28, 1923

Dearest Clara:—

At this moment CCC is rearranging her speech (Presidents Address at
IWSA Congress) and an expert typist is getting it ready for her and I have
a few minutes free. ——Well, we landed in Havre in due time and got into
Paris. Then we raced round like anything to get our clothes into shape in
a week. As I had splendid addresses from very good friends who live there,
we really managed beautifully, altho everywhere we went they told us blue
was not the fashion. We managed to have five hats with blue for the Chief,
three blue dresses, and everything is very satisfactory. She is as proud as a
peacock and can hardly wait to get on her new things. My mother and
father, who could not wait any longer, came to spend a week with us in
Paris. They came in the Pearce-Arrow,[1] and that was a great delight. Father
took us to the finest restaurants to lunch and dinner, and CCC loved it and
enjoyed the delicious food so much, especially as she had a cavalier to pay
the bills.

One evening we took her to the Casino de Paris, a most shocking real
Paris Veau de ville [vaudeville] with a quantity of naked women. She had
never seen anything like that, and I think it was good for her education.
In the meantime, we worked hard at the correspondence of the Alliance,
which poured in.

On Monday 23rd we arrived in a beautiful train de luxe here and have
been very busy. The Headquarters have not done anything, nor for the program nor for the Amendments, so the Chief had to start from the beginning. She is working like Hell.

However she is in very good health, looks very well and feels so happy
at the idea she will soon be released from it, but in her heart I think she
will feel it dreadfully, as after all the whole Alliance is Mrs. Catt, and no
one else feels the spirit and knows all about it. Everybody is in despair,

and they do not know who to have. Mme. Schlumberger[2] wants to be it, but she is really impossible, <u>too</u> <u>old</u>, <u>too</u> <u>slow</u>, <u>too</u> <u>French</u>.

Altho it was first planned Mrs. Catt should come home with me for a week and then sail from Holland, she now decided to take the Berengaria, (former Imperator) on the 26th and will be home the 1st of June.

May 5. Altho I would have loved to cuddle her up for a week at our lovely country home in Holland, I can quite imagine the Chief is so longing to get home to her dear farm, her dear friends, that I try not to be disappointed. I have had her for 8 lovely months, and I ought to be grateful. Well, Clara, you know I am. Every moment has been a delight for me, and I think the Chief does not regret too much having had me. We really have had such a good time, have laughed—laughed sometimes dreadfully. She looks so happy and well, and I do hope she will return looking as she does now,—if the Congress wont take it all out again.

She cant stand quite as much as formerly and gets sooner tired after a hard days work. However, then we have nice little dinners up in our sittingroom, and we are quite happy.

The Congress will be very well attended. Bertha Lutz is on her way as Govt. Delegate! Tonight the Chief and I are going to see Mussolini. Yesterday, historic pictures have been made of her with the Collos[s]eum in the background, the Arc[h] of Titus, etc. They are splendid. You shall have one, Clara, and so will Mary Peck. In Paris, I had ripping fotos made of her, and do hope you will like them. I ordered quite a good deal. This week I at last got your press pictures, you sent me in Sept., so I use them here.

Thanks again for all your letters, dearest Clara, I enjoy every bit of them and so does CCC. We now talk about our next trip, she seems so full of pep and so do I. Do write to me when you have seen her, and tell me what you think of her. She bought heaps of paintings and fotos to be framed for the farm. I will send this letter off now, as otherwise it may never go. I am so busy, but love the work.

Good bye, dear girl. I wish you were coming.

My love for always,

Your Dutchie

1. The Pearce-Arrow was a limousine. See Peck 1944, 390.

2. Marguérite de Witt-Schlumberger (1856–1924) was a social feminist and, from 1914, chairman of the Union Française pour le Suffrage des Femmes (UFSF; French Woman Suffrage Association). She was the French delegate to this congress and was one of the vice presidents until her death. See Hause with Kenney 1984.

Rosa Manus with Catt in a horse-drawn tram in Santiago, Chile, 1923.

Aboard the Little Venezuela.

Aboard the Little Venezuela.

At home again in Baarn, 1923. Left to right: *Rosa Manus with Carmen, Henry, and Egon, her small niece and nephews.*

From Rosa Manus' picture album, 1923: Margery Corbett Ashby.

Margery Corbett Ashby, her son Michael, Carrie Chapman Catt, and two unidentified men.

Carrie Chapman Catt and Rosa Manus at the Forum, 1923.

61. Aletta Jacobs to Miel Coops-Broese van Groenou[1]

[Rome] May 18, 1923

Dear Miel,

I should have written before but I know you understand that Congresses leave very little time for correspondence. We are attending meetings, committees, teas, etc., from nine in the morning until late at night. Tomorrow we start at 8:30. Our whole days are spent speaking in various languages about numerous subjects.

The women from the Orient are speaking this evening. There are four from Egypt, eight from the British Indies, women from Japan and China, Peru, Chile, Brazil, Argentina, etc. A total of forty-three countries is represented. I am exhausted and didn't go this evening, so I'm using some of the time to write to you.

I am hoping to get to bed, for once, by ten o'clock.

Jerusalem is now also represented by Mrs. Dr. Welt Strauss.[2]

I've been meeting many old friends from all over the world. Even those whom I thought had long passed on are as energetic as ever. The old guard is proving to be infinitely more vigorous and progressive than our followers. We are often shocked to see how their dedication to the cause in no way matches ours—such as working without vanity for an ideal and not thinking of personal gain. This morning Catt said, "If only I could make the old guard twenty years younger, together we could restore order, peace, and prosperity in the world. But we are too old, and the young lack energy and devotion." And she is right!

Poor Mien hasn't seen much of the Congress. She arrived last Sunday evening still suffering from her old ailment and hoping to conquer it. She attended the opening on Monday morning but by the afternoon wasn't feeling well and spent the rest of the week in bed. It's the usual trouble, but bad enough. She left her bed for the first time this afternoon and accompanied me to the Capitol, where we were received by the mayor and the local authorities. It was splendid. But on the way home Mien began to feel unwell. Luckily, Richard[3] has arrived, so they will be able to decide what to do. She would be better going home than spending all her time in a hotel bedroom. Catt has stepped down and appointed Mrs. Corbett Ashby as our president. However, her fellow board members are not very able. It is too bad!

You will be interested to know that the French delegation has urged that many of us return via Paris. A peace rally is to be held on May 25 at the Sorbonne, with speakers from many countries. The delegation asked us to speak out as freely as we would in other countries. They assured us that half of France and almost half of Paris condemns the policy of the French government, but that they alone will not be able to bring about a change. So I shall be returning via Paris and will stay at the Hotel des Saints Pères, rue des Sts. Pères. The French ladies will make the arrangements. I expect Mien has written to you about Mussolini. He imitates Napoleon in all his movements, and looks like him, too. Early tomorrow we will be marching to hand over to him a conference resolution. Carrying banners and wearing our friendliest faces, we shall march through Rome. The general attitude here is that enfranchised women belong to the third sex. This will be the first lesson in street propaganda for the Italian women. Mussolini has asked that we present ourselves to him. This should take a couple of hours.

The weather is reasonable, dry and cold. Many are walking around in fur coats, which are necessary, but a warm cloth coat is quite adequate. I won't start a new page; I'll go to bed now. Would you pass on my regards to your family and all dear friends in the Parkweg? I don't have time to write, and a postcard says so little.

The Mondinis[4] were so kind and extremely helpful. They were hoping I would visit them on the way home, but now I'm going to Paris I shall not be able to.

Give Letteke a big kiss from me.[5] I know you are greatly inspired by what we are doing here, so I shall do my best to remember everything and tell you all about it.

Affectionately yours,

Aletta

1. Printed by permission of W. E. S. Coops, one of Miel Coops' three daughters. Published earlier by De Wilde, 1984b.

2. A Jewish Women's Society of Palestine was formed and entered the IWSA in Rome. Rosa Welt Strauss was delegate.

3. Richard van Wulfften Palthe was Mien's husband.

4. A couple from Milan whom Miel knew from her student days. De Wilde 1984b, 37.

5. Letteke (born in 1920) was Miel Coops' youngest daughter and Aletta Jacobs' godchild.

62. Rosa Manus to Carrie Chapman Catt

Baarn, June 22nd, 1926

My dearest Mother Catt,

I am actually home again since a few days and my very first duty is to write you an explaining letter about the doings and the goings on of the congress.[1] How I am to begin and how I am to end I don't dare to think of at present.

My short little note which I gave to Miss Sherwin[2] to hand to you with the watch sent to you with love and gratitude of the delegates from the Paris congress, as well as the Paris hat will have come into your hands I hope and will have given you some pleasure. Miss Sherwin will have told you much about the congress.

There were some very nice french women on the committee who were very charming indeed. They gave dinners and teas and lunches no end and I don't think that ever the delegates had so many invitations in private houses as this time. I am proud to say that never in all those weeks there was one quarrel or one struggle with them. We parted as the best of friends, both appreciating each other. I also managed never to loose my temper. I suppose now I grow older this is not so difficult for me.

The evening meetings were an enormous success, crowded and crowded every evening. To think that in our Sorbonne we could have 5000 people and that large Trocadero peacemeeting was filled untill the very last seat! But oh Mother Catt, I never missed you so much in my whole life as that peace-evening. There was really not one speech worth mentioning. There was no impression made at all and instead of stirring up the people and feeling that we could get hold of somebody, I felt absolutely as if I was left in the cold. Your message who [which] was really so wonderful and which I read and reread many times myself, was read by one of the american delegates who made nothing of it, so that I felt ashamed and wished they would have let me read the message, as I felt positively that I could have given it in the way you sent it. However I am almost sorry to say that the meeting was an enormous success and that it was a kind of spectacular performance what the french liked. What made me more mad still was that at the table on the huge platform was seated Mrs. Ashby from the board only, as we had got the message from the french committee that there was no room to put all the other boardmembers on the platform and they gave us a seat in some box far away. But there was room to put at that very same table THE MARCHIONESS OF ABERDEEN AND TEMAIR, MADAME AVRIL DE ST. CROIX AND MISS LOUKY VAN EEGHEN!!!! WHAT DO YOU THINK OF THIS![3] Can you understand my rage? Margery that evening made a very innocent little speech.

Let me tell you a funny little thing that happened one afternoon in our congress meeting. The Marchioness was sitting on the platform behind the board wrigged out in one of her beautiful get-ups, a dress with chiffon, silver and lace, long white gloves and on the top of her lightcoloured wig was seated a tremendous black chiffon hat, the form of a pan-cake and in three corners a big blue plume sticking out. Unluckily after 10 minutes she dozed away and the plumes said "yes" to one side and "no" at the other side and allmost wig and hat dropped off. It was too funny to look at. This is not all however. At the end of the afternoon meeting we went out into the street and somy [some] lady came up to Mme Malaterre[4] and asked her the address of her mill[i]ner. A journalist who was just passing and who overheard the conversation said: "Madam do you also want the name of the mill[i]ner of the lady who was asleep at the platform this afternoon?" In the middle of the afternoon messages were sent up by the pages asking the name of the lady who was asleep at the platform. Surely this was the most amusing incident of the congress. I am sure you will appreciate this and I can see the naughty twinkle in your eyes when you read it. Luckily for us the Marchioness called her boardmeeting for the council simultaneously with the congress, so the council people could never be with us, which was rather fortunate, but I do think it was a mean trick of them to do it. The best joke of all was that the last afternoon Lady Aberdeen sent in a letter to Mrs. Ashby of about ten pages telling her that the Alliance had no right at all to call a peace meeting and to have an afternoon speaker for the League of Nations. When people get to that stage they had better stay at home, I think!

The official receptions were grander than anywhere else. Surely the french do know how to receive. It was absolutely in the South-American style. Ovations, flowers, etc., etc. And the buildings in Paris are all so beautiful that it is quite a treat to be shown through. Not only the "Maire" received us officially and gave out one thousand invitations for a teaparty, but also the Senat received officially and gave champaign and flowers. When going out Plamínková[5] in her witty way said to the president: "We thank you for your nice reception, we thank you for the flowers and the champaign and the postal cards, if only now you would give your women the vote, we should be perfectly satisfied."

The congress proceedings in general went peacefully and happily. We were able to keep up to the program and there was no unfinished business. I am only afraid that at times the "chair" did not always know what was to be voted and I think sometimes a resolution was voted down one day and voted up another day.

The British delegation behaved most uncourteous to their British president and did all they could to go against everything. Macmillan was more in a position than ever and she and Mrs. Abbott were dreadful.

I am afraid the Shuler-family[6] was not very satisfied either with the American delegation. Mrs. Shuler wanted to have been in the delegation and she had much to say about the delegates. I suppose one day they will come and tell you something about it. Mrs Paige was very sweet and charming. She even came to pay a short visit here in Baarn and I think she will tell you herself about it.

I am so pleased that Ruth Morgan[7] is actually elected on the board. I took a lot of trouble in telling the delegates what a wonderful woman she is. But of course it is always difficult to get someone elected who is not in the delegation. So therefore I am double proud we succeeded. She has also been made the president of the peace committee and I have been made secretary of her committee, as the board thought I could be of some use to her in Europe and always come in direct contact with her as soon as she comes. I do hope Mother Catt that you will give some direction to that essential committee, as your views on that point are the only right ones.

It is our intention to go to Geneva in September to be present at the Assembly[8] and we should hold the boardmeeting at that time. Mrs. Ashby and Miss Sterling[9] were wondering if you could not come over. Surely that would not be half as fatiguing as a congress and I am sure that would be wellworth for yourself to do it. Think it over and let me know. Then I will see for rooms.

The board of 21 consists of 17 countries. There are some wonderful elements in it. Miss Walin from Sweden seems a very good choice. I am one of the vice-presidents now and I wonder if you approve of it.

Well my dear I think I had better stop to-day as I am afraid there won't be even time in between your garden duties to read this congress "story". Of course I worked very very hard all the weeks in Paris. I always got up at 6 o'clock and started work and as Paris meetings and parties never finish untill after midnight, I never was in bed till after one o'clock. However I managed to keep going and not to look or act tired.

On the platform I missed you every minute and will never get used to have [having] a congress without you. I found all the nice parcels you sent. The corsets are quite allright and so is everything else. The dear gloves with the frills are perfectly charming and I thank you very much. Now to business, please. Will you send me a bill for all you spent? Then I shall send you a cheque in return. Thank you again for all the trouble I gave you.

The dogwood trees are really growing!

Aletta was not able to come to the congress. She had been ill again. It was a great pity she was not there. Many of your old friends like Signe Bergman and Mrs. Coit were so disappointed you were not there.

Please send me a line in return and say if you are satisfied with your stepdaughter.

who sends you love and lots of it,

Rosa

1. Rosa had attended the IWSA's tenth congress in Paris.

2. Belle Sherwin, one of the American delegates, was until 1924 president of the National League of Women Voters, the successor to the NAWSA. See NAW.

3. Ishbel Marjoribanks, Marchioness of Aberdeen and Temair, better known as Lady Aberdeen (1875–1939), was president of the ICW from 1893 to 1936, with exception of the years 1899–1904 and 1920–22. See WWT.

Ghenia Avril de Sainte-Croix (1855), a Frenchwoman, was present in 1888 at the founding of the ICW in Washington. For years she was chairman of the ICW committee on the White Slave Trade (Commission of the ICW for the Up-lifting of Morality and against White Trade). In 1926 the Joint Committee appointed her its delegate to the League of Nations. See WWT.

The Dutchwoman Louise Cathérine Antoinette (Louky) van Eeghen (1884) had been on the ICW Board since 1920. She knew Rosa from the organization committee of the exhibition *Woman, 1813–1913*. See WWT.

4. The Frenchwoman Germaine Malaterre-Sellier (1889) had been active in the women's movement since 1920 and was vice president of the Alliance. During the thirties she was the French delegate to the League of Nations.

5. Františka F. Plamínková (1875–1943), a Czech, had been active from the beginning of the century in the women's movement. Jacobs and Catt met her while traveling through Central Europe in 1906. From the founding of the independent state of Czechoslovakia at the Peace Conference in Versailles, Plamínková played a prominent role in national politics. She sat on the Prague city council and later in the Senate. From 1925 she was vice president of the ICW, and in the thirties she was appointed delegate to the League of Nations. See Kern 1930; WWT.

6. Probably Nettie Rogers Shuler (1862–1939), a suffrage activist, and her daughter Marjorie. With Catt, Nettie Shuler wrote *Woman Suffrage and Politics*. She also played a role in the Woman Suffrage Party. See NAW.

7. The American Ruth Morgan and Rosa Manus were the driving force behind the International Committee for Peace and the League of Nations of the Alliance, which was founded in Paris. The committee organized important study conferences, the first in 1927 in Amsterdam. Catt attended. In 1932 Ruth Morgan succeeded Catt as chairman of Cause and Cure of War. She died in 1934.

8. The Assembly is the General Assembly of the League of Nations. At the suggestion of the Swiss board member Emilie Gourd, each year when the League Assembly was in session, a temporary Alliance office was opened in her home in Geneva to facilitate more direct contact with League delegates. Schreiber and Mathieson 1955, 38.

9. Frances M. Sterling, who was from Great Britain, was treasurer to the Alliance.

63. Rosa Manus to Lucy E. Anthony

Baarn, 15 November 1926

My dearest Lucy,

Your letter send to Dr. Jacobs was also send to me and I was very pleased to read its contents. What a delightful plan that Mrs. Harper is writing an other volume about Dr. Shaw and how very nice that Caroline Reilly is helping you.[1] I wish I were near, as I would love to say some special wonderful things which are in my mind about Miss Shaw in the International Congresses. I shall never forget how in Buda-Pest and Stockholm she got up in the American deligation and explained matters with her clear ringing voice helping to solve and save the situation.

I have myself too a bundle of letters of Miss Shaw and it is my intention to look them through and see if there is anything which would be well worth printing. Miss Shaws visit to the "Exhabition of Woman" in Amsterdam in 1913 and her speech given there was more than wonderful. Haven't you got some snapshots too of our trip to Copenhagen? What fun we had!

Well Lucy I think it is wonderful that you are doing this work and please note me down for one of the first volumes coming from the press and I shall send you a check by return when I know how much it is.

I can imagine what a lovely time you and Caroline are having, she is such an amusing personality full of spirit. I am only sorry she is not helping Mrs. Catt in her difficult task for the second[2] Conference on the "Cause and Cure of War," and I am wondering who will take her place.

Yes, Lucy you are right in saying that for my love of Mrs. Catt I was inspired to give my very best to the Paris Congress; every minute and every thing I did for it I thought of her and it was dreadful not having her with us, however her watching eye and leadership was still with us.

I suppose you have heard that we erected in the Alliance a Committee on Peace and the League of Nations? Miss Ruth Morgan is President of that Committee and I am the Secretary for Europe.

And Mrs. Catt is the Honorary President of that Committee.

This means that she has given us her full attention.

It really was a wonderful Congress in Paris and I had my hands full as President of the Committee of Arrangements.

I am sorry you did not turn up Lucy, you would have enjoyed it and so many of the old friends came and they all said it was their last visit and they real[l]y came as they thought Mrs. Catt would be there. I am now one of the Vice Presidents of the Alliance, poor Miss Shaw would rejoice in that if she knew it.

Well real[l]y and truly much of my inspiration has come from the dear Lady. Her picture is always before me and gives me strength in different times.

Dr. Jacobs has real[l]y been very ill in spring. She has been doing a cure in Nauheim and came to stay with us in the country for a month. She is much better again.

My parents are still well also growing older. The grandchildren are a delight to us all, some of them turning out good specimen[s].

Mia Boissevain, who has two adopted girls lives at the sea-side place. We do not see so much of each other, but when we are together we are the real old friends and enjoy each others company.

Well Lucy I hope you don't mind this gossip. Give my love to Mrs. Harper and to Caroline. We shall all meet one day again.

With much love,

from Rosa.

1. As far as we know this volume was never published. Caroline I. Reilly was head of the library of the National League of Women Voters (formerly the NAWSA).

2. This was the third gathering. Since its founding in 1925, a Cause and Cure conference had been held each January.

64. Aletta Jacobs to Lucy E. Anthony

Den Haag, 21 July 1928

My dear Lucy,

You do not know how glad I was this morning after I found your letter on my breakfast-table. In years I have not heard of you. All my letters, postcards, informations remained unanswered and no one could tell me where you was, or in Moylan or somewhere else.

Now at last there came a letter in the nice old style of Lucy out of Moylan. And now I am going to answer it at once before you will go away or that I loose track of you.

In 1926 I was looking out for you and longing to see you, because I was very ill and could not go to the Conference in Paris, where I surely thought you should come to. I was ill for months. At last my doctor sent me to Nauheim to a Sanatorium. The first women I met there were the two sisters McMurtrie from Philadelphia by which I slept for a night the day I had to speak in the Business and Professional women's club. We remained there 6 weeks together. Did you ever me[e]t them afterwards[?] I gave them a message for you.

Yes I am following the political situation in U.S.A. closely. I have here an American relation living in the same street as I live, they read the newspapers of U.S.A. and sent them to me. Besides I read the Nation of Oswald Villard,[1] the Woman Citizen,[2] the Birth Control Review, and I never receive a letter of one of my American friends who does not send me some interesting press-clippings, and it is now the time that the Americans come to Holland and nearly daily I receive a visit from one or another American friend.

I envy your visit to Californië. It is the part of the world where I should like to live and to die. I know there were some of the Anthony-relations living there, because my husband and I we met there some of them in 1904.

You wish to know how I feel about the multilateral peace-treaty of your government.[3] I do not think anything of it. A State Department what declares war for a crime, and in the same time sends troops to Nicaragua to kill the people there,[4] who fight for their freedom, a government which let[s] every boy drill to become a soldier, a country that does not disarm, but have an army and a navy bigger than ever before, such a government is not serious when it declares war as a crime. Let them show us deeds, then we can believe its words.

The disarmament-question in the League of Nations is the same. One country does not trust the other and only to satisfy the people of the different countries they appoint a committee for internat. disarmament but they never come to one deed. Talks, talks, and nothing else.

You know of course that Mrs. Catt is going to celebrate her 70th birthday the 9th of Januari next. Rosa Manus is coming over for the celebration and to bring her the presents of the women of Europe. Rosa is now travelling with a niece of 14 and a nephew of 13 in Switzerland and will return in the beginning of August. As soon as she returns she will come to see me and then I shall give her your love and greetings.

Will it now be sure you are coming to Europe the next winter? Let me know it as soon as you have decided. It is possible we could meet then somewhere in the South of France or in Spain. I do not like to go to Italy under the Mussolini system. That is too dangerous.

I was very much interested in the meeting you have had in your house in Moylan and in the photograph you sent me from the garden. I shall show our friends the trees of Holland in it. Mia Boissevain who lived for 3 years with her two children in the mountains of Switzerland is now living here again. She shall be interested in it.

How Rosika Schwimmer always finds a way to propagate her person and her name. In that way she is the real journaliste. I hope for her that she will receive the 17000 dollars that man Marvin[5] has to pay her, than [then] perhaps her international beggary will take an end.

I feel sure she shall try to play a role in the celebration of Mrs. Catt. She will find a way again to bind her name again together with the names of all well-known people of the world.

What is Mrs. Harper doing now, and where is she living[?] About my self I can not tell you much in a letter. You must come and we must talk together. But that is sure I am going to sell my house and my belongings and than [then] I will become the wandering Jewess, perhaps a tramp. But it is possible that I shall die before it is so far. One does not know.

Now, dear Lucy, will you promise me to write me soon again. I love you very much and ought [not] to remain for months and months without news about you. Have I done something wrong that that was the reason of your long silence? Tell me, because than it must have been a mistake and I shall apologize.

Lovingly yours

Aletta H. Jacobs

1. Oswald Garrison Villard was well known in the suffrage movement. In 1905 Anna Howard Shaw had asked him to organize a male league, which was founded in due course.

2. In June 1917, the Leslie Commission purchased the already historic *Woman's Journal.* Merged with other publications, it has since appeared under the name *The Woman Citizen.*

3. This refers to the Kellogg-Briand pact, the agreement between the French foreign minister Aristide Briand and the American secretary of state Frank B. Kellogg to outlaw war. Catt was enthusiastic about "this remarkable proposal to the American people" (Van Voris 1987, 206).

4. Between 1900 and 1933 the Monroe doctrine legitimated twenty-five United States military interventions in Latin America, including the two-year occupation in Nicaragua.

5. Fred R. Marvin, an important blacklister, had charged Rosika with being a German spy. She won charges brought against him for libel. See Wynner 1974.

65. Aletta Jacobs to Carrie Chapman Catt

Den Haag, 23 Oct. 1928
Tobias Asserlaan 5

My dear friend,

Your kind letter of Sept. 20th came to me when I was staying in the hospitable home of the family Manus in Baarn. I was glad to hear from you directly how sudden but how enviable Miss Hay died. It is good you survive her. You can [do] better without her than she without you.

But it makes me feel unhappy to know that you do not feel well and that already for a long time. What is the matter? I know you have a weak heart but that did never prevent you from doing more work than a strong, healthy man could do and you never complained of it. Can it be that your nerves are shocked and you will feel better after a while? It is a comfort for me to know that Rosa is soon leaving Holland to go to you. I feel sure she will bring the necessary sunshine and comfort in your house and in your heart which is needed for your health and happiness.

Of course the first thing you have to do is to make everything ready and to write down all your wishes what people have to do after you have passed away. I did it sometime ago. That will comfort you after you have done it. At least I felt that.

Since 3 weeks I am now in my new home[1] and I feel at present perfectly happy. I take the meals together with the family and only when I feel tired or if there are some guests I do not care to meet one of the servants serves me in my room.

My room is a very comfortable, large, sunny room, with [which] allows a beautiful view on [of] large trees on two sides of the room. Especially now the trees are in their fall-colours, all red and gold. After what I have gone through I feel now as if I am in heaven.

Rosa is in Germany now. She has developed in[to] an extremely useful member of the different boards she belongs to. There are of course certain things she can not do, but then there is easily someone found who is willing to take that work over. But Rosa possesses qualities no one has and it are these peculiar qualities which are of great value in at least one of the members of a board.

The question . . . if W.S. was worth the fight we made for it . . . is often asked me, just as someone did you.

People who ask that are blind for the great change in the world after we have got it. Since ten years ago women are beginning to play a rôle in the building of a new world and men are beginning to look to women more as comrades than as a creature only for their pleasure.

I feel happy that I have seen the 3 great objects of my life come into fulfilment during my life and that I see the great value of it for a happy woman['s] life.

They were: the opening for women of all opportunities to study and to bring it into practice; to make Motherhood a question of desire, no more a duty; and the political equality for women.

With these three newly obtained rights the women are able to get their full legal, social and econ. equality easily if they really wish it. And I feel it every day more, it will not take a long time before the women of the world have reached that goal. No, my dear Carrie, I feel sure we have not lived for nothing. We have done our task and we can leave the world with the conviction that we have left it in a better condition than we have found it.

As soon as Rosa is with you I hope to hear from you both and that you can send me good news about your health and your comfortable feelings. I feel sure both of us will pass away one day or another on the same quiet way as our friend Molly did.

But you ought not to remain alone in your house. Someone of your long list of good friends ought always to be with you to share your daily life in summer as well as in winter.

I love you and I have admired you from the first day I have met you and I know you deserve to be happy.

With many kisses

Yours

Aletta H. Jacobs.

1. Jacobs spent the last year of her life in the home of her friend Mien van Wulfften Palthe-Broese van Groenou.

66. Aletta Jacobs to Carrie Chapman Catt

's-Gravenhage, May 28th 1929

My dear Carrie,

I was staying in Baarn with the Manus-family during the Whitsunday-week when your letter arrived in which you gave the sad news that you could not come to Berlin in June.

After what Rosa had told me before concerning your health I had doubted already that your doctor would allow you to go. All the emotions and fatigues such a Conference brings with it must be too much for you just now.

However it was a great desillusion to me not to see you again and for all the women who will attend the meeting the great charm of the Conference will have gone.

You know of course that Rosa is again in Berlin to help the women there organising the meeting and to take care that the Congress will be received in a good way by the author[it]ative men and women of the country.

The German women are good organisers themselves but German women always quarrel when they have to work together. Rosa must now be the tie to keep them quietly together to fulfill their task.

It is certainly very wise of you to stay this summer at home and to arrange your business so that you feel quite at ease if something might happen. If that is done you will feel much more calm and can give the coming years of your life to the work you like.

Now, after you have passed the 70, you will soon feel that your muscular force has lost a great deal but that your brain power kept its full strength. And that is what you will need mostly for the coming work.

Rosa told me of the beautiful house you are now living in and that you have a nice lady-companion.[1] I hope you never will feel lonely.

One of the consequences of you[r] not coming to Berlin is the fact that now Clara Hyde and Mary Peck do not come. That is a great disappointment too. I felt so glad to meet them again. Will you give both my love.

I hope to be able to go to Berlin and if Mrs. Palthe is not kept at home by illness of her old mother she is accompanying me. I feel quite happy here in her family-circle, enjoying family-life and full freedom in my rooms.

My social work is now not much more than to give the younger generation advise [advice] in their feministic and peace work. Here in Holland we have now roused in every town a large group of young women who are interested in our work and who are fully convinced that they ought to continue our work will they not loose again the freedom we have gained for them. It were these young, clever, enthousiastic women who have put a stone in the house in the Tesselschade straat in Amsterdam, (which was built by me and my husband), on which is engraved that I have lived and worked

IWSA board members relax. Berlin, 1929. Left to right: *Kathleen Bompas, Margery Corbett Ashby, Anna Jacobi-Manus (?), Rosa Manus, Frances Sterling.*

The old guard. Berlin, 1929. Left to right: *Lida Gustava Heymann, Aletta Jacobs, unidentified, Annie Furuhjelm, unidentified, Helene Lange.*

there and that the generations to come might not forget what I have done for them. They did it on March 8, when it was 50 years ago that I as the first woman doctor in Holland took my degree at the University of Groningen.

Such a thing does not mean much in U.S.A. because the houses in your country often do not last many years, but in Holland it means more where the houses are mostly built for centuries and where such a ceremony most times only takes place after the death of the person.

I feel sure that the young group of women I got to take up our task shall not be satisfied before they have brought the world a good deal farther in the direction of full equality between the sexes and peace among the nations and the sexes.

Rosa is a strong pushing-power under the younger generation. She knows what she is able to do and what not and she leaves the things she does not understand to others.

I hope, my dearest friend, you will soon find your strength again and feel that there is still something to do for you in the world and although we both are willing and ready to die at the moment we can still make something of our old days and need not to feel as if we are living a parasite life.

If I die conscious it will be with a kind thought for you upon my lips.

Wholeheartedly yours,

Aletta H. Jacobs.

1. This is Alda Wilson, an architect. After Hay's death she went to live with Catt.

67. Carrie Chapman Catt to Rosa Manus

[New Rochelle] July 19, 1929

My dear Rosa:

I have a dim recollection of having started a long letter to you by hand and that I never completed it. I, therefore, do not quite remember where my end of the correspondence ought to begin. I do know that I thought while you were in Berlin I would not bother you with letters about things that would only turn your mind from the duties at hand. I, therefore, do not know whether I have thanked you in proper terms for the beautiful little coat you sent me and for my cheese long ago devoured. The little coat will last me a long time and is a most useful garment in a climate so changeable as ours.

I have also received a book-rack by mail and then yesterday Mrs. Slade[1] handed to me the big package of night gowns, kimono and bed shoes. It is a perfect trousseau. I am now prepared to have a long spell of sickness or to get married and go away on a honeymoon. I noticed with great pleasure the especial arrangements on the night gowns for permitting the doctor to examine a badly behaving heart. Now, Rosa dear, I am provided with night gowns to the very end of my life so check that off your list. You have provided your step-mother with that necessity of life and you need think of it no more. The bed shoes are delightful and my cousin who is now here is about to knit some like them for all her friends at Christmas. I cannot thank you enough for this wonderful gift. It would be foolish for me to say that I do not like it for it just fits into my needs. Now, however, being supplied, I want to tell you that I have not another need in the whole world. This must be the last present you ever send me because I have no need for anything more. I have a good many things I do not need. I do not want any more things that I cannot use so please be guided by this instruction. You are a most generous and dear girl but now you must turn your attention to somebody else who is in need of presents because I am not. In nearly every direction I turn in the house I see something that you have given me and my cousin asks concerning each new thing, "Did Rosa give you that?"

I have this morning received the bill for the flags and we hasten to send you an international draught for $47.32. I will make this $4. bigger and that extra $4. is to pay for the waffle pitcher.

It was quite right to pay for the yellow dresses and everybody says the picture was most beautiful.

I have seen several of the persons who were present in Berlin and I have heard from others and everyone tells me how wonderful you were and how splendidly the Congress was arranged. I think by and by you will forget the disagreeable moments and only remember what a fine Congress it has been. They all tell me that it was the best Congress ever held and that the Alliance shows a permanence never manifest before. I am very, very glad.

Now, concerning myself, let me say to my stepdaughter that I am very much better for not having gone to Berlin. They all say it was a fatiguing experience whereas I had a fairly restful time at home. More, I have accomplished a great deal of work in clearing up my accumulated work which would have piled still higher had I gone to Berlin. I am feeling pretty well now and am taking no medicine and am not going to see the doctor. I do not know how long this good record will last. I do not mean to say that I am quite as well and able to do things as I was a few years ago but I am certainly better than I was last summer and a great deal better than I was last winter.

My cousin, Helen, is here now. Miss Wilson is going to take a little business trip to Iowa for three or four weeks. Mary Peck now lives in New

Rochelle and pays us a call every day. We, therefore, have a very good time reading in the evenings and that is a good preparation for sleep at night.

Very lovingly, and with love to all the family, I am

Yours,

[Carrie Chapman Catt]

1. F. Louis Slade was present in Berlin as a member of the Leslie Suffrage Commission.

68. Carrie Chapman Catt to Rosa Manus

[New Rochelle] September 18, 1931

Dear Rosa:

I have a cable from Miss Schain,[1] saying that the Ad Hoc Committee[2] got itself organized; that Miss Dingman is Chairman, and you are Secretary. Of course I do not yet know what the Committee is to do and probably I will not know until those two girls of ours return. They will arrive in New York on the 21st and I am now trying to find a day when the two of them can meet with me and two or three others, so that we may hear what they have to say. Very soon, therefore, I shall hear what you are up to.

I am terribly sorry to hear that Mrs. Ashby is so ill. Perhaps she will surprise everybody by coming through it faster than they think. If you write to her, will you be so kind as to give her my love and sympathy and tell her I am grieved, indeed, to learn that she is ill. Tell her not to worry about it as I am sure she will be all right again. She is young and optimistic and both are qual-[i]ties which lead to rapid recovery. Tell her I am not writing to her, because I learn that mail is not acceptable in the estimate of the doctor.

I hope, dear Rosa, that you are sufficiently recovered to carry on your work in Geneva as you want to do it. When I think of the little Dutch girl who sat in the hall by the side of a blackboard in the beginning of this century and looked so cute as she took the names of the delegates who wanted to go on excursions, and I now think of the matronly Miss Manus who is going to manage all the folks who go to Geneva in February, I am proud of her development and I want to say to her that I have the utmost confidence that everything will be done just right.

Most sincerely do I hope that your father and mother are doing well.

Very lovingly,

[Carrie Chapman Catt]

1. Josephine Schain (1886–1972) had been active in the suffrage movement and also in the Henry Street Settlement in New York. In 1925 she assumed the organization of the secretariat of Cause and Cure of War, of which she became chairman after Ruth Morgan's death. She was also chairman of the Peace Committee of the Alliance from 1934 to 1939. Extensive correspondence between her and Rosa Manus is in JS-SSC.

2. The Ad Hoc Committee is the Dingman Committee. See p. 177.

69. Rosa Manus to Carrie Chapman Catt

Geneva, Sunday Jan: 24th 1932

Dearest Mother Carrie: –

Nobody better than you will understand how lonely I feel, sitting in my Hotelroom left all by myself since saturday noon. Everybody here seems to leave work and home to go into the mountains, no secretary available. How many times in your life you have found this same experience in all countries? However I am not complaining as it gave me ample time after a most busy and hectic week to get all my papers in order and getting ready all new things which must be attended to first thing on monday morning. Well since I am in Geneve 10 days to day I have not been idle as you can imagine. I have not left a stone unturned as you told me to and I think at last things look a bit more promising. I have had many talks with people at the secretariat and on friday afternoon Miss Dingman and I had a most sympathetic talk with Sir Eric Drummond.[1] With him were the two secretaries who will serve with Mr Henderson. We explained our wishes and asked for his collaboration. I must say it looked hopeful to us and Sir Eric said that he thought every-thing could be arranged. That of course we must wait for the final decision of the special Conference Committee which will only be named and in action the 3rd or fourth of february. He told us to write an explanative letter to Henderson[2] to find upon his arrival.

It looks as if the women shall be officially received the same day when many other petitions will be offered, but the women apart of course.

They want the petitions brought in and a speech made I think. And then in french and english. Two callers to name the countries and numbers. Well if that we be allowed we must be satisfied. I have been working hard on the program. Took some of your valuable advice. Untill now nobody had time to look at it. I brought it into the meeting of last thursday and showed the "dummy" I had made. They seemed to like it and left it further to me. I am hoping that Miss Courtney[3] who will arrive in a few days will take it up with me.

Oh Mother Carrie it seems so strange to talk about this presentation from the women of the world and then really <u>all</u> the arrangements are left to me. Of course it is flattering in one way that everybody has such confidence in me but I wish I had someone with me to share the responsibilities. Never mind I am all the time thinking that <u>you</u> are with me and when I get a bit discouraged I look at your picture standing near me and I feel better.

I have been making a tremendous card board to count the signatures as they come in. I will show you how. (x–Have been received)

Name of Country	L.P.F. I	L.P.F. II	Alliance III	Cause & Cure IV	Total
Africa	5.912 X		4.031 X		9.943
Albania					
Australia	112.040 X		100.000 X		212.040
Austriche [Austria]		32.750 X			32.750
	117.952	32.750	104.031		[*sic*] <u>454.733</u>

In this way I have made it from the 56 countries actually received in Geneva we have them from 38 countries and many announced to be sent off. I think its this way I will show the final in the program as it is clear for every body.

It is of course very exciting to receive all these parcels and even if from some countries a few signatures have arrived it seems good. Many difficulties are of course arrising, f.i. several societies would like to show the number they have collected but I think this will be too complecated and will not make things easy for those who do not understand the women's organisations. We may however give it on a separate page.

Also if possible the names of the women representing the countries but there again difficulties arrise as for those countries for which we have no women, but we shall put other nationalities in, it is hardly fair to put those names.

No flags will be allowed with the presentation, it must be as simple as possible.

All the petitions will be bound with a green ribbon as this is the color of the Int. Disarmament Com. of the Womens Organizations.[4]

Everybody who will be allowed to come in the hall with us will get from me a green ticket to wear with their name on.

No procession is allowed in Geneva as many other people have asked for processions, the communists etc.–and they are afraid for disturbance. I saw the Pres. of the Council of Geneva and the Chief of Police. However we shall go to the Palais Eyriand with a big garden around. We shall make speeches there have loudspeakers–press–movies etc. The presentation will be probably between the 9th and 13th. I think the 10th as on thursdays in Geneva it is a free afternoon for schools etc.

To the Broadcasting Com. we went but it will be difficult to do this as when 3 o'clock in Geneva it is about 8.30 in New York and earlier still South. We are trying however, and we shall cable.

I am much looking forward to your American women of course. Mrs Ben Hooper[5] I know very well and you may be sure I shall do all I can to help them.

We are planning for a public meeting on febr. 9th and then we shall hope the women delegates to the Conference will speak, also, the representatives of Int. Org.—Thus far we have

Miss Woolly	—U.S.A.
Miss Kydd	—Canada
Mrs Ashby	—Gr. Br.
Mrs Szelagowska	—Poland and probably
Dr. Lüders	—Germany[6]

Mrs Ashby will stay in my Hotel that is why I came here as it is more useful to be near. I wonder where your Am. women will stay. Her[e]by I am sending a picture of the meeting in Amsterdam, which was a tremendous success. Left: your stepdaughter speaker for the Int. Dis. Com. Right: the women standing adopting the resolution and singing the League of Nations Song.

Well my dear dear friend I think this is the last letter before the presentation as I shall be inundated with work. I promise to do my utmost. I [think] it must be a success. I suppose when it is a failure I shall be the one person blamed.

I have just eaten some rolls-and butter in my room. I often pic-nic as it is too expensive to go down to the restaurant always. I wish you were here.

I hope to reach 10 million signatures! and then think that little Holland collected 2 1/2 million in 6 weeks.

I love you dearly as always and your inspiration helps me along these difficult days.

Your only stepdaughter

<u>Rosa</u>

I forget to say that the day before the presentation we shall have tremendous waggons passing through the town with the petitions. This Hotel is next to the Hotel de la Paix where we stayed in 1920. I went twice to the local Com. meeting and really the Genevese women are waking up.

---

1. Sir James Eric Drummond, an Englishman, was the first secretary-general of the League of Nations, 1919–33.

2. Arthur Henderson was an English politician, member of the Labour Party, and minister from 1924 to 1931. In 1932 he presided over the disarmament conference of the League of Nations. In 1934 he was awarded the Nobel Peace Prize.

3. Kathleen D. Courtney (1877–1974) was an English pacifist and chairman of the English section of the WILPF (she attended the 1915 Women's Congress in the Hague), and was a member of the IWSA Peace Committee as well as vice president of the Dingman Committee.

4. The Dingman Committee.

5. Jessie Ben Hooper (1865–1935) took the American women's signatures to Geneva. Until 1920 she was active in the NAWSA, then in the Democratic Party. She was cofounder of Cause and Cure of War and its secretary from 1928 to 1932.

6. There were five women delegates to the conference: Mary Woolley from the United States, Winnifred Kydd from Canada, Margery Corbett Ashby from Great Britain, Anna Szelagowska from Poland, and Paulina Luisi from Uruguay. According to Whittick, Winnifred Kydd resigned from the Alliance board in 1937, a statement that I have not been able to prove or disprove. Paulina Luisi became a member of the board in 1923. Anna Szelagowska, who was also a member of the Polish senate, is mentioned as an officer of the Alliance in 1939. Mary Woolley had no such international experience. She was a long-time president of Mount Holyoke College whom President Hoover appointed as a result of the women's lobby in the United States. (Whittick 1979, 109ff.; Wells 1978, 211ff.; cf. NAW, s.v. "Woolley.")
Marie-Elisabeth Lüders (1878–1966) was a German feminist and a doctor of political science. During World War I she led the Committee of Women's Work in the Department of War. From 1920 to 1932 she was a delegate to the Reichstag for the German Democratic Party. Weiland 1983, 161.

70. Rosika Schwimmer to Carrie Chapman Catt

[New York] May 23, 1932

Mrs Carrie Chapman Catt,

Dear Mrs Catt:
The other day we saw a moving picture in which you spoke about the Woman's Suffrage campaign. We were delighted to see you wore the Hungarian Suffrage brooch, and I just can't refrain from mentioning this pleasure to you.[1] I have the duplicate of this brooch, and it is one of the very few keepsakes that I have of those good old times.
It was grand to see the smile with which you finished your speech. On the other hand, I wonder whether you have seen the whole film and realize that you have been put into the section which is plainly wet propaganda. I am not a dry, as you know, and this is not a denouncement, but I thought it was funny to have you speak in the dry section where Nicholas Murray Butler[2] was also shown with a caption as the Nobel Prize winner, yet made an exclusively anti-prohibition speech!

Excuse this intrusion, but seeing you with the Hungarian brooch just created a mood which I had to express. In memory of old times,

Devotedly,

[Rosika Schwimmer]

1. See letter 40.

2. Nicholas Murray Butler was president of Columbia University and leader of the Carnegie Peace Foundation. In 1931 he received the Nobel Peace Prize, together with Jane Addams.

71. Carrie Chapman Catt to Rosika Schwimmer

New York, June 11, 1932

My dear Rosika,

I was very glad, indeed, to get your letter the other day and I am very sorry to have been so negligent in my reply. You would be surprised to know how my time is frittered away in replying to many nonsensical appeals. I seem to be working all the time and yet nothing I do is very important.

I never go out in the evening and seldom in the daytime. I avoid crowds. I am trying to find out how to be an old lady with dignity. I am more reconciled then [than] I was and probably would be happier if this was a happier world in which I live.

I have often wondered how you and Franciska[1] are getting on. Of course you have had hard luck—everybody has.

Yes, I think a great deal of my Hungarian brooch. It is queer how, when one lives long enough, he feels that he has lived through several different and unrelated lives, and that was one and a very happy one. That was a wonderful, beautiful Congress at Budapest and it must have had a great deal to do with the movement afterwards which gave the vote to so many women. I think you can feel that you contributed a very great deal to the coming of woman suffrage.

None of us think that the enfranchisement of woman has brought any very great change to the world, but it might have been different if we had not had a war. Sometimes, I hope the world will discover that the worst thing about a war is getting over it.

I have not seen the film in which my picture appears and no one had told me that I was hobnobbing with President Butler. He manages to work two causes at the same time. Miss Schain wrote him to express thanks for a good peace speech he had made. In prompt return, he sent her an envelope full of wet literature.

I wonder if some day this summer when you and Franciska feel like having a vacation, you would come out and spend a day with me. I will send you the tickets and tell you how to come. We might gossip much about old times.

Lovingly,

(signed) Carrie Chapman Catt

1. Franciska Schwimmer was Rosika's sister, with whom she went to live in the United States in 1920. She tried to earn a living teaching the piano. See letters in VWP-IAV-IIAV and Coops-IAV-IIAV.

72. Rosa Manus to Carrie Chapman Catt

Baarn, October 5th, 1932

Dearest Mother Carrie:—

It seems such a long time since I saw a letter from you and I am so longing to get one from you again and hear how you spent the summer and who were your guests at Carrielaan.[1] Ruth Morgan writes and says how active you are and how much she enjoys working with you always. So at least I know you are pretty well and that is good to know. Just 10 years ago we were beginning our big trip together through Central Europe and South America. How time has gone and how much has happened since. My good Father who always knew every port when we came and when I found his letter waiting for me. Then the flowers which awaited you and me in Rome and Rio and the happy days I spent with you that trip. Often I sit and recollect some events and as you have always said: no one in the world can take away our remembrances.

That evening in Vienna when you had made a speech and we had to hurry for our train to Praag [Prague] and when the millions of Kronen were not enough to pay for our taxi and luggage. The 100.000 dollar knife!! The room in Lima!! Can you smell it yet? The hanging train of sugarloaf and the little "Venuzuala" ["Venezuela"] with the good food and the mass of passengers. Our arrival in Paris, the buying of clothes; the strike and then the Rome Congress. For me such happy and interesting days will never come back again. Mother Carrie when may I look into your sweet eyes again? I do want to kiss you and tell you how much I love you. But your step-daughter seems to have duties to fullfill.

We are packing up our beautiful Baarn home, it is just heartbreaking and yet I must be firm and never show my feelings.[2] Surely for my dear Mother it is a million times worse. Untill the first of September all the family was with us, then I began at once tyding [tidying] and packing, sorting out and making presents to all who need things. Beds and blankets, cots and sheets, tow[e]ls and serviet[te]s, glasses and dishes, pots and pans. The children and grandchildren had of course the first choice, pictures and armchairs, desks and sofa's are carried away to each of them. And it is quite amusing to see what every one chooses. Rosa makes lists of everything as I want to keep trac[k] where everything goes to. Then of course Mother and I take all we need for our new home but there is such a quantity of a 52 years married life. Then so many sheets and tow[e]ls when the family were all staying here. Big trunks are packed to go to Berlin to Anna who can use a great deal in these days. Packing, packing, always packing and never ready. The days not in Baarn are spent in the new house with carpenters, painters electricians. The difficulty is to make the house good looking with the real antique furniture and still pleasant to look at. We are using curtains in Mother's sitting room which were used by Father's grandparents and I assure you the material is better than one can bye [buy] today.

Father's writing table in empire style mahogany will be in my room and my whole library which was in my office is also there.

We each have our own sitting room, mine is my office. Then there is a dining room and we each have our nice bedroom and bath. A smaller room for Carmen.

A little kitchen. After long consideration I have decided to take an electric stove and your stepdaughter has taken cooking lessons with electricity.[3] It seems a real delight, no dirt, no dampness, it is much easier than any other way. Of course we need all new pans and pots, but I said to Mother there is just an opportunity now or never. I feel as if I am getting married and byuing [buying] everything new, beginning a new life, but I am glad to say no husband to worry the life out of me. Don't you think it is a good idea?

The plants in the greenhouse ares solt [sold], they look empty and forlorn, and when we have left Baarn, we shall sell everything that is left here. Antique china, furniture and the rest.

I have sent you some bulbs again a lovely kind of "perrot [parrot] tulips" which I think you will enjoy and some beautiful new orange tulips and some hyacint[h]s, I hope they will arrive safely. Try and put each lot together in a bunch that looks pretty.

Then Father's stamps are being solt in London and I have asked them to send you a cathalogue so that you can see what an immense object those stamps were. The auction will be in London that is to say 10 auctions beginning two days in October and each following month some days. People are coming from all countries to purchase them, so I hope they will fetch what is deserved. When I think of all the hours and hours Father spent with his stamps his love and energy for these bits of paper, it is quite amazing.

Oh Mother Carrie why are we so far away? I want to talk over so many things with you, so many things I cannot tell anybody but you. Still I know some day will come when we can chat together.

The world crisis is hard yet and the women cannot do much. Some of our good women are technical advisers at the Assembly—Malaterre for France, von Velsen for Germany—and the old staff of women has returned to Geneva—but what little good can they do[?] My heart sinks, yet we must march on and keep the banner floating. Mrs Ashby is doing her best, but everything seems so hopeless and difficult. The Alliance Board and the President will meet in Marseilles in March.[4] We shall have a meeting in Paris at the end of November to prepare. I shall go, but I feel so little can be done. We work in the dark.

Well dear good friend I will leave you. I am ashamed of this long letter but I expect it is the last letter from Baarn. I am so busy these next weeks. By the first of November I hope to have the house ready for Mother to go into it. Think of me sometimes and say you love me still it will comfort me again in these difficult times.

> Loving thoughts go out to you
>
> God bless you my wonderful friend
>
> Your only Rosa

1. Manus' play on words. In Dutch *laan* means *lane*. Catt's maiden name was Lane.

2. Manus' father died in 1931.

3. Manus was cofounder of the Vrouwen Electriciteits Vereeniging (Dutch Women's Electricity Society) in 1932.

4. The executive committee and presidents of the national branches met in Marseilles to discuss the Alliance's future, which was in doubt because of lack of funds.

7

Crisis within the IWSA

Despite the fact that Rosa Manus became a prominent figure within the IWSA, throughout the years she somehow contrived to remain away from center stage—literally. On almost every group photograph, and there are many, one can find her in the second row or even farther back: "On the foto you can see the board and also me sitting at the back of the platform, well my usual place," she wrote in a letter to Lucy Anthony (letter 57). And as a caption to one such photograph in *Journey towards Freedom*, we read: "In shadow: Miss Manus" (Schreiber and Mathieson 1955, caption to photo 22).

Was it only modesty that kept her in the background in this way? One of Rosa Manus' best friends, Mia Boissevain, in an unpublished essay[1] on Rosa's life, points out that Manus nearly always declined to take a leading position. Only rarely did she accept a chairmanship: "One of the reasons she gave me was that being a Jewess she did not want to come too much to the front. 'You have no idea how many people, even those of whom you would not expect it, are prejudiced against our race,' she would say. Though many of her friends tried to convince her of the contrary she never swerved from that idea. The Jewish question always remained a great point with her."[2] Boissevain then proceeds to illustrate this point:

In the spring of 1914 we spent a few weeks together in London. It was a most stirring time and as usual Rosa brought me into contact with many interesting people. Bad luck however would have it, that we went to two theatrical plays, in both of which the Jewish problem was the central point of interest. Back in our hotel, late at night, I found Rosa in her room prostrate with grief. I had never before seen her like that. Amidst tears she said: "You simply don't know how dreadful it is to be born a Jewess." We talked for a long time, but it seemed to give her little comfort. "It is a thing I find so difficult to accept," she said at last, "nothing will ever change the world's attitude towards our race."

These words were written with the knowledge that in 1943 Rosa Manus became a victim of the Nazis. Boissevain ends the description of this eve-

Mia Boissevain and Rosa Manus, Wiesbaden.

ning: "It struck me how deeply tragic she looked when she pronounced these words. Looking back on that night when I vainly tried to comfort her, it seems to me as if something prophetic and sinister was already in her mind."[3] Seldom in portraits of feminists are such incidents narrated, since these were considered to be private concerns. Indeed, one can wonder whether Boissevain would ever have written of the London incident and the Jewish question in Manus' life, had Manus not died at the hands of the Nazis.

Not that the feminists of the IWSA were blind to the ever-growing dangers of Fascism and anti-Semitism in Europe during the twenties and thirties. On the contrary. Margery Corbett Ashby, in her presidential address to the IWSA Jubilee Congress in Berlin in 1929, claimed: "Our prolonged struggle for the vote has given us unique political training" (IAW 1929, 46). Carrie Chapman Catt and Rosa Manus were in Rome in 1922 when the Fascist takeover took place, which brought Catt to the observation: "Mussolini is not only an antisuffragist, but one with no open mind" (Peck 1944, 365; Van Voris 1987, 174). Aletta Jacobs in 1926 refused to take a vacation in Italy, saying: "I do not like to go to Italy under the Mussolini system. That is too dangerous" (letter 64). The march on Rome gave Catt and Manus a foretaste of what the remainder of their journey through Europe would be like. In Hungary, where less than ten years earlier they had held a triumphant congress, they were confronted with the Fascist dictatorship of General Horthy. In a report on the tour, Catt noted: "A sinister anti semetic [sic] movement sprung up and sorry vengeance has been wreaked on many an innocent Jew" (Elinor Lerner 1983, 20).[4] She linked this to a general climate of repression, which also produced a vicious form of antifeminism, and she told of a female medical student who was assaulted and thrown from the stairs of the medical facility.

Through the international network, women were kept informed of the state of affairs in various countries. Throughout the thirties, the Alliance was clearly affected by the disappearance of an increasing number of national branches. A letter written in 1933 by Dorothee von Velsen tells of the circumstances surrounding the dissolution of the German branch of which she was president.[5] In 1935, after the highly successful international gathering in Istanbul and the courteous reception of the IWSA officers by Kemal Atatürk in Ankara, the authorities dissolved the Turkish branch—women "no longer needed" their society now that they had been given the franchise and many other rights (Peck 1944, 454). When the Alliance met again in 1939 more organizations suffered a similar fate, for example, those of Italy, Austria, and Czechoslovakia. In Zürich, where in spring 1937 a study conference was held, a Jewish speaker, Cécile Brunschvicg, was pelted with eggs by a "Nazzi-man" in the audience. The incident caused Manus to comment: "Helas, the jewish question is infecting more and more other people and although many, and most let me say, get mad about it, we must reckon with it more than ever" (letter 77). A few weeks earlier, Brunschvicg had been banned from making a public speech in Strasbourg. A second study conference scheduled to take place in Poland in fall 1937 was canceled because prospective Jewish speakers were denied the right of admission.

To this point, it seemed as if only events on the outside had affected the Alliance. But by the time of the 1939 congress in Copenhagen, it was all too clear that international developments were exerting a dark influence on thinking and events inside the movement. The Egyptian delegate, Huda Shaarawi, who after her first congress in 1923 in Rome had enthusiastically done away with the veil, now proposed a resolution at a preliminary council meeting that the IAW should speak out against admitting more Jews into Palestine. On the eve of the congress an extra session was convened to try to dissuade her, but Shaarawi angrily left the meeting and subsequently declared that she would not be a candidate for office unless the council unanimously wished her to. Manus wrote to Catt: "I then for the first time spoke in this matter as I did not think it wise for me as a Jewess to have mixed myself into it" (letter 80). She went on to say that not once during the entire congress had Shaarawi spoken to her, despite the fact that they had always gotten on well and that in 1935 Shaarawi had invited Manus to Cairo. When the board was about to make a decision regarding Shaarawi's membership, Rosa asked if Shaarawi had anything against her because she was Jewish. Rosa continued: "The re-action of my Board Members was quite funny as some of them seemed never to have known that I was a Jewess and Malaterre pretended that it was out of the question that Shaarawi had anything against me for that reason. So there we had the jewish question right in our midst which really ought not to have been mentioned at all" (letter 80). The words "Malaterre pretended" suggest that Manus had her doubts about the sincerity of Malaterre's assurances. But Manus' words reveal as well that she was still undecided whether she should have brought the matter to a head, a doubt which is reinforced by the vehement negations of her coworkers. Rosa's strategy, and that of the Alliance as a whole, was simply not to discuss "that" issue: it "really ought not to have been mentioned at all," a strategy which had such deep roots that it survived even the Second World War.[6] How else can we explain, for instance, that Adele Schreiber in *Journey towards Freedom* (1955) describes herself as a refugee solely "on account of her liberal views"? In my opinion this explanation is a simplification of a much more complicated situation, leaving out such painful but significant facts as that her "Aryan" husband had divorced his "Jewish" wife (Schreiber and Mathieson 1955, 47; Peck 1944, 447).[7]

The letters of Rosa Manus and Carrie Chapman Catt in the thirties illustrate that the great political insight on which Margery Corbett Ashby had prided the IWSA in 1929 did not later help women to recognize the many-headed monster of Fascism in all its forms; nor did it stimulate a free discussion of anti-Semitism. When Hitler came to power in 1933, Manus was immediately aware, insofar as was possible in the circumstances, of the nature and the potential magnitude of the danger threatening Jews in Germany and elsewhere. And she acted true to character, vigorously organizing refugee work under the supervision of a Neutraal Vrouwen-Comité voor Vluchtelingen (Neutral Women's Committee for Refugees). Her activities kept her abreast of events in Hitler's Germany, and she passed on the many painful details in her letters to Catt who, in turn, duly informed the Council of Jewish Women in the United States. The American women's movement was therefore aware of what was going on in Germany. In 1933 Catt distributed a petition of protest against German anti-Semitism among non-

Jewish feminists, collecting nine thousand signatures. The petition was sent to several governments as well as to the League of Nations. To show its gratitude the American Jewish Committee in the United States presented Catt with the American Hebrew Medal.[8]

Yet, as Elinor Lerner observes in her article on anti-Semitism in the American women's movement during the first decades of the twentieth century, there is a difference between drawing attention to specific Jewish problems far beyond one's own borders and drawing attention to similar problems nearer home. Later in 1933 Catt formed a committee of ten to work on the relaxation of immigration regulations. But she restricted this action to the collection of no more than a hundred signatures attached to a detailed statement she sent to the government (Elinor Lerner 1983, 23). On the basis of her research, Lerner concludes: "The failing of many feminists like Catt was in their political opportunism and their determination to keep feminism, as they understood it, alive as a viable force, even if it meant discounting radical or inconvenient allies in times of political repression" (Elinor Lerner 1983, 45). The old adage that it was best to remain respectable and acceptable in the eyes of white Protestant America gained strength even during the twenties. Lerner convincingly argues that during this phase of the "Red Scare," conservative attacks on the women's movement contained an anti-Jewish element which feminists never openly combated. Various imputations and smears against Rosika Schwimmer, as well as the refusal to grant her citizenship, were also partly based on anti-Semitic feelings (Elinor Lerner 1983, 40).

Feminists including Catt reacted by not mentioning Schwimmer's Jewish descent, by denying that her ideas were "un-American," and by avoiding any hint of interest in communism or socialism. This attitude arose partly from the strategic optimism which formed the basis of Catt's existence: a belief in progress and universal sisterhood based on the assumption of an essential unity and equality prevailing over any difference of race, class, color, creed, or nationality. Such an optimism had been her strength politically in the international women's movement, but it could get in the way of a sober and realistic acceptance of less pleasant facts. This is the context in which we must read Catt's letters. They reflect her incapability to acknowledge the very real danger of Manus' being "different" in the eyes of the Nazis, going even so far as to obscure the reason for Manus' death. When in 1942 the report had reached her that Rosa Manus had died in the women's concentration camp in Ravensbrück,[9] Catt immediately sent a circular letter to friends and acquaintances, the last sentence of which ran: "She grew into a dependable worker in the woman movement and, curiously enough, was the first of us all to suffer and to die for our cause" (letter 85). Catt thus reduced the reason for Manus' imprisonment to her feminist and pacifist activities. The Nazis indeed arrested her for her "communist and international inclinations," but Manus knew that as a Jew she was particularly vulnerable. Clara Meijers, one of her closest friends, describes her anxiety and her constant awareness of danger from the moment the Germans marched into the Netherlands: "She always said about herself, even as nobody had as yet been taken away or sent to a camp: 'You'll see, they'll come to fetch me and they'll kill me!' and with every hard ring she inwardly trembled with fear" (Meijers 1946, 59).

Although IWSA history suggests a familiarity with the discourse of difference, neither Catt nor the Alliance managed realistically to come to terms with it. The concept of difference was used predominantly in a symbolic way, to dramatize the idea of universal sisterhood. The international suffragists never fully came to accept that not all women are the same and not all women want the same things, or that in fact all such concepts as difference, unity, equality, and sameness are full of complexities which need constant consideration. In this respect both Catt and the IWSA were burdened with the inheritance of a suffrage movement which, a quarter of a century earlier, had chosen Susan B. Anthony's harmonious model of organization through impartiality and unity instead of Elizabeth Cady Stanton's ideal. Stanton's suffrage movement would have built "women into a force for radical political change" (DuBois 1981, 222), encouraging a never-ending debate, instead of silence: "When any principle or question is up for discussion, let us seize on it and show its connection, whether nearly or remotely, with women's disfranchisement. There is such a thing as being too anxious lest someone 'hurt the cause' by what he or she must say or do; perhaps the very thing you fear is what should be done" (DuBois 1981, 226).

April 1933–July 1942
Letters 73–85

73. Carrie Chapmann Catt to Rosa Manus

Dear Rosa:

I received your nice letter a few days ago and I thank you for all that is in it. I was going to dictate a letter to you in any event, but now I have something quite special to say.

Mr. James McDonald, the leader of the Foreign Policy Association in this country, a few weeks ago very suddenly and unexpectedly departed for Europe.[1] It was whispered around by some people very near to him that some Jews had offered to pay his expenses in order that he might go to Germany and find out the whole truth about the Jews. He has just returned and the other day there was a meeting of the so-called pacifists for the purpose of organizing a committee to serve as a sort of clearing house. He came to that meeting and was asked to give a little account of his experiences.

Of course there is a good deal in the newspapers concerning German affairs, but we do not know how much of this is true and how much is exaggerated. In answer to the question: – "Just what is the aim of the Hitlerites concerning the Jews?" – he replied that they do not intend to put them out of Germany, but to put them down in Germany. He described the movement as a revolution unlike any other revolution that has ever taken place. We, on the outside, do not understand it, but it is a crazy idea of making a Germany that will pass the definition of the Hitlerites, but they have not revealed to others just what that definition is.

The subject so stirred my emotions that I was not able to sleep last night. I have been very much disturbed about this uprising in Germany. Now it would seem that if the world was not so poor, there might be a war immediately. Fortunately, the armies are not in good training and there is no money to support them. It looks as though we will have to behave ourselves for a little while

Mr. McDonald, you will remember, is a blond with reddish hair and in no respects does he look like a Jew. He was a good man to select, because they would not be suspicious of his race or aims. He has been to Germany so many times that he had many acquaintances to whom he could appeal.

I thought you would be glad to know all this, because it is testimony quite outside the realm of gossip.

I have thought a good deal of your brother-in-law who saved my life, with your good nursing, in Berlin. If you could find any way to slip him out of Germany, I think it would be a good thing to do, for as long as these queer people are in power, the Jews will have no opportunity to live up to their best. Worse things may happen to them than have yet come.

I believe that before the thing is over, Austria will have joined Germany in the same ideas. Perhaps a turn against the Jews may come in other states of Europe, because that has been the case before.

I hope your brother-in-law can get located in Holland, because that would bring your family all together. It is too terrible.

We were all entreatied to keep Mr. McDonald's story quiet and to give it no publicity. I beg of you, therefore, not to pass on his name, because he is a valuable person to go to Germany and we do not want them to get their backs up against him. He speaks German too.

It looks as though the Germans are a queer people for when they voted for the Hitlerites they must, in some degree, sympathise with their curious philosophy.

I have always thought that, perhaps, the chief reason why the Jews have been persecuted and driven from state to state was because they had originally claimed to be God's chosen people. That is not very unusual. You know, the Chinese call their nation "A Celestial Empire," meaning the only empire right from Heaven, and there have been many others who said similar things, but now it is curious that if this has been a reason for the attack upon the Jews, that the Germans claim, so it seems, that they are going to put the "pure, superior Nordic race" at the top and they make everybody else step aside. It is enough to make a dog laugh.

Well, dear Rosa, in every generation the human race does something ridiculous and when it gets around to the point where everything is nearly perfect and everybody is quite happy, the old earth will probably explode and go up in smoke. There is work for you to do.

I am so glad the Alliance voted to go on a little longer. I think those Hitlerites will take the vote away from women in Germany or do any other mean thing they can think of.

Give my love to your good Mother and tell her I hope she is doing well.

The very first of your tulips have just blossomed. There are many little buds coming along soon. I suspect you are missing your fine garden these days. That is the worst about an apartment. However, I got used to going without a garden during the years I lived in an apartment and I found it very comfortable. The trees are just coming out in leaf but it is still cold and we have fires.

Dear Rosa, do tell me what you learn about Germany when you do hear something. There is no haste about it.

Very lovingly yours,

[Carrie Chapman Catt]

1. The Assembly of the League of Nations decided in autumn 1933 to appoint a High Commissioner for Refugees. According to the Dutch historian De Jong, James G. McDonald, a trusted aide to President Roosevelt, was chosen for the purpose of underlining "that particularly the U.S. was prepared to offer asylum to refugees" (De Jong 1969, 497). At the end of 1935 McDonald stepped down, as he found no cooperation.

74. Rosa Manus to Carrie Chapman Catt

R.M.S. Berengaria,[1] August 31. 1933

Dear Mother Carrie:

Never before I found it difficult to write to you but today I simply do not know how to begin. I know I may not thank you for the wonderful time I had with you and still my heart is just po[u]ring over with gratitude to you my very dear friend for the real and true friendship you have shown me again. More than ever you can realise yourself, more than I can possibly say is the great help you have been to me in these so very difficult times and "thank you" seems so small and insignificant to say. But you understand me without saying again how grateful I am for your love and friendship which means to me more than anything in this world. Dear Stepmother may you be spared years to come to be a benefacting blessing for your true friends.

It is a good thing you cannot see under which emotion I am writing this to you. But surely real friendship is the best thing on earth.

My stay with you seems a wonderful dream, and when I let the days and hours go by since my arrival on July 14th so much seems to have been that is almost impossible that I have been only 5 weeks there. Seeing you at work for the protest of the Jews moved me more than I can tell you and the words written by one of those man [men] "you are a blessing to the world" is real true and the Jews of the world can never be grateful enough to you for having done this masterly piece of work.

Well let me express the thanks of the hundreds and thousands of Jews and you may be sure that I will not stop telling about it to every one Jew I meet.

All the work you have done in the past seems small in comparison with this wonderful, daring jest [gesture].

Now I suppose you would say: Rosa you have not inquired how I feel; well mother Carrie tell me how are you by now? Does the mouth feel very sore yet, or does it feel better. I suppose pretty soon that wonderful capable dentist will arrive once more and take away the two other tooths—well you wont be half as nervous then as you exactly know what will happen now, the first time one expects all sorts.

It was such a pity to have had that glan[d] trouble as before you were so well and I found you ever so much better and stronger than when I left you 5 years ago. I trust however that when this tooth episode is past you will soon pick up again and [be] quite ready to start on another job. Dont forget to let me know what it will be.

On the steamer there is not much excitement, the first two days I slept a good deal you remember that the sea and the train always have that effect on me.

Rosa Manus and Carrie Chapman Catt. Paris, 1923.

I found a "Dean's box" full of good things from Mrs Parsens. Very kind of her. And many steamer greetings and telegrams from others. I have decided to land at Cherbourg and go to Paris and fly home from there. It saves another day on the steamer.

It is quite wonderful to think I left you on Saturday morning and the next Saturday morning before lunch I am with Mother in Amsterdam, and one day there may be an areoplane that takes me in two days to you. It might be dangerous as I would be tempted to come for a long weekend pretty often.

There are two midgets on the steamer, a boy from 21, a girl from 22. They are as sweet as they can be. Their father is with them a big tall good-looking man. It seems that the Mother is also quite normal, that they had first a normal child, then twice a midge[t] and 3 other normal children. It does seem strange. I think they are going over to a music hall in London; they will perform to us tonight.

The public in this tourist class is the funniest lot I ever saw. First they put me at a table with 5 other women. I had lunch the first day with them. 3 of them dropped their H., and belonged more to the class of [?] and cooks, as a matter of fact, one used to (h)ave a boarding (h)ouse in Brighton; they each told stories of loosing a brother—berrieng [burying] a sister etc. etc.

So after lunch I asked the purser to put me at another table so I am now seated well with three Irish people. One couple and another man a lawyer. They are not very talkative, but it is just as well. In the daytime I am on deck and do not talk to any body so it left me plenty of time to think and there is so much to think and plan in the near future. I hope I can get ready to go to Geneva towards the end of September if I find I can be useful. My first job home will be to write to Miss Dingman and find what she thinks about my plans. If you hear any more or can give me some advice or hints do let me know. My second job will be to make the report for Miss Ginsberg.[2] Both these I could not do on the steamer as they both need duplicates.

I do want to say that I am feeling very well and that my degestion is very good although I do miss the nice homemade food of your house. I manage to get stewed fruit every day and I eat salad and tomatoes with french dressing, but oh how different these tomatoes are to your huge ones. They taste quite differently.

I think I will surprise my people by eating all sorts of things I was not allowed to eat for so long. Well dear Mother Carrie that is all your doing. So you see your call has not been in vain. I came at once when you called and you have not only restored my health but you have given me new energy, new pep in life and I will try to use it the best I can—always thinking of you; who has been my helping power, ever since I knew you. Think, 25 years of real sound friendship—that is worth something to both of us!! I hope it will make you feel good to know how much <u>you</u> are and have been to me always and especially these past weeks.

> Thank you
>
> dear Mother Carrie
>
> one more kiss from your
>
> truly loving stepdaughter
>
> Rosa

1. The RMS *Berengaria* was the ship in which Manus returned to Holland after visiting Catt.

2. Marie Ginsberg, a Swiss, was a member of the Alliance board. She was also assistant to the director of the library of the League of Nations.

75. Carrie Chapman Catt to Rosa Manus

[New Rochelle] July 17, 1935

Dear Rosa:

I enjoyed your letter of June 25th very much with all its news and gossip. I passed it on to Miss Wilson and Miss Peck to read and both enjoyed it very much.

First, let me say I am very glad, indeed, that Carmen[1] has found employment and I hope that she will continue to like it and live a long, prosperous, happy and contented life. That was a curious story you told about Carmen and the dentist with whom she has found employment. I was not able to treat her as well as I wished while she was in New York. I wanted to do some more things for her than I could do.

My last year was an extremely busy one with more work than I could do. I was not at all well. I am now better than I have been for some months past and hope it will continue. The weather now is hot,—almost as hot as some of the weather we met in South America.

I have now seen Miss Ogden, Miss Schain and Mrs. Beggs and have heard their reports. The National Committee on the Cause and Cure of War gave a small luncheon for the delegates, and Mrs. Simonson, Miss Ogden, Miss Schain and Mrs. Beggs told their story. On the whole, I feel I have had a pretty good report. I have not seen Miss Fast.[2] She returned, but I was not well enough to go to town and she could not come out here as she had to return to her home in Ohio where she had to attend to some business at once. She expected to come back to New York, but she has not done so yet and I do not know why. There is a new executive secretary for the National Committee on the Cause and Cure of War, so Miss Fast will not come back for work at the office. Perhaps she will change her mind and not come back at all.

There was only one sad thing about the Congress and that was that the Turkish women had been squeezed out. That, however, is quite in line with a dictatorship and some day there will be something different in Turkey. Meanwhile Kemal seems to be doing pretty well for his country, although it is not the kind of government we would like.

I was very glad that Adele Schreiber was made Honorary Vice-President. I am afraid she is in a sad condition. I imagine that that Aryan husband of hers availed himself of the Hitler attitude and divorced her because she was a Jewess. That would make any woman angry and would hurt her feelings beyond expression. I am very sorry for her. If you hear anything about her, I would be glad to know what you learn.

You said you were about to fly to London. You are such a go-ahead, you will not go anywhere except in an airplane.

I shall be glad to know what comes out of the discussion of merging the Council with the Alliance. Our American delegates did not like Miss van Eeghen. Perhaps they were prejudiced.

I am especially interested in what you tell me about your sister Anna and Felix. I doubted that they would like to go there. They have been accustomed to civilization, but they surely must get away from Germany. They will have no comfort there. Our delegates spoke very highly about Erica.[3] I am glad she is so promising.

There is not much of interest to tell you of myself, or about my plans. When I came to New Rochelle,[4] it was because I was too old to move around as I had formerly done and I wanted to find a place where I could stay all the year around. Our summers are very nice even though we have occasional warm spells. We do not get real summer until the first of June and it is over by the middle of October, so we have about four months of spring and fall that are not too cold, but not very agreeable. The other six or seven months are wonderful and now I find the winter rather too cold, but I am quite comfortable in this house except for the fact that I am shut in a good many days in the winter.

I always have plenty to do and one of the things that is amusing me now is assorting photographs of my own journeys—some of them made with you. I have planned to do several things with them and will send some sets to my College if they will accept them. I am thinking that when I was young and going to school, I would have been glad to have seen some of these collections and so I think they may be useful to the young people of this day. I am thinking that all I can get rid of while I am here will be appreciated by my executors when I am gone. This is very pleasant work as I am living over the old days. Now there is a very nice new hotel at Lima where we would be very much more comfortable were we to go again.

I think you must stay with your mother as much as you can, because you are about all she has left now and it must mean a great deal to her to have you with her. You will not be too old to travel even when she is gone and that may be a fine way to spend time and money. Your experience with the Alliance will fit you for it much better than you would have been had you never worked in its circles.

I feel a sense of disappointment whenever I think of the absence of progress concerning the enfranchisement of women in Switzerland and the rather slow progress being made in France.[5] I do not mind other countries so much. I would think that the Alliance might very well come to an end now were it not for the possibility it has to do some good in the peace movement. Nothing in that campaign looks promising at present. That does not matter, however, for time will give the world more common sense than it now possesses. It does mean, however, that a very great deal of intelligent work must be done to convert nations to see the wisdom of getting on without war. It will be a long and tedious process and very much work must be done to bring about that change. Women are better adapted to change the world's mind than are men. I hope the Alliance will go on to uphold the flag of peace and that the women of many lands will be brave enough to do effective work on its behalf.

At present it looks as though Italy would tempt the world into another war. It is sickening. Apparently, there is no power on earth that can do anything to stop Mussolini's madness.[6] I would like to have the last war paid for before we go into another one.

Give my love to your mother, Carmen and to Felix and Anna if they happen to be with you.

With great love to yourself, I am

[Carrie Chapman Catt]

1. Carmen Manus is a niece of Rosa. She survived the war and wrote to Catt on November 11, 1945 (CCC-LC).

2. Esther Ogden, Josephine Schain, Mrs. Frederick Beggs, and Mrs. Charles Simonson as well as L. K. Fast were the American delegation to the Alliance's twelfth congress in Istanbul.

3. Erica was the daughter of Anna Manus and Felix Jacobi.

4. After Mary Garrett Hay's death Catt moved to New Rochelle.

5. French women won the vote in 1946, the Swiss not until 1971. Women in some parts of the district of Appenzell still did not have the franchise in 1989.

6. Italy marched into Abyssinia (Eritrea and Ethiopia) in October 1935.

76. Rosika Schwimmer to
Mien van Wulfften Palthe-Broese van Groenou

Private Pavilion, Room 441,
March 23, 1936

My dear Mien,

Ever since we had the pleasure of seeing your darling grandsons and the two young ladies, I have wanted to write to you fully. I also wanted to thank you for the beautiful calendar and the war picture book; but I have been so awfully miserable that I kept on waiting for a better moment.

In health and spirits I was in a worse condition since the Ethiopian business began than I have been for many years. I should have come to the hospital in September, but could not manage it financially.[1]

I have now a very serious reason for writing to you. Several months ago I sent you the prospectus and press clippings about the Archive Center campaign[2] and asked you several questions concerning Aletta Jacobs', Martina Kramers' and other Dutch suffrage leaders' archives. You never answered my question and, as I say, I was too sick to write to you again urging an answer, which I needed badly. Three weeks ago here in the hospital I got a hurried inquiry about the Dutch plan for a World's Center for women's archives. With a great amount of trouble and work, I finally found the February issue of the "International Women's News," which contained the paragraph the copy of which I here enclose.[3]

The campaign here is in the hands of the foremost American women. I keep away from any official appointment and act only as adviser, so that no one should have an excuse for withholding cooperation because of my hated personality. In my capacity as adviser, I was asked to comment on the Dutch news for an executive meeting that was held in New York. I was disgusted and sick to the bottom of my heart when I found that that unspeakable creature, Rosa Manus, who has neither intellect, learning, nor character, put up a campaign for a similar institute in Amsterdam.[4] It is Aletta's and Mrs. Chapman Catt's crime that an empty-headed nobody like Rosa Manus can arrogate to herself the role which she has now assumed. Those two ladies have patronised her to the extent that she can now play such tricks as confuse the clearcut issue. I would commit a similar crime if I did not express my protest to you, who perhaps could have held her back.

My dear Mien, please take the trouble of going through all the enclosed material – and you will see the gigantic document of women's efforts can be created if the proper forces pull together and do not permit mean self-seekers, intellectually unequipped for the task, to insert their nebulous personalities.

The foremost women of all parties and shades of opinion in feministic pacifistic activities are now united here. They try to induce some of these

Rosika Schwimmer (with Jus Suffragii *brooch) at her desk. The books and documents behind her became the Schwimmer-Lloyd Collection.*

fabulously rich women who give every year millions of dollars to universities, colleges, missions and charities to put up from five to ten million dollars for this planned institution. Women architects and builders should for the first time have a chance in international competition to erect a proper building, etc., etc. But this grandiose plan cannot be carried out if mushroom actions will confuse the issue. It would be a tragedy if we permitted the endangering of this vast enterprise.

I personally would accept neither an honorary nor a paid office in it; so nobody can suspect in my criticism anything but the deepest anxiety for its most perfect realisation. The situation worries me very much, and you would help me greatly if you would answer the questions about Aletta's and the other archives of which I inquired in my latest letters to you.

The irradiation of my pituitary gland is again improving me, but the process keeps me rather weak; so I will not now go into a personal letter, though I long to have a good, thorough chat with you about world affairs, and our own private matters, too. I hope some windfall will suddenly enable you to take a little trip to this crazy part of the world, as a release from your crazy part.

Please do answer this letter immediately, with all the personal information you care to add. Please address the letterr to New York, because the physicians do not know how long they are keeping me. At present it is settled that I will have to stay here until the 20th; only then will they be able to decide whether to continue irradiation or to send me home.

With lots of love to your family, I embrace you,

As always,

Your affectionate old friend.

[Rosika Schwimmer]

P.S. How much is the Aletta Jacobs' Fund, and for what purposes had it been collected? Has Rosa Manus the right to dispose of it?

It will interest you that I have learned now from the Crerar Library authorities that their representative paid Mr. Gerritsen 7.000 pounds sterling ($35.000) for their collection on April 18, 1904 in London. Through all my connection with Aletta she told me about having <u>donated</u> the collection to the Chicago library.[5]

In a recent speech the 80-year old Mrs. Stanton Blatch said:

"Strange that a group wholly inexperienced in political action should have been expected to play chess with perfect skill from the first move of the men on the board. <u>H. G. Wells, with a great</u> deal of looking down his <u>nose at the sex, declares women have not contributed an idea—much less</u> <u>carried it to fruition—in connection with their enfranchisement. What a</u> <u>humbug that man is! Does he know of another group in the whole history</u> <u>of the growth of democracy who conceived the idea of gaining the ballot</u> <u>for itself without the slightest aid of the powerful within the fortress, and</u>

without shedding a drop of human blood? When, Mr. Wells, has anything more original and striking been achieved?

"Women doubled the electorate. And that is progress, even if it does not mean greater wisdom and efficiency. To represent more points of view, tends to keep life calmer, more satisfied by peace, better fitted in time to sit in council.

"We learned as we toiled in our campaign that sermons and logic never convince. Emotions stir us to action. Human beings move because they feel, not because they think. For that reason we began to march to Votes-for-Women music, for that reason we began to dance about our cause in the early nineteen hundreds, at great balls; instead of sitting in corners and arguing. No one is stirred to action by somnolent words. Men's idea was different—they couldn't ask for the vote for village constables without getting into a brawl over it. Their democracy grew by riots, revolutions, wars. Women conquered in peace and quiet, with some fun, right off their own bat. If that was not a new idea. I do not think there's been one. . . ."

And Mrs. Catt always reminded us that women have brought this novelty in the world's activities: that they fought and struggled for their rights and liberation internationally in a way that men never have done.

The world Center for women archives should be a mighty monument and proof of all that.

1. Rosika Schwimmer had had diabetes since 1920. She often mentioned her illness in her letters to Mien (SL-NYPL and VWP-IAV-IIAV).

2. Rosika Schwimmer was the force behind the founding of the World Archives Center, contacting numerous feminists, among whom were Jane Addams, Carrie Chapman Catt, and Harriot Stanton Blatch. Various women suggested that Schwimmer ask the support of Mary Beard, which was forthcoming. On September 17, 1935, Beard wrote to influential women and women's organizations while Schwimmer stayed in the background. Numerous meetings were held. Just before the outbreak of the Second World War they decided to abandon the idea because of insufficient funds. Most of the material they had collected was given to women's colleges. See Turoff 1979 and Relph 1979.

3. The announcement of the founding of the IAV appeared in the *International Women's News* 30/5 (Feb. 1936): 37–38.

4. It seems unlikely that Manus wanted to pre-empt the American initiative made by Schwimmer. The IAV became official on December 3, 1935. It was not the first time that Schwimmer had written negatively about Manus. In 1925, Schwimmer also contacted Manus (see CCC-LC). In 1936 she asked Catt to forward her letter to Manus, probably with a request to resolve the events of 1915. Cf. chap. 5, n. 11.

5. Cf. chap. 3, n. 3.

77. Rosa Manus to Carrie Chapman Catt

[Amsterdam] April 1st, 1937

Dear Mother Carrie,

It is indeed a long time since I wrote to you but I have been to Switzerland, Zürich for the Study Conference the Alliance held the end of February. Unfortunately my health was not very good at that time; in fact I was laid up in bed and my doctor did not give permission even that I should leave. However after two days in bed I made up my mind to get up and go, as I had promised to help Miss Heneker[1] with the organisation and to hold an international press gathering before the others would arrive.

My newest sister in law, the young woman who married my youngest brother Carel two years ago, offered to come along with me and take care of me. So I went and although I was not very well I managed to pull through during the conference; then afterwards she and I went to Arose, a real winterplace, 1800 Meters altitude where I enjoyed a few weeks of complete rest in the snow and sun.

I have just now returned and I must say I feel 20 years younger again (when I left, I felt about 100!). All the events of the last years have pulled me back tremendously and the many difficulties in our family are weighing heavily upon me. My nerves are much better however and I hope I can face the difficulties which are before us, much more bravely.

The Conference in Zürich has been indeed a good success. For the first time we introduced in the international conference the "Round-Table" discussions.[2] Of course internationally this is not such an easy matter as one always needs not only a chairman who thoroughly understands the questions but also one who understands the languages and who has next to her an efficient translator. Before the Swiss, as you will understand, were not very enthousiastic neither of our coming to hold a conference nor of our introducing these round-table sessions. They predicted we should not get any audience at all, that the Swiss people are not interested and that the young people are only interested in sports during the winter. You will remember the difficulties before our Geneva Congress when Gourd[3] told you everything was "impossible"!

As we had appointed Miss Heneker to be our organiser and she is a splendid levelheaded, intelligent person, she managed to go ahead wonderfully well, got very good friends with the people in Zürich and by the time I arrived, we could [a]rouse the international press very well and indeed although it had been predicted that no more than 6 people would come, we had about 30 journalists and they go[t] so much interested that during the Conference and weeks after that even we had splendid reports in all the Swiss papers with pictures in all their magazines too. This is quite astonishing as even in September last when Mrs. Ashby was asked to speak through the Radio in Geneva and she wanted to talk about the Status of Women, they said they wanted no talk about such strong feministic lines!, and in Zürich about 9 of us were asked to speak on the Radio, each one giving another attitude of the feministic cause. Instead of a few people, hundreds came and therefore the halls were overcrowded and for the first time in their lives in Zürich for the evening-meeting we had an overflow of five times more people than they had imagined.[4]

There was a most interesting youth-meeting where we had young men and women from different countries speak and where a young Swiss girl presided. About 800 young people came that evening!!, and their re-actions were quite remarkable. We have now formed a Younger-Group in our International Alliance and we will see what happens with it.

In Holland we have a Younger-Group in our Auxiliary since two years of young, active women, several lawyers, economists etc. It works splendidly and they go ahead in a different way than the others which is a good thing too.[5]

At the public meeting there was a nasty incident: when Mme Brunschvicg[6] came on the platform, a fascist or Nazzi-man found it necessary to throw raw eggs at her, crying out: "we do not want jews." Mrs. Brunschvicg did not move, just waited for some people and the police to take the man away and then gave us a very good address telling what her work as underminister of education in Paris is. Mme Malaterre who was on the platform, told me that Mme Brunschvicg had been forbidden to speak at the Meeting at Strassbourg a few weeks before.

Helas, the jewish question is infecting more and more other people and although many, and most let me say, get mad about it, we must reckon with it more than ever.

We were going to have a conference of the Alliance in Poland,[7] Varsovia [Warsaw], in spring but on account of the political situation this was absolutely impossible just now but it was quite clear to hear from the Poland Ladies that no jews could speak there at this moment. Of course the Minority question is quite difficult there. It is tragic indeed but true and I know how sad you feel about it.

You will know Mrs. Ashby will be in the States in May where she is to receive the doctor's honours at Mount Holyoke College May 8th. I hope you will have time to talk with mrs. Ashby about many of the European questions.

Do you know that Margery's Michael, the fairhaired boy, won the boat race this year; he is indeed a wonderful boy but I am afraid that by too much sport he sometimes forgets he is to become a doctor; however he says and he is quite right there, that when once a doctor, he will not get time to enjoy himself.

The International Archives are going ahead very well indeed. We are getting many documents etc. from many countries and I do hope that

The board of the IWSA in the newly opened IAV. Amsterdam, 1936. Left to right: *Margery Corbett Ashby, Ingeborg Walin (?), Nina Spiller (?), Anna Szelagowska, Halina Siemienska (?), Alison Neilans, Marie Ginsberg, Senta Rama Rau, Kathleen Bompas, Emilie Gourd, Rosa Manus, Františka Plamínková, Mrs. Piepers.*

some of your international co[r]respondance you have kept, may come along here too although I understand that most of your things will remain in the United States.

You ask in your last letter when I could come for a visit to you; well, it will be difficult to get away from all my family surroundings but I wonder if you would be ready to have me in June or July for a short visit. I have not looked up boats yet but will await your answer to say when it would be most convenient for you to have me. I would love to spend a short time with you again!! We shall have so much to talk about. So please, let me know when you can have me.

Meanwhile I send you love, and heaps of it.

Your loving stepdaughter

Rosa.

Much love to Alda, Mary and all the friends around.

1. Dorothy A. Heneker, a Swiss, was secretary of the Dingman Committee.

2. Posthumus-van der Goot wrote: "In 1932, Mrs. Catt discovered a method of passing on knowledge which was applied successfully, the so-called Marathon roundtable." Groups of women sat at round tables during congresses discussing issues. They were also expected to organize round-table discussions in their own homes. Posthumus-van der Goot 1961, 228.

3. The Swiss Emilie Gourd (1879–1946) had been secretary to the board of the IWSA since 1920.

4. After years of lobbying by women's organizations, in September 1937 the League of Nations set up a work committee which was to study the position of women in all countries. The International Women's Year (1975) was a legacy of these women's activities.

5. Those taking part included the historian Jane de Iongh and W. H. Posthumus-van der Goot (Posthumus-van der Goot 1977, 263ff.).

6. The Frenchwoman Cécile Brunschvicg (1877–1946) was active in the suffrage movement and national politics. She was cofounder of the French suffrage association in 1910 and a committee member of the French national council of women and the ICW. In 1936 she was state secretary of education in the Popular Front government of the social reformist Léon Blum.

7. The congress took place in Copenhagen, not Poland, and at the request of the ICW, one year later, in 1939, because the ICW was to celebrate its fiftieth anniversary in 1938.

78. Rosa Manus to Carrie Chapman Catt

[Amsterdam] January 5th 1938

Dear Mother Carrie,

We are living in a most difficult time in Holland! Our Minister of Social Affairs, a catholic, has put a new proposal of law before Parliament to discriminate all married women from paid work.[1] This includes really every married woman in every career, the charwomen as well as actresses, teachers, professors etc. etc. will be all debarred from paid labour. Only married women who create or have created an independent career can go on, but any married woman who earns a salary shall not be able to keep her post if this law is accepted.

You can imagine the women of little Holland are getting stirred up and the academic women who never wanted to join the women's movement are now in the end feeling they also must become feminists.

We have been advised to organise a tremendous press campaign and we have been able to raise quite a sum of money and we are holding a mass meeting quite soon in Amsterdam.

A special Committee has been appointed to advise the High Court where the proposal is to come to first. There are only a few women in this commission of which one is one of our women and the other one is a member of parliament,[2] who used to be the president of the National Council of women, from the christian-historic party who will vote with most of the men and as many are catholics, it seems that not much can be done.

We are really in an unworthy and dreadful position.

I have been asked if it would be possible at all to ask Mrs. Roosevelt[3] to write an article of about 400 words for our dutch weekly paper about the value of women's work.

Do you think it would be possible for you to send Mrs. Roosevelt the enclosed letter and press her to write that article for us. It will make all the difference in Holland to get a few words from your first lady of the land. I thought it would be better not to send a letter directly to Mrs. Roosevelt but to beg you, my dear Mother Carrie, to send it along with a few words from you. If however you think it can or may not be done, then I leave it of course entirely to you but I do hope it can be done.

It may be when you get this letter you are just on the verge of going to Washington and it may make things easier as you will surely see Mrs. Roosevelt.[4]

Hope you are well. I am longing to hear your plans for the winter.   .

Loving greetings,

Rosa.

2 enclosures

1. The Dutch women's movement protested en masse against a bill put forward by Romme, a minister in the fourth Colijn cabinet (1937–39). The first major protest rally was held on February 7 in the Concertgebouw in Amsterdam and was followed by meetings all over the country. The change of government in 1939 resulted in Romme's post being taken over by a social democrat who rejected the bill.

2. This refers to Ch. L. Polak-Rosenberg, who sat on the board of Women's Interests, and C. Frida Katz, who was a member of parliament for the Christelijk Historische Unie (Christian Historical Union) and from 1932 to 1938 chairman of the National Council of Women.

3. First Lady Eleanor Roosevelt was a strong feminist. She was a journalist by profession and supported women's issues in her writings. Her letter is not printed here. She did not write a new article but sent Manus one already published in the United States. See NAW.

4. Catt was on the point of going to the thirteenth meeting of Cause and Cure of War.

79. Rosa Manus to Carrie Chapman Catt

[Amsterdam] Nov. 29th 1938

Dear Mother Carrie,

The events of the last few weeks are so terrible that my thoughts have only been in one direction, that is with those who suffer so dreadfully in Germany.[1]

The appeals for help I get by letter and telephone are simply terrific and my only aim is to try and relieve some of the troubles as far as I possibly can.

The Committees in Holland are doing splendid work and the devotion of people from all religions is wonderful but to save lives and help the men out of the concentration camps is very, very difficult indeed.

We have begun opening the frontiers for the children but this also has taken quite some time of consideration. All those who come in, have to go into quarantaine for at least 2 weeks before they can be distributed in the homes which have been got up for them as well as in private houses.

The latest in Germany is that they are not only taking away the men but several young girls from 14 to 16 and boys of that age have disappeared or been taken away. I could write volumes about all the tragedies. I get urgent letters and telephone messages from different places in Germany and many sacrifices are needed finantial and otherwise to <u>begin</u> to help.

One blessing is that Felix and Anna are out even though they have lost everything they had in Germany, it is better to be away. It seems incredible that one single man can go on in that despotic way like is done now. Five years ago when this madness began, I felt how things would be for the Jews in reality; I felt it coming and worse things have happened than the darkest view could ever have predicted.

It is quite natural that the amount of Jews coming into the other countries will have to make in the long run an antisemitism which cannot be avoided and for which one cannot blame them.

You were right in saying there was something wrong with the Jews from the beginning, that they ought to have formed their own group with their own soldiers and their own country.

The Colonisation plan which is being got up and which they asked me to join, is in full swing, that is to say a discussion is being held with the different governments and each country will have to take shares for the undertaking which ought to be made rendable [profitable].[2]

The worst of course of everything are the young children which are now being sent away to different countries; the mothers rather prefer sending them away than keep them not knowing what will happen to them or their children.

The other day one of my friends went to Hambourg to fetch a pair of twins of 1½ years old of whom the mother had been killed and the father been put in a concentration camp. Another tragedy which the same women met with yesterday was when she went to the frontier to fetch about 40 children; the conductor of the night train came to her at 6 o'clock in the morning telling her that they had found three children in a compartment; the children 1 ½ year, 3 and 12 years belonged to no one and they had no identification whatsoever! Six more children were also handed out to her which had been found near the Dutch frontiers, nobody knowing where they had come from. Oh, it is all too dreadful for words.

You can understand that I have no wish to go to our Board Meeting in Paris next week. To go and talk about Alliance work at this moment seems to me not the work for me to do.

I suppose you will have read my letter of resignation I sent to the Board Members a few weeks ago. I feel it is no longer me who have to be on the Board of the Alliance and I suppose you agree with my decision.

I am still living in hopes to come to you, dear Mother Carrie. I have taken my ticket to sail December 24th and hope to arrive either January 1st or 2nd. If my boat should arrive Sunday the 1st, I suppose it will be better for me to spend the night in a hotel and only go to you on Monday as I know it is always difficult for your chauffeur to be ready on a Sunday. It will not be so difficult as I have hand luggage and can easely take it to the hotel and I hope the car will then meet me the next day.

If only I need not cable to you that I cannot come as it is my greatest desire to spend those days with you to get new strength and energy from your wonderful personality.[3]

Love, dear Mother Carrie

Your always loving stepdaughter

Rosa

1. She refers to the violent attack on Jews on Kristallnacht (November 9–10, 1938) and the arrest of thirty thousand Jews who were sent to concentration camps. The Jewish community in Germany was also "fined" one billion R-marks.

2. Throughout the thirties numerous colonization plans were developed for (refugee) Jews. In 1938, there were hopes for colonization in San Domingo.

3. Manus went to the United States for Catt's eightieth birthday. See Peck 1944, 459. While Manus was on her way back to the Netherlands, her mother died.

80. Rosa Manus to Carrie Chapman Catt

[Amsterdam] July 31st 1939

Dear Mother Carrie,

I am ashamed of myself that I have not had the energy to write to you since my return from Copenhagen. There is really no excuse, but the Congress really this time overwhelmed me a bit and I could not come to my senses and get my thoughts in order so as to write to you about my impression.

This Congress in Copenhagen has surely been one of the most difficult and one with the most ups and downs I have ever been through. It was a real reflection of the world situation of the present moment. The day I left by airplane to Copenhagen, some of my man-friends at the aerodrome said to me: "how dare you go to Copenhagen on a day when the world situation is so earnest [serious]; you will have to return no sooner than you have arrived," but as I had made up my mind and Mrs. Ashby was waiting for me at the other end I decided to go and I am glad I went.

As usually is the case it was found that the Danish Auxiliary had not executed what we had planned with them and the final arrangements as always had to be done by ourselves.[1] Mrs. Ashby who had been there for more than a week did what she could but she had to go to Sweden to a big Meeting organised for her there, so that real final arrangements were still left for me and I was glad to take hold of them.

Instead of hundreds and hundreds of delegates and many more hundreds of visitors like we used to have in former days, there came about 250 Delegates and visitors altogether, except of course a large number of Danish Visitors attending the Congress.

It me[a]nt however that on the whole we had women who really me[a]nt to do earnest work and who were interested in it which made things in one way more efficient and easy. Also we only had English and French for our Congress and translations in German were not needed.

Mrs. Ashby herself was terribly nervous and exhausted and I am sorry to say (but <u>this I only tell you in secret</u>) she was not a good presiding officer at all which was much felt in the Congress. On other congresses I always sat next to her and helped her watching speakers, handing in the names to her and keep[ing] her going a little, but in Copenhagen the platform was divided in two and in between was the speaker's desk. Mlle Gourd sat next to Mrs. Ashby but she was so busy with her own duties that she could not assist her really.

Some of the sessions were presided over by Mme Malaterre and these were a great success so that even the three British Societies of each of which Delegates were present, said to me: "why do you always keep Mrs. Ashby as your President. Malaterre is much better" and I must confess that Malaterre kept them much more in order. It is a pity however that Malaterre does not speak enough English to preside in English at times. She understands it however and is indeed making progress in her English. When it came to the voting it was surely Malaterre who got the most votes so I think next time there will not be any difficulty in letting her pass as President.

The Declaration which was put to the Congress was very much discussed and debated and some of the Delegations amongst whom were the three British ones, did not want to vote for it and when the Declaration was finally put to vote it was only with a slight majority that it was accepted.[2] My Dutch Delegation also voted against it. They had prepared another one which might have been more to the point. I myself was not much in favour of this Declaration and do not think it means much as it is much too weak. I am enclosing a copy for you just to see and give your opinion to me about it. In due time you will get the resolutions voted I suppose; they will appear in "Jus." If I have enough copies, I will send you one of each.

Lady Astor was especially invited by the Danish Members to come. She was tremendously applauded and was a great attraction the few days she was there.

There was a special Meeting organised by the Danish Members of Parliament and Members of the Town Council for all the women Members of Parliament in other countries, ex-Members of Parliament and Members of Town Councils. They seem to have had a very good and interesting meeting and a special Committee was set up which will be one of the Alliance Committees now to keep the international contacts with these women who will then meet in different places. I think they want Szelagowska of Poland to preside over the next meeting; she certainly is a most prominent woman who is a Member of Parliament since many years and is sitting in four official commissions of her parliament, also the budgetary one. They seem to think that those women who are really on duty ought to have more contact with the feminists and their wishes.

At the Board Meeting, where about 17 of the 20 Members were present, a terrible incident happened. Mme Shaarawi[3] came to present a resolution to the Board which she wanted the Board to accept and put to the Congress in which it was asked that we should take a vote that from now on Palestine would not let in anymore Jews. She said that the Arab population was too badly treated by them, that it was the country of the Arabs and that we ought to protest against more Jews going to Palestine.

You can well imagine that the Board Members did not want to go in for any discussion about it as it was not within the scope of the work of the Alliance but meant mere politics.

A special session was then called in the evening on which Shaarawi got hotter and hotter. She said it was all very well the Alliance having in its Constitution that it was for all races and creeds and why then could not they accept her resolution. Poor Shaarawi was so beseated [besotted] with that one idea that nobody could bring her to reason; she was like a tiger and finally in rage left the room. This was a very nasty incident and happened on Friday evening when on Saturday would be the official opening.

It was then decided that on Saturday morning Mrs. Ashby and Mme Malaterre would go together and see her and beg her to come to the opening session as it would have been a very bad thing if she would not have been there when it was all planned for her to speak at the Opening Meeting. I for myself must confess that I thought it a weakening point to beg her to return as this was a matter of principle and there was quite a few of the Board Members who had no patience with her standpoint but still it may have been better for the Congress at this moment not to have a fuss of this kind right in the beginning.

So after two hours talk they left Shaarawi who said she would consider to come at the Opening Session.

As you know we have since many years the organisation of the Jewish Women of Palestine affiliated to the Alliance and three of them had come to the Congress, fine, intelligent women.

The Arab Society of Palestine with whom we had been in contact before the Istanbul Congress does not belong anymore to the Alliance and therefore it is their own fault that the Arab Women are not officially represented. We could not make Shaarawi see this point and she said that Palestine was not really represented as there were only Jewish women.

Well, finally Mme Shaarawi came to the Opening Session. She entered like a queen as she always does en [and] she was treated with great honour but incidentally she did not salute some of her Board Members.

On Sunday morning was the opening of the Congress at 9.30 but the Egyptian Delegation came at about 11 o'clock, however they came! They sat through some of the sessions of the Congress but it was quite clear that in reality they were not much interested and were only concentrated upon their own hobby.

When it came to the election and it was asked if Mme Shaarawi would stand she said that she would not stand. Again private discussions took place and then a special Meeting of the Board Members without Shaarawi.

She was of course all the time talking against the Jews. We then learned that Shaarawi said she would stand again if the Board unanimously wished her to. I then for the first time spoke in this matter as I did not think it was wise for me as a Jewess to have mixed myself into it but then I spoke up and said that ever since Mme Shaarawi had come she had not spoken to me, that all those years before she had thought me her best friend on the Board, that she had invited me to come to Cairo, that she had discussed all the special matters of the Alliance over with me, that on the whole she had been rather not too friendly with Mrs. Ashby on account of the political situation with the Mandates etc., so I said to the Board that if they would unanimously decide to beg Mme Shaarawi to stand for re-election that I wanted to know if Mme Shaarawi was against me as a Jewess and that if the Board wanted her to stand I wanted to know before Mme Shaarawi's opinion.

The re-action of my Board Members was quite funny as some of them seemed never to have known that I was a Jewess and Malaterre pretended that it was out of the question that Shaarawi had anything against me for that reason. So there we had the jewish question right in our midst which really ought not to have been mentioned at all. Malaterre went to see Shaarawi again and we learned that she was as fond of me as ever, that she had put me forward on her voting paper, that the Jewish question was not the matter but only the Palestine-Jewish question, so on the election paper Shaarawi appeared. Naturally she did not get as many votes as she would have liked as she had propagated before that she would not stand.

You can well imagine my feelings those days as I had just after much pressure from your side tried to overcome my standpoint and after my Board Members had each of them made a speech to me at the Board Meeting to beg me to re-consider and stand for election, I had indeed given in but at that moment you can understand what I felt like.

Well the elections went off fairly well and a great number of countries put me forward as usual and after Malaterre and Plamínková I had the most votes. Funnily enough Mme Shaarawi had said that the only member of the Board she could not stand was Mlle Gourd because 15 years ago she had said something she did not like. That was quite an amusing incident and it shows that the mentality of the Moslem woman is rather different to ours.

Well then it came to the last day when resolutions were put forward by the Resolution Committee and although the Egyptians had put their resolution in quite a different form, they still put it into the Congress which as you can imagine was a dreadful thing in which for the first time they stirred the Palestine women.[4] To my mind it was <u>wrong</u> to have any discussions on it at all as it was really not within the scope of the Alliance and ought to have been ruled out, but Mrs. Ashby let it for discussion and even let Shaarawi or her Delegates talk two to three times. The Palestine women got so heated up that it was really terrible. One of the Indian Women got up and said this was out of order and that the Indian women did not talk about their Indian politics and that it was wrong to do so. Finally the egyptian resolution was put to the vote and was of course voted down with a great majority, so then the three egyptian Delegates walked out.

It was a dreadful thing to happen and I think it could have been avoided if we had been strict in the beginning.

Funnily enough we first got a letter of resignation from Mme Shaarawi and then she wrote again saying she had to re-consider and talk with her Auxiliary at home. Well honestly, we ought to have a firm president although I agree that for Mrs. Ashby as a british woman it was a very delicate matter, but if politics get into our Alliance, we better stop. What do you say?[5]

A good feature of the Copenhagen Congress was that there was a great number of younger women under thirty interested in the work and anxious to carry the work on. They had an interesting meeting of the Youth Council where young men and young women came in great numbers. This was most peculiar because it was holiday time and they feared that everyone was away. There were quite capable young women from England and many

Delegations had brought young women with them. It was quite interesting to hear their speeches and their discussions, also Miss Betty Shield Collins who was one of the head persons of the Youth Congress at Waser [Vassar] College last year. They intend carrying the work on in a special Youth Council but nobody over 30 years is allowed there so I am afraid you and I are no more accepted!

As I have mentioned already in the beginning I stood again for re-election and more than 15 countries put me forward and I was re-elected with almost the highest amount of votes and now I am in again for three years. I hope you received my cable telling you I have been re-elected.

We have eight new Board Members now amongst whom some very valuable ones. An outstanding woman from Sweden, Dr. Hanna Rydh, who was in the U.S.A. last year; she is an archeologist. Then a charming, capable woman, Kunwa Rani Lady Maharay Singh from British India, further a young french woman who is at the head of a wood manufactury in Marseilles, as well as a young french lawyer from Maria Verona's Society and then a young Danish girl who had been sent last year to the Youth Congress and who did a great deal for our Congress this time.[6] Then the president of Denmark, Mrs. Edel Saunte, a young lawyer and president of our auxiliary came in and instead of our polish member of parliament Mrs. Szelagowska who has no more time, we have a capable polish woman, Mrs. Siemienska.

Bertha Lutz has not been re-elected. It is always difficult to get people elected if not at the Congress and as she had not been at the Istanbul Congress either, the people who come now, do not even know her. I think poor Bertha will be very disappointed.

Instead Mrs. Rocha from Brasil was elected. She is an official at the Ambassy of Brasil in Paris, a nice intelligent young woman who since a few years is a Delegate to the Assembly and the Labour Office[7] for Brasil and she can come to the Board Meetings which of course, is a great help.

It was indeed a great <u>loss</u> to the Congress that we had <u>no</u> American Delegation. This was the very first time such a dreadful thing happened. Although Mrs. Potter was made american delegate and Miss Dingman, to us insiders, it did not mean the same at all. Mrs. Potter has been for so many years at Geneva so that although she keeps in touch with the League of Women Voters she is no longer to my mind, a real delegate of that body and Miss Dingman has never been really in touch with them, so although Mrs. Potter was put forward by some countries, there was no chance of getting her elected. We have discussed it with our new Board Members and everybody thought it was dreadful not to have the United States represented. You will understand how badly I feel about it personally but I think Josephine[8] never had the real interest in the Alliance.

I wonder what could be done about it and if it would help if two good Alliance Members would make a tour in different places for the Members of the League of Women Voters. Do give us your advice!!

I am going to spend a week or ten days with my sister at Miss Sterling's from August 8th and I shall be home again for my birthday when my young nieces and nephews will be with me that day, August 20th. In September I shall go to Geneva.

My house is not rented yet so I think I will have to keep it on for another year. I have a friend staying with me now.

Now I leave you again for the moment and send you my love and heaps of it.

I am sorry this letter seems such a long one but I know you like to hear—There is much more to tell but I shall leave that till next time. Much love from old <u>fighting Rosa</u>.[9]

1. Manus may be referring to stories she undoubtedly heard from Catt about preparations for the 1906 congress. On June 11, 1906, Catt wrote to Jacobs that the Danish women were good women but "I have not yet discovered one with leadership qualities and this is going to present difficulties." CCC to AJ, June 11, 1906 (AJ-IAV-IIAV).

2. The declaration ran: "The sacredness of human personality has always been the keystone of the women's movement. If women believe the state to be an organisation to secure peace, freedom, justice and well-being for all they must hold this conviction with passionate sincerity. Women must keep alive the belief of democracy. There can be no freedom for women when freedom is no longer a recognised right of every individual. The woman's battle is that of all mankind." Remarkable, Schreiber notes that the resolution was unanimously carried. Schreiber and Mathieson 1955, 52.

3. Huda Shaarawi (in Alliance records spelled Hoda Charaoui; here spelled according to Margot Badran's edition of Huda Shaarawi's memoirs) was an Egyptian who grew up in a harem and later became a feminist and nationalist. In 1923, four years after the Egyptian women took to the streets for the first time on March 16, 1919 to protest British rule, Huda Shaarawi founded the Egyptian Feminist Union, of which she was chairman. In May 1923, together with two other Egyptian women, she formed a delegation to the Rome congress. When they reached the Cairo railway station Huda Shaarawi threw back her veil in front of all the women who had come to meet them. Her fellow delegates followed suit. See Shaarawi 1986.

4. Manus means Jewish women here. The Palestinian-Jewish question had so far been discussed only within the board. The issue still sparks off commotion at United Nations women's conferences, in Mexico (1975), Copenhagen (1980), and in Nairobi (1985).

5. Palestine was under British mandate. At the end of 1917, Britain had supported Zionism by recognizing the right of Jews to create "a national refuge" in a Palestine mostly inhabited by Arabs (Balfour). During the thirties, the British tried to appease the Arab world by curbing immigration of Jews. Margery Corbett Ashby (probably late in life in view of the handwriting) recorded differing, detailed memories of this "sad incident which nearly sent our much loved pioneer from Egypt . . . Madame Shaarawi home." According to Ashby, Shaarawi had proposed a resolution condemning the system of capitulations—the right of foreigners (the English) in Egypt to stand trial in their own courts of law, a system dating from the Ottoman era. Because a motion which involved two affiliated countries could not be passed without approval of both country's organizations, and because the British society was opposed, it was not brought forward. Ashby contines: "Poor Madame Shaarawi could not understand my hesitation and dissolved into tears at my British imperialism" (MICA-FL). Certainly Ashby had a difficult position in Copenhagen. Manus' criticism of her may be colored by criticism of British policy with regard to Jewish refugees. Nevertheless, the different reports of the events, even if biases and lapses of memory are taken into account, are intriguing.

6. The young French woman was Marguérite Boyer. The French lawyer was Andrée Lehmann. The Danish woman was Margot Petersen.

7. The International Labour Office of the League of Nations.

8. Josephine Schain, who had chaired the Alliance's Peace Committee since 1934. She left the committee to devote her time to Cause and Cure of War.

9. On June 8, 1939, Manus wrote Catt: "I am now beginning a new period in my life: will it be one of the old maid sitting and knitting or will it be a fighting Rosa who still believes in the cause of equality and righteousness[?] Catt answered by return of post, on June 20: "Do be a fighting Rosa. The world is going to need fighters, because most people are terribly confused and bewildered over the present situation" (CCC-LC).

81. Rosa Manus to Carrie Chapman Catt

[Amsterdam] August 22nd 1939

Dear Mother Carrie,

I have before me your letter of August 4th and another one of August 7th and since I have had my birthday on August 20th I have had your most welcome greetings on that day. It was so nice to know that day you were thinking of me!

It was strange to have that day pass by without my mother being there. One is so used having her around all the day but still I am satisfied to know she has had until the last a good time and that last year when we went together in the country she enjoyed it so much and we spent my last birthday with her.

The young ones all spent two days with me as it was on a Sunday, so Erica came and Carmen and Egon. We were fourteen at midday dinner and as it was a hot day, I had it served on the terrace and I gave them a real dutch east-indian meal. How you would have enjoyed it. The real "Rice-tafel" with the "Kroepoek" etc. It was served in soup-dishes and they drank beer with it and they all had a good time.

Do you remember the seeds I took away two years ago from your climber with the blue bells; they all came up of a sudden this time and so I was surrounded in fact by the American blue bells!

I had a good many nice presents and amongst them was a blue table cloth with little serviettes, all blue and beautifully embroidered. I am going to use it to day as I am going to have a friend just now.

In the morning of my birthday at about 10 o'clock I was called at the telephone by your Mr. Josefa[1] of the Philippines telling me they had arrived in Amsterdam the evening before and were leaving for Hambourg the very same morning at 11.29 –. I begged them to make me a flying visit as I thought

I did want to see them, so they spent 20 minutes with me. Mrs. Josefa certainly is a charming woman and we would have liked a few days of talk and discussion. I told her as much as I could about our Archives and she wants to send material for it and she also wants some of our stuff. What a pity they are in such a hurry as one really cannot get to understand a new country only in a few minutes time. Nevertheless I was pleased to see her and hope one day to meet her again in the Philippines.

Now as to your questions:

1. My health at present is better than it has been for many years. I look sunburned and well after a ten days stay with my sister at Miss Sterling's beautiful home. I enjoyed the garden and the rest and my sister[2] for the first time after Edgar's death came away and seemed to enjoy it very much. We were one day in London shopping and remembered the happy days with you at Liberty's etc. We went to the tea place where we went with you in Regent Street.

   The blood test showed that the streptococcen have gone, so there is no reason why I should have a relapse. My finger itself is not normal yet but that must take its time.

2. About Plamínková I have told you in my last letter and I think I said already what you wanted to know. She really said that the materials used for automobiles, flying machines, agricultural machinery etc. are all of inferior quality; things collapse by the road and she thinks that for war time they simply would be no use. On the other hand people told me the good materials have been stored away under the ground and piled up for use during the war.

   Plam indeed must be very careful. She came away to Copenhagen and to a Congress of the University Women at Oslo; she took away some amount of clothes. I think she had a quantity of new dresses made for fear she would not be allowed back and would then have enough clothes to last her for a number of years. I suppose she left quite a number in Denmark to have them at her disposal when they should chase her away.

   Mrs. Bompas[3] got her news saying she was over the Tsechoslovakian frontier again, so we think she is safe there now.

   She was busy building a little cottage outside Prague where she intends to go and stay for the rest of her life. If this is an optimistic idea I do not know. She was not allowed to take any jewelry out of the country unless she would put down a big sum of money as a caution and as she did not think it safe she did not take the jewelry away but gave everything officially by notary act to her sister who was still in Prague. Plam is as always, a plucky woman. It was plucky of her to come and she did not hesitate to speak, of course within the scope of our programme, and not one word of politics.

Nevertheless one evening in Copenhague one of our Congress people was rung up from Prague asking to give Plam a message to say she would better not return as it would be dangerous for her. Plam did not mind and did go back! I told Plam when I saw her about the interest you were taking in her and she was very, very pleased. I begged her to write a letter to you from Copenhague but she was so terribly busy there that I am afraid she did not write at all but she asked me to send her warm love to you.

3. No, there were no german, austrian, hungarian, italian nor spanish women at the Congress.

4. Has been answered in my last letter, that the Alliance would go on; not one word was said about dissolving it.

I for myself am not so convinced that we did rightly and that there is still a reason for the Alliance to go on with so many countries not attending. One can hardly call it really international nowadays but on the other hand it is in some way [of] keeping contacts with the women of the other countries, seeing there were so many present all the same (34 countries).

5. Yes, we have camps in Holland where refugees are kept temporarily until they can go to a permanent place. Now that we cannot really diggest [digest] anymore refugees in this country, they can only enter Holland now if they have a definite certificate, a real railroad or steamer ticket for another country and if their passport is officially marked off for the country they definitely go to. These refugees with their permits etcl, are allowed to stay here for a short period until they can continue their ultimate yourney and the Government has had camps errected [erected] where these people are kept; if possible the families have to pay for their relations thus kept in camps a fee of about $30,– a month to enable them to live there. If refugees appear not to have the necessary permits, tickets and so on, they are sent back at the frontiers.

There are camps of this sort outside Rotterdam, also in the north of our country; in fact there are several, also near Amsterdam. Such camps also exist in England. I think England on the whole is a <u>little</u> easier to take people in than they are in Holland. As a matter of fact Holland has taken in such enormous quatities of refugees in proportion to other countries, that it can hardly diggest anymore and the government must be as strict as they are now.

We also have a great number of children here; f.i. in Amsterdam an empty orphelinage [orphanage] has been filled with them; amongst these children there is a young cousin of 17 from my sister. We are taking care of that child paying a monthly fee to keep her there. Unfortunately lately they took in some children who seemed to have the dipht[h]eria-baccil [bacterium] and directly about 24 children were infected; these were put into quarantaine-hospital and some more followed. A few weeks later the little cousin was also taken to the hospital suddenly as she seemed to be infected too. That is the risk when one has to take care of someone else's children and the parents are so far away (in Chili this instance, trying to build up a new living. The mother is trying to earn her bread by making hats and it is quite remarkable how they seem to succeed).

As to Mrs. Urban,[4] I had a letter from her again this week. She also told me that her son is at work in the United States and that she hopes that her son will soon be able to have them come to America. I do not know how it will be possible to give them a preference visum [visa] but one thing I have learned in these last years, namely that the germans themselves manage always in some way or other to get affidavits[5] and permissions for parents etc. to join them whereas we outsiders trying to help, do not succeed at all. Over and over again I have tried myself lately with our own Government and I absolutely did not succeed to get any further people into the country whereas the Germans themselves managed to get them in. So I am at the point not to intervene with the Government any further as regards these matters.

As to Felix and Anna I have had several letters from them lately. They seem to like their new home. They have received the antique chairs from the dining room which Anna very much wanted to have. A cousin has brought them over with several other pieces of furniture, porcelain etc. from the parents' home. Anna seems very pleased with everything. Felix writes that he has a few patients and in his letter he was not so depressed.

The reason why he seemed so depressed when they come [came] to dinner with you will have been I am sure, as I have seen that so often before, that for some reason or other Anna before going out to you, Anna has made no end of a row with him and she does that in such a terrible way that Felix gets immensely downhearted and depressed. I myself always feel quite scared by one of these scenes of Anna; she herself after a few minutes quite forgets she has hurt your feelings and she does [acts] as if nothing has happened. A scene of that sort with Anna upsets Felix for days and I would not be surprised if this depression from Felix did not result again from a similar outbreak of Anna's. I am so sorry for him as instead of helping him, she always for one reason or other bothers him and worries him.

It was indeed lucky for them that at that moment they received the money from my mother; just at the right moment when they needed it most.

Anna has always been impossible and will remain so for the rest of her life.

First she bothers him that she wants a certain thing to happen and no sooner has it been arranged then she worries him that she wants something else to happen. So for that.

I am sorry I was not there when you read over the letters to Molly about South-America. I would have enjoyed it immensely and would have loved to hear you putting in some words of praise. I remember indeed very well the moment when you hurt your foot. Indeed at first it looked rather serious although I did not tell you so but I was glad that by dressing it two or three times a day, it got well so soon. It might easely have given you some blood poissoning. It was quite funny you saying I would have been a good doctor or a good nurse.

When I was in England I read a book about Mary Garrett Anderson,[6] the first woman Doctor of Gr. Br., a sister of Mrs. Fawcett. It gave me a big thrill; it is quite wonderful what she has done and made of her life. I go indeed so enthusiastic that I kept on saying: why did not I become a woman doctor, why did not I erect a women-hospital with women-doctors and women-patients. Why have I made such a failure of my life! I told my little sister I still wanted to be a doctor but coming to my senses again I quite well realize that my brains would not be ready for doing the examens [examinations] that are needed nowadays but I am still thinking hard in what way I can make muself [myself] useful in that direction. It may be that some day shortly a new plan will appear!

I am so glad to hear you are feeling so much better. That sounds wonderful and I am sure your garden will have given you much pleasure this summer.

My plans are not settled yet for the future. If the Inter-Continental Conference will take place and the European situation will allow it, I intend coming over to Washington Conference, but it may be that our situation gets thus that it will not be likely that we can travel, but I will write later about that.

In England I found that war-psychose [psychosis] is most horrible! If it was artificially done, I do not know; because as a rule the British nation is so very flegmatic it has been considered necessary to buck them up, I do not know; at any rate one felt as if war was to break out at any moment.

To day I will simply thank you for all your loving thoughts to me. Your friendship has been amongst the greatest assetts in my life and you know it. Your understanding has been most helpful and I hope you will be able to help me solve my problems of to day when I have to start a new life in many ways.

Dear Mother Carrie,

blessing upon you.

Your loving stepdaughter, Rosa.

Lots of love to dear Alda.

1. The Philippine couple Josefa had visited Catt earlier. Catt asked Rosa to receive them and show them the IAV. CCC to RM, August 7, 1939 (CCC-LC).

2. Rosa's youngest sister, Bé, who was married to Edgar Stern. They had one son, Egon.

3. Kathleen Bompas was secretary at the Alliance headquarters in London.

4. Gisela Urban-Stern was an Austrian feminist writer who attended many international suffrage congresses. From the beginning of 1939, the Catt correspondence gives evidence of her attempts to emigrate to the United States (CCC-LC). See WWT.

5. This refers to a sworn statement by which an American citizen could stand as guarantor for the maintenance of an immigrant or refugee.

6. Rosa means Elizabeth Garrett Anderson. The biography was written by her daughter, Louisa Garrett Anderson, *Elizabeth Garrett Anderson, 1836–1917* (London, 1939).

82. Rosa Manus to Carrie Chapman Catt

Amsterdam, February 2nd 1940

Dear Mother Carrie,

I have been wanting to write to you many a time but I am so full of work that there is hardly a moment to stop.

With our Women's Voluntary Corps[1] we have our hands full of work. The municipality reckons very much upon co-operation with us and although we are not paid neither by the Government nor by the municipality we only do the things which the municipality asks us to do but we think we keep free without having them finance us.

We are very popular and therefore big concerns, banks etc. up to now have secured us enough funds to go on. All the work to be done in the headquarters (there are about a 100 women working there daily) is done without pay.

Yesterday we had a lecture from the Chief of the Airraid-Protection Service and he tried to tell us in what way we women could be of the greatest use to our country.

The European situation is certainly very grave and one cannot think who will make an end to it. I fear this desaster may last a few further years.

I have started to clear out many things, f.i. a great part of my documents and letters which I have gathered since 30 years have gone to our International Archives; much of my library had already gone there too. It will prove more useful in the future to have it all there and as everything was already filed, it was quite easy to remove things.

Still having this big department [apartment] which is really too expensive for me, is really a burden but helas, I cannot get rid of it. I have so many obligations to fulfill towards family and relations that I must try to knock down my expenses. To begin with I have done away with my faithful chauffeur Herman, the one who drove you about during the study conferences, the one who has been with us for 21 years. Three months ago I told him that really I could not go on keeping him, I have not enough work for him to do and the expenses are much too high, it is very sad indeed, as with him really go all the family souvenirs. But I think it is better to do it in time. Next November I shall get rid of this big department [apartment] and will try to find a small, three-room flat with a kitchen. That is all I need and even if I have to go and live in one room I would not mind. Nothing seems to matter nowadays with this world catastrophe hanging about our heads. At any rate I will stay here and hope I shall not be chased away.

The Alliance Board is planning to come together in the first days of March possibly Paris, and in connection with it we are inviting some special people to have a consultation and see in how far the women can join up and have their influence when the time comes, of the peace settlement. Travelling in Europe however, is very very difficult. To get a visum [visa] from England to France or to Switzerland takes about six weeks at least and then one is not sure to get it. From our country it is even more difficult, so I do not know if I will be able to get permission to leave. Secondly my Corps of Voluntary Women keeps me in my own country.

Kathleen Courtney and Margery very much want me to join them, so I will see what I can do.

Anna wrote and told me she dined with you for your birthday. I am glad one of the family was there. How I wish I could come and see you and have a heart to heart talk. There is so much I would need your advice about. At times I feel horribly lonely. Do you know that your stepdaughter is 58 years old now? So I am getting on to be a real old lady! We in Holland have organised a campaign for donations of [to] the brave women of Finland.[2] We have little books with the flag of Finland on the outside, just not too big to put in your handbag. Every women we meet we ask to sign her name and to give us a small gift. All the women's organisations of Holland are playing their part in it and we mean to get thousands of these little books filled and they will be sent by the Ambassy and handed over in March to those splendid women showing them how the women of Holland are admiring them. In that way we hope to collect a big sum of money which these women can use as they like. We read in the papers that gifts come in from many countries for Finland, but these are all sent through the Red Cross to Finland, so we thought it would be a nice idea to have a collection especially for the women who certainly show their energy and perseverence. I have had a letter from one fin[n]ish woman, Miss Hallsten Kallia who writes us a great deal about the terrible things they have to endure but she says that they are all willing to serve and help their country.

I am so pleased that another University has given you a[n] honor[ar]y degree. Have they given you another coat and cap?

I send you much love and be assured, dear Mother Carrie that my thoughts wander often and often out to you. It is wonderful to have had you as a friend for so many years and I hope and pray that one day I shall be in your home again.

> Bless you dear old friend,
>
> lovingly always
>
> Rosa

1. Manus and others, for example, Jane de Iongh, were board members of the Women's Voluntary Corps (Korps Vrouwelijke Vrijwilligers), founded in 1938. The corps provided aid in fields of social life and offered courses for women in anticipation of the war. It was forced to dissolve in February 1941 during the German occupation but came back to life after the war as the Union of Women Voluntaries (Unie van Vrouwelijke Vrijwilligers).

2. The Russians marched into Finland on November 30, 1939. The war between the Soviet Union and Finland lasted until March 12, 1940. A special women's regiment was publicized in the international media, and collections were carried out for the regiment in the Netherlands.

83. Rosa Manus to Carrie Chapman Catt

Amsterdam, January 16th 1941

Dear Mother Carrie,

I was so pleased to receive your letter of December 12th telling me about the Congress.[1] From different sides I have heard what an immense success it was and how remarkable you were.

Anna was enchanted and was very thankful that you gave her and the doctor the opportunity to sit at your guest table. I could all picture it so well as I have been so often amongst you all that I know exactly how the preparations and the congress proceedings were.

I was much thinking of you those days when you were at the Commodore Hotel and my thoughts were daily with you. I am so glad you are saving a book for me, please write something in it; you know how much it will be appreciated.[2]

Erica is trying to get her visum [visa] but this is not an easy matter at present. She is working daily at the Laboratorium but I am convinced that when she gets over there she will have to do some new sc[h]ooling.

My health is not as good as it might be but that is a minor fact. I am still doing my work, go to the office a few times a week; the board meetings take place in my house as they do not want me to get too tired, so you see I am now getting the old lady with all those youngsters who come on their bicycles through the snow and rain but they simply do not let me go, so I am trying to help them, if it is only trying to give them some of my experience. It is so wonderful to feel in these days how the friends who are real friends keep coming. We go through difficult times and I may say that I long for the time when we can have a heart to heart talk again like in olden times. After five o'clock we do not go out. We have a severe winter, and Holland is on skates again like one sees it on the pictures. I wonder if you have seen Miss Hage.[3] I received a cable from her and Josephine for the New year, so I know she was there. She is a very remarkable person and you will enjoy her talk although she may be a bit fatigueing at times, but she is very, very nice. I hope you will be able to take a holiday with Alda. In one way it is nice to get out of the regular home life but on the other hand one is always best in one's own bed and surroundings. Still I know a few weeks in a good sanatorium where one is looked after, is also a good plan.

I suppose you read about the happenings in Europe. Margery seems to be well and one day I hope to get a letter from her; I have not seen her paper.[4]

You have always told me that a memory can never be taken away and you are right. In these days I just sit and think of all the nice things which have gone, the wonderful times I have had with you arise amongst them and it seems to be helping me to pull along, but it is difficult sometimes. Let us hope that the time may come that we can sit chatting. I will be the first to come over when it will be possible.

I try to be brave. Blessings on you, dear Mother Carrie and may you be spared for many, many years to come. Love to dear Alda and to all the friends over there.

Your ever loving

stepdaughter

Rosa

1. The Woman's Centennial Congress (Peck 1944, 464) marked the anniversary of the international antislavery congress in 1840 in London, where women like Lucretia Mott and Elizabeth Cady Stanton shared their indignation at women's not being allowed to take part in the meeting. They were allowed only to follow the discussion from the public gallery. Stanton 1971, 71ff.

2. The book refers to *Victory: How Women Won It* (1940) to which Catt had contributed the introduction and a chapter.

3. Miss Hage, a friend of Manus', safely reached the United States via Lisbon.

4. This may refer to the *International Women's News,* successor to *Jus Suffragii.*

84. Carrie Chapman Catt to Rosa Manus

[New Rochelle] August 6, 1941

Dear Rosa:

This is a birthday letter to congratulate you upon your sixtieth birthday. You will surely live as long as I have lived, twenty-two years longer. My brother, whom you never saw, is still living and is eighty-five and a half years old.

At Anna's urgent request, we drove to Riverdale on Saturday and took tea with Anna and Felix. It is only about a half hour's ride from here. They have a very comfortable little apartment with a tiny garden, but they are not quite satisfied with it because it is so far from Felix' office.

Perhaps you remember Madam Palencia.[1] She has written a book which is very good indeed. She is a good writer and what she has to say is very pleasing. She has told about her early life which gives one an idea of how the people in Spain lived. She is a refugee now with her husband and she has been lecturing this last winter, and it has been very satisfactory. People like her very much.

Our garden would be very nice if it did not have so many visitors. The latest visitor is the Japanese beetle. It came to this country with some bulbs from Japan about twenty years ago. Now we take a good sized can of soap suds and put some ammonia in it. We then go around and fill it full of these pests. They eat flowers and leaves, but their favorite is roses. Fortunately, we are between the two blossoming seasons. The June roses have passed and the October ones have not yet come. Before that time, the beetles will leave us and go down into the ground and lay eggs, so more beetles can come next year. Many varieties of poison for them are being recommended, but none of them can kill them off fast enough; however, they will not last forever.

We had a little visit from Mrs. Van den Bergh[2] and her granddaughter Ada who is a friend of Erica. We were very glad to see them. I have also met some other people from Holland.

Anna is very much disturbed about her daughter and is very anxious to have her come over. It is not so easy to do and I have an idea that perhaps the daughter prefers to remain there.

Our bulbs do not blossom more than once a year, although I believe there are some kinds that blossom in the autumn. We have none of that variety. Everybody misses the Dutch bulbs this year for many of us were accustomed to ordering them direct from Holland. The bulbs do not continue to remain large and free blossoming. We have many squirrels and the naughty little creatures sometimes go down into the earth and eat the bulbs.

Mary Peck lives where she has always lived and is getting on very well.

At this present moment she is taking a little trip, visiting some relatives and friends, but will be back before the week is over.

We do not go to New York often during the hot summer, but we shall be going some day soon and we shall not forget to look for a rubber apron for you. However, our country has discovered that it must curtail the use of many things for the present. We are being limited a little on gasoline and no longer is silk allowed to come in from Japan, so there are no silk stockings to be made after today. Some women are worried about this, but they forget that silk stockings are quite new and we can get along without them in the future as well as we have done in the past.

With the warmest of love and the hope that ships will soon be crossing the ocean in such numbers that they will furnish a place to bring you over, for you have many friends here who would love to see you, I am, as ever,

Lovingly,

[Carrie Chapman Catt]

1. Isabel de Palencia, president of the Spanish feminist association, wrote *I Must Have Liberty* and *Smoldering Freedom*. After the war she published a biography of Alexandra Kollontai.

2. Betsi van den Bergh-Willing was in various committees of the Dutch National Council of Women. In 1908 she was made an honorary member of the Alliance. She was very wealthy, probably made many donations, and was one of the women who supported Jacobs financially after 1918. VWP to RS, June 11, 1947 (SL-NYPL).

85. Carrie Chapman Catt to Friends of Rosa Manus

[New Rochelle] July 10, 1942

To Friends of Rosa Manus:

I take this means of reply to numerous inquiries concerning Rosa's death which have come to me.

At some date between August 10th and 14th 1941, the Gestapo arrested her at her home. She probably had no intimation that this would ever happen.[1] She spent a month in a hotel in Holland used by the Germans as a place of detention.[2] While there, she wrote one letter to her sister in Amsterdam, asking for wool to knit and a hot water bottle. Whether she received these things is unknown to me. From Holland, she was moved to Düsseldorf and from there to Berlin where she was kept in what was once a Woman's Prison. She received no letters or messages and her family did not know where she was until they received a letter in the early spring of

1942, asking them to send her 200 marks with which to purchase clothing. She acknowledged the receipt of the money and said that she now had permission to write to her sister, but to no one else, once a month, and to receive one reply. No further news came from her. She is supposed to have died in the camp May 29th.[3] She was therefore a German prisoner for nearly ten months without communication with any outside person.

She left an unfinished letter to me on her desk at her home, dated August 10th, 1941.[4] It was personal only and her sister sent it to me via Switzerland.[5] She said in it that since she had developed gall stones, she felt miserable and suffered from cold. I therefore am amazed that she lived so long. No one knows anything about her life or treatment in her prison camp. In similar camps, prisoners were not permitted to speak with each other and in others they were made to crawl on their hands and knees. That happened to a Czeck member of the Alliance Board[6] whom I have known for years. We probably will never know the details of Rosa's experience there.

Why was she seized? She was not accused of any offense. It is my understanding that she was one of many Dutch who were caught in the strategy of military politics. When the Germans attacked Holland, it was apparently their plan to seize the East Indies at the same moment. They had organized all the Germans living there and had sent several ships which were anchored in the ports and had never been seen there before. The local Dutchmen, however, arrested all Germans on the Islands and seized the ships before the Germans had had time to set. The Hitlerites were furious about that and at once arrested by way of reprisal one hundred of the most prominent Dutch citizens in Holland as hostages and, from time to time thereafter, added groups to this number. Rosa was taken a year later.

Rosa had been active for some years in the organization and maintenance of the International Women's Archives, a library at Amsterdam designed to be a research center for all subjects concerning the woman['s] movement. Its most valuable asset was the library and collection of Dr. Aletta Jacobs. I was somewhat familiar with it and regard its loss as irreparable. Rosa was the President. She also organized and was President of the Amsterdam Women's Volunteer Corps, sponsored by the Dutch government and which was devoted to the care of refugees and victims of the Nazi oppression. The Germans dissolved the Corps and the Archives. They seized the entire contents of the Archives Headquarters, including all books and correspondence. It is believed that they were burned.

Rosa remained quietly at home thereafter. Previous to the war, Queen Wilhelmina had awarded her the Order of the Orange Nassau. This was a further indication of her importance as a citizen.

Rosa had been an officer of the International Alliance of Women for Suffrage and Equal Citizenship for some years and had been conspicuous in the preparations and conduct of all the conventions held since the World War.

One friend writes: "Memories of Rosa have been crowding in my mind. I can see her bustling around in Paris, Amsterdam, Berlin, Istanbul. I'm sure that when the crisis came, she met it with courage. The same persistence which made her an organizer would stiffen her against the blows of fate. At least we may know that she was spared more suffering."

I may add that she became a dear personal friend and visited me in my home three times. She came for my seventieth birthday and for my eightieth. She also took two long trips with me, one in Europe and one through South America. Yet, for ten months, I could not send her one cheering message.

Rosa was a little Dutch girl, dancing with other boys and girls in Dutch costumes for the entertainment of the delegates in the Amsterdam convention of 1908. Then she scarcely knew what we were about. She grew into a dependable worker in the woman movement and, curiously enough, was the first of us all to suffer and to die for our cause.

Carrie Chapman Catt

1. In spring 1941 Rosa Manus was interrogated several times by the Gestapo. She was arrested on August 17 in Noordwijk, a resort, where she was on vacation.

2. Catt was mistaken. Rosa was at the "Orange Hotel," the rather cynical nickname for the prison at Scheveningen. Orange is the color of the Dutch royal family and was a symbol of liberty in World War II.

3. There are a number of accounts describing Rosa's last months. Clara Meijers, a good friend of hers for many years, wrote in her sympathetic biography that according to eyewitnesses Rosa was transported to Auschwitz in March 1942. She wrote hopefully of a rumor that Rosa was shot dead during the transport because of "unseemly" behaviour, which would have saved her the horror of the gas chamber (Meijers 1946, 62). Diligent research on the part of An du Burck, Mieke van Vugt, and Aukje van der Heu-Wildschut has recently brought new documents to light which suggest a totally different outcome, namely that Rosa died on April 28, 1943, in Ravensbrück after spending a year in hiding somewhere in the hospital where she was at the time of her disappearance in March 1942. It appears from an unsigned note that between May 24 and May 30, 1942, attempts were made through the Swedish embassy in Berlin to obtain information about her whereabouts. During a meeting on May 29, 1942, the prison authorities declared that Rosa Manus had never been in Ravensbrück and was not known. On June 13, 1942, the family in Amsterdam received a message that she had died at Ravensbrück on May 29, 1942. According to a letter from the Red Cross several witnesses have confirmed April 28, 1943, as the day of Manus' death. The death certificate from the Ravensbrück registry office, together with items like her last passport and a letter from fellow prisoner Nelia Epker, are now in her archive at the IIAV. See Burck, Van Vugt, and Van der Heu-Wildschut 1988.

4. We were unable to find this letter in the IAV collection or in the Library of Congress.

5. Via Switzerland means via Emilie Gourd. As Catt wrote to Margery Corbett Ashby, Emilie Gourd was a "heaven-sent friend to the people in this country." CCC to MCA, August 14, 1942 (MICA-FL). Rosa's sisters Bé and Anna corresponded through Emilie Gourd.

6. Františka Plamínková, who was hanged by the Germans. See letter 62, n. 5.

Rosa Manus, by Marthe Antoine Gérardin. The Hague, 1930.

Appendixes

A. Abbrevations[1]

AHS	Anna Howard Shaw
AJ	Aletta Jacobs
AM	Anna Manus
AWSA	American Woman Suffrage Association
Cause and Cure	Conference on the Cause and Cure of War
CCC	Carrie Chapman Catt
CH	Clara Hyde
Dingman Committee	Committee of International Women's Organizations for Peace and Disarmament (of Liaison Committee)
HWS	History of Woman Suffrage (see bibliography)
IAV	Internationaal Archief voor de Vrouwenbeweging (International Archive for the Women's Movement)
IAW	International Alliance of Women for Suffrage and Equal Citizenship
ICW	International Council of Women
IIAV	Internationaal Informatiecentrum en Archief voor de Vrouwenbeweging (International Information Center and Archive for the Women's Movement)
IISG	Internationaal Instituut voor Sociale Geschiedenis (International Institute for Social History)
IWSA	International Woman Suffrage Alliance
International Committee	International Committee of Women for Permanent Peace (later WILPF)
JA	Jane Addams
Joint Committee	Joint Standing Committee of International Women's Organizations
LEA	Lucy E. Anthony

---

1. For abbreviations of archives and collections, see Appendix B, below.

Liaison Committee	Liaison Committee of International Women's Organizations
NAW	Notable American Women (see bibliography)
NAWSA	National American Woman Suffrage Association
NUWSS	National Union of Women's Suffrage Societies
NWSA	National Woman Suffrage Association
Peace Committee	International Committee for Peace and the League of Nations (of IWSA)
RFA	Rachel Foster Avery
RM	Rosa Manus
RS	Rosika Schwimmer
SBA	Susan B. Anthony
VVVK	Vereeniging voor Vrouwenkiesrecht (Woman Suffrage Association)
VWP	Mien van Wulfften Palthe-Broese van Groenou
WCTU	Woman's Christian Temperance Union
WILPF	Women's International League for Peace and Freedom
WSPU	Women's Social and Political Union
WWT	Well-Known Women of Today (see bibliography)

B. Archives and Collections

AJ-IAV-IIAV	Aletta Jacobs Papers. In the IAV collection, Internationaal Informatiecentrum en Archief voor de Vrouwenbeweging (IIAV), Amsterdam.
AJ(JA)-IAV-IIAV	A small collection of photocopies from the Jane Addams Papers (in the Swarthmore Peace Collection, Swarthmore College), which have been added to AJ-IAV-IIAV.

CCC-IAV-IIAV	Carrie Chapman Catt Papers. In the IAV collection, IIAV, Amsterdam.
CCC-LC	Carrie Chapman Catt Papers. In the Manuscript Division, Library of Congress, Washington, D.C.
CCC-NYPL	Carrie Chapman Catt Papers. In the Rare Books and Manuscripts Division, The New York Public Library, Astor, Lenox and Tilden Foundations, New York.
CCC-Schl	Carrie Chapman Catt Papers. In the Arthur and Elizabeth Schlesinger Library, Radcliffe College, Cambridge, Mass.
CCC-SSC	Carrie Chapman Catt Papers. In the Sophia Smith Collection, Smith College, Northampton, Mass.
Coops-IAV-IIAV	E. Coops-Broese van Groenou Papers. In the IAV collection, IIAV, Amsterdam.
CPG-Schl	Charlotte Perkins Gilman Papers. In the Arthur and Elizabeth Schlesinger Library, Radcliffe College, Cambridge, Mass.
DC-Schl	Dillon-Collection. In the Arthur and Elizabeth Schlesinger Library, Radcliffe College, Cambridge, Mass.
FHAG-CRPA	Familie-en Huisarchief Groenoue. In the Central Register of Private Archives, The Hague.
IAW-SSC	International Alliance of Women Records. In the Sophia Smith Collection, Smith College, Northampton, Mass.
JS-SSC	Josephine Schain Papers. In the Sophia Smith Collection, Smith College, Northampton, Mass.
MICA-FL	Margery I. Corbett Ashby Papers. In the Fawcett Library, City of London Polytechnic, London.
SL-NYPL	Schwimmer-Lloyd Collection. In the Rare Books and Manuscripts Division, New York Public Library, Astor, Lenox and Tilden Foundations, New York.
SL(EWN)-NYPL	Edith Wynner notes (copyright Edith Wynner). In SL-NYPL. Edith Wynner, consultant to the Schwimmer-Lloyd Collection, kindly shared with us

the research notes she had made for the biography of Rosika Schwimmer which she is preparing.

RM-IAV-IIAV   Rosa Manus Papers. In the IAV collection, IIAV, Amsterdam.

VWP-IAV-IIAV   F. W. van Wulfften Palthe-Broese van Groenou Papers. In the IAV collection, IIAV, Amsterdam.

WRC-Schl   Woman's Rights Collection. In the Arthur and Elizabeth Schlesinger Library, Radcliffe College, Cambridge, Mass.

C. Letters and Locations

1. Aletta Jacobs (AJ) to Rosika Schwimmer (RS), November 5, 1902. German; manuscript. SL-NYPL.

2. AJ to RS, November 18, 1903. German; manuscript. SL-NYPL.

3. Susan B. Anthony (SBA) to AJ, December 17, 1904. English; typescript. AJ-IAV-IIAV.

4. AJ to RS, February 16, 1905. German; manuscript. SL-NYPL.

5. Anna Howard Shaw (AHS) to AJ, February 24, 1905. English; typescript. AJ-IAV-IIAV. Missing page from De Iongh 1938, 74–75.

6. Carrie Chapman Catt (CCC) to RS, March 4, 1905. English; typescript. SL-NYPL.

7. AJ to RS, May 7, 1905. German; manuscript. SL-NYPL.

8. AJ to RS, [July 1905]. German; manuscript. SL-NYPL.

9. CCC to AJ, December 1905. English; manuscript. AJ-IAV-IIAV.

10. AJ to RS, January 1, 1906. German; manuscript. SL-NYPL.

11. Lucy E. Anthony (LEA) to AJ, April 3, [1906]. English; typescript (and manuscript). AJ-IAV-IIAV.

12. Rachel Foster Avery (RFA) to AJ, April 9, 1906. English; manuscript. AJ-IAV-IIAV.

13. AJ to RS, September 10, 1906. German; typescript. SL-NYPL.

14. CCC to AJ, March 17, [1907]. English; manuscript. AJ-IAV-IIAV.

15. AHS to AJ, March 26, 1907. English; typescript. AJ-IAV-IIAV.

16. AJ to RS, May 15, 1907. German; manuscript. SL-NYPL.

17. AJ to RS, December 16, 1907. English; manuscript. SL-NYPL.

18. LEA to AJ, April 27, 1908. English; typescript. AJ-IAV-IIAV.

19. AHS to AJ, May 22, 1908. English; typescript. AJ-IAV-IIAV.

20. AHS to AJ, December 14, 1908. English; typescript. AJ-IAV-IIAV.

21. CCC to AJ, March 11, [1909]. English; manuscript. AJ-IAV-IIAV.

22. Rosa Manus (RM) to Catherine Waugh McCulloch, June 2, 1909. English; manuscript. DC-Schl.

23. AJ to RS, July 7, 1909. English; manuscript. SL-NYPL.

24. CCC to AJ, September 27, 1909. English typescript. AJ-IAV-IIAV.

25. AHS to AJ, December 11, 1909. English; typescript. AJ-IAV-IIAV.

26. AJ to RS, April 8, 1910. English; manuscript. SL-NYPL.

27. LEA to AJ, June 10, 1910. English; typescript. AJ-IAV-IIAV.

28. RFA to AJ, July 14, 1910. English; typescript. AJ-IAV-IIAV.

29. CCC to AJ, July 16, 1910. English; manuscript. AJ-IAV-IIAV.

30. AHS to AJ, August 5, [1910]. English; manuscript. AJ-IAV-IIAV.

31. CCC to AJ, May 15, 1911. English; typescript. AJ-IAV-IIAV.

32. RM to Anna Manus (AM), [June 1911]. Dutch; manuscript. RM-IAV-IIAV.

33. AHS to AJ, July 16, 1912. English; manuscript. AJ-IAV-IIAV.

34. CCC to AJ, December 7, 1912. English; manuscript. AJ-IAV-IIAV.

35. CCC to AJ, February 26, 1913. English; manuscript. AJ-IAV-IIAV.

36. AJ to Mien van Wulfften Palthe-Broese van Groenou (VWP), May 16, 1913. Dutch; manuscript. VWP-IAV-IIAV.

37. Martina Kramers (MK) to RS, June 2, 1913. German; manuscript. SL-NYPL.

38. CCC to MK, May 21, 1913. English; typescript (copy?). SL-NYPL.

39. MK to CCC, June 2, 1913. English; typescript (copy?). SL-NYPL.

40. CCC to RS et al., [June 1913]. English; manuscript. SL-NYPL.

41. AHS to AJ, July 11, 1913. English; manuscript. AJ-IAV-IIAV.

42. AHS to AJ, March 19, 1914. English; manuscript. AJ-IAV-IIAV.

43. LEA to AJ, October 7, 1914. English; typescript. AJ-IAV-IIAV.

44. CCC to AJ, November 13, 1914. English; typescript (and manuscript). AJ-IAV-IIAV.

45. AHS to AJ, January 4, 1915. English; manuscript. AJ-IAV-IIAV.

46. AJ to VWP, February 5, 1915. Dutch; manuscript. VWP-IAV-IIAV.

47. AJ to RS, April 7, 1915. English; typescript copy. SL(EWN)-NYPL.

48. CCC to AJ, June 30, 1915. English; typescript (and manuscript). AJ-IAV-IIAV.

49. AJ to Jane Addams (JA), September 8, 1915. English; photocopy of manuscript. AJ(JA)-IAV-IIAV.

50. Emily Hobhouse to AJ, August 21, 1915. English; photocopy of manuscript. AJ(JA)-IAV-IIAV.

51. AJ to RS and Chrystal Macmillan, September 13, 1915. English; typescript copy. SL(EWN)-NYPL.

52. AHS to AJ, [October 1915]. English; manuscript. AJ-IAV-IIAV.

53. AHS to AJ, April 18, 1916. English; manuscript. AJ-IAV-IIAV.

54. AHS to AJ, [August 30, 1917]. English; manuscript. AJ-IAV-IIAV.

55. CCC to AJ, September 4, 1918. English; typescript. AJ-IAV-IIAV.

56. AHS to AJ, Thanksgiving Day 1918. English; manuscript. AJ-IAV-IIAV.

57. RM to LEA, June 1920. English; manuscript. RM-IAV-IIAV.

58. CCC to AJ, October 11, 1920. English; typescript. AJ-IAV-IIAV.

59. Clara Hyde (CH) to RM, September 29, 1922. English; typescript, minute. CCC-LC.

60. RM to CH, April 28, 1923. English; typescript. CCC-LC.

61. AJ to Miel Coops-Broese van Groenou, May 18, 1923. Dutch; typescript. Coops-FHAG-CRPA.

62. RM to CCC, June 22, 1926. English; typescript. CCC-LC.

63. RM to LEA, November 15, 1926. English; typescript. RM-IAV-IIAV.

64. AJ to LEA, July 21, 1928. English; manuscript. AJ-IAV-IIAV.

65. AJ to CCC, October 23, 1928. English; manuscript. CCC-NYPL.

66. AJ to CCC, May 28, 1929. English; manuscript. CCC-LC.

67. CCC to RM, July 19, 1929. English; typescript, minute. CCC-LC.

68. CCC to RM, September 18, 1931. English; typescript, minute. CCC-LC.

69. RM to CCC, January 24, 1932. English; manuscript. CCC-LC.

70. RS to CCC, May 23, 1932. English; typescript (copy?). SL-NYPL.

71. CCC to RS, June 11, 1932. English; typescript (copy?). SL-NYPL.

72. RM to CCC, October 5, 1932. English; manuscript. CCC-LC.

73. CCC to RM, April 25, 1933. English; typescript, minute. CCC-LC.

74. RM to CCC, August 31, 1933. English; manuscript. CCC-LC.

75. CCC to RM, July 17, 1935. English; typescript, minute. CCC-LC.

76. RS to VWP, March 7, 1936. English; typescript. SL-NYPL.

77. RM to CCC, April 1, 1937. English; typescript. CCC-LC.

78. RM to CCC, January 5, 1938. English; typescript, minute. CCC-LC.

79. RM to CCC, November 29, 1938. English; typescript. CCC-LC.

80. RM to CCC, July 31, 1939. English; typescript. CCC-LC.
81. RM to CCC, August 22, 1939. English; typescript. CCC-LC.
82. RM to CCC, February 2, 1940. English; typescript. CCC-IAV-IIAV.
83. RM to CCC, January 16, 1941. English; typescript. CCC-LC.
84. CCC to RM, August 6, 1941. English; typescript, minute. CCC-IAV-IIAV.
85. CCC to friends of RM (circular letter), July 10, 1942. English; typescript. CCC-IAV-IIAV.

D. Countries Affiliated with the IWSA, 1904–42

The list is based upon the often unclear congress reports. Countries are named only at their first official affiliation with the IWSA. One or more associations may have been affiliated. Since the map has changed more than once (and the reports do not explain such changes and even use old and new terms next to each other), I have chosen to copy the reports with respect to historical geographical terminology, sometimes indicating changes only parenthetically. To give one instance, Serbia is later listed as "Kingdom of Servia, Croatia and Slovenes" and later still as Yugoslavia (or Jugoslavia). In my list I record only the entrance of Serbia (later Yugoslavia), thus skipping over dramatic political changes. The same is true for Bohemia (later Czechoslovakia). Here I do not mention the fact that after the foundation of the Republic of Czechoslovakia after World War I a second association of German women became affiliated, which reflects the political situation of growing German (Sudeten) nationalism in Bohemia, the Czech part of Czechoslovakia. Contemporary names are placed in square brackets, as with Ceylon [Sri Lanka]. A full list of affiliated countries is given for 1939 to show which countries were still in the IWSA.

1904

Australia
Germany
Great Britain
Netherlands
Sweden
United States

1906
Austria
Canada

Denmark
Hungary
Italy
Norway
Russia

1908

Bulgaria
Finland
South Africa
Switzerland

1909

Belgium
Bohemia (later Czechoslovakia)
France

1911

Iceland
Serbia (later Yugoslavia)

1913

China
Galicia (later Poland)
Portugal
Romania

1920

Argentina
Greece
Poland (first entered as Galicia)
Spain
Uruguay

1923

Brazil
Egypt
India

Ireland
Jamaica
Japan
New Zealand
Newfoundland
Palestine [Israel]
Lithuania
Ukraine (SSR)

1926

Bermuda
Cuba
Luxemburg
Peru
Puerto Rico
Turkey

1929

Ceylon [Sri Lanka]
Dutch East Indies [Indonesia]
Syria
Rhodesia [Zimbabwe]

Complete list of affiliated countries in 1939:

Argentina
Austria
Belgium
Bermuda
Bohemia
Brazil
Bulgaria
Canada
Ceylon
Denmark
Dutch East Indies
Egypt
Finland
France
Great Britain
Greece
Hungary
Iceland

India
Ireland
Japan
Luxemburg
Netherlands
New Zealand
Norway
Palestine
Poland (i.e., the Ukraine)
Romania
Sweden
Switzerland
Syria
Uruguay
United States
Yugoslavia

E. Boards and Officers of the IWSA, 1904–42

This list is based on the congress reports, which are not always unambiguous with respect to names, countries, and other details.

1904

Susan B. Anthony (United States)	Honorary President
Carrie Chapman Catt (United States)	President
Anita Augspurg (Germany)	1st Vice President
Millicent Garrett Fawcett (Great Britain)	2nd Vice President
Rachel Foster Avery (United States)	Secretary
Käthe Schirmacher (Germany)	1st Assistant Secretary
Johanna W. A. Naber (Netherlands)	2nd Assistant Secretary
Sophie Rodger Cunliffe (Great Britain)	Treasurer

1906

Carrie Chapman Catt (United States)	President
Anita Augspurg (Germany)	1st Vice President
Millicent Garrett Fawcett (Great Britain)	2nd Vice President
Rachel Foster Avery (United States)	Secretary
Käthe Schirmacher (Germany)	1st Assistant Secretary
Martina Kramers (Netherlands)	2nd Assistant Secretary
Sophie Rodger Cunliffe (Great Britain)	Treasurer (through 1906)

1907

Adela Stanton Coit (Great Britain)   Treasurer

1908

Carrie Chapman Catt (United States)   President
Anita Augspurg (Germany)   1st Vice President
Millicent Garrett Fawcett (Great Britain)   2nd Vice President
Rachel Foster Avery (United States)   1st Secretary
Käthe Schirmacher (Germany)   2nd Secretary
Martina Kramers (Netherlands)   3rd Secretary; Editor, *Jus Suffragii*

Adela Stanton Coit (Great Britain)   Treasurer

1909

Carrie Chapman Catt (United States)   President
Millicent Garrett Fawcett (Great Britain)   1st Vice President
Annie Furuhjelm (Finland)   2nd Vice President
Martina Kramers (Netherlands)   Secretary; Editor, *Jus Suffragii*
Anna Lindemann (Germany)   Secretary
Signe Bergman (Sweden)   Secretary
Adela Stanton Coit (Great Britain)   Treasurer

1911

Carrie Chapman Catt (United States)   President
Millicent Garrett Fawcett (Great Britain)   1st Vice President
Annie Furuhjelm (Finland)   2nd Vice President
Martina Kramers (Netherlands)   Secretary; Editor, *Jus Suffragii*
Anna Lindemann (Germany)   Secretary
Signe Bergman (Sweden)   Secretary
Adela Stanton Coit (Great Britain)   Treasurer

1913

Carrie Chapman Catt (United States)   President
Millicent Garrett Fawcett (Great Britain)   1st Vice President
Annie Furuhjelm (Finland)   2nd Vice President
Anna Lindemann (Germany)   3rd Vice President
Marguérite de Witt-Schlumberger (France)   4th Vice President
Katherine Dexter McCormick (United States)   1st Corresponding Secretary

Rosika Schwimmer (Hungary)	2nd Corresponding Secretary
Chrystal Macmillan (Great Britain)	1st Recording Secretary
Marie Stritt (Germany)	2nd Recording Secretary
Adela Stanton Coit (Great Britain)	1st Treasurer
Signe Bergman (Sweden)	2nd Treasurer

1920

Carrie Chapman Catt (United States)	President
Marguérite de Witt-Schlumberger (France)	1st Vice President
Chrystal Macmillan (Great Britain)	2nd Vice President
Anna Lindemann (Germany)	3rd Vice President
Anna Wicksell (Sweden)	4th Vice President
Margery Corbett Ashby (Great Britain)	Recording Secretary
Katherine Dexter McCormick (United States)	Treasurer
Eleanor Rathbone (Great Britain)	committee member
Antonia Girardet-Vielle (Switzerland)	committee member
Margherita Ancona (Italy)	committee member
Adele Schreiber (Germany)	committee member

1923

Carrie Chapman Catt (United States)	Honorary President
Margery Corbett Ashby (Great Britain)	President
Marguérite de Witt-Schlumberger (France)	1st Vice President
Anna Lindemann (Germany)	2nd Vice President[1]
Margherita Ancona (Italy)	3rd Vice President
Mrs. Gifford Pinchot (United States)	4th Vice President
Emilie Gourd (Switzerland)	Corresponding Secretary
Avra Theodoropoulos (Greece)	Recording Secretary
Frances Sterling (Great Britain)	Treasurer
Adele Schreiber (Germany)	committee member
Julie Arenholt (Denmark)	committee member
Paulina Luisi (Uruguay)[2]	committee member

1926

Carrie Chapman Catt (United States)	Honorary President
Margery Corbett Ashby (Great Britain)	President
Adele Schreiber (Germany)	1st Vice President
Margherita Anconra (Italy)	Vice President
Germaine Malaterre-Sellier (France)	Vice President
Rosa Manus (Netherlands)	Vice President

Františka Plamínková (Czechoslovakia)	Vice President
Emilie Gourd (Switzerland)	Corresponding Secretary
Avra Theodoropoulos (Greece)	Recording Secretary
Frances Sterling (Great Britain)	Treasurer
Suzanne Grinberg-Aupourrain (France)	Assistant Treasurer
Julie Arenholt (Denmark)	member
Milena Atanatskovitch (Yugoslavia)	member
Huda Shaarawi (Egypt)	member
Paulina Luisi (Uruguay)	member
Frederikke Mörck (Norway)	member
Ruth Morgan (United States)	member
Eugenie de Reuss Jancoulescu (Romania)	member
Bessie Rischbeith (Australia)	member
La Marquesa del Ter (Spain)	member
Avra Theodoropoulos (Greece)	member
Dorothee von Velsen (Germany)	member
Ingeborg Walin (Sweden)	member

1929

Carrie Chapman Catt (United States)	Honorary President
Margery Corbett Ashby (Great Britain)	President
Adele Schreiber (Germany)	1st Vice President
Rosa Manus (Netherlands)	2nd Vice President
Germaine Malaterre-Sellier (France)	Vice President
Františka Plamínková	Vice President
Emilie Gourd (Switzerland)	Corresponding Secretary
Milena Atanatskovitch (Yugoslavia)	Assistant Secretary
Frances Sterling (Great Britain)	Treasurer
Huda Shaarawi (Egypt)	member
Suzanne Grinberg-Aupourrain (France)	member
Ingeborg Hansen (Denmark)	member
Paulina Luisi (Uruguay)	member
Ruth Morgan (United States)	member
Alison Neilans (Great Britain)	member
Eugenie de Reuss Jancoulescu (Romania)	member
Bessie Rischbeith (Australia)	member
Belle Sherwin (United States)	member
La Marquesa del Ter (Spain)	member
Avra Theodoropoulos (Greece)	member
Dorothee von Velsen (Germany)	member
Ingeborg Walin (Sweden)	member

1935

Carrie Chapman Catt (United States)	Honorary President
Margery Corbett Ashby (Great Britain)	President
Adele Schreiber (Germany)	1st Vice President
Rosa Manus (Netherlands)	2nd Vice President
Germaine Malaterre-Sellier (France)	Vice President
Františka Plamínková (Czechoslovakia)	Vice President
Emilie Gourd (Switzerland)	Corresponding Secretary
Milena Atanatskovitch (Yugoslavia)	Assistant Secretary
Dorothee von Velsen (Germany)	Treasurer
Huda Shaarawi (Egypt)	member
Marie Ginsberg (Switzerland)	member
Suzanne Grinberg-Aupourrain (France)	member
Ingeborg Hansen (Denmark)	member
Paulina Luisi (Uruguay)	member
Alison Neilans (Great Britain)	member
Dhanvanthi Rama Rau (India)	member
Bessie Rischbeith (Australia)	member
Josephine Schain (United States)	member
La Marquesa del Ter (Spain)	member
Avra Theodoropoulos (Greece)	member
Ingeborg Walin (Sweden)	member

1939

Carrie Chapman Catt (United States)	Honorary President and Founder
Adele Schreiber (Germany)	Honorary Vice President
Margery Corbett Ashby (Great Britain)	President
Germaine Malaterre-Sellier (France)	1st Vice President
Frantiska Plamínková (Czechoslovakia)	2nd Vice President
Rosa Manus (Netherlands)	3rd Vice President
Kunwar Rani Maharaj Singh (India)	4th Vice President
Hanna Rydh (Sweden)	5th Vice President
Emilie Gourd (Switzerland)	Corresponding Secretary
Nina Spiller (Great Britain)	Treasurer
Milena Atanatskovitch (Yugoslavia)	member
Margarete Bonnevie (Norway)	member
Marguérite Boyer (France)	member
Huda Shaarawi (Egypt)	member
Marie Ginsberg (Switzerland)	member
Dimitrana Ivanova (Bulgaria)	member
Andrée Lehmann (France)	member

Alison Neilans (Great Britain) member
Margot Petersen (Denmark) member
Bessie Rischbeith (Australia) member
Héloise Rocha (Brazil) member
Edel Saunte (Denmark) member
Halina Siemienska (Poland) member
Anna Szelagowska (Poland)[3] member

1. According to the 1926 report, this was Paulina Luisi.

2. Germaine Malaterre-Sellier in 1926 report.

3. Mentioned in the list of delegates/members of the board in the 1939 report.

Notes

Chapter 1

1. In 1888 there were still two national suffrage organizations, the NWSA (or the "National") and the American Woman Suffrage Association (or the "American"). I have based my description of the early period of American suffragism predominantly on Dubois 1980 and Dubois 1981.

2. In her autobiography Elizabeth Cady Stanton (1815–1902) wrote extensively about her friendship with Susan B. Anthony (1820–1906) (Stanton 1971). See also Spender 1983 and DuBois 1981.

3. The first separatist suffrage organization grew out of disagreement with Radical Republicans, former abolitionists, and equal rightists over the Fifteenth Amendment, which intended to prohibit disenfranchisement explicitly on the grounds of race. DuBois gives a sensitive analysis of the combination of racism and feminism that emerged in feminist debates over the Fifteenth Amendment. DuBois 1980, 162ff.

4. Shaw 1915, 251. Shaw identifies "foreigners" also as "Russian Jews." Cf. Elinor Lerner 1986, 316.

5. Kraditor (1981) introduced the clarifying distinction between "arguments of justice" and "arguments of expediency."

6. Shaw 1915, 190. Shaw dedicates two chapters in her autobiography to "Aunt Susan," whom she saw almost daily for eighteen years.

7. Until recently Lucy E. Anthony has been largely ignored in the historiography of the suffrage movement, although she left her imprint on several important archival collections. In the context of a special issue on lesbian history of *Frontiers*, she received attention for the first time because of her importance in the life of Anna Howard Shaw. See Finn 1979.

8. They were: equal access to higher education and vocational training, equal pay for equal work, and an equal standard of morality for men and women.

9. Anita Augspurg (1857–1943) and Lida Gustava Heymann (1868–1943) lived and worked together in the woman's movement for more than forty years. In the nineties they both belonged to the radical wing of the Bund Deutscher Frauenvereine (Federation of German Women's Associations), which was organized separately in 1899 as the Bund Fortschrittlicher Frauenvereine (Federation of Progressive Women's Associations). Since Prussian law forbade women to organize themselves for a political goal, a separate suffrage organization did not yet exist. However,

Augspurg, who in 1893 had taken up university studies in law to become a legal adviser on women's issues, found out that Hamburg law offered the possibility of
founding such a woman suffrage organization. Thus in 1902 Augspurg and Heymann founded the Deutsche Verein für Frauenstimmrecht (German Woman Suffrage Association) and later played an important role in Berlin in 1904. See Heymann 1972; Schwarz 1983; *Feministische Studien* 1984.

    10. For instance, Schreiber and Mathieson 1955. I do think such interpretation
of the origins of the IWSA reflects a bias and uncritically repeats the historical domination of the IWSA by American suffragism in general and Catt in particular. It is
always important to make a distinction between chronicle and history, in this case
between IWSA chronicle and IWSA history. IWSA chronicles are most often, but
not always, written by members of the IWSA and are based on the records of the
Alliance. The chronicle may provide the (academic) historian with "facts," but it
must be considered as a reflection of the collective identity of the IWSA–of how
the IWSA wants to see its past. IWSA history, as written by (academic) historians,
is based on a broader range of source materials. A critical analysis of the IWSA chronicle is one part of research into the history of the IWSA. This distinction accounts
for the difference in interpretation of the "roots" of the IWSA. The chronicles, lean-
ing heavily upon Alliance reports and Peck's biography of Catt, repeat the influence
Catt had on the IWSA and discard the 1899 incident. But that incident is given
greater weight by scholars, who have access to sources besides IWSA records. See
Hurwitz 1977; Sherrick 1983. In this respect it must be said that Van Voris' narrative
of international suffragism is unsatisfactory. Not only does she romanticize Catt's
internationalism into an individual act of altruism (Van Voris 1987, 55), she is also clearly
mistaken on several issues, as when she calls Catt's questionnaire the first research on
the status of women in different countries (p. 56), or says that the IWSA was founded
in 1902. Fowler (1986) does not elaborate on Catt's internationalism but places it much
more convincingly in the context of American progressivism. Such a view gives room
for a more sophisticated interpretation of the history of the IWSA, which acknowl-
edges the fact that the International Alliance was dominated by American suffragism
and may reach beyond a simple repetition of such domination to grasp some of the
diversity of the suffrage politics and cultures bearing on the IWSA. See also Bosch 1989.

    11. Vida Goldstein (1869–1949) in 1899 became suffrage leader of Australia,
where since 1894 suffrage had begun being granted to women in different parts of
the country. When in 1902 federal suffrage was won (federal suffrage came before
all the states had granted it and did not include all levels of government), she set
out to organize a Woman's Party, for which she stood as the Women's Candidate
in the first federal elections in 1903. See Weiner 1983.

    12. Peck 1944, 138; Schreiber and Mathieson 1955, 4. One of the Dutch reporters
felt it necessary to explain Jacobs' motion, which was much quoted and widely condemned, by pointing out that it was customary in the Netherlands to discuss internal
matters like principles and constitutions in closed meetings so as to promote a free and
spirited exchange of arguments. In my opinion such a difference of method may point
to other differences between American and Dutch (European) suffragism. See Bosch
1989. By ascribing this motion to a "suspicious Dr. Aletta Jacobs" Van Voris without
any further evidence goes beyond Peck, who wrote that Aletta Jacobs made this first
motion "with the best of intentions" (Van Voris 1987, 61; Peck 1944, 138).

13. Schreiber and Mathieson 1955, 5. The use of the term *fraternal* needs further analysis. It may signify an adherence to parliamentary politics and a distancing from sentimental notions of sisterhood.

14. Millicent Garrett Fawcett (1847–1929) played an important role in the English suffrage movement for several decades. She was president of the National Union of Women's Suffrage Societies (NUWSS) from its founding in 1903 until 1918. In 1924, she published her autobiography, *What I Remember*. The sister institution of the IIAV in London, the Fawcett Library, is named after her.

Sophie Rodger Cunliffe fell ill soon after 1904 and died in 1907. Her task was taken over by Adela Stanton Coit.

Rachel Foster Avery (1859–1919) became active in the suffrage movement at the same time as Shaw, who became a good friend. From 1890 to 1900 she was secretary to the NAWSA, and from 1907 to 1909 vice president. See NAW.

Johanna W. A. Naber (1859–1941) was active in the Dutch women's movement as organizer, publicist, and feminist historian. Daughter of a professor who was sympathetic to his first women students but did not allow his own child to take up university studies, Naber worked herself up to the position of a well-known historian. She began her publishing career with a prize-winning book on the art of embroidery. The competition had been held by Tesselschade, a middle-class women's organization that promoted paid (anonymous) work for their impoverished sisters. This was her first contribution to the women's movement. Ten years later, however, she became more of a radical under the influence of the first large feminist exposition in the Netherlands, the Nationale Tentoonstelling van Vrouwenarbeid (National Exhibition of Women's Work) in The Hague in 1898. She was the editor of the exhibition's journal and commemorated this (for her, particularly) historic event two times, in *Na tien jaren* (After ten years) and *Na XXV jaren* (After twenty-five years). Recently a bibliography of her work has been published that has brought to light all of her numerous books about historical subjects in addition to her articles and pamphlets on political issues. A précis of her thought must include the notion of continuity and the passing of knowledge and wisdom from one generation to the next. She practiced this tirelessly, making connections between "great-aunts, aunts, and nieces." Her commitment to the history of women surely explains her involvement in the foundation of the IAV in 1935.

Käthe Schirmacher (1865–1930) was a German suffragist who for years lived in France but maintained close ties with the German movement. She published several works, including a particularly thorough review of the international women's movement, *Die Frauenbewegung* (1905), which was also translated into English. She was a fervent supporter of the militant English suffragettes, as is illustrated by her book *Die Suffragettes*, reprinted in 1976. Today's scholars regard Schirmacher and her friend Klara Schlekel as the only feminist couple to have portrayed themselves more or less openly as lesbian. She became more and more nationalistic and anti-Semitic. See Pieper 1984, 117; cf. letter 39 and Weiland 1983, 240.

15. Martina Kramers (1863–1934) was a journalist, publicist, and, as a long-time board member, played a prominent role in the Dutch Woman Suffrage Association. In 1895 she had been one of the founding members of the Vereeniging ter Behartiging van de Belangen der Vrouw (Association to Promote Women's Interests) in Rotterdam, which worked on a broad scale by organizing community clubs, setting up courses, and planning lectures and meetings. When Aletta Jacobs for the first time

publicly lectured on the issue of prostitution, it was for the Vereeniging in Rotterdam. In 1897, at the request of ten Dutch women's organizations, Kramers went to London to attend the meetings in preparation for the ICW Quinquennial in 1899. Impelled by what she had learned in London, in 1898, at the National Exhibition of Women's Work in The Hague, she argued the usefulness of such an umbrella organization, with the result that the Dutch National Council of Women was founded. Until 1904 she was on the board of the Dutch Council, and she remained a board member of the ICW until 1909.

16. I do not think it is correct to say, as is often done, that Jacobs was the first to open a birth-control clinic. She did give free medical help and taught hygiene courses to women from the poor quarters of Amsterdam. She may have helped these women to practice birth control, but this was not her main objective.

17. Jacobs had failed to persuade the authorities in charge to have her registered and thereupon filed a complaint against the state. The supreme court finally dismissed her argument, saying that although women were not explicitly excluded from the vote in the relevant section of the law, it had certainly not been the intention of the legislators that they should vote. In 1887 the "omission" was "corrected" by adding the word *male* to the specification of the electorate (Jacobs 1924, 99).

Anthony, in 1872, had done something similar, thereby risking three years' imprisonment. She was summoned to appear in court and sentenced to pay a fine of five hundred dollars, which she never paid (Peck 1944, 142; Flexner 1977, cf. 169).

18. Marie Lang (1858–1934) was an Austrian feminist who campaigned for woman suffrage, the legal rights of illegitimate children, and abolition of prostitution. In 1893 she was one of the founders of the Allgemeiner Österreichischer Frauenverein (General Austrian Women's Association) and in 1899 she became an editor of *Dokumente der Frauen* (Documents of women), as well as of the Austrian journal *Die Zeit*, in which Rosika Schwimmer published several times. See Weiland 1983, 147.

Marianne Hainisch (1839–1936) was a prominent Austrian feminist. She did much to promote higher education for women. She was a founder and long-time board member of the Bund Österreichischer Frauenvereine. See Weiland 1983, 124; WWT.

19. CCC to RS, Feb. 10, 1947 (SL-NYPL).

20. See letter 4, n. 4.

21. Since 1945 a few friends have undertaken to edit biographical essays about Rosa Manus. Parts of an unfinished manuscript written by Mia Boissevain, Carrie Chapman Catt, and Hans van der Meulen are in RM-IAV-IIAV.

22. Mary Anthony to AJ, April 7, 1906 (AJ-IAV-IIAV).

23. CCC to RS, May 28, 1911 (SL-NYPL).

24. Whereas the IWSA chroniclers present the organization's history most often as an undifferentiated mixture of politics and culture, academic historians have been so much occupied with suffrage feminism as a social and political movement that until recently they analyzed "suffrage text" only on the basis of the content, not the form, of written documents. They have ignored the representational aspects of image and propaganda as well as the narrative structures and the use of anecdote as a means of expression. Lisa Tickner's (1987) study is a wonderful start at redressing the imbalance. She concentrates upon the visible images; the history of suffragism is still in need of an analysis of narrative forms.

25. Of course, the procession did more than give visible form to class dif-

ference. It also made a clear statement about working women's need for the vote.

26. See chapter 4.

Chapter 2

1. Gerda Lerner was in 1969 the first—after Mary Beard—to suggest this "new approach" to the study of women. In an article she drew the conclusion that the achievements of women must be measured on a different scale: "To define and devise such a scale is difficult until the gaps in our knowledge about the actual contributions of women have been filled. This work remains to be done" (Gerda Lerner 1969, 13). An important step in the revision of the scale was the proposal to abolish the feminist concept underlying most early women's history research, the universal subordination and victimization of women. The concept of women's culture developed in close relation to this change of direction.

2. Joan Scott did much to introduce poststructuralist ideas in women's history which have immensely enriched the field. However, in her powerful plea for a new, "more radical" women's history, she reduces the history of women's history to a rather simple scheme. For one thing, she ignores completely the debate on lesbian history. Moreover she identifies all earlier approaches to women's history as a naive combination of positivism and pluralism, an assessment which I find inadequate and counterproductive. It is too easy to discard feminist political differences with an appeal to epistemological arguments. Not all feminist historians had such static ideas about the historical process and the role of historical concepts in the writing of history as Scott once had as a social historian of the Thompson school. Her reductive interpretation of the concept of women's culture (in her article on gender as a category of historical analysis she identifies it almost completely with the theories of Chodorow and Gilligan) was introduced (and reinforced) in the Netherlands in an article by two editors of the *Jaarboek voor vrouwengeschiedenis* (the main publication on women's history in the Netherlands). The concept of women's culture was exposed as "moralistic," and Dutch women's historians were warned against "circular arguments" and "demagoguery" on the part of Gerda Lerner and Carroll Smith-Rosenberg (Jansz and Van Loosbroek 1985,28).

3. In my article "Women's Culture in Women's History: Historical Notion or Feminist Vision?" (Bosch 1987), I have analyzed the ambivalence of the concept of women's culture. On the one hand, it represents a paradigm shift, from a women's history which records the eternal subjection of women to a history which vindicates "women as a force in history." In this sense it stands for a feminist *vision*, a new perspective on the past, which borrows its vitality from the self-conscious feminist culture in which women's history is practiced. On the other hand, the concept of women's culture is used as a well-defined historical concept which wants to do justice to the experiences of women in sex-segregated communities in the past, and thus deals with historical "reality."

4. Of course the terms *prosaics* and *poetics* have strongly valued connotations. My reason for using them is not to introduce a new, fixed, binary opposition, but to structure the narrative temporarily.

5. This is clear not only from the content of the letters, but also in the forms they take. The letters are written on all kinds of paper. Anna Shaw, for instance,

wrote her letters on NAWSA paper, her own paper, ICW paper, and hotel paper. Headings and signatures range from the very formal to the most intimate.

6. Martha Carey Thomas (1857–1935) became dean and professor of English at Bryn Mawr when it opened its doors in 1885. In 1894 she became president, a position she held until 1922. In 1908 she became the first president of the National College Equal Suffrage League. From 1906 she lived with Mary E. Garrett (1854–1915) in the deanery of Bryn Mawr College. Mary Garrett was cofounder of the Bryn Mawr School for Girls and a great sponsor of both the college and the suffrage movement. See NAW.

Jane Addams (1860–1935) was a social feminist and founder of Hull House, a center in the immigrant neighborhoods of Chicago. She wrote articles and books on peace and welfare. From 1911 until 1913 she was vice president of the NAWSA, and in 1915 she chaired the Women's Congress at The Hague. She became president of the International Committee of Women for Permanent Peace in 1915, and from 1919 until her death president of its successor, the Women's International League for Peace and Freedom. See Addams 1961; NAW; chap. 5, below.

Lillian D. Wald (1867–1940) was a social feminist and founder of the Henry Street settlement in New York, an institute similar to Hull House. She was also a peace activist and a president of the American Union against Militarism, founded in 1914. See Cook 1979; NAW; chap. 5, below.

7. AHS diaries, vol. 26, July 25 and Aug. 13, 1912 (DC-Schl.).

8. CCC to AJ, May 1, 1907 (AJ-IAV-IIAV).

9. According to Van Voris (1987, 219), the epitaph runs: "Here lie two, united in friendship for thirty-eight years through constant service to a great cause."

10. Mary Gray Peck (1867–?) came to New York in 1909. She became one of Catt's closest friends and lived the rest of her life near her. She completed her biography of Catt in Catt's lifetime.

11. AHS to AJ, March 26, 1907 (in AJ-IAV-IIAV).

12. Shaw's reference is to Mary Garrett Hay, and it is far from the most hateful comment Shaw made about her (see chap. 4).

13. Helene Stöcker (1869–1943) was active in the German radical women's movement and developed a theory of a "new ethic," which pleaded for male-female relationships legitimated only by (sexual) love instead of marriage. In 1905 she founded the *Bund für Mutterschutz und Sexualreform* (Association for the Protection of Mothers and Sexual Reform). She was also active in pacifist organizations (Weiland 1983, 260–61; Schlüpmann 1984).

14. CCC to AJ, Dec. 7, 1912 (AJ-IAV-IIAV).

15. Letter 39.

16. Ibid.

17. Gerda Lerner has suggested distinguishing *feminism* from *women's emancipation* and *women's rights feminism* from *women's emancipation feminism*. The first member of each pair represents a reformist striving for equality with men without challenging the existing power and value systems; the second is more radical in its aim of freedom and autonomy on women's own conditions.

18. Charlotte Perkins Gilman, *Women and Economics: The Economic Factor between Men and Women as a Factor in Social Revolution* (Boston: Small Maynard, 1899). Jacobs translated the book into Dutch as *De economische toestand der vrouw. Een studie over de economische verhouding tussen mannen en vrouwen als een factor in de sociale evolutie* (Haarlem: H.D. Tjeenk Willink, 1900).

19. AJ to RS, July 12, 1904 (SL-NYPL).

20. Edith Wynner suggested this explanation to me.

21. German suffragism was deeply divided over political differences, as was its French counterpart. Even the Netherlands possessed three different woman suffrage organizations by 1916. See Bosch 1989.

22. Letter 5.

23. Frances Squire Potter (1867–?) was professor of English literature at the University of Minnesota until, in 1909, she was appointed to the post of corresponding secretary of the NAWSA board. With her friend Mary Gray Peck she then came to New York. See *Woman's Who Is Who of America, 1914–1915.*

24. CCC to Frances Squire Potter, n.d. (CCC-LC). Though I do appreciate Fowler's decision to look "below the public surface to catch her basic concerns and tensions as revealed in her letters especially to close friends" in his chapter "The private Catt," I do not agree with his interpretation of Catt's friendship with Mary Gray Peck, which he characterizes as one of "unique intimacy," yet downplays in a predictably heterosexual manner. Although there is scarcely a scrap of paper to testify to the existence of Catt's second husband, George Catt, Fowler declares that "she fell in love with and married George Catt." He does not question what lay behind Catt's and her friends' assertions that "the Catts' marriage was happy and successful." Where Catt's relationships with Mary Garrett Hay and Mary Gray Peck are concerned he needs much more space, not only to do justice to the enormous amount of evidence they left of their presence in Catt's life, but also to "explain" Catt's friendships with these women. He does not mention the word *lesbian*, although lesbianism is clearly his point of reference—which makes the "explanation" all the more difficult:

> Peck never married, and there are no indications of romantic or sexual involvements with men. Her letters never mention men, and rarely, for that matter, other women. She had some other friends, but her devotion to Catt was obviously intense—and exclusive. There can be no question that the center of Peck's adult emotional life was Catt. Though it can be said of their friendship that it was of the species of "romantic friendships" that "were love relationships in every sense except perhaps genital" [Faderman], Catt was also attracted to men, having married twice. Moreover she had many other friends and, in Hay at least, one other who was very close to her. . . . If they were lovers, they were so only as far as Catt's traditional and unquestioned acceptance of heterosexuality permitted. [Fowler 1986, 52]

Indeed it is difficult to find words to describe love between women. I doubt, however, whether mentioning marriage, the absence of romantic or sexual involvements with men, and so forth does help to "clarify" the Catt-Peck relationship.

25. Mary Garrett Hay (1857–1928) sat on the NAWSA Organisation Committee with Catt from 1895 to 1900. She was active in the New York suffrage movement. Her successful attempt to lobby the support of the General Federation of Women's Clubs for the suffrage movement was significant. After enfranchisement, she was active in the Republican Party. See NAW; letter 20, n. 5; chap. 4, n. 6.

26. AJ to VWP, Sept. 30, 1928 (VWP-IAV-IIAV).

27. RM to Selma Lagerlöf, Oct. 4, 1928 (CCC-IAV-IIAV). Manus wrote to Lagerlöf for a contribution to Catt's seventieth birthday album. See chaps. 4 and 6.

28. Adoption was not yet regulated as it is today. It is striking how many single women adopted children. Mia Boissevain, for instance, adopted two girls. See the remarkable testimony of Olive Renier, who was, to her delight, adopted by Alice Corthorn, one of the first female doctors in England and a friend of Olive Schreiner (in Alice Corthorn, *Before the Bonfire* [Shipston-on-Stour, Warwickshire: P. Drinkwater, 1984]). Shaw also describes her not-so-fortunate adventure with the small son of an "alcoholic mother." She took him home with her, washed and clothed him, and begged the mother to give the child to her. But the mother refused and Shaw had to return the child, to her regret (Shaw 1915, 144–45).

29. Boissevain in her essay on Rosa Manus also speaks of "prophetic words." Cf. chap. 7.

30. RM to CCC, Feb. 2 and 16, 1933 (CCC-LC).

31. CCC to RM, Feb. 16, 1933 (CCC-LC).

32. CCC to RM, May 29, 1938 (CCC-LC).

33. CCC to RM, Oct. 6, 1933 (CCC-LC).

34. CCC to RM, Oct. 14, 1933 (CCC-LC).

Chapter 3

1. Theodore Stanton to AJ, Oct. 17 and 28, 1882 (AJ-IAV-IIAV). The book is: *The Woman Question in Europe: A Series of Original Essays*, ed. Theodore Stanton, with an introduction by Frances Power Cobbe (New York: G.P. Putnam's Sons, 1884).

2. Alexandra Gripenberg to AJ, November 17, 1892; May 25, 1893 (AJ-IAV-IIAV).

3. A large part of Jacobs' correspondence with women in other countries deals with women's periodicals, books, and pamphlets for the section on the "woman question" in her and her husband's library. H. J. Mehler, a librarian of the University of Amsterdam, catalogued this material in 1900 under the title *La Femme et le féminisme: Collection de livres, périodiques etc. sur la condition sociale de la femme et le mouvement féministe. Faisant partie de la bibliothèque de M. et Mme. C. V. Gerritsen (Dr. Aletta Jacobs) à Amsterdam.* The Gerritsen Library, including this section, was sold to the John Crerar Library in Chicago in 1903, which expanded the collection with publications about the American women's movement. In 1951 this augmented collection was sold to the Kenneth Spencer Research Library of the University of Kansas, and in 1974 the Microfilming Corporation of America decided to put the collection on microfilm as *The Gerritsen Collection of Women's History, 1543–1945*. A provisional *Short Title List* was published in 1976. See De Wilde, 1982; letter 76.

4. The first regular international correspondence Jacobs took up was with Rosika Schwimmer. The fact that Jacobs carefully eliminated any trace of Schwimmer from her archives reminds us of the limited extent to which archives reflect historical reality.

5. CCC to AJ, April 12, 1907 (AJ-IAV-IIAV). See also letter 14, nn. 3 and 4.

6. Catharina van Rennes was a member of the League and, according to Wij-

naendts Francken-Dyserinck (1953, 22) asked permission to cooperate with the Association.

7. The Union Française pour le Suffrage des Femmes was organized in February 1909 to join the IWSA. (An effort of French suffragists to join the IWSA had failed in 1904.) Catt seems to have been unimpressed by the French movement and appears to have been prejudiced against the Catholic countries of "Latin" Europe. For their part, French feminists did not want to adapt to the tastes and policies of foreign suffragists (Hause with Kenney 1984, 74–75).

Chapter 4

1. CCC's seventieth birthday album (CCC-IAV-IIAV).

2. Two candidates from Anthony's point of view: in fact initially there was also a third candidate, Lillie Devereux Blake (1833–1913) who ran for the office at the urging of Elizabeth Cady Stanton. She withdrew her candidacy when it became apparent that Anthony supported Catt (Peck 1944, 105–6). See NAW.

3. See letter 20. It is interesting to see that Van Voris and Fowler cite rather indirect sources on this issue, when almost every other letter to Aletta Jacobs contains a diatribe against Hay: that she has such a bad influence on Catt; that Catt is lovable when outside the presence of Hay; that it is almost impossible for Shaw to meet Catt without Hay, and so on. Probably Shaw was more frank in conveying her dislike for Hay in letters to a relative outsider like Jacobs than to any insider. See Van Voris 1987, 227 n. 12; Fowler 1986, 193 n. 34.

4. If one thing has become clear during this study, it is that where health is invoked as a reason, further research is necessary. Cf. chap. 2, at n. 14.

5. Certainly this interpretation is a partial one. Shortly after suffrage was won historical accounts of the struggle were dominated by NAWSA interests and sentiments. Flexner's study, with its heavy emphasis on the NAWSA, is still rooted in this tradition. See letter 42, n. 4.

6. For futher details on the world tour see Jacobs 1915; Jacobs 1924, 174ff.; Peck 1944, 181ff.; Van Voris 1987, 85ff.

7. Peck adds: "Olive Schreiner's husband later wrote her biography, and if Dr. Jacobs had been able to read it she would probably have moderated her viewpoint." A recent biography of Olive Schreiner addresses the question of how to understand Schreiner's home life.

8. Both Catt and Jacobs wrote extensively about Sing Pey Zung (whom Jacobs referred to as "Miss Sung" and Catt as "Captain Sheng"). Both compared her with the militant suffragettes in England (Jacobs 1915, 656–61; Van Voris 1988, 101–2, 240 n. 8).

9. In the same way Fowler dismisses Catt's travel diaries and reports in the *Woman's Journal* as impressing him as rather banal (Fowler 1986, 28; I was similarly disappointed when I saw them [see preface]), I had written off Jacobs' *Reisbrieven*. They seemed to be good only as a source for exotic anecdotes to flavor historical narrative, a vision Feinberg has taught me to revise. Van Voris seems not to have been negatively impressed by the Catt diaries and reports—rather the reverse. She makes ample use of them in her description of Catt's travel experiences. Implicitly addressing the same question Feinberg raised, she does not build up her own inter-

pretation on the basis of the diaries, but rather unsatisfactorily quotes Catt from her homecoming address, saying: "Once I was a regular jingo but that was before I had visited other countries. I had thought America had a monopoly on all that stands for progress, but I had a sad awakening" (quoted from Van Voris 1987, 105).

Chapter 5

1. One of the central ideas in the peace movement at the turn of the century was the idea of permanent arbitration, for the purpose of which in 1899 the World Court for Permanent Arbitration was set up in The Hague. Since no warring country would submit to arbitration, peace activists now started to campaign for permanent mediation, to be realized in the form of a permanent conference of neutrals which would offer peace proposals to the belligerents.

2. Wiltsher 1985, app. 2, shows the result of the voting.

3. In many countries Women's Relief Committees were set up in August. In the Netherlands organization began when Belgian refugees poured into the country. See Posthumus-van der Goot and De Waal, eds., 1977, 153. For Rosa Manus' role, see [Mia Boissevain], "Rosa Manus," unpubl. typescript, 17 (RM-IAV-IIAV).

4. Emmeline Pethick-Lawrence, who with her husband Frederic belonged to the nucleus of the WSPU, was turned out of the Union in 1912. The militant suffragettes of the WSPU adopted a program of militant support for the war. The NUWSS became more or less pacifist, but a division appeared in the ranks. For more insight into the intricate English situation see Vellacott 1987; Wiltsher 1985; Oldfield 1984, chap. 9.

5. This plan was printed (anonymously, because Julia Grace Wales was Canadian) by the Wisconsin Peace Society and became known as the "Wisconsin Plan" or "Canadian Plan." It was widely distributed in the United States and Europe, and in January 1915 was called to the attention of the president. In April the Wisconsin Legislature endorsed it and recommended it for consideration by the Congress. From the very beginning of the war Rosika Schwimmer advocated a similar idea of a continuous conference of neutrals which would offer to mediate between the belligerent powers. She issued a manifesto which was printed in the October issue of *Jus Suffragii*. It is difficult to assess what exactly were the differences between the two plans. Randall urges that Wales' plan for a continuous mediation without armistice was more elaborate and differed from Schwimmer's in not calling for an immediate armistice. At the Women's Congress at The Hague, the resolution on mediation which embodied the Wisconsin Plan was presented by Schwimmer. See Randall 1964, 161–63; Wiltsher 1985, 94; Internationaler Frauenkongress 1915, 154.

6. During the war, the NAWSA maneuvered between propaganda against U.S. intervention and loyal support of government policy. In April 1917, when the United States finally entered the war, the NAWSA engaged in numerous war activities such as raising money for hospitals (Lemons 1975, 9). Catt's attitude was based on strategy and so differed from Jane Addams', who was first and foremost a pacifist.

7. A letter dated December 1917 to the German "Chef des Stellvertretenden Generalstabes der Armee" describes her as follows: "Frau Jacobs is a fanatic supporter of the women's movement and will not subject herself to bribery of any de-

scription, whether from the German or the enemy side" (quoted from EWN [Jacobs], SL-NYPL; trans. from German). Jacobs was registered with British Intelligence because of her contact with Emily Hobhouse. See Fisher 1971, 243–44; letters from Hobhouse to AJ (AJ-IAV-IIAV).

8. In January 1919 the peace conference at Versailles began. In May 1919 the second International Women's Congress was held in Zürich, instead of in Paris, to enable German women to take part as well. At this congress the Women's International League for Peace and Freedom (WILPF) was founded. Its headquarters were opened in Geneva.

9. I have restricted myself here to the outline of this story. Much has already been written about the 1915 congress, though mostly in the context of other narratives. Thoroughgoing research which would focus especially on the congress is still wanting. In AJ-IAV-IIAV there are handwritten reports by Jacobs of her trip to the United States, and by Balch and Macmillan of their visit to London in July. The report of the congress (Internationaler Frauenkongress 1915, [317]–18) gives a detailed list of delegates' conversations with government leaders.

10. Emily Balch (1867–1961) was a peace advocate and social reformer, and a professor of economics and sociology at Wellesley College, from which post she was dismissed in 1919 because of her peace activism. After World War I she played an important role in the WILPF, and in 1946 she was awarded the Nobel Peace Prize. See Randall 1964; NAW; WWT.

Chrystal Macmillan was a Scottish barrister who was active in the suffrage movement. In 1914, together with Mrs. Coit and Mrs. Fawcett, she formed the IWSA Relief Committee. Macmillan, Kathleen Courtney, and Emmeline Pethick-Lawrence comprised the small English delegation to the congress at The Hague in 1915. She took a seat on the International Women's Committee for Permanent Peace (later the WILPF), which was founded during the congress. Emily Balch, Rosa Manus, and she were responsible for the congress report. See Wiltsher 1985.

Cornelia Ramondt-Hirschmann was a Dutch pacifist. She was involved in organizing the 1915 congress and travelled as part of the delegation to the neutral countries of Denmark, Norway, Sweden, and Russia. From 1919 to 1937 she was a board member of the WILPF and president of its Dutch branch. See WWT.

11. When I wrote elsewhere: "Differences of opinion in 1915 led to a final break," Edith Wynner, consultant to the Schwimmer-Lloyd Collection, informed me that she considers this a falsification of the reason for the break between Jacobs and Schwimmer (Edith Wynner to Mineke Bosch, personal communication, Sept. 13, 1987). According to Wynner the break was caused by Jacobs' insane rage, which induced her to slander Schwimmer viciously for the rest of her life. In conversations with me in the summers of 1984 and 1987, Wynner told me she had known Aletta Jacobs as a pathological liar and a sufferer from dementia praecox. Although I am the first to admit that "differences of opinion" are far from sufficient to explain the whole story, especially not the vehemence of the emotions involved, I find it difficult to be satisfied with Wynner's explanation, since I have found no other evidence to confirm her view of Jacobs' state of mind. In this I share the position of Rosa Manus. In a letter to Catt in 1937, Manus declined a request relayed from Schwimmer via Catt to talk about past events, saying: "I do not like her to call Aletta un-

sane as up to the last she was not unsane, but as I say, it is no use beginning to write about it" (RM to CCC, Dec. 7, 1937, CCC-LC).

It must be said that both women were, to put it mildly, "strong characters." Jacobs had her own peculiarities and personal pride, which made her several enemies. The controversies around Schwimmer in her own time seem to repeat themselves in present-day research. Kraft, in her book about Henry Ford's peace ship, passes a negative judgement on Schwimmer. Wiltsher also recognizes the ambivalence of her legacy, but judges Schwimmer differently. Schwimmer is clearly the heroine of Wiltsher's book about the 1915 peace efforts. See Kraft 1978, 205; Wiltsher 1985, 10.

12. The difference of opinion sketched here between Jacobs and Schwimmer can be traced to the parties pro and con the last resolution at the congress. Jacobs also objected to making a second round of the belligerent powers, according to Wiltsher and Kraft, because she wanted the Netherlands to take the mediation initiative. Schwimmer favored Sweden. See Randall 1964, 198–99; Posthumus-van der Goot 1961, 155.

Certainly Rosika's efforts to bring the women's activities to the attention of a wider public had their effect. In the fall of 1915 her energies were devoted to inspiring the industrialist Henry Ford, who decided to finance a "peace ship" to take American pacifists to Stockholm, where they hoped to bring about a conference for continuous mediation. Schwimmer was jubilant and sent golden promises to the International Committee of Women for Permanent Peace in Amsterdam. The money pledged, however, never arrived, which led Jacobs to complain to the press about Schwimmer when the Peace Ship expedition arrived in the Netherlands in February 1916. In the end the Ford Peace Ship expedition was a fiasco (Kraft 1978). According to Bussey and Tims (1980, 26), Jane Addams had telegraphed Jacobs to keep the International Committee separate from the Peace Ship expedition. Bussey and Tims attribute the International Committee's survival after the Peace Ship's failure to this strategy.

Chapter 6

1. Women in the Netherlands got passive suffrage in 1917. In 1918, for the first time, women could be elected–but they could not vote. This they did first in 1922. Women in the Dutch colonies, both East Indies and West Indies, were excluded from voting since Dutch law did not apply to the colonies. Even long after 1919, whenever a census system was designed for the East or West Indies, women were treated differently from men.

2. These organizations were the WILPF, the World Union of Women for International Concord, the World's Young Women's Christian Association, the International Federation of Business and Professional Women, the International Federation of University Women, the World's Women's Christian Temperance Union, and the St. Joan Political and Social Alliance. The Joint Committee worked for more women in the delegations to the League of Nations (Reinalda and Verhaaren 1989, 56–57; Posthumus-van der Goot 1961, 208).

3. Willemijn H. Posthumus-van der Goot (1897–1989), who in the preface was mentioned as one of the founders of the IAV, in 1930 was the first woman in the

Netherlands to become a doctor of economics. At the end of the twenties Aletta Jacobs convinced her of the importance of feminism. When in the thirties younger women began to organize to protest state restriction of women's work, she took the lead. She used her academic training to develop economic counterarguments on the basis of research into working women, putting strong hopes on the forcible power of scientific argument. Her marriage to N. Posthumus, founder of the International Institute for Social History (IISG) in Amsterdam, facilitated the realization of the IAV in 1935. He invited the newly founded organization to take up residence in the same building as the IISG. Posthumus-van der Goot is best known for her editorial and organizational activities in connection with the book *Van moeder op dochter* (From mother to daughter), which is still the most comprehensive history of the women's movement in the Netherlands. She was also active in the women's peace movement. With her death on 16 January 1989, one of the last living links between the first and the second wave of feminism died as well.

4. It has been hinted that Jacobs "sold" the idea of a women's list in exchange for the Radical Democrats' full parliamentary support for the law to secure active woman suffrage in 1919 (Jacobs law). See Posthumus-van der Goot and de Waal, eds., 1977, 255–56.

5. Apart from the attempts in 1919 and 1922 to organize a women's list, attempts in part supported by women of the VVVK, every now and then new initiatives sprang up to found a women's political party, but never with any real chance of success.

6. See Freedman 1979 for a convincing analysis of the dissolution of women's institutions in the twenties.

7. Seventieth birthday album for Carrie Chapman Catt (CCC-IAV-IIAV).

8. See invitation and correspondence in CCC-IAV-IIAV.

9. *Vrouw en Gemeenschap* 4/8 (January 15, 1934). Manus could not attend the celebration. Instead she wrote on January 9, 1934: "I do hope the gramophone discs have given you some moments of pleasure and you can understand the words spoken to you at that moment came right out of my heart but there are more unspoken words which I could not say as you can well imagine" (CCC-LC). Francisca de Haan brought the article in *Vrouw en Gemeenschap* which explained this passage in detail, to my attention. Where have these records gone?

10. To be precise, Manus coordinated the work of the Dingman Committee, which was the disarmament committee of the Liaison Committee of Women's International Organizations.

11. See Rupp 1981. Rupp's skepticism about the death of feminism resulted in a fine analysis of the history of the American women's rights movement between 1945 and 1965, which was published under the appropriate title *Survival in the Doldrums*. See Rupp and Taylor 1987.

Chapter 7

1. See chap. 1, n. 20.

2. [Mia Boissevain], "Rosa Manus," unpubl. typescript, 21–22 (RM-IAV-IIAV).

3. Ibid., 22.

4. Elinor Lerner's 1983 article (published in 1986 in slightly altered form) provides a clear insight into the relationship between the women's movement and anti-Semitism in the United States before World War II. My references are to the unpublished 1983 version.

5. Manus enclosed a copy of this letter (dated June 7, 1933) in a letter to Catt (RM to CCC, June 13, 1933 [CCC-IAV-IIAV]).

6. Whittick (1979, 145) writes that during a large dinner reception at the Congress in Copenhagen, Rosa Manus' hotel room was searched, which of course distressed her even more.

7. Letter 35.

8. In Wyman's book *The Abandonment of the Jews*, on the American reaction to the Holocaust after June 1942, the reluctance of Americans actually to help Jews is seen as a continuation of their passive and even negative attitude with regard to Jewish refugees of the thirties. In this light Catt's action is significant, yet Wyman does not mention her. Virtually the only woman he does include in his book is Mercedes Randall, who with the booklet *The Voice of Thy Brother's Blood* (1944) produced "the only comprehensive discussion of the European Jewish disaster issued by an American Christian source during the Holocaust" (Wyman 1984, 317–18). Randall was the biographer of the pacifist Emily Balch. Both were active in the sister organization of the Alliance, the WILPF. In her biography of Balch, Randall mentions facts which should have been included in Wyman's book (Randall 1964, 358, 361). Wyman's analysis of America's great reluctance to act would have carried more weight if he had included women (and their organizations) in his research. I myself look forward to a comparative analysis of the IWSA and the WILPF on the issues of antifascism and protest against anti-Semitism.

9. Rosa actually died in 1943. See letter 85, n. 2

Bibliography

Addams, Jane. 1961. *Twenty Years at Hull House. With Autobiographical Notes*. Foreword by Henry Steel Commager. New York: New American Library. (First published 1910.)

Advokaat, Marjan, Trees Moll, and José Niekus. 1980. "Geboortenregeling: een vrouwenzaak? Aktiviteiten van vrouwen en de vrouwenbeweging ten aanzien van geboortenregeling, 1881–1940." In *Jaarboek voor Vrouwengeschiedenis, 1980*. Ed. Josine Blok et al., 111–40. Nijmegen: SUN.

Ammers-Küller, Jo van. 1933. *Twaalf interessante vrouwen. Korte biographieën, geschreven na persoonlijke kennismaking*. Amsterdam: J.M. Meulenhoff. See the chapter on Rosa Manus (136–64).

Banner, Lois W. 1980. *Elizabeth Cady Stanton: A Radical for Woman's Rights*. Boston: Little, Brown.

Bilder vom Internationalen Frauenkongress, 1904. 1904. Ed. Eliza Ichenhäuser. Berlin: der "Woche."

Boissevain, Mia. n.d. *Een Amsterdamsche Familie*. Photocopy of unpublished typescript in IAV-IIAV (Library).

Bosch, Mineke. 1982. "Blauwkousen en hobbezakken in een witte jas. De eerste vrouwelijke artsen in Nederland, 1872–1913." In *Jaarboek voor Vrouwengeschiedenis 1982*. Ed. Josine Blok et al., 63–97. Nijmegen: SUN.

————. 1983. "De geschiedenis van een en ander. Naar een discussie tussen lesbische en vrouwengeschiedenis." In *Lover* 10/3: 115–25.

————. 1987. "Women's Culture in Women's History: Historical Notion or Feminist Vision?" In *Historiography of Women's Cultural Traditions*. Ed. Maaike Meijer and Jetty Schaap, 35–52. Dordrecht-Providence: Foris.

————. 1989. "Gossipy letters in the context of international feminism." In *Current Issues in Women's History*. Ed. Arina Angerman et al. London: Routledge.

Buhle, Mari Jo, and Paul Buhle (eds.). 1978. *The Concise History of Woman Suffrage: Selections from the Classic Work of Stanton, Anthony, Gage and Harper*. Urbana: University of Illinois Press.

Burck, An du, Mieke van Vugt, and Aukje van der Heu-Wildschut. 1988. *Laat ze maar lachen. Wij komen er toch wel!! Een ontmoeting met Rosa Manus (1881–1943)*. Den Haag. Photocopy of typescript in IAV-IIAV (Library).

Bussey, Gertrude, and Margaret Tims. 1980. *Pioneers for Peace. Women's International League for Peace and Freedom, 1915–1965.* London: WILPF. (First published as *Women's International League for Peace and Freedom 1915–1965: A Record of Fifty Years' Work* [1965].)

Catt, Carrie Chapman, and Nettie Rogers Shuler. 1926. *Woman Suffrage and Politics. The Inner Story of the Suffrage Movement.* New York: Charles Scribner's Sons.

Cook, Blanche Wiesen. 1979. "Female Support Networks and Political Activism: Lillian Wald, Crystal Eastman, Emma Goldman." In *A Heritage of Her Own: Toward a New Social History of American Women.* Ed. Nancy F. Cott and Elizabeth H. Pleck, 412–44. New York: Simon and Schuster.

Crawford, Anne, et al. (eds.). 1983. *The European Biographical Dictionary of British Women. Over 1000 Notable Women from Britain's Past.* London: Europa.

Crezee, Marianne. 1978. "Martina G. Kramers (1863–1934): Een leven gewijd aan vrouwenemancipatie, socialisme en internationaal contact." Unpublished master's thesis, Vrije Universiteit Brussel. Photocopy of typescript in IAV-IIAV (Library).

David, Ann. 1986. "Het Belgisch burgerlijk feminisme tussen 1914 en 1936: Een verkenning." Unpublished master's thesis, Rijksuniversiteit Gent [Ghent]. Photocopy of typescript in IAV-IIAV (Library).

Deutsch, Regine. 1929. *The International Woman Suffrage Alliance: Its History from 1904 to 1929.* London: IAW.

DuBois, Ellen Carol. 1980. *Feminism and Suffrage: The Emergence of an Independent Women's Movement in America, 1848–1869.* Ithaca: Cornell University Press.

DuBois, Ellen Carol (ed.). 1981. *Elizabeth Cady Stanton–Susan B. Anthony: Correspondence, Writings, Speeches.* New York: Schocken.

DuBois, Ellen, Mari Jo Buhle, et al. 1980. "Politics and Culture in Women's History: A Symposium." In *Feminist Studies* 6/1: 26–64.

Eerste feministische golf, De. 1985. In *Zesde Jaarboek voor Vrouwengeschiedenis.* Ed. Jeske Reys et al. Nijmegen: SUN.

Evans, Richard J. 1979. *The Feminists: Women's Emancipation Movements in Europe, America and Australasia, 1840–1920.* Rev. ed. London: Croom Helm; New York: Barnes & Noble. (First published 1977.)

Faderman, Lillian, and Brigitte Eriksson (eds.). 1980. *Lesbian-Feminism in Turn-of-the-Century Germany.* Weatherby Lake: Naiad.

Feinberg, Harriet. 1988. "Aletta Jacobs' Reisbrieven uit Afrika en Azië." Unpublished article. Cambridge, Mass.

Feith, L. W. 1968. "Proeve van een bibliografie betreffende de werken geschreven door en over Dr. Aletta H. Jacobs, 1854–1929." [Amsterdam]: Bibliotheek- en Documentatieschool. Stencil.

Feministische Studien. 1984. *Die Radikalen in der alten Frauenbewegung.* 3/1. Special issue.

Finn, Barbara R. 1979. "Anna Howard Shaw and Women's Work." *Frontiers: A Journal of Women Studies* 4/3: 21–25.

Fisher, John. 1971. *That Miss Hobhouse.* London: Secker & Warburg.

Flexner, Eleanor. 1977. *Century of Struggle: The Woman's Rights Movement in the United States*. Rev. ed. Cambridge: Harvard University Press, Belknap Press. (First published 1959.)

Fowler, Robert Booth. 1986. *Carrie Catt: Feminist Politician*. Boston: Northeastern University Press.

Freedman, Estelle. 1979. "Separatism as Strategy: Female Institution Building and American Feminism, 1870–1930." *Feminist Studies* 5/3: 512–29.

Gedenkboek. 1919. *Bij het 25-jarig bestaan van de Vereeniging voor Vrouwenkiesrecht, 1894–1919*. Amsterdam: Privately printed.

Gerritsen, C. V., and Aletta H. Jacobs. 1906. *Brieven uit en over Amerika*. Amsterdam: F. van Rossen.

Hackett, Amy. 1976. *The Politics of Feminism in Wilhelmine Germany, 1890–1918*. 2 vols. Ann Arbor: University Microfilms International.

Harper, Ida Husted (ed.). 1922. *The History of Woman Suffrage*. Vols. 5 and 6 (1900–1920). [New York]: National American Woman Suffrage Association. Abbreviated as HWS.

Hause, Steven C., with Anne R. Kenney. 1984. *Women's Suffrage and Social Politics in the French Third Republic*. Princeton: Princeton University Press.

Heymann, Lida Gustava, and Anita Augspurg. 1972. *Erlebtes–Erschautes. Deutsche Frauen kämpfen für Freiheit, Recht und Frieden, 1850–1940*. Ed. Margrit Twellman. Meisenheim am Glan: Anton Hain.

Hinding, Andrea, Ames Sheldon Bower, and Suzanna Moody (eds.). 1979. *Women's History Sources. A Guide to Archives and Manuscript Collections in the United States*. 2 vols. New York: R.R. Bowker.

Holton, Sandra Stanley. 1986. *Feminism and Democracy: Women's Suffrage and Reform Politics in Britain, 1900–1918*. Cambridge: Cambridge University Press.

Hurwitz, Edith F. 1977. "The International Sisterhood." In *Becoming Visible: Women in European History*. Ed. Renate Bridenthal and Claudia Koonz, 325–45. Boston: Houghton Mifflin.

International Alliance of Women for Suffrage and Equal Citizenship. 1926. *Report of Tenth Congress, La Sorbonne, Paris, France, May 30th to June 6th, 1926*. London: Privately printed.

———. 1929. *Report of the Eleventh Congress, Berlin, June 17th to 22nd, 1929*. London: Privately printed.

———. 1935. *Report of the Twelfth Congress, Istanbul, April 18th to 24th, 1935*. London: Privately printed.

———. 1939. *Report of the Thirteenth Congress, Copenhagen, July 8th to 14th, 1939*. London: Privately printed.

International Committee for Peace and the League of Nations. 1927. *Report and Resolutions of the First Peace Study Conference*. London: Privately printed.

International Woman Suffrage Alliance. 1906. *Report [of the] Second and Third Conferences, Berlin, Germany, June 3, 4, 1904/Copenhagen, Denmark, Aug. 7, 8, 10, 11, 1906*. London: Privately printed.

302 *Bibliography*

25

25

——. 1908. *Report of the Fourth Conference, Amsterdam, Holland, June 15, 16, 17, 18, 19, 20, 1908.* London: Privately printed.

——. 1909. *Report of Fifth Conference and First Quinquennial, London, England, April 26, 27, 28, 29, 30, May 1, 1909.* London: Privately printed.

——. 1911. *Report of Sixth Congress, Stockholm, Sweden, June 12, 13, 14, 15, 16 and 17, 1911.* London: Privately printed.

——. 1913. *Report of Seventh Congress, Budapest, Hungary, June 15, 16, 17, 18, 19, 20, 21, 1913.* Manchester: Privately printed.

——. 1920. *Report of Eighth Congress, Geneva, Switzerland, June 1920.* Manchester: Privately printed.

——. 1923. *Report of Ninth Congress, Rome, Italy, May 12th to 19th, 1923.* London: Privately printed.

Internationaler Frauenkongress, Haag vom 28. April–1. Mai 1915/Congrès International des Femmes, La Haye 28 April–1 Mai 1915/International Congress of Women, The Hague April 28th–May 1st 1915. Bericht/Rapport/Report. [1915]. Internationales Frauenkomitee für Dauernden Frieden/Comité International de Femmes pour une Paix Permanente/International Women's Committee of Permanent Peace. Amsterdam.

Iongh, Jane de (ed.). 1938. "Letters from Dr. Anna Howard Shaw to Dr. Aletta Jacobs." In *Internationaal Archief voor de Vrouwenbeweging. Jaarboek II/International Archives for the Women's Movement. Yearbook II,* 71–134. Leiden: E.J. Brill.

Jacobs, Aletta H. 1905. *Uit het leven van merkwaardige vrouwen.* Amsterdam: F. van Rossen.

——. 1915. *Reisbrieven uit Afrika en Azië, benevens eenige brieven uit Zweden en Noorwegen.* 2d ed. Almelo: W. Hilarius Wzn. (1st ed. 1913.)

——. 1924. *Herinneringen.* Amsterdam: Van Holkema & Warendorf.

Jansz, Ulla, and Tineke van Loosbroek. 1985. "Nieuwe literatuur over de eerste feministische golf: 'herschrijven van de geschiedenis.'" In *De eerste feministische golf: Zesde Jaarboek voor vrouwengeschiedenis.* Ed. Jeske Reys et al., 10–29. Nijmegen: SUN.

James, Edward T., Janet Wilson James, and Paul S. Boyer (eds.). 1971. *Notable American Women, 1607–1950: A Biographical Dictionary.* 3 vols. Cambridge: Harvard University Press, Belknap Press. Abbreviated as NAW.

Jong, L. de. 1969. *Het Koninkrijk der Nederlanden in de Tweede Wereldoorlog.* vol. 1, *Voorspel.* The Hague: Staatsuitgeverij.

Jus Suffragii. Published by the International Woman Suffrage Alliance, 1906–17. After 1917 it became *International Woman Suffrage News.*

Kern, Elga (ed.). 1930. *Führende Frauen Europas.* n.s. Munich: Ernst Reinhardt.

Kloek, Els, and Yvonne Scherf. 1982. "De vrouwenbibliotheek van de man van Aletta Jacobs. Een bibliografie van de nederlandstalige titels." In *Jaarboek voor Vrouwengeschiedenis, 1982.* Ed. Josine Blok et al., 256–94. Nijmegen: SUN.

Kraditor, Aileen S. 1981. *The Ideas of the Woman Suffrage Movement, 1890–1920.* New York: W.W. Norton. (First published 1965.)

Kraft, Barbara S. 1978. *The Peace Ship. Henry Ford's Pacifist Adventure in the First World War.* New York: Macmillan.

Lauretis, Teresa de. 1986. "Feminist Studies/Critical Studies: Issues, Terms, and Contexts." In *Feminist Studies/Critical Studies.* Ed. Teresa de Lauretis, 1–19. Bloomington: Indiana University Press.

Lemons, J. Stanley. 1975. *The Woman Citizen: Social Feminism in the 1920s.* Urbana: University of Illinois Press.

Lengerke, Christiane von. 1984. "'Homosexuelle Frauen': Tribaden, Freundinnen, Urninden." In *Eldorado: Homosexuelle Frauen und Männer in Berlin, 1850–1950 Geschichte, Alltag und Kultur,* 125–48. Berlin: Frölich und Kaufmann.

Lerner, Elinor. 1983. "American Feminism and the Jewish Question." Unpublished article, Stockton State College, Pomona, N.J.

———. 1986. "American Feminism and the Jewish Question, 1890–1940." *Antisemitism in American History.* Ed. David Gerber. Urbana: University of Illnois Press.

Lerner, Gerda. 1969. *The Majority Finds Its Past: Placing Women in History.* New York: Oxford University Press.

Mackenzie, Midge. 1975. *Shoulder to Shoulder: A Documentary.* New York: Alfred A. Knopf.

Meijers, Clara M. 1946. *Een moderne vrouw van formaat: Leven en werken van Rosa Manus.* Leiden: E.J. Brill.

Mossink, Marijke. 1986. "Tweeërlei strooming? 'Ethisch' en 'rationalistisch' feminisme tijdens de eerste golf in Nederland." In *Socialistisch-Feministische Teksten 9.* Ed. Selma Sevenhuijsen et al., 104–20. Baarn: Ambo.

Naber, Johanna W. A. 1923. *Na XXV jaren, 1898–1923: Het feminisme in zijnen bloei en in zijne voleinding.* Haarlem: H.D. Tjeenk Willink & Zoon.

Naber, Johanna W.A. (ed.). 1939. *Samuel Pierre l'Honoré Naber, Schout bij Nacht t.t. naar de correspondentie met zijn Ouders, loopende 1880–1913, en bewerkt door zijn zuster.* The Hague: Privately printed.

Oldfield, Sybil. 1984 *Spinsters of This Parish: The Life and Times of F. M. Mayor and Mary Sheepshanks.* London: Virago.

Outshoorn, Joyce. 1973. *Vrouwenemancipatie en socialisme: een onderzoek naar de houding van de SDAP ten opzichte van het vrouwenvraagstuk tussen 1894 en 1919.* Nijmegen: SUN.

Pankhurst, E. Sylvia. 1977. *The Suffragette Movement. An Intimate Account of Persons and Ideals.* New introduction by Richard Pankhurst. London: Virago. (First published 1931.)

Peck, Mary Gray. 1944. *Carrie Chapman Catt: A Biography.* New York: H.W. Wilson.

Pfeffer, Paula F. 1985. "'A Whisper in the Assembly of Nations': United States Participation in the International Movement for Women's Rights from the League of Nations to the United Nations." *Women's Studies International Forum* 8/5: 459–71.

Pieper, Mecki. 1984. "Die Frauenbewegung und ihre Bedeutung für lesbische Frauen (1850–1920)." In *Eldorado: Homosexuelle Frauen und Männer in Berlin, 1850–1950. Geschichte, Alltag, und Kultur,* 116–24. Berlin: Frölich und Kaufmann.

Posthumus-van der Goot, W. H. 1961. *Vrouwen vochten voor de vrede.* Arnhem: Van Loghum Slaterus.

———. 1975. *Aletta Jacobs. Pionierswerk naar alle kanten.* Amsterdam: Internationaal Archief voor de Vrouwenbeweging.

Posthumus-van der Goot, W. H., and Anna de Waal (eds.). 1977. *Van Moeder op Dochter: De maatschappelijke positie van de vrouw in Nederland vanaf de Franse tijd.* Rev. ed. Nijmegen: SUN. (First published 1948.)

Raalte, E. van. 1958. "Esther Welmoet Wijnaendts Francken-Dyserinck." In *Jaarboek van de Maatschappij der Nederlandse Letterkunde te Leiden, 1957–1958,* 84–96. Leiden: E.J. Brill.

Randall, Mercedes M. 1964. *Improper Bostonian: Emily Greene Balch, Nobel Peace Laureate 1946.* New York: Twayne.

Rasmussen, Janet E. 1983. "Sisters across the Sea: Early Norwegian Feminists and Their American Connections." In *Reassessments of "First Wave" Feminism.* Ed. Elizabeth Sarah, 647–54. Oxford: Pergamon. Previously publ. in *Women's Studies International Forum* 5/6 (1982).

Rauther, Rose. 1984. "Rosika Schwimmer. Stationen auf dem Lebensweg einer Pazifistin." *Feministische Studien,* special issue: *Die Radikalen in der alten Frauenbewegung* 3/1: 63–75.

Reinalda, Bob, and Natascha Verhaaren. 1989. *Vrouwenbeweging en internationale organisaties, 1868–1986. Een vergeten hoofdstuk uit de geschiedenis van de internationale betrekkingen.* De Knipe: Ariadne.

Reiss, Mary-Ann. 1984. "Rosa Mayreder: Pioneer of Austrian Feminism." *International Journal of Women's Studies* 7/3: 207–16.

Relph, Anne Kimbell. 1979. "The World Center for Women's Archives, 1935–1940." In *Signs: Journal of Women in Culture and Society* 4/3: 597–603.

Romein, Jan. 1967. *Op het breukvlak van twee eeuwen.* 2 vols. Leiden: E.J. Brill; Amsterdam: Em. Querido.

Rupp, Leila J. 1981. "Reflections on Twentieth-Century American Women's History." *Reviews in American History* 9/2: 275–84.

Rupp, Leila J., and Verta Taylor. 1987. *Survival in the Doldrums: The American Women's Rights Movement, 1945 to the 1960s.* New York: Oxford University Press.

Schirmacher, Käthe. 1976. *Die Suffragettes.* Berlin: Frauen-Clitverlag. (First published 1913.)

Schlüpmann, Heide. 1984. "Radikalisierung der Philosophie: Die Nietzsche-Rezeption und die sexualpolitische Publizistik Helene Stöckers." *Feministische Studien,* special issue: *Die Radikalen in der alten Frauenbewegung* 3/1: 10–34.

Schreiber, Adele, and Margaret Mathieson. 1955. *Journey towards Freedom. Written for the Golden Jubilee of the International Alliance of Women.* Copenhagen: I.A.W.

Schwarz, Gudrun. 1983. "Women support networks in Germany at the end of the 19th and beginning of the 20th century." In *Among Men, Among Women: Sociological and Historical Recognition of Homosocial Arrangements.* Ed. Mattias Duyves et al., 420–30. University of Amsterdam conference on gay studies and women's studies, June 22–26, 1983. Amsterdam: Sociologisch Instituut.

Schwimmer, Rosika. 1924. "Women Pioneers of a New International Order." *B'nai B'rith News* (April), 231–33.

[Schwimmer, R. 1947.] *Rosika Schwimmer: World Patriot.* Rev. and enl. ed. London. (First published 1937.)

Scott, Anne Firor, and Andrew MacKay Scott. 1982. *One Half the People: The Fight for Woman Suffrage.* Urbana: University of Illinois Press. (First published 1975.)

Scott, Joan Wallach. 1983. "Women in History: The Modern Period," *Past and Present: A Journal of Historical Studies* 101: 141–57. Translated as: "Vrouwengeschiedenis: de geschiedenis herschrijven. De 'discussie' in de afgelopen tien jaar." In *Jaarboek voor Vrouwengeschiedenis (1984).* Ed. Jeske Reys et. al., 131–52. Nijmegen: SUN. A revised version was published as "Women's History" in Scott 1988, 15–27.

———. 1988. *Gender and the Politics of History.* New York: Columbia University Press.

Shaarawi, Huda. 1986. *Harem Years: The Memoirs of an Egyptian Feminist (1879–1924).* Trans., ed., and with an introduction by Margot Badran. London: Virago.

Shaw, Anna Howard. 1915. *The Story of a Pioneer.* With the collaboration of Elizabeth Jordan. New York: Harper & Brothers.

Sherrick, Rebecca L. 1983. "Toward Universal Sisterhood." In *Reassessments of "First Wave" Feminism.* Ed. Elizabeth Sarah, 655–61. Oxford: Pergamon. Previously published in *Women's Studies International Forum* 5/6 (1982).

Smith-Rosenberg, Carroll. 1975. "The Female World of Love and Ritual: Relations between Women in Nineteeth-Century America." *SIGNS: Journal of Women in Culture and Society* 1/1: 1–29. Reprinted in *The SIGNS Reader: Women Gender & Scholarship.* Ed. Elizabeth Abel and Emily K. Abel. Chicago: The University of Chicago Press, 1983.

Spender, Dale. 1983. *Women of Ideas and What Men Have Done to Them: From Aphra Behn to Adrienne Rich.* London: ARK. (First published 1982.)

Stanley, Liz, with Ann Morley. 1988. *The Life and Death of Emily Wilding Davison. A Biographical Detective Story.* With Gertrude Colmore's *The Life of Emily Davison.* London: Women's Press.

Stanton, Elizabeth Cady. 1971. *Eighty Years and More: Reminiscences, 1815–1897.* New York: Schocken. (First Published 1898.)

Stern, Madeline B. 1970. *Purple Passage: The Life of Mrs. Frank Leslie.* Norman: University of Oklahoma Press. (First published 1953.)

Stevens, Doris. 1976. *Jailed for Freedom: The Story of the Militant American Suffragist Movement.* Introduction by Janice Law Trecker. New York: Schocken. (First published 1920.)

Stimmrecht, Das. 1913. Festschrift herausgegeben vom österreichischen Frauenstimmrechtskomitee anlässlich der internationalen Frauenstimmrechtskonferenz in Wien, 11. und 12. Juni 1913. Vienna.

Strachey, Ray. 1978. *The Cause: A Short History of the Women's Movement in Great Britain.* New preface by Barbara Strachey. London: Virago. (First published 1928.)

Tickner, Lisa. 1987. *The Spectacle of Women: Imagery of the Suffrage Campaign, 1907–14*. London: Chatto & Windus.

Turoff, Barbara K. 1979. *Mary Beard as Force in History*. Dayton, Ohio: Wright State University. Monograph Series No. 3.

Van Voris, Jacqueline. 1987. *Carrie Chapman Catt: A Public Life*. New York: Feminist.

Vellacott, Jo. 1987. "Feminist Consciousness and the First World War." *History Workshop: A Journal of Socialist and Feminist Historians* 23: 81–101.

Vicinus, Martha. 1982. "'One Life to Stand Beside Me': Emotional Conflicts in First-Generation College Women in England." *Feminist Studies* 8/3: 603–28.

Victory: How Women Won It. 1940. A Centennial Symposium, 1840–1940, by the National American Woman Suffrage Association. New York: H.W. Wilson.

Vreede-de Stuers, Cora. 1985. *Johanna W. A. Naber 25.3.1859–25.5.1941. Bibliografie*. Amsterdam: Internationaal Archief voor de Vrouwenbeweging.

Vries, Petra de. 1984. "Alle vrouwen zijn moeders. Feminisme en moederschap rond de eeuwwisseling." In *Socialistisch-Feministische Teksten 8*. Ed. Selma Sevenhuijsen et al. Amsterdam: Feministische Uitg. Sara.

Weiland, Daniela. 1983. *Geschichte der Frauenemanzipation in Deutschland und Österreich. Biographien – Programme – Organisationen*. Düsseldorf: ECON (Hermes Handlexicon).

Weiner, Gaby. 1983. "Vida Goldstein: The Women's Candidate (1869–1949)." In *Feminist Theorists*. Ed. Dale Spender, 244–55. London: Women's Press.

Well-Known Women of To-Day. 1938? Vol. 1. Composed by the International Biographic Edition with the literary assistance of P. Husárek. Prague: Privately printed. Abbreviated as WWT.

Wells, Anna Mary. 1978. *Miss Marks and Miss Woolley*. Boston: Houghton Mifflin.

Whittick, Arnold. 1979. *Woman into Citizen: The World Movement towards the Emancipation of Women in the Twentieth Century with Accounts of the Contributions of the International Alliance of Women, the League of Nations and the Relevant Organisations of United Nations*. London: Athenaeum with Frederick Muller.

Wijnaendts Francken-Dyserinck, W. 1953. *De strijd voor het vrouwenkiesrecht herdacht*. n.p.: Privately printed.

Wilde, Inge de. 1979. *Aletta Jacobs in Groningen*. Groningen: Studium Generale/Universiteitsmuseum/Rijksuniversiteit.

———. 1982. "De bibliotheek van C. V. Gerritsen, de echtgenoot van Aletta Jacobs." *Jaarboek voor Vrouwengeschiedenis, 1982*. Ed. Josine Blok et al., 245–55. Nijmegen: SUN.

———. 1984a. "Inleiding bij zes brieven van Aletta Jacobs." *Tijdschrift voor Vrouwenstudies 17*. 5/1: 18–26.

Wilde, Inge de (ed.). 1984b. "Aletta Jacobs: Strijdlust is er nog genoeg in mij, maar strijdkracht ontbreekt mij – zes brieven." *Tijdschrift voor Vrouwenstudies 17*, 5/1: 27–40.

Willems-Bierlaagh, C. J. M. 1983. "Aletta Jacobs, persoonlijk bekeken, 1854–1929: Een visie op het leven, denken en werken van de eerste Nederlandse feministe." Literatuurrapport (Amsterdam). Photocopy of typescript in IAV-IIAV (Library).

Wiltsher, Anne. 1985. *Most Dangerous Women: Feminist Peace Campaigners of the Great War.* London: Pandora.

Woman's Who is Who of America, 1914–1915. 1915. *A Biographical Dictionary of Contemporary Women in the United States and Canada.* Ed. John William Leonard. New York [n.p.].

Women in a Changing World. 1966. *The Dynamic Story of the International Council of Women since 1888.* London: Routledge & Kegan Paul.

Women's International League for Peace and Freedom. 1919. Report of the International Congress of Women, Zürich, May 12 to 17, 1919. Geneva: WILPF.

Wyman, David S. (1984). *The Abandonment of the Jews: America and the Holocaust, 1941–1945.* New York: Pantheon.

Wynner, Edith. 1974. "Rosika Schwimmer." In *Dictionary of American Biography.* Suppl. 4, 1946–50. Ed. John A. Garraty and Edward T. James, 724–28. New York: Charles Scribner's Sons.

Index

Names

Abbott, Mrs. [Elizabeth], 197
Aberdeen, Ishbel Maria Gordon, 173n.6, 177, 196–97, 198n.3
Addams, Jane, 21, 25, 136–38, 138–40, 154–55, 156, 157–58, 159, 160, 169, 171, 214n.2, 238n.2, 290n.6, 294n.6, 296n.12
Ancona, Margherita, 187, 280
Anderson, Elizabeth Garrett, 10, 256, 257n.6
Andrews, Fannie Fern, 138
Ankersmit, Heleen, 152
Anthony, Lucy E., 5, 25–26, 27, 58, 60n.3, 71–72, 77, 93, 109, 114, 133, 160, 171, 219
    correspondence with Aletta Jacobs, 66–67, 75, 77, 103–5, 106–7, 147–48, 201–3
    correspondence with Rosa Manus, 40, 187–88, 199–201
Anthony, Susan B., 1–5, 6–7, 8, 9, 11, 28, 40, 49, 55–56, 66, 67n.2, 71–72, 78, 91–93, 116, 128, 224, 278, 288n.17, 293n.2
Anthony, Mary S., 15, 66, 67n.1, 68, 72
Arenholt, Julie, 280–81
Ashby, Margery I. Corbett, 105, 106n.2, 116, 181, 187, 194, 196, 198, 209, 212, 213n.6, 217, 221, 222, 239–40, 246, 248–49, 251n.5, 260, 264n.5, 280–82
Ashby, Michael, 240
Asmundsson, Briet, 16, 18
Asquith, Herbert H., 47
Astor, Lady Nancy, 107n.1, 247
Atanatskovitch, Milena, 281–82
Augspurg, Anita, 7, 9, 31, 33, 62n.2, 82, 85n.4, 127, 278–79, 285n.9
Avery, Julia, 108, 109, 110n.3
Avery, Rachel Foster, 9, 17, 27, 28, 67–68, 71–72, 75, 77–78, 79–80, 82, 92, 107–10, 111, 113, 147, 278–79, 287n.14

Avery, Rose, 109, 110n.6
Avril de Sainte-Croix, Ghenia, 196, 198n.3

Balch, Emily Greene, 138, 140, 295nn.9, 10, 298n.8
Balen-Klaar, Frederike S. van, 163
Bakker-Nort, Elisabeth (Betsy), 163
Banks, G. Linnaeus, 64n.2
Bataerds, Mme, 121
Beard, Mary Ritter, xii, 289n.1
Bedy-Schwimmer, Rozsa. See Schwimmer, Rosika
Beggs, Mrs. Frederick, 232, 234n.2
Belmont, Alva, 87, 89n.1
Bergh-Willing, Betsi van den, 107n.2, 261, 262n.2
Bergman, Signe, 82, 85n.6, 125, 155, 198, 279–80
Besant, Annie, 10
Blackwell, Alice Stone, 131n.1
Blackwell, Henry, 2
Blake, Lillie Devereux, 293n.2
Blatch, Harriot E. Stanton, 88, 89n.2, 237–38
Blum, Leon, 242n.6
Bobbie, 66n.2, 125
Boersma, Nettie, 95
Boissevain, Mia, 14, 152, 200, 202, 219–20, 288n.21, 292n.28, 294n.3
Bompas, Kathleen, 253, 257n.3
Bonner, Bradlaugh, 73, 74n.1
Bonnevie, Margarete, 282
Boyer, Marguerite, 252n.6, 282
Bradlaugh, Charles, 10, 74n.1
Breshovskaja, Catherine, 104n.1
Briand, Aristide, 203n.3
Broese van Groenou-Wieseman, Jeannette, 170n.2
Brunschvicg, Cecile, 221, 240, 242n.6
Burns, Lucy, 134n.4
Butler, Nicholas Murray, 213, 214n.2
Buuren-Huys, Jo van, 163

Cauer, Minna, 62n.2
Cameron, Amelia, 95, 115
Catt, Carrie Chapman, 6–8, 9, 12, 14,
   15–16, 19, 20, 22, 24, 25–26, 27,
   28–29, 31, 33, 44, 47–49, 55–56, 57,
   65, 69, 73, 74–75, 77, 79–80, 82–84,
   91–99, 103–4, 106–7, 109, 116–17, 119,
   125, 131–33, 135, 136, 141, 143, 147, 150,
   151, 162, 171, 173, 178, 179, 181–82, 187,
   189, 190–91, 194, 200, 202, 203n.3,
   221, 222–24, 235, 238, 278–82,
   286n.10, 288n.21, 290n.10, 291n.24,
   293nn.2, 3, 8, 293n.9, 294n.6,
   295n.11, 297n.7, 298n.8
   correspondence with Aletta Jacobs,
      63–64, 70–71, 81, 87–89, 110–13,
      114–15, 120–24, 148–49, 154–57,
      167–70, 178, 188–89, 203–7
   correspondence with friends of Rosa
      Manus, 262–64
   correspondence with Martina Kramers,
      126–29
   correspondence with Rosa Manus,
      38–42, 195–99, 207–13, 215–17,
      227–34, 239–62
   correspondence with Rosika Schwim-
      mer, 60–61, 130, 213–15
Catt, George W., 6, 64n.1
Cecil, Robert, 182
Chapman, Leo, 6
Chaponniere-Chaix, P., 188, 189n.2
Charaoui, Hoda. See Shaarawi, Huda
Chu Chia Hua, 175
Coit, Adela Stanton, 114, 122, 129n.1, 148,
   187, 198, 279–80, 287n.14, 295n.10
Collins, Betty Shield, 250
Conners, Miss, 104, 105n.3
Cooke, Frederica, 121n.2
Coops, Letteke, 195
Coops-Broese van Groenou, Emilia
   (Miel), xi, 124n.1, 152, 170n.2, 179,
   194–95
Coops, W. E. S., 195n.1
Corbett, Margery. See Ashby, Margery I.
   Corbett
Cort van der Linden, P. W. A., 141
Corthorn, Alice, 291n.28
Costelloe, Ray. See Strachey, Ray
   Costelloe
Courtney, Kathleen D., 210, 213n.3, 258,
   295n.10
Cunliffe, Sophie Rodger, 9, 279, 287n.14
Curie, Marie, 16

Daugaard, Thova, 138
DeBey, Cornelia, 104
Derment, Frau, 81
Despard, Charlotte, 143

Deutsch, Regine, 17, 175
Dingman, Mary A., 177, 209, 210, 231,
   250
Docters van Leeuwen-van Maarseveen,
   Geertruida W. P., 152
Dorp, Elisabeth C. van, 44
Dorp-Verdam, A. E. van, 58, 60n.1, 73,
   74
Drummond, James Eric, 210, 212n.1
Drucker, Wilhelmina, 55n.3, 69n.2, 70,
   71n.4
Drysdale, Charles, 10, 125

Eastman, Crystal, 22
Ebert, Friedrich, 181
Eeghen, Louise C. A. (Louky) van, 196,
   198n.3, 233
Epker, Nelia, 264n.3

Fast, L. K., 232–33, 234n.2
Fawcett, Millicent Garrett, 9, 10, 75, 83,
   89n.3, 107n.1, 148, 155, 187, 196–97,
   278–79, 287n.14, 295n.10
Ford, Henry, 295n.11, 296n.12
Fuchs, Malvi, 55, 56n.6, 62
Furuhjelm, Annie, 16, 82, 85n.7, 168, 187,
   279
Fürth, Henriette, 62n.2

Garrett, Mary E., 25, 290n.6
Genoni, Rosa, 138
Gerardin, Marthe Antoine, 265
Gerritsen, Carel Victor, 10, 12, 44, 54, 61,
   62n.1, 64, 237, 292n.2
Giesswein, Alexander, 153, 154n.4
Gill, Miss, 105–6
Gilman, Charlotte Perkins, 11, 33, 57,
   58n.3, 62n.2, 66, 290n.18
Ginsberg, Marie, 231, 232n.2, 282
Girardet-Vielle, Antonia, 187, 280
Glücklich, Vilma, 12, 33, 57, 58n.4, 62, 65
Goldman, Emma, 22
Goldstein, Vida, 7, 286n.11
Gomperts-van Emden, S., 163
Gourd, Emilie, 199n.8, 239, 242n.3, 246,
   249, 264n.5, 280–82
Grenfell, Helen Loring, 65, 66n.1
Grinberg-Aupourrain, Suzanne, 281–82
Gripenberg, Alexandra, 43–44
Groeneweg, Suze, 170n.1
Groot, Cornelia (Kee), 163
Grossmann, Janka, 53, 55n.1, 62

Haakon, King of Sweden, 16
Hage, Miss, 260
Hainisch, Marianne, 12, 66, 68, 81,
   288n.18
Hansen, Ingeborg, 281

Hansson, Emma, 138
Harper, Ida A. Husted, 55, 56n.2, 77, 80, 87, 131, 189, 199, 200, 202
Hauser, Elizabeth J., 77, 108–9, 110n.4
Haver, Theodore P. B., 55n.3, 69, 122n.5
Hay, Mary Garrett, 27, 38, 80, 92, 109, 117, 123, 131, 169, 170n.4, 203, 207n.1, 234n.4, 255, 290n.12, 291nn.24, 25, 293n.3
Henderson, Arthur, 210, 213n.2
Heneker, Dorothy A., 239, 242n.1
Herzl, Theodor, 33
Heymann, Lida Gustava, 7, 62n.2, 136, 285n.9
Hitler, Adolf, 40–41, 222
Hobhouse, Emily, 136, 157–59, 294n.7
Hodge, Pauline Chapers, 25
Hoeve-Bakker, S. van de, 163
Hoeven, E. van der, 163
Holbrook, Florence, 138
Hooper, Jessie Ben, 212, 213n.5
Horthy, General, 221
Hubrecht. *See* Lanschot Hubrecht, Jeanne C. van
Hyde, Clara, 189–91, 205

Iongh, Jane de, 242n.5, 259n.1
Ivanova, Dimitrana, 282

Jacobi, Erica, 85n.3, 233, 234n.3, 250, 259, 261
Jacobi, Felix, 85n.3, 233, 234n.3, 244, 255, 261
Jacobi-Manus, Anna (*also* Jacobi, Anna Manus), x, 39, 82, 85n.3, 116, 181, 233, 234n.3, 244, 255, 258, 259, 261, 264n.5
Jacobs, Aletta H., 2, 7, 8, 9–12, 20, 22, 24, 25, 26, 27, 28, 30–31, 43–45, 60, 91, 94–99, 125, 127, 135, 136–37, 138–42, 175, 178, 181, 199, 221, 235, 237, 251n.1, 263, 286n.2, 287n.14, 288nn.16, 17, 292nn.3, 4, 295n.7, 295n.11, 296nn.3, 12, 297n.4
correspondence with Jane Addams, 157–58
correspondence with Lucy E. Anthony, 66–67, 75, 77, 103–5, 106–7, 147–48, 201–3
correspondence with Susan B. Anthony, 55–56
correspondence with Rachel Foster Avery, 67–68, 107–10
correspondene with Carrie Chapman Catt, 63–64, 70–71, 81, 87–89, 110–13, 114–15, 120–24, 148–49, 154–57, 167–70, 178, 188–89, 203–7
correspondence with Miel Coops-Broese van Groenou, 179, 194–95

correspondence with Emily Hobhouse, 158–59
correspondence with Rosika Schwimmer, 53–55, 56–58, 61–63, 65–66, 68–70, 73–75, 86, 105–6, 153–54, 160
correspondence with Anna Howard Shaw, 58–60, 71–72, 77–80, 103–5, 113–14, 116–19, 130–34, 149–51, 160–66, 170–73
correspondence with Mien van Wulfften Palthe-Broese van Groenou, 124, 151–52
Jacobs, Charles E., 19, 64n.3, 65, 68, 73, 86, 87–88, 105, 107, 164n.3, 170n.2
Jacobs, Julius K., 64n.3
Jordan, Elisabeth, 133n.2
Josefa, Mr. and Mrs., 252–53, 256n.1

Kapteyn-Muysken, Geertruida A., 152
Katz, C. Frida, 243n.2
Kellogg, Frank B., 203n.3
Kemal Atatürk, 221, 233
Key, Ellen, 62n.2
Keyser, Dr., 122
Klemàn, Anna, 138
Kollontai, Alexandra, 262n.1
Kramers, Martina, 9, 7, 26, 30–31, 56–57, 58n.2, 66, 70, 74, 81, 105n.3, 107, 109, 111, 121, 131–32, 235, 278–79, 287n.15
correspondence with Carrie Chapman Catt, 126–29
correspondence with Rosika Schwimmer, 125
Kulka, Leopoldine, 153, 154n.3
Kydd, Winnifred, 212, 213n.6

Lagerlof, Selma, 39, 292n.27
Laidlaw, Harriet Burton (Mrs. James Lees), 117, 119n.1
Laidlaw, James Lees, 119n.1
Lang, Marie, 12, 66, 288n.18
Lange, Helene, 206
Lanschot Hubrecht, Jeanne C. van, 122n.5, 152, 157–58
Lansing, Robert, 171, 173n.5
Lawrence. *See* Pethick-Lawrence, Emmeline
Lehmann, Andree, 252n.6, 282
Leslie, Mrs. Frank, 25–26, 148n.1
Lindemann, Anna, 82, 85n.8, 125, 279–80
Lischnewska, Maria, 62n.2
Lloyd George, 136
Louise, Queen of Denmark, 15
Luders, M. Else, 62n.2, 212, 213n.6
Luisi, Paulina, 213n.6, 280–82, 283n.1
Lutz, Bertha, 181, 191, 250

McCormick, Katherine Dexter, 279–80
McCulloch, Catherine Gouger Waugh, 38, 82–85
McDonald, James G., 227, 278n.1
Macmillan, Chrystal, 136, 138, 140, 141, 148, 153, 154, 155, 157–59, 160, 197, 280, 295nn.9, 10
McMurtrie, Misses, 201
Maday, Andre, 69
Malaterre-Sellier, Germaine, 197, 199n.4, 217, 222, 240, 246–47, 248–49, 280–82, 283n.2
Manus, Bé, 257n.2, 264n.5
Manus, Carel, 215, 239
Manus, Carmen, 216, 232, 234n.1, 252
Manus, Rosa, 13–14, 22, 27, 33, 81, 82–85, 117, 122, 131, 151, 152, 158, 176–77, 179, 181–82, 203–4, 207, 219–20, 221, 222–24, 235, 237, 238n.4, 262–64, 280–82, 288n.21, 294n.3, 295n.10, 295n.11, 297nn.9, 10, 298nn.5, 6, 9
    correspondence with Lucy E. Anthony, 187–88, 199–201
    correspondence with Carrie Chapman Catt, 195–99, 207–13, 215–17, 227–34, 239–62
    correspondence with Clara Hyde, 189–91
    correspondence with Anna Manus, 116
Manus, Anna. *See* Jacobi-Manus, Anna
Marvin, Fred R., 202, 203n.5
Masaryk, Th. G., 179
Mayreder, Rosa, 153, 154n.3
Medley, Dr., 77
Meer van Kuffeler, V. C. van der, 163
Mensinga, Dr., 10
Meijers, Clara, 40, 224, 264
Meulen, Hans van der, 288n.21
Misar, Olga, 153, 154n.3
Mohr, Miss, 62
Mollie. *See* Hay, Mary Garrett
Mondini, Mr. and Ms., 195
Montefiore, Dora B., 74, 75n.1
Morck, Frederikke, 281
Morgan, Ruth, 197–98, 199n.7, 200, 210n.1, 215, 281
Muldern van der Graaf-de Bruijn, Clara, 163
Mussolini, Benito, 179, 191, 195, 221, 234
Mott, Lucretia, 260n.1

Naber, Johanna W. A., 9, 14, 46, 69, 106, 111, 278, 287n.14
Nathan, Maud, 120, 121n.2
Neilans, Alison, 281–83
Norrie, Charlotte, 56, 58n.1

Ogden, Esther, 232, 234n.2
Overduin, Anna, 19, 86, 105, 164n.3

Paige, Mrs. James, 197
Palencia, Isabel de, 261, 262n.1
Palthe, Mrs. *See* Wulfften Palthe-Broese van Groenou, Frederika Wilhelmina (Mien) van
Pankhurst, Christabel, 83, 85n.10, 149
Pankhurst, Emmeline, 83, 85n.10, 88, 112n.1, 113, 123, 124n.1, 133
Pankhurst, Sylvia, 85n.10
Parsens, Mrs. (Alice Parsons?), 231
Paul, Alice, 134n.4
Peck, Mary Gray, xi, 6, 27, 36–37, 38, 94, 95, 104n.1, 109, 121n.2, 141, 181, 191, 205, 208–9, 232, 261–62, 286nn.10, 12, 290n.10, 291nn.23, 24, 293n.7
Petersen, Margot, 252n.6, 283
Pethick-Lawrence, Emmeline, 136, 149, 150, 294n.4, 295n.10
Pethick-Lawrence, Frederick, 83, 85n.9, 113, 294n.4
Piepers, E. H., 241
Pinchot, Mrs. Gifford, 280
Plaminkova, Františka, 197, 199n.5, 249, 253–54, 264n.6, 281–82
Pogany, Paula, 130
Polak-Rosenberg, Ch. L., 54, 55n.2, 243n.2
Posthumus, N., 296–97n.3
Posthumus-van der Goot, Willemijn H., ix, 136, 177, 242nn.2, 5, 296nn.3, 12
Potter, Mrs. [Pitman], 92, 250
Potter, Frances Squire, 38, 108, 109, 291nn.23, 24

Quam, F. Marie, 187, 188n.1

Ramondt-Hirschmann, Cornelia, 138–39, 140, 159, 295n.10
Randall, Mercedes M., 294n.5, 296n.12, 298n.8
Rankin, Jeannette, 176
Raschke, Marie, 62n.2
Rathbone, Eleanor, 187, 280
Rau, Senta Rama (Dhanvanti Rama Rau), 282
Rees-Broese van Groenou, Suzanne (San) van, 124n.1, 170n.2
Reilly, Caroline I., 199–200, 201n.1
Renier, Olive, 292n.28
Rennes, Catharina van, 46, 292n.6
Reuss Jancoulescu, Eugenie de, 281
Rischbeith, Bessie, 281–83
Rocha, Heloise, 250, 283
Roosevelt, Eleanor, 243

Roosevelt, Franklin D., 228n.1
Rosenberg. *See* Polak-Rosenberg, Ch. L.
Rueling, Anna, 85n.4
Rydh, Hanna, 250, 282

Safford, Mary A., 84
Saunte, Edel, 250, 283
Schain, Josephine, 208, 210n.1, 214, 232,
    234n.2, 250, 252n.8, 282
Schirmacher, Kathe, 9, 13, 82, 85n.4, 127,
    278–79, 287n.14
Schlekel, Klara, 287n.14
Schlumberger. *See* Witt-Schlumberger,
    Marguerite de
Schreiber, Adele (*also* Schreiber-Krieger),
    17, 176, 187, 222, 233, 251n.2, 280–82
Schreiner, Olive, 11, 95, 292n.28, 293n.7
Schwimmer, Franciska, 12, 214–15
Schwimmer, Rosika, 11–12, 13, 22, 48,
    58n.4, 62n.2, 81, 127, 136, 138–41,
    148, 149, 154, 157, 159, 171, 173, 179,
    202, 203n.5, 205, 223, 279, 288n.18,
    292n.3, 294n.5, 295n.11, 296n.12
  correspondence with Carrie Chapman
    Catt, 60–61, 130, 213–15
  correspondence with Aletta Jacobs,
    53–55, 56–58, 61–63, 65–66, 68–70,
    73–75, 86, 105–6, 153–54, 160
  correspondence with Martina Kramers,
    125
  correspondence with Mien van
    Wulfften Palthe-Broese van
    Groenou, 235–38
Sewall, May Eliza Wright, 8, 54, 55n.5
Shaarawi, Huda, 221–22, 247–49, 251nn.3,
    5, 281–82
Shaw, Anna Howard, 3, 5–6, 8, 15, 22,
    25–26, 27, 33, 44, 48, 56, 60n.4, 66,
    67n.2, 68, 73, 75, 77, 80n.5, 83, 87,
    91–93, 106–7, 111–12, 120, 122–23, 124,
    141–42, 147–48, 157, 168, 176, 187,
    199–200, 285n.7, 289n.5, 290n.12,
    293n.4
  correspondence with Aletta Jacobs,
    58–60, 71–72, 77–80, 103–5, 107–9,
    113–14, 116–19, 130–34, 142, 149–51,
    160–66, 170–73
Shaw, James, 73, 151
Shaw, Pauline Agassiz Quincy, 157, 158n.2
Sheepshanks, Mary, 136, 153, 154n.1, 156
Sheng, Captain. *See* Sing Pey Zung
Sherwin, Belle, 196, 198n.2, 281
Shuler, Marjory, 199n.6
Shuler, Nettie Rogers, 197, 199n.6
Shuster, W. Morgan, 121
Siemienska, Halina, 250, 283
Simonson, Mrs. Charles, 232, 234n.2

Sing Pey Zung, 97, 293n.8
Singh, Kunwar Rani Maharaj, 250, 282
Slade, Mrs. F. Louis, 208, 209n.1
Smith, Mary Rozet, 158
Snowden, Ethel Philip, 88, 89n.3
Spiller, Nina, 282
Stanton, Elizabeth Cady, 1–5, 78, 89n.2,
    182–83, 224, 260n.1, 285n.2, 293n.2
Stanton, Theodore, 43
Sterling, Frances M., 198, 199n.9, 251, 253,
    280–81
Stern, Edgar, 253, 257n.2
Stern, Egon, 252, 257n.2
Stewart, Ella Seass, 82, 85n.2
Stöcker, Helene, 31, 62n.2, 290n.13
Stone, Lucy, 2, 133n.1
Straaten, E. W. van, 105, 106n.1
Strachey, Ray Costelloe, 106, 107n.1
Strauss, Rosa Welt, 194, 195n.2
Stritt, Marie, 69–70n.4, 125, 127, 280
Sulyok, Ylda, 69
Suttner, Bertha von, 62n.2
Szelagowska, Anna, 212, 213n.6, 247, 250,
    283

Teleki, Iska, 153, 154n.2
Ter, La Marquesa del, 281–82
Theodoropoulos, Avra, 280–82
Thomas, M. Carey, 25, 107n.1, 110n.3,
    162, 164n.1, 165, 290n.6
Thorbecke, Rudolf, xi, 9–10
Tiffany, Katherine Charles L., 169,
    170n.4

Upton, Harriet Taylor, 92, 104, 105n.2,
    109n.1
Urban-Stern, Gisela, 255, 257n.4

Velsen, Dorothee von, 217, 221, 281–82
Verona, Maria, 250
Villard, Oswald Garrison, 201, 203n.1

Wald, Lillian D., 21–22, 25, 158, 290n.6
Wales, Julia Grace, 136, 138, 294n.5
Walin, Ingeborg, 198, 281–82
Wallenberg, Knut A., 139–40
Weininger, Otto, 154n.3
Wells, H. G., 237–38
Welt Strauss, Rosa. *See* Strauss, Rosa
    Welt
Wibaut-Berdenis van Berlekom,
    Mathilde, 152
Wicksell, Anna (*also* Bugge-Wicksell), 127,
    129n.2, 187, 280
Wijnaendts Francken-Dyserinck, Esther
    Welmoet, 44, 70, 71n.3, 73, 74
Willhelm, Sidonie, 53, 54n.1

Wilhelm II, Kaiser, Emperor of Germany, 149, 170, 173n.2
Wilhelmina, Queen of the Netherlands, 106, 263
Wilson, Alda, 207n.1, 208, 232
Wilson, Woodrow, 119n.3, 136, 140, 165
Witt-Schlumberger, Marguerite de, 173n.6, 191, 279–80
Woolley, Mary, 212, 213n.6

Wulfften Palthe-Broese van Groenou, Frederika Wilhelmina (Mien) van, 124n.1, 130, 133, 204n.1, 205
correspondence with Aletta Jacobs, 124, 151–52
correspondence with Rosika Schwimmer, 235–38
Wulfften Palthe, Richard van, 194, 195n.3
Wynner, Edith, 63n.1, 295n.11

Organizations

Allgemeiner Deutscher Frauenverein (General German Women's Association), 69n.4
Allgemeiner Österreichischer Frauenverein (General Austrian Women's Association), 288n.18
American Woman Suffrage Association, 23, 285n.1
Bund Deutscher Frauenvereine (Federation of German Women's Associations: the German council of women), 285n.9
Bund Fortschrittlicher Frauenvereine (Federation of Progressive Women's Associations) (Germany), 285n.9
Bund für Mutterschutz und Sexualreform (Association for the Protection of Mothers and Sexual Reform) (Germany), 290n.13
Bund Österreichischer Frauenvereine (Federation of Austrian Women's Associations: the Austrian council of women), 288n.18
Committee on Suffrage and Rights of Citizenship of the ICW, 58, 60n.2
Congressional Union (*later* Woman's Party) (United States), 134n.4, 150
Deutscher Verein für Frauenstimmrecht (German Woman Suffrage Association) (*from 1903* Deutscher Verband für Frauenstimmrecht), 285n.9
Egyptian Feminist Union, 251n.3
Equality League of Self-Supporting Women (*later* Women's Political Union) (Great Britain), 89n.2
Equal Suffrage League of New York, 121n.2
Feministák Egyesülete (Feminist Association) (Hungary), 12, 58n.4
General Federation of Women's Clubs (United States), 291n.25
Internationaal Archief voor de Vrouwenbeweging (International Archive for the Women's Movement) (Netherlands), ix–xi, 41, 238nn.3, 4, 240–41, 263
Internationaal Informatiecentrum en Archief voor de Vrouwenbeweging (International Information Center and Archive for the Women's Movement) (Netherlands), 269
International Alliance of Women for Suffrage and Equal Citizenship, x, 26, 176, 222, 240, 245, 258, 263
International Committee of Women for Permanent Peace (*later* WILPF), 138, 155, 157n.1, 173n.4, 290n.6, 295nn.10, 11
International Council of Women, 1–2, 6–8, 11, 43–44, 53, 135, 173n.6, 176, 181, 242n.6, 287n.15
International Federation of Business and Professional Women, 296n.2
International Federation of University Women, 296n.2
International Woman Suffrage Alliance, 1, 7–9, 13, 15–20, 21–42, 43–49, 56, 60–61, 62, 98–99, 127, 128–29, 135–43, 173n.6, 175–83, 219–24, 286n.10, 288n.24
International Women's Relief Committee of the IWSA, 136
Interparliamentary Union, 12
Interurban Suffrage Council of Greater New York, 80
Joint Standing Committee of International Women's Organizations, 296n.2
Korps Vrouwelijke Vrijwilligers (Women's Voluntary Corps) (Netherlands), 257, 258, 259n.1
League of Women Voters (United States), 178, 198n.2, 250
Liaison Committee of International Women's Organizations, 177
Mannenbond voor Vrouwenkiesrecht (Men's League for Woman Suffrage) (Netherlands), 46

Men's League for Woman Suffrage, 119n.1
Munkásnö Egyesülete (Association of Working Women) (Hungary), 12
National American Woman Suffrage Association, 3, 4, 5–7, 24, 28, 92–94, 134n.4, 141, 198n.2, 293n.5, 294n.6
National College Equal Suffrage League (United States), 290n.6
Nationale Vrouwenraad (National Council of Women) (Netherlands), 54, 58n.2, 60n.1, 287n.15
National Union of Women's Suffrage Societies (Great Britain), 10, 44, 48, 107n.1, 156, 287n.14, 294n.4
National Woman Suffrage Association (United States), 1–3, 285n.1
Nederlandsche Bond voor Vrouwenkiesrecht (Dutch Woman Suffrage League), 44, 71nn.1, 3, 4
Nederlandsche Unie van Vrouwenbelangen (Dutch Union for Women's Interests), 178
Nederlandsche Vereeniging voor Vrouwenbelangen en Gelijk Staatsburgerschap (Dutch Union for Women's Interests and Equal Citizenship), 178–79
Neutraal Vrouwen-Comité voor Vluchtelingen (Neutral Women's Committee for Refugees) (Netherlands), 222
New York Suffrage Party, 170n.4
Nöegyesületek Szövetsége (Council of Women) (Hungary), 12, 53, 54, 55n.6
Nötisztviselök Országos Egyesülete (National Association of Women Office Workers), 12, 54, 55n.7
Rechtschutzverein für Frauen (Women's Legal Aid Society) (Germany), 69n.4
St. Joan Political and Social Union (Great Britain), 296n.2

Tesselschade (Netherlands), 287n.14
Union Française pour le Suffrage des Femmes (French Women's Suffrage Union), 191n.2, 293n.7
Vereeniging ter Behartiging van de Belangen der Vrouw (Association to Promote Women's Interests) (Netherlands), 287n.14
Vereeniging van Staatsburgeressen (Association of Women Citizens) (Netherlands), 178
Vereeniging voor Vrouwenkiesrecht (Woman Suffrage Association) (Netherlands), xi, 10, 13, 28, 30, 43, 44, 49, 55, 57, 71nn.1, 3, 178, 297n.5.
Vrije Vrouwen Vereeniging (Free Women's Association) (Netherlands), 55n.3
Vrouwen Electriciteits Vereeniging (Women's Electricity Society) (Netherlands), 217n.3
Woman Suffrage Party (United States: New York), 80n.4, 94, 119n.1
Woman's Peace Party, 136, 141
Women's Christian Temperance Union (United States), 3, 5, 28, 117
Women's Freedom League (Great Britain), 143
Women's International League for Peace and Freedom, 58n.4, 142, 173n.4, 213n.3, 295n.8, 296n.2, 298n.8
Women's Social and Political Union (Great Britain), 44–45, 48, 75n.1, 85n.10, 89n.2, 112n.1, 294n.4
World Center for Women's Archives (United States), 235, 238n.2
World Union of Women for International Concord, 296n.2
World's Women's Christian Temperance Union, 296n.2
World's Young Women's Christian Association, 296n.2